THE CIVILIZATIONS OF EUROPE

THE CIVILIZATIONS OF
EUROPE

MICHAEL GRANT

*President and Vice-Chancellor of
the Queen's University, Belfast*

An NAL Book
Published by The New American Library

© 1965 by Michael Grant

Library of Congress Catalog Card Number: 65–26113

First Printing

Published by The New American Library, Inc.
1301 Avenue of the Americas, New York, New York 10019

Published simultaneously in Canada by
General Publishing Company Ltd.

Printed in Great Britain

CONTENTS

CONTENTS

CONTENTS

ILLUSTRATIONS

ILLUSTRATIONS

ILLUSTRATIONS

ILLUSTRATIONS

Ovid among the Scythians by Delacroix. National Gallery, London

Drawing of a young girl by Renoir. Private Collection, Paris

Emile Zola by Manet. Louvre (*Archives Photographiques*)

Balzac by Rodin. Tate Gallery, London

Self-portrait by Cézanne. Louvre (*Archives Photographiques*)

Plan for the cemetery at Chaux from Ledoux's *L'Architecture*

Halle des Machines at the Paris 1889 Exhibition (*Collection Viollet*)

Painting of Gottfried Semper's Opera House at Dresden before it was destroyed by fire. Stadtmuseum, Dresden (*Deutsche Fotothek*)

Scene from Stanislavsky's production of *Uncle Vanya* in 1899 (*Garzanti Editore*, from *Storia del Teatro*)

THE TWENTIETH CENTURY   (*between pages 282 and 283*)

Detail of pinnacle on Gaudí's church of the Sagrada Familia, Barcelona (*Ampliaciones y Reproducciones Mas*)

Unité d'Habitation by Le Corbusier outside Marseille (*Roger-Viollet*)

Phoenix Rheinrohr building in Düsseldorf (*Ullstein Bilderdienst*)

Bottle, Glass and Pipe by Braque. Mrs E. Hulton Collection (*Arts Council of Great Britain*)

Composition by Mondrian. Marlborough Fine Art Ltd.

Reclining Female Figure by Henry Moore. Marlborough Fine Art Ltd.

Déjeuner sur l'herbe by Picasso. Marlborough Fine Art Ltd.

Programme heading for a performance of *The Firebird* by the Russian Ballet. Monte Morris Collection

Scene from *The Cabinet of Dr Caligari* (*British Film Institute*)

Penguin: a black-and-white 'ryijy' rug by Lea Eskola (*Finnish Society of Crafts and Designs*)

Swedish Orrefors Glass (*Swedish National Travel Association*)

Page from an electronic score by Stockhausen. Universal Edition, Vienna

Bicycle Wheel by Marcel Duchamp. Gimpel Fils

COLOUR ILLUSTRATIONS

Heracles and Cerberus, from an Attic amphora by the Andocides painter. Louvre (*Hirmer Fotoarchiv*) — 18

Lion of St Mark, from the Echternach Gospels. Bibliothèque Nationale — 66

Icon of the Annunciation from the church of St Clement, Ochrida. Skoplje Museum (*Hirmer Fotoarchiv*) — 114

St Michael, from a triptych by Simone Martini. Fitzwilliam Museum, Cambridge — 130

Polychrome bust of Charles V by Conrad Meit. Gruuthuse Museum, Bruges — 162

The Opening of the Fifth Seal by El Greco. Metropolitan Museum of Art, New York — 194

Detail of interior of the pilgrimage church of Die Wies (*Toni Schneiders*) — 226

Rouen Cathedral: the porch in morning sunlight, harmony in blue (1894) by Claude Monet. Louvre (*Giraudon*) — 258

The author and publishers would like to thank the trustees and authorities of the museums and institutions mentioned above, by courtesy of whom the photographs are reproduced.

MAPS

The maps for this volume were specially prepared by Design Practitioners

INTRODUCTION

This book is meant to be a history of Europe with emphasis on art and thought: a sketch of cultural developments indicating a few of the principal political, social and economic events which formed their background.

Great men are now widely regarded as mere labels for events or for developments. Yet historians of art and letters, however reluctant to award 'first classes' to individuals, would concede that a few creations achieve a startling, miraculous energy and perfection in their kind. Such apocalyptic works are the principal hall-marks of an authentic civilization, and not just the sugar-icing on top of the cake; and they come not only from evolving tendencies but from single human beings. Nevertheless, we do not have to go right back to the Victorian idea of a row of Great Men's images lining the Hall of Fame. A proverb of the same period proclaimed the (rather improbable) antithesis that 'servants talk about people, gentlefolk discuss things'. We want an *entrée* on both sides of the baize door. There is no need to *choose* between the behaviour of individuals and the action of all those social, economic and political forces which John Stuart Mill grouped together as 'the state of society'. For the significant man is only able to express himself with, or against, his group. He inherits traditions, adjusts them to his own time with personal and environmental additions, and pushes the resultant amalgam into the hands of his successors. For such reasons I have started this book at the period when European cultural manifestations first have detectable social backgrounds, in the region of the Aegean.

To select one's great men is perhaps slightly less difficult in the cultural than in the politico-military sphere,[1] because, in the latter, moral judgments more readily creep in – and indeed perhaps they should, since international politics are conducted, as Hobbes observed, 'in continual jealousies and in the

---

[1] The dates of rulers given in this book are those of their reigns; the dates of others are those of their life-spans (in so far as these are known).

I

state and posture of gladiators'. One of the most remarkable European phenomena has been the co-existence of that hate-filled destructiveness with literary
and artistic brilliance and variety. This blinding contrast is one of the reasons
why a cultural history of Europe should not be attempted unless political,
social and economic developments are briefly suggested also. We must get
away from the old formula of a ten-chapter book in which nine chapters are
devoted to public life and one, lamely tagged on at the end, to culture – or
vice versa.

The interaction of cultural and public life is a complex question on which
it is notoriously hard to generalize. Perhaps, however, the whole collection
of rash generalizations of which this sort of book inevitably consists should
be regarded as an attempt to suggest some answers. Being one man's attempt
(although every word is indebted to someone else), it obviously reflects all
his limitations, one of which is ignorance both of history and, doubtless, of
his own biases; a quality which Lytton Strachey comfortingly described as
'the first requisite of the historian'. This ignorance extends to science, of
which my treatment is accordingly limited to an occasional reference to its
impacts upon other aspects of life. To write a cultural history of Europe dealing with science less perfunctorily – in other words, devoting half the book to
it – would have been a different task, which I hope someone will undertake.

By Europe, I mean that area lying within its present recognized geographical boundaries – that is to say, including 'European' Russia and Turkey, and
(in the past) Moslem Sicily and Spain. To interpret the term otherwise would
be to give it a private significance, or to implement a private wish or political
topicality; and to do any of these things would be merely confusing. We
therefore reach the position, unusual in some cases, of having to treat those
Russian and Islamic rulers, writers, architects and artists alongside their fellow-
Europeans. Most westerners, including myself, are ill-equipped for this task.
Nevertheless, I feel that the attempt needs no apology. True, it is sometimes
said that we spend too much time on European history and not enough on
other continents. After living for nearly a decade in Asia and Africa, I sym-
pathize with the second part of this suggestion. But when such critics say we
have too much 'European' history, surely they must be thinking of *western*
European history or, more probably still, of their own national history plus
some slight attention to other immediately related countries. We surely do
not hear too much of European history as a whole.

Because of the intricacy of this picture my title is *The Civilizations of
Europe*. Ought the word instead to be in the singular? But physical and spirit-
ual geographers usually lose sight of European unity some way west of the
Urals, or at the Pyrenees, or even at the English Channel. Europe can only be

made into an 'intelligible field of study' if one does not expect it to yield too many universal generalities: for there are quite a number of European civilizations, and this has been true, with some coming and others going, for a very long time.

Furthermore, these civilizations are interrelated and overlap and fluctuate in such an involved fashion that their boundaries or even their very names cannot usefully be defined for more than the most transient moment, if at all. When, therefore, sections of the present book are divided according to geographical areas, this is a matter of convenience and does not mean that I am trying to indicate where, for example, the borders of German civilization (if there was one at a given time) should be placed, or where central, western and eastern Europe begin or end, or whether Ireland is part of the British Isles, or if one could speak, say, of a specifically Bohemian or Burgundian civilization. Rather than attempt (in every case) strictly racial or national classifications, it seemed more important to indicate the cultural and other manifestations which these territories, or groups of territories, actually produced.

Considerations of the same kind apply to the way in which I have divided the book into periods. Obviously, however seamless the garment of Clio may be, however continuously the stream of history may flow, some sort of division is necessary – since otherwise one could not write any history at all. But some readers will perhaps be surprised to see from my chapter-headings that I have chosen to adopt a purely mechanical division, according to periods of time. Would it not have been more helpful to label the chapters the Dark or Middle or Gothic Ages or the Age of the Renaissance, Reformation, Discovery, Baroque, Political or Industrial or Technological Revolution? In my opinion, granted the pan-European range of my subject, such labels would have been the reverse of helpful, and would indeed have loaded the picture in a very misleading fashion. The 'Middle Ages' for example (whether split into two, or three, or even four) are notoriously far more confusing than enlightening as a designation. Moreover, when there may have been a 'dark age' in parts of northern Europe, there was nothing of the kind at the other end of the continent at Constantinople; and Gothic architecture, again, had no meaning either there or to the Russians when it flourished in the north and west. Moreover, the Italian Renaissance and Baroque movements were phenomena which were at first strictly localized and only spread gradually and over a considerable period: so that, on a European scale, one is hard put to it to define a single 'Age' for either of them. Similarly, a work about Europe becomes too parochial if it heads chapters the 'Age of the Reformation', or of Discovery, or of this or that variety of Revolution. Such titles, though perfectly satisfactory when they accurately indicate what a book is about, would be inappropriate in a volume that attempts to look at the wider European canvas; since they would ignore areas of the continent to which, although they were of major historical and cultural importance, no such term could be applied. For concepts of this kind depend for their delimitation, or even for their very existence, on whether one is at Paris or Granada or London or Moscow or Istanbul.

For such reasons I would solicit support for the view that it is not merely defensible, but positively desirable, to divide a history of Europe not according to Ages or Movements but according to a chronological succession of epochs. The philosophy (if the word is not too pretentious here) behind this choice should, I hope, be more acceptable than any effort to fit things into ideological frameworks which are inadequate because they only concern relatively limited portions of the continent's most significant activities at whatever period is being discussed. Naturally, I shall try to pin-point what seems to me important; but I should not wish to erect these processes of selection into summings-up which claim to embrace Europe as a whole. I suggested earlier that, although a book like this is bound to contain all too many sweeping generalizations, one must not expect, as one goes along, to find it possible to make *universal* generalizations about European history or culture at any given date. Since this is meant to be a book about Europe, rather than about part of Europe, I have felt that I have to ration such statements very severely: this kind of approach seems more likely than others to cast unbiassed light on the successive situations that have arisen and developed upon the European continent as a whole. It throws up, incidentally, some strange and significant simultaneities and juxtapositions that are nothing like so apparent if one has to force all one's material into the Age of something or other. (Having accepted this method of periodization, I have adopted the most convenient period available, the century, or in earlier epochs a group or pair of centuries – undeterred by the obvious fact that neither great movements nor great men stop when centuries do: or by the schoolboy's definition of the eighteenth century as something which began in 1715 and ended in 1789.)

'No European', said Burke, 'can be a complete exile in any part of Europe'; and many had already detected in it some peculiar, unitary, fragrant superiority over all other continents. But this can scarcely be religious, since the principal religious revelations, although elaborated, interpreted and fought over by Europeans, have invariably originated outside Europe. Is it political? But Europe's political tradition, though exceptionally inventive – and inventive of totalitarian as well as various democratic devices – has also been exceptionally divisive and belligerent. Scientific and industrial? It is true that Europe made scientific and industrial revolutions, but America has equalled and is perhaps exceeding the former, and has certainly exceeded the latter. Cultural? But there have also been almost continual artistic developments of extraordinary quality, if not perhaps quite so sensationally varied, in China, Persia and India, not to speak of the shorter-lived efflorescences of Cairo and Baghdad.

As it happens, these developments in other continents are not valuable for purposes of comparison alone, they are also very relevant to our problem of the individuality of Europe. For one of this continent's most essential features has been, not only the influence of European groups and individuals upon the outside world, but their own extreme receptivity to external influences. For Greeks, Romans, Byzantines and Moslems, there were no divisions between Europe and Asia and Africa. The ancient role of the Mediterranean, as a bridge not a barrier, is expressed by the myth of Europa carried off from Asia to her new home. And now Europe is being changed again by the new world across the Atlantic.

All these factors combine to give the Europeans their distinctive character – ideological bellicosity, political inventiveness and fragmentation, creativity in science and industry, cultural manifestations unsurpassed in talent and un-equalled in diversity, and an extraordinarily active two-way traffic and inter-relation with other continents. Something original and remarkable is always going on in Europe. Even during the present century, amid its appalling convulsions, this fertility in new ideas has continued. The current political lop-sidedness of the continent, and its partial external dependence, are no indica-tions – provided total destruction is avoided – that European achievement will cease. I believe it to be more probable that the civilizations of Europe will continue their millennial task of constantly exploiting and amending tradi-tion in order to produce unprecedented, astonishing, profoundly evolutionary or revolutionary results.

I want to thank Mr Derek Hill and Professor Stuart Piggott for showing me books of theirs in advance of publication. I am very grateful for assistance I have received from Mrs Maura O'Hara, the Hon. Sir Steven Runciman, Mrs Tamara Talbot Rice and Miss Irene Taylor. I have also derived much benefit from the co-operation of Mr P. Havard Williams, Librarian of the Queen's University, Belfast, and from Mr A. K. McMillan and other members of the library staff. I owe a very special debt to Mr Richard Cocke and Mr Paul Hyam who have offered many invaluable suggestions and criticisms. I should also like to offer acknowledgment for the use of certain material to Mr Don Pottinger my co-author of *Greeks* and *Romans*, to the publishers of those books Messrs Thomas Nelson & Son Ltd, and to Messrs Thames & Hudson who published *The Birth of Western Civilisation*. In conclusion I wish to express my appreciation for all the help that I have received from the staff of Messrs Weidenfeld & Nicolson and particularly from Mr Nicolas Thompson, Mr Anthony Burton, Mr Michael Raeburn who has collected the illustrations, and Mrs S. Robinson who has made the maps.

BELFAST, 1965   MICHAEL GRANT

THE ANCIENT WORLD

Crete, Mycenae and Early Greece

As the second millennium BC began, the wealth and civilization of the kingdoms of western Asia overflowed to the island of Crete, itself producer of a surplus of wine and oil as well as timber for its ships. The scattered communities of the island, non-Greeks whose ancestors had come from Asia some two thousand years earlier, probably coalesced into a single kingdom with its capital at Cnossus, which was connected by paved roads to the rest of the island.

Secure in their sea-power and sea-borne Mediterranean trade, the priest-kings of Cnossus had no need to fortify their luxurious though cramped stone palace, the complex 'labyrinth' of legend; and they developed an imaginative and lively civilization. Their best wheel-turned vases and fresco paintings enliven Egyptian motifs by a confidently sophisticated blend of abstraction and impressionism, displayed in crowd scenes, bull-fights, and pictures of animals and birds that reveal profound sympathy with nature both at rest and in movement. The Cretans seem chiefly to have worshipped goddesses (forerunners of Athene, Hera and Artemis), though there was also apparently a cult of Zeus, as child of Mother Earth.

The first wave of peoples speaking a language something like Greek reached mainland Greece in about 2000 BC. Worshipping Zeus as lord of the sky, and practising a cult of the dead, these new arrivals in Greece introduced porched and gabled houses going back to the timber forms of more northern climates. They also brought the use of the potter's wheel, by which they made a scaly surfaced pottery with shapes imitated from metal-work. Possessing better tools than their predecessors, and better soil, forests and game than exist today, they built royal fortresses in the Peloponnese, notably Mycenae not far from the strategic Isthmus of Corinth. Mycenae's rulers monopolized new armaments – long bronze rapiers, huge shields and light horse-drawn chariots of oriental origin. The grandeur of the royal graves within their citadel (*c.* 1600) recalls earlier tombs at Alacahüyük in Asia Minor – just as the later Lion Gate continues to echo the architectural styles of Asia Minor and Syria. Mycenae also imported valuable objects from Crete, and made others itself.

By 1500 BC the Mycenaeans in their turn were influencing and indeed controlling the civilization of Crete. Thousands of clay writing tablets found at Cnossus as well as at the mainland Greek centres of Mycenae, Tiryns and Pylos are written in a language which has been interpreted as an early form of Greek ('Linear B' script). Whether – as is still disputed – the government at Cnossus fell in about 1400 BC or survived for another two centuries as a Mycenaean outpost, command of the seas had passed, in this period, to mainland monarchs. Mycenaean Greeks now travelled all over the Mediterranean, establishing settlements and commercial links which gave them a place among the great powers of the near east. They had become a major seafaring nation, and their fortified towns were centres of small but powerful land empires, controlled by war-chariots and good roads. The vases they exported far and wide are made of buff terracotta with lustrous brown ornament. Though based upon Cretan models, and occasionally upon the vivid animal art of Eurasian nomads, the shapes and designs of this Mycenaean pottery also foreshadow the Greek feeling for less fluid structural values and proportions.

The late fourteenth century BC witnessed the decline of this culture and wealth. Exports to Egypt and the Levant ceased abruptly in *c.* 1250 or a little later – a time of mighty disturbances and migrations, resulting in the dissolution of Aegean cultural uniformity. In about 1200 BC Greek invaders besieged and burnt Troy across the Dardanelles, where there had been six successive earlier settlements. The siege, confirmed by archaeologists, inspired the Homeric *Iliad* which, although not written down for another four hundred years, presents a plausible picture of the Greek besiegers as a loose confederacy of jealous, recalcitrant, hunting and chariot-racing meat-fed chiefs.

Within a century after this aggressive expedition, the palaces of the Mycenaeans were destroyed – probably by a last stream of Hellenic invaders, who differed from their predecessors by cremating their dead instead of burying them. These Dorians (*c.* 1200–1000), perhaps propelled from the rear by even more barbarous hordes of Illyrians, passed through the Balkans into northern Greece, driving before them earlier Greek arrivals who migrated to Asia Minor. Among such settlers upon its coasts and islands were the Ionians, who passed through Attica; some stayed at Athens, and others moved across the Aegean to establish Miletus, Smyrna, Ephesus and other towns.

The Dorians occupied or subdued almost all the Peloponnese except mountainous Arcadia in its centre, and finally reached Crete, Rhodes and south-western Asia Minor. Iron began to be used (*c.* 1100), the iron slashing sword started to play a formidable part, and tools became much more readily available, making people less dependent upon the state and its monarchs and priests. Yet the epoch following the destruction of the palaces is a 'dark age' in which the Greeks, having lost control of the sea to the Phoenician navies of Sidon (and later Tyre), were cut off from the rest of the world. There were evidently sharp changes of political régime, but, although the use of writing diminished, a fair measure of cultural continuity prevailed.

Moreover, a new Ionian school of pottery soon became active, particularly at Athens which was relatively unaffected by the upheavals of the times. Athenian Protogeometric pottery (*c.* 1025–900), developing from earlier schematic designs, displayed an effectively balanced and disciplined simplicity. Its Geometric successors (*c.* 900–700) evolved richer patterns, often within horizontal bands. Such vases, containing the ashes of the dead, began to show silhouetted scenes of chariot and funeral processions.

The construction of temples can also be traced back to the eighth century BC. They include shrines of Artemis at Sparta and Ephesus, and of Zeus' wife Hera at Samos and Argos, which had superseded its neighbour Mycenae.

Holy places such as these became the centres of early religious and commercial unions. Homer probably recited at religious festivals of the Ionian League. Created like Teutonic, Slavonic and Celtic sagas from orally transmitted material, the *Iliad*, with its natural, picturesque, imaginative style suited perfectly to its theme, created a heroic ideal which was the most important unifying, civilizing factor in Greek and Roman history and in the cultures that have flowed from them. The slightly later *Odyssey*, too, assembling with genius a vast collection of folk-tales and fairy-tales derived in part from Sumerian and Babylonian epics, has appealed to the imagination of innumerable searchers after spiritual truth.

Another poet of about the same date was Hesiod, to whom is attributed the *Works and Days* and the *Theogony*. The author of the former work, who describes himself as the son of an immigrant to mainland Boeotia from Asia Minor, stresses divine concern with human justice, but reflects a hard-working impoverished life embodying many centuries of agricultural lore. The writer of the *Theogony* originates, in mythological guise, the Greek vein of religious and moral speculation. Meanwhile the earliest of the 'Homeric Hymns' combine heart-felt human warmth and religious solemnity in their praise of Demeter the earth-mother at Eleusis near Athens, and of the Hellenic spirit's flashing embodiment Apollo, whose shrines were at Delos and Delphi.

Isolated from other lands, Greek communities were also cut off from each other by their mountainous countryside; so they were often at odds, and asserted their local peculiarities and independence. In about the eighth century BC the city-state or *polis*, often very small, re-emerged to become the normal unit of society, as in ancient Mesopotamia and Asia Minor. Developing from one village or several – especially in areas with a historic past – the city-states centred round a citadel (*acropolis*), usually a safe distance from the sea and with arable land attached. Unlike eastern towns, each of these Greek cities possessed not only its religious centre but a central market-place (*agora*) and, in due course, a theatre and gymnasium too.

Except at a few places such as Sparta where monarchy survived, local kings were first weakened and then superseded by their aristocratic councils of landowning chieftains of clans. With the disappearance of the kings, who had conducted religious observances, there remained no widespread professional priesthood. Communities generally comprised citizens, slaves and resident aliens, and two free non-citizen classes: artisans or professionals – smiths, potters, carpenters, minstrels, doctors – and rural serfs or hired labourers.

Among the citizens, it was the rising mercantile class which gave these states their heavily armed infantry (*hoplites*). With Ionia as intermediary, this was one of the innovations which originated from the Levant. As Greek navies began to challenge Phoenicia's monopoly of the seas, Greek people met its traders and learnt much from them. For instance, in the eighth century BC, they borrowed a Phoenician alphabet in which the signs, including vowels, represented the simpler sounds of language. The diffusion of this alphabet, despite varying details in different regions, rapidly increased literacy and emancipated political and philosophical thought.

Into Greek art, too, flowed novel orientalizing motifs, particularly conspicuous on pottery of Corinth (*c*. 675), the city which bridged east and west. Corinthian paintings replace geometric designs by floral patterns and animals and winged monsters, and there are experiments in technique: incised black-figure outline drawing instead of silhouette, varied colours, a widening range of martial and mythological subjects, and an increasing naturalism of the human form which released new and manifold creative forces. By the end of the seventh century, large-scale Greek sculpture had also begun, with the islanders of the Cyclades in the lead. Though retaining for a time the Egyptian male statue's conventional pose and a stylized formalism which kept realist tendencies under control, sculptors displayed an ever keener curiosity about the structure of the human body.

The Greek temple (p. 9) also took a more definite shape, with its structural principles based on the vertical and horizontal 'post and beam', wooden in origin but now of stone. Doric temples of the seventh century BC echo Minoan and Mycenaean traditions in the forms of their capitals and columns. Some fifty years later appeared the graceful Ionic Order with its curling capital reminiscent of Hittite and Iranian models.

During the eighth and seventh centuries, internal political strife, rising populations and new overseas contacts at the expense of declining Phoenicia caused large-scale movements of emigration from Greece – anti-aristocratic in motive, yet encouraged by the ruling classes as a salutary vent. New communities, independent of their mother cities, extended from the Black Sea, Syria and Cyrenaica to Sicily, south Italy, France and Spain. At first many of the settlers came from the Greek mainland, where conditions were most cramped. But then Ionian Miletus, threatened by the non-Greek Lydian kingdom in its hinterland, occupied the mouths of the great Black Sea fishing rivers, the Danube, Dniester, Bug and Dnieper. New colonies required laws which could be written down, seen, and criticized. So the age of colonization is also the age of the lawgivers – or gradual codifications – seeking to conciliate class disturbances. At Athens Solon, appointed 'archon and reconciler', reserved the chief offices for the nobility, but appealed to the rising middle class by defining the rights of the Assembly and accepting the principle that all citizens should share in the government and the courts. Solon also pointed the way towards a more mobile society by adding wealth to landownership as a criterion of privilege.

Encouraged by the introduction of the alphabet, poets received further stimulus from the establishment of a musical scale, fitted both to the eastern flute and to the lyre. The result was the creation of new sorts of poetry: elegy and lyric. To the accompaniment of the flute, the seventh-century Ionian Archilochus of Paros wrote and sang about many subjects – in a new individualistic poetry of personal likes and dislikes which reflected his own wandering, frustrated life. For choral groups singing to the lyre, Alcman of Sparta wrote with fresh musical imagery and homely vivid phrase. This poetry for choirs found its chief home in Dorian lands where communal feeling was especially marked. But the lyric ode for one voice reached its climax round the Asian coasts, where individualism was at its strongest; and Alcaeus (c. 600) and Sappho introduced personal poetry concerned with their own interests, loves and hatreds.

The distinction between mainland and oriental Greece now becomes increasingly noticeable in the arts. Mainland sculptors stress the structural mechanism of bodies, whereas the subtler, more superficial eastern work exploits the decorative possibilities of female drapery. Athens gradually took over from Corinth the artistic as well as the commercial leadership of Greece, producing black-figure pottery with superbly economical designs that include Execias' masterpieces both of action and of classic restraint. Then, from c. 530, a new red-figure Athenian technique opened the way to a variety of vigorous anatomical and facial explorations and foreshortenings (c. 500).

By this time coinage had come westwards from the Ionian cities and from non-Greek Lydia in the hinterland of Asia Minor. Its employment as currency, first by the island city of Aegina which for a time successfully rivalled Athens, and then by Corinth and Athens, revolutionized Greek society, enabling farmers to specialize and manufacturers to make cheap goods. But the use of money also resulted in oppressive usury and mortgages, and the enslavement of debtors. With the backing of restive proletariats, as well as of the middle classes who provided cities with their armies (p. 10), powerful new-rich financiers assumed dictatorial positions. These 'tyrants', who were particularly to be found in advanced areas such as the Corinthian isthmus, Athens, Ionia (Samos) and Sicily (p. 22), adopted imperialist foreign policies, and tackled economic pressures by mobilizing unemployed labour for major public works, and developing export industries. However their dynasties, harassed by exiled noblemen, mostly succumbed either to more democratic governments – as at Athens under Cleisthenes – or to the old oligarchic régimes.

Sparta had not developed like most other Greek city-states. The Spartans were a military aristocratic caste, living under two joint kings, five 'overseers' and a Senate, among a population of subject peasant serfs (*helots*) who outnumbered them by at least seven to one. The permanent threat inherent in this situation enforced on the ruling race a peculiar way of life involving a rigorous, totalitarian discipline which made them the best soldiers in Greece – and the enemies of democratic states.

This was also an age of restless orgiastic worships, such as the cult of Dionysus (Bacchus) from Thrace. Guilt feelings were reflected in tales of posthumous punishments and rewards. Among the many holy women whose pathological trances attracted reverence, the most influential was the Pythia who presided over the Delphic oracle; its priests, guiding a political league of city-states, exalted Apollo (p. 9) as the omniscient moral imposer of law and order. While half-Ionian, half-Asian thinkers of Miletus, in contact with Egyptian and Mesopotamian learning, formulated semi-scientific conceptions of the world as an intelligible whole, Pythagoras, who left his native Samos for Croton in south Italy (c. 531) (p. 22), was closer to contemporary mysticism in his doctrine of reincarnation. Yet he also foreshadowed modern physics by seeking to explain nature in terms of mathematics, which he saw as the key to the universe.

Classical Greece

Before tackling mainland Greece, the Achaemenid Persian empire conquered Croesus of Lydia (546 BC) and then the Asian and Ionic Greeks. However, Darius I (522–486) of Persia attempted in vain to secure a Danube frontier against the Scythians of south Russia (512), whose unique artistic talents are illustrated by the fantastic blends of naturalism and stylization with which, inheriting earlier Eurasian nomad traditions, they depicted rams' heads, eagles, lions, fishes, boar and deer. After an unsuccessful Ionian attempt to revolt against the Persians (494), there followed the triumphant mainland resistance to their invasions. The epic battle of Marathon (490) against Darius, and the no less heroic engagements of Thermopylae, Salamis, Artemisium (480) and Plataea (479) against Xerxes I (486–465), have done more than anything else to hand down to history a specifically European image in opposition to Asia.

During the next forty years, by means of its fleet created by Themistocles victor of Salamis, Athens took the political lead, adopting an imperialist policy which intensified under Pericles (d. 429). Corinthian sea-power, clashing with Athens, was supported by the land-power of Sparta which finally defeated the Athenians in the Peloponnesian War. This long drawn out series of hostilities (431–404) was the theme of the historian Thucydides, whose scientific concern with the laws of human nature in politics – in contrast with his more discursive but also less tendencious predecessor Herodotus of Halicarnassus in Asia Minor – extracted permanently valid political lessons from the downfall of his city and empire.

Next Sparta was briefly in the ascendancy (404–371), and then Thebes under its military genius Epaminondas (d. 362). Soon however, in spite of the warnings of the Athenian Demosthenes – the outstanding public speaker of all time – the battle of Chaeronea (338) brought the whole of Greece under half-Hellenized Macedonia, where Philip II (359–336) had created from the proceeds of his gold mines an irresistible army and an equally competent system for bribing the politicians of the Greek city-states.

Founder at Athens of 'the first European University', for the training of orators and statesmen, Isocrates (d. 338) had urged Philip to lead a Persian expedition on a new, national, pan-Hellenic basis; and the League of Corinth, into which Philip formed the Greek cities, appointed him for the task. When he died, his son Alexander the Great (336–323) took up the challenge and conquered all the territories of Persia (334–329), extending his frontiers as far as Russian Turkestan and the Punjab. A general of unprecedented quality, he was increasingly worshipped as a god – in his lifetime, unlike

13

earlier recipients of this hero-cult who had received its attentions after their death. Yet Alexander displayed outstanding insight by his desire for Macedonian and Persian partnership, and by the founding of perhaps as many as seventy new cities; the greatest of these Alexandrias was in Egypt, but others were established on the farthest Indian borders. A homogeneous Greek civilization was thus extended for enormous distances towards the east, and for a time the centre of gravity shifted away from Greece and Europe.

After the Persian wars, Greek art had developed the severe Hellenic idealism that shines from its sculpture such as the statue identified as Leonidas, Spartan hero of Thermopylae, and the figure of Apollo at Olympia (c. 456) whose human splendour is so formidably transfigured into superhuman strength. At about the same time Myron, designer of narrative sculptural groups, studied new problems of pose and the austere geometry of taut, continuous movement. Polyclitus, working in bronze, determined a fixed set of proportions for his athletic male nudes, in the *Canon* (now lost) which illustrated the intellectuality of this century's unparalleled creative output. On the Athenian Acropolis, Pallas Athene's Parthenon, rebuilt in the Doric order after Persian destruction, has bequeathed the novel and sophisticated reliefs of Pheidias, with their deeply cut and shadowed draperies; while the mathematical subtlety of the temple's almost imperceptibly curving lines pays equal tribute to the classic doctrines of balance and moderation.

Another leading art of the day was painting. The large-scale pictures (now lost) which were executed on walls and wooden panels by Polygnotus of Thasos seem to have possessed a new *trompe l'oeil* plasticity; and surviving red-figure and white-figure vases achieve a novel transparency of clothing and liveliness of facial treatment. At the end of the fifth century Apollodorus developed fresh techniques of light and shade to emphasize his modelling. The most remarkable painter of all was held to be Alexander's court artist Apelles, who no doubt went further in exploring three-dimensional effects; but his work too, like so much else, has disappeared or is no longer identifiable. Meanwhile the fourth-century sculptor Scopas of Paros emphasized the emotional expressions of his subjects. Praxiteles of Athens, who was said to model from life, evolved the female nude, and endowed male statues such as his Hermes at Olympia with a novel, insinuating, languorous balance between the ideal and the individual. Lysippus of Sicyon, creator of an original heroic type from the features of Alexander, decreased the proportion of head to body in his robust figures, but above all liberated his free-standing statues by designing them to be seen from every side.

In the days of their fifth-century imperialism, the Athenians had used the

Ancient Greece and the Mediterranean

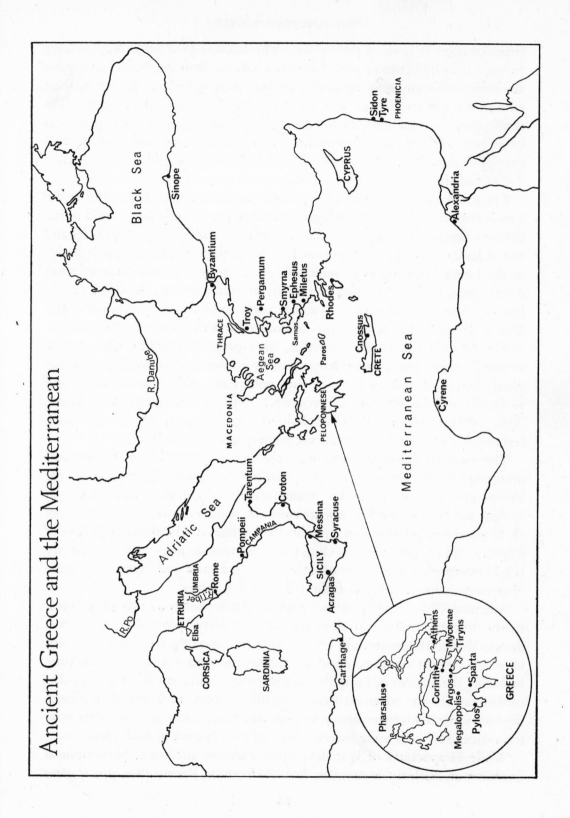

financial contributions of their allies – who became their subjects – not only to build temples but to improve the city's narrow dirty streets, and to furnish the baths and gymnastic institutions which played so large a part in their educational system; though women enjoyed few of these amenities, spending much time in their dark insanitary houses. The economy of Athens was based not only on 'allied' contributions but on its 70,000 slaves (nearly half the population) who mainly came from Asia Minor, Thrace and south Russia, and included the city's doctors, musicians, policemen and minor civil servants.

The great times of the Athenian tragic dramas, presented annually at the spring festival of the Great Dionysia, extended between the first award of the prize to Aeschylus at the competition of 484 and the deaths of Sophocles and Euripides in c. 406. Their exceptional talents brought the flexible, rich clarity of the Greek language to its zenith. Greek tragedy is often concerned with *hubris*, presumptuous conduct or speech, and with *nemesis*, the anger or dislike – resulting in retribution – which such conduct or speech provokes. 'Know yourself' (know that you are human) was the other enduring lesson.

The *Oresteia* trilogy of Aeschylus, his *Agamemnon*, *Libation-Bearers* and *Eumenides* with their densely charged, stiffly gorgeous, doom-laden wealth of poetic language, link or identify Fate with Zeus, who is omnipotent and perilously jealous. Sophocles, preoccupied with the sufferings of mankind, depicts the horrifying downfall of Oedipus as his illustration of human powerlessness in the face of god-given yet incomprehensible destiny.

The plays of Euripides, who won the annual prize only five times and emigrated to Macedonia, were moulded by the rigours and tensions of the Peloponnesian War. Euripides' dramatic approach, formal in manner yet violent and fraught with passionate conflicts, turns a disturbingly critical eye upon cherished traditions of morality and religion. The moving praises of heroism and of nature in sparkling lyric choruses do not conceal an utterly tragic interpretation of his morbidly conceived male and especially female characters, helpless victims of blind and amoral forces.

Athenian Old Comedy, in the hands of Aristophanes (c. 450–383), welds many different traditional elements into masterly, poetical, conservative dramas that lavish penetrating wit and invective upon the absurdities inherent in every current opinion, custom, controversy and cultural innovation – including the manner of Euripides. Astonishingly frank as a war-time, pacifist spokesman for the common man who suffers worst in wars, Aristophanes directed some of his strongest abuse against radical leaders such as Cleon, who for a time, and with some success, directed the conduct of hostilities.

While Hippocrates of Cos developed scientific medicine, philosophical doctrines on dualistic or monistic lines (Heraclitus, Parmenides, p. 22) gave way to the Theory of Atoms elaborated by Leucippus of Miletus and Democritus of Abdera in Thrace (*c.* 460–370), who postulated innumerable, tiny, various-shaped, solid particles colliding and agglomerating in empty space. Democritus also argued in favour of a rising cosmopolitan spirit – 'the native land of a good soul is the whole universe'. His compatriot Protagoras (*c.* 480–400), one of the 'sophists' who claimed to teach efficient living, called man the measure of all things, and doubted the existence of the gods – whom Critias called bogeys invented by governments. Antiphon foreshadowed Marx in another way, by identifying inequality of wealth as a primary cause of dissension.

Socrates of Athens (469–399 BC), condemned and executed as a subversive influence, left nothing in writing; but he gave human thought a decisive shift from cosmology to ethics. Insisting that virtue is knowledge – knowledge of the individual's happiness or good – he applied serious critical thought, and systematic definition of terms, to personal conduct. His pupil Plato (*c.* 427–347 BC), who founded the Academy and taught there for nearly forty years, inherited from Socrates the conviction that man's first aim should be to understand his own Ultimate Good, determinable by *a priori* reasoning. In the *Republic*, Plato outlines a Utopian city-state community, requiring censorship, conscription, and state control of economics and education and thought by an expert *élite*. His *Laws*, while reiterating the theoretical perfection of communist unity, favour in practice a 'mixed constitution' without extremes of poverty or wealth. His metaphysics bequeathed idealism.

Diogenes (*c.* 400–325) 'the Cynic', who came to Athens from Sinope in northern Asia Minor, believed like Plato that virtue was all-important. But he went further by elaborating cosmopolitan tendencies (p. 19) and saw no difference – except in so far as individuals might differ in virtue – between Greek and barbarian, rich and poor, master and slave. Diogenes also pointed the way to many a Hellenistic philosophy aiming at impregnability against circumstances, when he asserted and practised the renunciation of all personal possessions; while Pyrrho of Elis (*c.* 360–270) saw scepticism, a suspension of judgment so that nothing will surprise us, as the best means towards the same end.

On the other hand, Plato's pupil Aristotle of Stagira in Macedonia (384–322) still based his *Politics* on the assumption that the city-state, obsolete though it was now becoming, gave men the best lives. But his absorbing concern was with the world's scientific phenomena, and his *Metaphysics*, with their orderly certainty that speculation must be based on systematic empirical investigation, have handed down to us, often through Islamic intermediaries (p. 87), the basis and much of the terminology of modern classifications.

Aristotle's works on logic, which were his only writings known in the west between *c.* AD 500 and 1200, developed the science of reasoning based on the syllogism. His two books on *Ethics* conclude that, although the ideal is to contemplate truth, ordinary men must find their happiness in two things, between which he distinguished: intellectual good sense, and moral decency, identified by him as the Mean between two extremes of conduct. This definition caused many later thinkers, in Rome as in the eighteenth century, to emphasize moderation as an ideal (p. 32). No less influential was his systematization of the extraordinarily pervasive art or science of rhetoric or public speaking, the basis of classical education: while from the twelfth century AD onwards his *Organon*, known at first only in part through a Latin version, provided the staple for current dialectic and the largest single influence (outside theology) upon educational practice.[1]

Greece after Alexander

Alexander's death was followed, after forty years of warfare, by the consolidation of three multi-national kingdoms (*c.* 280 BC). The Seleucids ruled a heterogeneous realm extending from the Aegean to the remotest confines of Persia and, at first, as far as India. The Ptolemies, who made Egypt the ancient world's most thoroughgoing instance of state control, had their capital at Alexandria; it rivalled or excelled Athens as the cultural centre of this new Hellenistic world. In Macedonia, the monarchy was revived by Antigonus II Gonatas (276–241), who not only rejected the ruler-worship accepted by his eastern colleagues, but (like Asoka and Marcus Aurelius, p. 36) nearly made philosophy practical politics, interpreting his kingship as 'a glorious slavery' – something that seems glorious to the world, but is really a job of hard work.

Antigonus' dynasty protected Hellenism against the barbarians of the north, such as the Celts (Gauls) who had overrun most of the Balkans and occupied the territories of central Asia Minor that were called Galatia after them (278). Many Greek city-states, though still internally self-governing, depended on Macedonia. Others, for mutual protection, banded together in federal institutions such as the Achaean and Aetolian Leagues. The island of Delos was a trading-centre for corn, of which the half-Hellenized kingdom of the Cimmerian Bosphorus, the Crimea, was the largest exporter. But the most prosperous and cultured city-state in the eastern Mediterranean was that of the Rhodians, whose carrying trade was stimulated by Alexander's conquests and backed by an efficient fleet.

[1] Aristotle's *Poetics* likewise dominated literary criticism for centuries.

Opposite: Heracles and Cerberus, from an Attic amphora
by the Andocides painter (*c.* 530-525 BC)

Elsewhere in the Hellenistic world this was a period of warfare and famines, and of down-and-outs swelling the slave-markets. From *c.* 279 serious outbreaks occurred among slaves; and the cause of the non-slave proletariat was espoused by two communistic, Stoic-influenced Spartan kings Agis IV (244–241 BC) and Cleomenes III (235–222). Cleomenes was suppressed by the Macedonians. But then an appeal against the overlordship of Macedonia heralded the end of the Hellenistic state system: for opposition to its ambitious King Philip V (221–179) prompted Rhodes and Pergamum (an Anatolian offshoot of the Seleucid realm) to call in Rome (p. 25).

In a world of huge states where man was defenceless and afraid, escape was sought through the worship of Chance or Babylonian astrology, or through the deities of the emotional mystery religions which with their thrilling cult-dramas and initiations likewise offered immortal refuge from destiny: Dionysus (p. 12), the Anatolian earth-mother Cybele, the Egyptian moon-goddess Isis – beloved of women – and the Indo-Iranian sun-god Mothras, whose lofty rejection of weakness provided another non-philosophical route to the goal of Hellenistic man, imperviousness to fortune's blows.

But it was Athens, though now of secondary political importance, which produced not only a humanely individualistic expression of contemporary ideas in the polished New Comedy of Menander (*c.* 341–290) – ancestor of European comic dramatists – but also the leading philosophical schools working towards this contemporary ideal of imperturbability. Epicurus (*c.* 342–270) saw sense perception as the only basis of knowledge, far more reliable than fear of the gods or of death; though his concession of a 'swerve' to the atoms of Leucippus (p. 17) rejected a wholly mechanistic view in favour of some measure of free will. Led by his trust in sensations, Epicurus argued that the highest aim of personal conduct, with which like all contemporary philosophers he was preoccupied, is *happiness*. By this he meant pleasure of a negative kind: renunciation, independence, freedom from trouble and pain.

A deliberately opposed attempt at this same purpose of rising above the vicissitudes of life was made by the Stoics. Inaugurated in the Painted Porch at Athens by Zeno from Citium in Cyprus (*c.* 300), they held, in opposition to Epicureanism, that the universe is animated by a divine spark, of which all human beings have a share: so that they can, and should, attain to part of its goodness. A man is the captain of his own soul, and has a conscience and a duty. Moreover, this shared divine spark makes mankind a universal brotherhood, a world-state which transcended the traditional city-state – a cosmopolis instead of a polis. Although social revolutions were envisaged only by later followers of this doctrine, it indicated that men are equal, because they are equal in their souls.

Hellenistic cities were lavishly adorned with amenities including porticoes and colonnaded halls. The outstanding sculptural masterpiece known to us from the epoch immediately following Alexander was found on the north Aegean island Samothrace; it is the Victory of Pythocritus, with its superb wings and diaphanous drapery. The kingdom of Pergamum (p. 19) elaborated a style of theatrical, restless, pathetic virtuosity. Sculptors in many Greek lands also contributed to a remarkable development of portraiture, moving on from Sumerian and Egyptian achievements to more subtle blends between idealism and realistic observation. The charm of the commonplace, too, was exploited in the graceful little terracotta figures named, wrongly, after the town of Tanagra.

In literature Alexandria was unquestionably in the forefront, with its polished, experimental, individualistic poetry (c. 300–260) led by Apollonius Rhodius who romanticized the epic, and by the Cyrenean, Callimachus, who preferred poems of miniature dimensions. Moreover, researchers from all over the Mediterranean area worked at Alexandria's Museum. Among them were Euclid (c. 323–285) who developed theoretical geometry, Eratosthenes of Cyrene the creator of scientific geography, and Aristarchus of Samos (c. 310–230) who made use of trigonometry and conjectured that the earth goes round the sun.

Early Italy and Sicily

The Etruscans, living in the plains and hills of western Italy north of the Tiber, organized themselves in loosely federated piratical city-states (c. 700 BC) which were at first monarchies and then republics. Their strength came from horse-chariots, which they introduced into Italy, and from the working of Tuscan copper and the iron of Elba.

The ritualistic religion in which they believed was a fear-ridden business requiring vast cities of corridor- and chamber-tombs. The Etruscans loved bloodthirsty games, feasting and music. Their language, though largely incomprehensible to us, was evidently non-Indo-European. Moreover, their granulated jewellery and dynamically rhythmical paintings and sculptures, though adapted from Greek artistic imports, display an un-Greek lack of concern for anatomic realism. All these features suggest affinities with the middle east as well as with Hellas. So the belief of the Etruscan-influenced Romans that they themselves had come from Troy reflects historical migrations of cultural themes, if not of a ruling class, from Asia Minor or the Levant.

In the seventh century BC the cities of southern Etruria near the coast (Caere, Vulci and the religious centre of Tarquinii) were particularly rich in resources and sea-power; then Clusium (Chiusi) farther to the north became strong. On the other flank of Latium, in Campania, there was an Etruscan federation dominated by Capua – rival to the Greek Cumae – while Felsina (Bologna) and Melpum (Milan) dominated a group of Etruscan settlements in northern Italy.

Tarquinii specialized in painting, Vulci in bronze-work, Caere and Veii in terracotta, Clusium in sculpture. These centres drew successively, without loss of individuality, upon artistic models from Assyria, Phoenicia and elsewhere in the east (*c.* 650–600), from Rhodes and the Peloponnese, from Ionia and finally from Athens (*c.* 500). Then the Etruscans lost their political impetus and eastward cultural links, before classical Greek art, the successor of these archaic styles, had been able to impinge upon them. Yet long after their suppression by the Romans (Veii *c.* 396, Etruscan League *c.* 351), their art retained its peculiar strength through the medium of a portraiture of expressive concreteness and realism which profoundly influenced Rome and Rome's medieval inheritance.

Rome, fifteen miles from the Tiber's mouth, was a well-watered, well-pastured and protected site commanding a river-crossing from Etruria to the south. Its Palatine hill was settled (traditionally in 753 BC) by the lowland, iron-using agricultural Latins, an offshoot of forty or sixty tribes who had crossed the Alps not long before 1000 BC. The adjoining Esquiline and Quirinal slopes were occupied by hill-men, the Sabines, who, though Indo-European-speaking like the Latins, sometimes interred their dead instead of cremating them as their neighbours did. Latins and Sabines at Rome united, draining their joint burial ground for conversion into the Forum (*c.* 600–575), and building upon the Capitoline hill a citadel which guarded their cattle-market and dominated their wooden bridge and its traffic of salt.

While the city-states of Etruria dominated Italy from the Po valley to Campania, an Etruscan dynasty known to history and myth as the Tarquins conquered Rome and developed its government, ceremonial, and physical appearance (*c.* 575–550). Upon the Capitoline hill they built the largest temple in Italy, dedicated to Jupiter, Juno goddess of women, and Minerva patroness of handicrafts: deities whom the Romans, although formally identifying them with Greek counterparts (Zeus, Hera, Athene), did not endow with mythological personalities to nearly the same extent, regarding religion more as a matter of bargaining in which both sides had to do their bit.

The Romans also owed a great deal to the Greek settlements in southern

Italy (p. 11). Most influential was the city-state which was also the earliest Greek colony in the west, Cumae (Cyme), founded by Chalcis (Euboea) a hundred miles south-east of Rome (*c.* 750). Soon afterwards (*c.* 734), Corinthians and others settled in Sicily, the most fertile of Hellenized lands. The Greek communities of the west were menaced both by Etruria and by north African Carthage, which had succeeded its Phoenician motherland Tyre (p. 9) as the leading Mediterranean maritime power. Etruscans and Carthaginians defeated the Greek colonizers of Massilia (Marseille) in a sea-battle off Corsica (*c.* 535), but during the next sixty years Cumae, in various coalitions, got the better of Etruria. Early in the fifth century, the Greek part of Sicily was dominated by the dictators of Syracuse, Acragas (Agrigento), Messana and Himera. The Carthaginians, invited in by Himera, were annihilated there by Gelon of Syracuse and Theron of Acragas (480). After Gelon's brother and successor Hieron had finally eliminated the Etruscan threat (474), Syracuse, under the democracies to which its dictators soon gave place, was free to develop its increasingly spectacular prosperity.

Already in the seventh century BC, Stesichorus of Himera had written grand and dignified narrative lyrics. Pythagoras (p. 12) migrated in *c.* 531 to Croton in south Italy, ruling the city as a religious brotherhood. His conviction of a mathematical universe was carried further by Parmenides of Elea (*c.* 500), who, although critical of observational science, superseded mythical cosmology by methods of historical description. Rejecting apparent diversity as 'mere evidence of the senses and so delusion', he envisaged the universe as single, spherical, and eternally immobile; and his fellow-citizen Zeno supported this monism by arguments which have caused him to be described as the founder of dialectic.

Empedocles of Acragas (*c.* 490–430), a wonder-working medicine-man and democratic leader, refused to believe in Parmenides' absence of movement. Instead, he adopted the dualist view (p. 16) of the universe as an everlasting battleground between Love (attraction) and Strife (repulsion). Empedocles was also credited with the invention of rhetoric, of which however the most famous exponent was his compatriot and pupil Gorgias of Leontini (*c.* 483–376), the creator of artistic Greek prose. Gorgias was a pan-Hellenist who also contributed to the critical, sophistic brand of philosophy (p. 17) by propounding that if anything exists (which it does not) it is unknowable.

Called in by the enemies of Syracuse during the Peloponnesian War (p. 13), Athens launched against that city the catastrophic expedition so movingly described by Thucydides (415–413). The next invaders of Sicily came from Carthage; their capture of Acragas caused a revolution at Syracuse, where a muleteer's son Dionysius I (406–367) gained power and maintained resplendent autocratic control for nearly forty years by military improvements, naval strength, extortion from the rich, favours to the proletariat, and the liberation of thousands of slaves. Although the biggest city in the world was Pataliputra (Patna) on the Ganges, Syracuse was the largest in Europe. After pushing back the Carthaginians (392) and subduing the native Sicels, Dionysius ravaged Etruria and occupied Corsica. The dimensions of his state and its capital Syracuse were unprecedented among the Greeks. But a further Carthaginian war failed (c. 383), and his successors lost more ground. Some prosperity was regained under a moderate democracy set up by the Corinthian general Timoleon (344–337), but Agathocles (317–289) weakened the city again, by wars and internal violence.

Thereafter, Syracuse gained fame from antiquity's greatest engineer and mathematician Archimedes (c. 287–212). It was also the birthplace of Theocritus (c. 310–250), who, moving to Alexandria and Cos, invented the long-lived pastoral which transfigures into elegant, humorous and urban poetry the shepherds' songs of his native Sicily.

During the general decline of Etruscan authority in Italy (p. 21), Rome had asserted its independence, becoming a republic (c. 510 BC?) under two consuls whose annual election seemed an adequate safeguard against autocracy. Guided by an inner circle of ex-consuls, the Senate controlled finance, foreign policy, and the wars and laws promulgated by the national Assembly – a collection of thrifty farmer-soldiers grouped in their ancestor-venerating families.

The quasi-regal Roman patrician clans' occupation of the best land, combined with severe laws of debt, caused the lower classes (plebeians) to agitate successfully for the recognition of their own protectors (tribunes of the people) and for the legal code of the 'Twelve Tables' (451–450), framed in a Latin already possessing its historic qualities of concrete terseness and precision. The plebeians gained admission to the main offices of state (366, 351), and when their resolutions were given the force of law (c. 287) popular sovereignty had come into being. But the tribunes attended and assisted the Senate, in an atmosphere of compromise hitherto almost unknown in the ancient world. The short-term office of dictator, provided in the constitution for emergencies, was rarely needed.

A setback to Roman expansion occurred in c. 390 when a force of Gauls briefly occupied the city, though the Capitoline citadel held out. This was one of the farthest points reached by these Celtic peoples who, from a nucleus in the Upper Danube and Rhine basin, had extended their military power and culture into Spain, Britain (and later Ireland), most of France, the Balkans and now north Italy where Etruria became their link with the world of

Greece. The Hallstatt culture of the seventh and sixth centuries was replaced by the La Tène culture (*c.* 450), in which the Celts, extracting, working and distributing their native metallurgical resources, adorned gold- and bronze-bedecked chariots, harnesses and weapons with an exuberantly plastic, rhythmically patterned asymmetrical curvilinear art. Contemporary classical themes were transfigured by an essentially geometric and abstract discipline; but this again was modified by fantastic animal motifs echoing the oriental period of Greek art (p. 10), as well as Etruscan and Scythian styles (p. 13).

Having occupied Rome, the Celts, who lacked political cohesion and pertinacity, accepted a ransom and withdrew. The Romans resumed the quarter-millennium-long process of winning more land and food by the reduction of their Sabine, Etruscan, Latin and Samnite neighbours; of whom the last finally succumbed in 272. The causes of Roman successes – usually gained after an initial disaster – were ruthless endurance and thoroughness, unflinching self-confidence, skilful diplomacy, the refusal to accept defeat, and the disciplined employment of open-order formations with accurate javelin-throwers in their front rank.

The Gallic invasion was followed by the construction of a new Roman city wall (*c.* 378) and all-weather roads. By 260 BC the confederacy based upon Rome extended over 52,000 square miles, exceeding in size all contemporary Mediterranean empires except that of the Seleucids (p. 18). Many central Italians from sea to sea were incorporated into the Roman state as full citizens or half-citizens; there was an elaborate system of bilateral or unilateral alliances with 120–150 treaty states in the peninsula, including newly established fortresses.

Roman citizens paid a direct capital tax assessed on means. Allies contributed military service, providing just over half the total force of the confederacy. Few had a voice in determining peace or war, but the Pax Romana and its spoils were theirs. Rome's methods were non-interfering compromise, 'divide and rule', and the allurements of increased privilege for collaborators. Gradually, the Latin tongue and Roman law tended towards a common culture.

The Imperial Roman Republic

Rome's southward expansion alarmed the most prosperous Greek city of southern Italy, Tarentum, which called for help to Pyrrhus, the half-Greek king of Epirus across the Adriatic; a second appeal came to him from Syracuse, faced with a new Carthaginian threat. Pyrrhus invaded both Italy and Sicily (280–272), but without ultimate success. The Romans were now free to reduce western Hellenism to subject status; and in two traumatic wars (264–

241, 218–201), the second involving Hannibal's prolonged invasion of Italy, they eliminated the Carthaginian menace. The hero of final victory was Scipio Africanus.

The first Punic War, in which the Romans had built themselves a fleet, also brought them into closer contacts with Hellenistic culture. Their own crude, Etruscan-influenced song-and-dance shows progressed to Latin versions of Greek plays. Then came the first original Latin comic dramatist, Plautus from Umbria (c. 254–184), who during and after the Second Punic War (in spite of uncertain popular taste and suspicious governmental reactions) produced a varied and unequalled series of plays 'in Greek dress' but in vivid Latin, far more explosively farcical than the Athenian New Comedy (p. 19) from which their themes were drawn. Meanwhile, under Scipio Africanus' patronage, the works of Ennius from Calabria (239–169), 'father of Roman poetry', included a ruggedly grand first national epic, the *Annals*, much revered by later Romans. The younger Scipio (Aemilianus) befriended the satirical poet Lucilius (c. 180–102); and another of his protégés, the north African comic dramatist Terence (c. 195–159), developed the Plautine drama for more sophisticated audiences, employing skilful construction, graceful well-made dialogues and fluent soliloquies which have inspired the theatres of Europe.

Rome was now drawn into the affairs of the large Hellenistic states. Responding to an appeal from Rhodes and Pergamum (p. 19), Flamininus defeated the Macedonian king Philip V at Cynoscephalae (196), declaring Greece 'free'. Next, an expansionist Seleucid ruler, Antiochus III, by crossing into Europe, caused the alarmed Romans to retaliate by landing for the first time in Asia; where the flexibility of the legions enabled them to win against numerical odds at Magnesia in 189. An imperialistic group in the Senate now made withdrawal from the Greek world impossible. Instead, amid a deteriorating moral atmosphere, the Romans crushed and annexed Macednitia (168, 147), plundered Corinth (146) and dissolved the Achaean League (p. 18). The enormously wealthy provinces of Africa and Asia – in Tunisia and western Asia Minor – were the next to be established, by the conquest of Carthage (146) and inheritance from a king of Pergamum (133) respectively.

One result of the wars was the rise of an important class of Roman businessmen (*equites*, knights) who, organized in joint stock companies, handled the influx of plunder, indemnities and mineral wealth, lent and banked money (based on the silver *denarius*), and through their agents (*publicani*) organized trade and farmed the collection of taxes from the state. The leading Roman families, with their traditional flair for management which had won the Second Punic War, not only exacted their percentage from the knights, but maintained control over successive consular elections as well as over foreign policy. Their instruments, in lieu of political parties which were not yet known, included prestige, bribery, popular entertainments, armies of supporters ('clients') and indefatigable marriage alliances. The capitalist but austere farmer-statesman Cato the Censor (d. 149) stood for conservatism. The circle of his opponent Scipio Aemilianus (d. 129), notable for its freedom of thought and discussion, included not only Latin writers but an outstanding Greek historian who illuminated the imperial rise of Rome, Polybius of Megalopolis (c. 203–120). Another of Scipio's friends was the Rhodian philosopher Panaetius (c. 185–109), who adapted Stoic rigours (p. 19) to Roman careers by leaving room for 'imperfect' progression towards virtue.

While Hellenistic art produced the Venus de Milo (Melos) and the Laocoon of Rhodes with its baroque contorted rhythms, there were also signs of a Greek-inspired but national Roman art. Influenced by flourishing Hellenistic schools – particularly at the Graeco-Italian trading-centre of Delos – and by a native Roman tradition of preserving death-masks, portrait-sculpture began to develop. But above all, there were striking advances by architects working on the new marble temples, bridges, quays, houses and high tenements of Rome. The town-Forum, with its colonnaded porticoes and aisled and storied hall (basilica), was evolved from Hellenistic models (p. 20); and there appeared the characteristically Roman ceremonial arch, with its reliefs and its statuary decoration. At Pompeii, a commercial port and residential town, the earliest houses recall by their peristyles the buildings of Delos, but display an un-Greek symmetry round the open atrium. The Stabian Baths of Pompeii have a room which displayed the novelty of a dome, so fruitful for the future.

After the wars, Italian small-holders gave way to huge ranches grazing cattle rather than growing corn. The brutal ill-treatment of the slaves on these estates provoked savage outbreaks by gangs of deserters; in Sicily 70,000 slaves under the Syrian Eunus temporarily seized several towns (135–132). These large properties also dispossessed the free poor, who now, and during the civil wars which were to follow, drifted to the cities, unemployed, starving and violent. Two high-minded young noblemen, the brothers Tiberius and Gaius Gracchus, proposed land-laws, which Gaius endeavoured to follow up by extending the Roman franchise in Italy. But both Gracchi met their deaths at the hands of conservative opponents (133, 122 BC), and a century of internal political violence had begun.

Moreover, from now on, the legions placed their formidable *esprit de corps* no longer at the command of the increasingly impotent Roman state, but at the disposal of talented generals who disregarded traditions but could produce

Outstanding features of the Minoan (Cretan) art, which in the second millennium BC created something wholly original from near eastern models, were these female statuettes with curved aprons, conical hats and exposed breasts

Lead statuette of c. 1500 BC from Kampos (south Peloponnese). Egyptian and Asian models have been left behind in a blend of abstraction and natural movement. Much Hellenic myth seems to have come from the Minoans and Mycenaeans

After a 'Dark Age' had succeeded Mycenae, Athens led a new Geometric style of vase-painting. There were also lively local schools in the islands. This generously shaped jar with its uncrowded design comes from Thera (Santorin) (c. 700 BC)

BELOW: Corinthian wine-jug (625–600 BC). As is suggested by the place where this was found (Rhodes), the trade of Corinth dominated the Mediterranean – east as well as west – until Athens took over commercial supremacy
OPPOSITE: Marble Gorgon from the pediment of the temple of Artemis at the Corinthian colony of Corcyra (Corfu); early sixth century BC. Archaic Greek art reflected the terror and hysteria of contemporary religion

LEFT: In the seventh century BC, the coastal cities of southern Etruria, north of Rome, were immensely powerful and luxurious. This opulent, intricate gold clasp and pendant from a tomb at Caere (Cerveteri) reflects oriental models; later it was Ionian and Attic work that influenced the Etruscans

ABOVE: Colonising Greeks (Phocaeans) for a time interrupted the Phoenician (later Carthaginian) commercial monopoly of south Spain. This 'Lady of Elche' (near Alicante) – once polychrome – with her mitre, roundlets and necklaces, arrestingly illustrates the creative impact of archaic Hellenism on local cultures

ABOVE: The western Greeks, in south Italy and Sicily, were wealthy but discordant. Acragas (Girgenti) helped to repel Carthage, produced the wonder-worker and philosopher Empedocles, and built numerous magnificent Doric temples of which this is the best preserved (c. 450–440 BC)

LEFT: Even minor Greek city-states employed outstanding artists for their coinage. This silver piece of Terina in south-west Italy (c. 425 BC) shows a head of its patron nymph in an olive-wreath, and Nike (Victory) seated on an overturned vase

BELOW: At Athens red-figure painting first accompanied and then succeeded black-figure. The great murals have not come down to us, but outstanding artists decorated vases; this shows a rhapsode chanting a poem (c. 480 BC)

RIGHT: Bronze horse-trappings in the form of the Great Goddess and her beasts; from near Amiens. The nomad animal art of the Scythian steppes, part naturalistic and part stylised, spread west and inspired the Celts

BELOW RIGHT: Hellenistic taste for baroque design and precious metal is fully indulged in this gold amphora from the Panagurishte hoard (Plovdiv, Bulgaria, c. third century BC). It depicts the Seven against Thebes, theme of Aeschylus' tragedy

Greek and near eastern sculptors derived
magnificent material from the expensive patronage
determined features and native portrait traditions
of Republican Romans, including women who
were as prominent as they had been in Etruscan
society

results on their own by strong-arm methods. This development was largely due to the tough, sly Marius who, with a partly volunteer force, eliminated a monarch who seemed to threaten Rome's new African possessions (Jugurtha of Numidia), and then annihilated in north Italy an enemy which had caused a panic by overwhelming several amateur Roman generals: the Cimbri and Teutoni, a half-million-strong horde of migrating Germans from Jutland.

Italians who did not possess the franchise or own state lands were imprudently rebuffed by the Roman government, and attacked it in the desperate Social or Marsian War. Rome won, but had to concede full citizenship to all men south of the Po, and certain rights to north Italians beyond the river (90–89). Civil war then broke out between Romans of the left and right; Marius (d. 86) and Cinna, backed by knights and Italians, were opposed by the extremely able but impoverished nobleman Sulla. After ridding Greece of the Asian invader Mithridates VI of Pontus, Sulla demolished his opponents at home, and had himself made dictator – without time-limit, other than 'the completion of national recovery'. However Sulla, cruel, mystic and dissolute, instead of destroying the Senate, packed its ranks, guarding against would-be destroyers by limitations upon overseas commanders; and then he abdicated.

He was the patron of a novel architecture full of exciting adaptations of Hellenistic ideas. In the reconstructed sanctuary of Fortune at Praeneste (Palestrina), an intricate choreography of vision and movement transformed the whole mountainside into an enormous stepped and vaulted axial series of terraces surmounted by the goddess's temple. Sulla also systematized the architecture of a substantial portion of Rome. As its population approached the million mark, public buildings were beginning to display unprecedented boldness in their arches and vaults, made of the revolutionary material of concrete consisting of a local sandy earth (*pozzolana*) which, fused in a monolithic mass by the admixture of lime, eliminated all thrust. Meanwhile the Greek or oriental designers of Roman portrait busts were stimulated both by the formidable physiognomies and by the lavish purses of their Roman models and patrons.

The final half-century of the Roman Republic was taken up with struggles between over-powerful politicians backed by military force. The outstanding contestants were Pompey, who had liberated Rome's eastern Mediterranean trade from pirates (67) and crushed Mithridates VI of Pontus; and Julius Caesar who, in a series of unprecedented campaigns, added to Rome's province in southern Gaul (annexed in 121) all the northern and central parts of that country (58–52), as well as landing twice in Britain. Caesar possessed an unerring sense of the moment to strike, a total comprehension of supply problems, and the supreme capacity for utilizing his unequalled legionaries.

When the empire became too small for these two men's pretensions, the Republican government, designed for a modest city-state, collapsed. Caesar crossed the Rubicon (49), pursued Pompey from Italy to the Balkans, and defeated him at Pharsalus (48). On landing in Egypt Pompey was murdered, and Caesar crushed Pompey's sons in north Africa and Spain (46–45). Master of the whole Roman world, he caused the dictatorship, which he had held at intervals since 49 BC, to be extended for life (44). A month later, amid grandiose schemes for capital development and demobilization, he was struck down by Brutus, Cassius and others who had enjoyed his favour or his pardon but could not endure his perpetual autocratic rule. At the time of his death Caesar was on the eve of an eastern expedition intended to outdo Alexander. Yet, despite his exceptional clearness of vision, he had not attempted any far-reaching reforms of the state – which reverted to anarchy.

His *Commentaries* are rapidly moving military narratives which, in taut and lapidary Latin, disarmingly evade war-guilt and present an unequalled picture of Roman drive and discipline. A younger historian who supported him, Sallust (86–34 BC), preferred an artificially rugged style for his moralizing philosophical *Histories* (now lost), and his surviving essays *Jugurtha* and *Catiline* which elevated Roman historiography to a new, though rhetorical, distinction. While Lucretius (*c.* 94–55) stated the calm Epicurean case (p. 19) in poetry of a paradoxically passionate grandiloquence, the poet of the smart upper class was Catullus. Although a leading Latin representative of the experimental perfectionism which takes its name from Alexandria (p. 20), he was as unswervingly direct as he was sophisticated. An emotionally tortured intellectual, Catullus wrote of his agonizing love for 'Lesbia', who has been identified with Clodia, the most notorious of the women leading uninhibited lives in the society and subliminal politics of Rome.

Cicero (106–43 BC), proud of rescuing the state from the eccentric right-wing conspiracy of Catiline (63), was not able by all his startlingly persuasive oratory to eliminate the war-lords. But just before and after Caesar's murder, during compulsory retirement made even more sorrowful by his own daughter's death, Cicero consoled himself by producing a series of guides to living – admirably written, undogmatic popularizations of Stoic and other Hellenistic works, claiming to provide Romans with the best of Greek thought. In the later 50's BC he had written a more original treatise *On the State*, envisaging a 'leader' for the disintegrating Republic. Other studies, relating to his own legal and oratorical profession, include an emphasis on moral and intellectual qualities alike which made them the most civilized theories of education that the world had yet seen. When Antony aspired to Caesar's autocratic role, Cicero, hesitant and conceited though he was, so greatly disliked autocracy that he launched against him the devastating *Philippics* (44–43) which caused the new Triumvirate – Antony, Octavian, Lepidus – to have him killed. Cicero's extensively preserved writings include an incomparable collection of over 800 letters, many of them addressed to Atticus, richest but least ostentatious of millionaires in an age of resplendent display. These letters, together with Cicero's other works, comprise our principal source of information for the period; his impact upon generation after generation of Europeans has been inestimably powerful and varied.

After Antony, in short-lived alliance with Julius Caesar's cold-hearted twenty-year-old heir Octavian, had forced Brutus and Cassius to suicide by defeating them at Philippi in Macedonia (42), the victors spent the next eleven years preparing for their final clash with one another. When it came, Antony, whose Roman prestige was damaged by his liaison (inherited from Caesar) with Cleopatra VI of Egypt, suffered defeat at sea off Actium (31). He and Cleopatra committed suicide (30), and Octavian annexed Egypt and took over its gigantic resources.

The Earlier Roman Emperors

Augustus – a name with sacred overtones by which Octavian chose to be called (27 BC) – maintained supreme authority for forty-four years because he had first-class helpers such as Agrippa, Maecenas, Tiberius and Drusus but kept the army and the empire's wealth in his own outstandingly efficient control. Yet, describing his position by the disarming term 'first man' (*princeps*) and officially regarding his powers as renewable, he revived and encouraged Republican forms and institutions. This publicity-enforced formula or fiction, despite a few sharply suppressed aristocratic conspiracies, proved satisfactory to most Romans, since Augustus at last gave them peace.

All branches of the Roman government, senators and knights alike, were now transformed into an organism capable of bearing imperial responsibilities. The Senate was encouraged to undertake its traditional duties. Nevertheless, its membership was purged, and the ruler influenced appointments to every important office; he was also 'persuaded' to take over huge regions where most of the army was concentrated, particularly on the Rhine, Danube and Euphrates frontiers.

The Augustan peace, accompanied by much road construction, made the empire a safe place. Agriculture, still its basic industry, was extended; trades and manufactures multiplied. Italy took the lead with new factories for woollen goods in Pompeii and the north, glass-blowing in Campanian workshops, and metal-work in Rome. Exporting wine, oil and many other goods throughout the west, Italians imported slaves, grain, metals, marble, papyrus, linen and more expensive eastern articles of luxury such as furs, ivory, silk and jewels. The state did not actively intervene, except to influence and then nationalize the principal Spanish and other mines, which provided the metals for an empire-wide network of coinages with inscriptions and designs commending the merits of the government and of its head.

Augustus' endeavours to create unhampered peaceful communications required much fighting and imperial expansion. The European frontiers were pushed forward to include Danubian territories from Switzerland to the Black Sea, and western and central Germany where a more compact line on the river Elbe was reached in 9 BC. But the inadequate dimensions of Rome's 28 legions and 150,000 provincial auxiliaries were shown by serious rebellions in Pannonia (Yugoslavia) and Germany (AD 6, 9). The first of these revolts prevented the conquest of Bohemia, and the second threw back the borders to the Rhine. Nevertheless Augustus succeeding in establishing, beyond many frontiers, a *cordon sanitaire* of kingdoms under monarchs who, though officially independent, were his 'clients' and kept invaders out. Notable among them was the king of the corn-producing Bosphorus (Crimea); less successful were his attempts to make Armenia into a buffer-state which would insulate Rome from the Iranian empire of the Parthians farther to the east.

The traditional and popular Italian religion was exploited to secure acceptance for Augustus' régime and to console and direct the many who felt that ruinous civil wars had somehow upset relations with heaven. Such anxieties were calmed by his restoration of ancient rites and crumbling religious buildings, and by the construction of splendid new shrines such as the Palatine temple of Apollo – Augustus' radiant patron who was intended to reflect the fusion, under Italian supremacy, between the Hellenic and Roman ideals. Augustus also developed Caesar's plan of an imperial Forum adjacent to the ancient city-Forum: a meeting-place which unified religious and secular business in a massive spatially dynamic axial composition of rectangular lines and colonnaded curves, centring upon a temple of Mars the Avenger and transverse basilicas. The sculptural and numismatic portraiture of Augustus likewise rang the changes skilfully upon the realistic and idealistic traditions of the past, and upon the gradual and varying approximations of his status to Hellenistic concepts of the all-powerful God Made Manifest (p. 18). Another sculptural novelty was attempted in the Altar of

Peace, with its processional and symbolic reliefs which elevate patriotic events by infusing Greek frieze techniques with a serene Augustan dignity. Contemporary wall-paintings, in the House of Livia and rich men's residences at Pompeii and Herculaneum, reveal a wide variety of colourful landscapes and architectural and mythological scenes, supplemented by vivid floor-mosaics.

Augustus rallied round himself Rome's greatest poets. Virgil, born near Mantua in 70 BC, startled the literary world by the novelty of his ten short *Eclogues*, adapting to Latin with hauntingly melodious artistry the pastoral, city-dwellers' Arcadia of Theocritus (p. 23). One poem, the fourth cryptically prophesies the birth of a boy who will inaugurate the Golden Age – in terms which were to make Christendom adopt Virgil as a prophet.

The *Eclogues* were dedicated to Octavian (Augustus), and the *Georgics* (36–29 BC) to his friend Maecenas. In verse of a new and subtle power the *Georgics* hymn the Roman homeland, the beauties labours and rewards of Italian rustic life, and the Augustan peace. Virgil was also master of the epic, but the sophistication of his *Aeneid*, with its romantic and pathetic *vignette* of Dido's tragedy, is far removed from Homer's extrovert, oral tradition; and so is the complex wealth of this poetry's musical texture, interweaving a thousand intimations of philosophy, legend, emotion and religious belief. For Virgil, wars turn to weariness, in spite of a radiant Augustan future ahead. At the last, melancholy yet unembittered, he seems to reckon martial conquest lower than the conquest of his own soul by man: whose goal and place in the Universe remain mysterious, though the *Aeneid* is unsurpassed among the books which have attempted to pierce the veil, and have influenced mankind.

Rome, as the selected instrument of providential destiny, receives further glorification in the poetically imaginative prose history of Livy from Patavium (Padua) (59 BC–AD 17). His evocation of Rome's beginnings and Hannibal's invasion (p. 25) dramatizes heroes who were to inspire the historians of Europe, just as its revolutionaries were fired by his idealized account of the young Republic.

The youthful years of Horace of Venusia (65–8 BC) produced his vituperative *Epodes*, and the quick-moving informality of the *Satires* which present his famous humane commonsense. The more mature *Epistles* have made a strong impact on the world as the well-turned products of a civilized and humorous, mildly philosophical personage, a follower of Maecenas and believer in Augustus, yet still politely independent and detached. Horace's lyric *Odes* came into their own during the Italian Renaissance. In their themes of love and wine, nature and the gods, friendship and *Romanità*, life's transience and the goodness of being moderate, poetic inspiration is extended by a calculated intellectual set of clever surprises, achieved by a boldly astute, compact word order and by the ingenious adaptation of Greek metres to the Latin tongue's wholly different qualities.

This was also the classic period of Roman elegiac love-poetry. Tibullus (*c.* 48–19 BC) reverences peace and the countryside, and sensitively seeks an endurable place in a hard world. The manic-depressive Propertius of Asisium (Assisi), before turning to antiquarian national themes, devoted his far more powerful gifts, in morbid yet ironical terms replete with sombre tortuous imagery, to the analysis of the disastrous affair with 'Cynthia' which had shattered his life. Ovid of Sulmo (Sulmona) (43 BC–AD 17) reacted against both personal emotionalism and patriotic ethics. His rapid, dexterous, glittering verses look at men and especially women with not unfriendly or unhumorous or altogether untender gaze, yet with a certain professional cold-bloodedness. Augustus the moralist exiled him to Tomis (Constanta) on the Black Sea, where he completed his elegiac Roman calendar (*Fasti*). The *Metamorphoses*, a hexameter poem of 15 books, displays Ovid's narrative genius in a multitude of poetic stories about magic changes of shape: a conglomeration of myth, legend, folk-tale and anecdote which largely created the medieval ideal of Romantic love, and inspired many of Europe's finest paintings.

The next four emperors each began with protestations of Republican and Augustan correctness, but were then induced by fears for their own isolated position to plunge the upper ranks of society in a series of blood-baths which lose nothing in the telling by Tacitus and Suetonius (p. 35). Yet Tiberius (AD 14–37) was an efficient and just ruler; Claudius (41–54), born at Lugdunum (Lyon), had a genuine regard for the provinces (to which he added Britain, to Severn and Trent); and Nero (54–68) achieved a durable diplomatic solution for Armenia (p. 30).

Latin literature, second-rate since Augustus, experienced a revival in its 'Silver Age'. Although philosophical ideas were hard for a minister of Nero to put into practice, the epigrammatic treatises of the Romano-Spanish Seneca (*c.* 5/4 BC–AD 65) are redolent, not only of belief in divine providence, but of Stoic tolerance, clemency and humanity, including sympathy with slaves. His nine tragic dramas are replete with the phantoms, madmen and tyrants whom Shakespeare and many another European playwright inherited from him. In equally rhetorical poetry, his nephew Lucan (AD 39–65) wrote a Latin epic second only to the *Aeneid*, namely his *Pharsalia* devoted to a historical theme, the war between Pompey and Caesar (p. 28). Both Seneca and Lucan met their deaths, by enforced suicide, because of alleged participation in a plot against Nero. So did the epicure Petronius 'the arbiter', who may be the author of the racy *Satyricon* – a picaresque novel famous for its set-pieces the Dinner of Trimalchio and Widow of Ephesus.

Nero seized the opportunity presented by Rome's destructive fire to eliminate the capital's squalors by applying orderly ideas of town-planning inherited, in part, from the Etruscans. His domed and arcaded Golden House, the first magnificent Roman palace, had elegant ceiling-paintings – depicting intricate filigree trellises and arabesques – of which some survived to attract Raphael; and Neronian wall-paintings at Pompeii and Herculaneum, buried until more recent times under the débris of Vesuvius' eruption (80), entered into a period of flashing, sophisticated scenic illusionism, with every baroque device of spatial recession and curve (p. 189). Nero and his successors also established an unprecedentedly high artistic standard for their portraiture on coins.

The Year of the Four Emperors (68–9), theme of Tacitus' trenchant *Histories*, showed that emperors need not have Julian or Claudian blood, and that they could be appointed by the Guard, or by legions far from Rome. The victor who emerged from these convulsions was a former governor of Judaea, Vespasian (69–79), suppressor of national rebellions first by the Jews and then by Gauls and Germans. This sensibly frugal, humorous, bourgeois Italian, founder of a new (Flavian) dynasty, reorganized the empire's army and ruinous finances, and created an aristocracy of provincial origin. After the brief reign of Titus (79–81), his able but twisted brother Domitian (81–96), who directed Agricola's advance into the Scottish highlands and carried the German frontier to the Neckar, gave the principate a more frankly monarchical, terroristic character which finally provoked his assassination.

The Arch of Titus, showing soldiers carrying spoils from the Jerusalem temple, is relief-sculpture transformed by shadow-effects and other spatial devices. The Colosseum (dedicated in AD 79), largest of the amphitheatres invented by Romans to house their bloodthirsty entertainments, towers in its final form to four storeys of massive arch-bearing piers. It has profoundly influenced many-tiered Renaissance architectural designs; while other buildings of early imperial date worked out its implications, and foreshadowed Romanesque styles, by even more decisively rejecting horizontal entablatures in favour of arches springing direct from the capitals. Domitian's Palatine palace, of which little but the ground-plan has survived, had a throne-room with a 100-foot-wide barrel vault, considerably exceeding the span of St Peter's. Already, too, there were enormous, elaborately integrated complexes of imperial Baths.

Poets active under Domitian included Statius of Naples (*c.* 45–96), revered in the Middle Ages for his epic *Achilleid* but more admired today for his sensitive smaller poems; and the Spaniard Martial whose vivid, humane but frequently obscene epigrams have imprinted their definition of this *genre* upon the literatures of Europe. Martial's compatriot Quintilian (*c.* 35–95) retired from the first state Chair of Rhetoric to write his *Training of an Orator*, a sensible, practical restatement of the classical system of education which contains famous advice on Greek and Latin reading. Pliny the Elder of Comum (Como) (*c.* AD 23–79) was a man of extraordinary industry and encyclopaedic though uncritical knowledge whose numerous works included his thirty-seven-book *Natural History*, a mine of curious information veering between fable and shrewdness. His death in the eruption of Vesuvius is picturesquely narrated by his nephew Pliny the Younger (*c.* 61–113), notable for his nine varied books of literary letters, and for a tenth containing correspondence which as governor of Bithynia, in Asia Minor, he exchanged with the emperor. These letters include Pliny's inquiries and the ruler's directives concerning the treatment of Christians, whom the governor was instructed to punish if they were recalcitrant, without, however, hunting them out.

The emperor who thus directed Pliny was the military expert Trajan (98–117), descendant of Roman settlers in Spain and first of a series of monarchs to be 'adopted' by their predecessors as the most suitable candidate for imperial responsibility. Before turning to the Parthian empire, in which he overran vast regions, Trajan reduced and annexed Dacia (Rumania), seizing its treasures and exploiting its mines.

These campaigns were commemorated by reliefs spiralling up to the skies upon the Column of Trajan; this vividly and variedly grouped, continuous narrative performs the dual task of concentrating upon the emperor's triumphant personality and bringing the Roman and barbarian worlds into dramatic confrontation with one another. Trajan's Column forms part of the colonnaded complex of his Forum, created by the town-planner and architect Apollodorus of Damascus. Another of its components was the double-aisled, clerestoried, apsidal Basilica of Trajan – place of social and commercial assembly, law-court and ancestor of Christian churches. There was also an extensive series of market-buildings hewn out of the rock. For Trajan, in spite of an aggressive foreign policy, was 'best of rulers', devoting great care to the welfare of Italy and the provinces alike.

When he died in Asia Minor his protégé and compatriot Hadrian succeeded him, but reversed his policy by evacuating Mesopotamia and Armenia. This restless, versatile administrator, soldier, sightseer and poet spent more than half his reign traversing the empire, throughout which he put into effect a new, provincial's conception of partnership between Rome and the provinces. His visit to Britain led to the construction of a frontier wall from Solway to Tyne (*c.* 122–9). But in Judaea a formidable rebellion cost over half a million Jewish lives, and the destruction of Jerusalem and fifty other fortresses.

Patron and practitioner of letters and architecture, Hadrian gave Rome a new Athenaeum, where poets and orators recited and lectures were given on philosophy, rhetoric and grammar. Legal studies were also taught there. They had flourished in many previous Roman centuries, throughout a majestic series of unprecedentedly skilful and increasingly humane developments; and now came a pre-eminent jurist and codifier, Salvius Julianus.

Hadrian's building projects reveal the breathtaking developments in dome construction which the exploitation of concrete (p. 27) had made possible. The best-preserved of all Rome's ancient structures, the Pantheon, has a monolithic dome 142 feet high and wide. Its sun-like central aperture and starry rosette decoration assist the harmonious grandeur of the whole edifice to reflect the heavenly powers and their majesty. Despite his keen Hellenism, expressed in the new sculptural ideal apparent in the features of his favourite Antinous, Hadrian's building schemes in the west are Roman in their tremendous vaults and cupolas and curves. The architects of his Villa at Tivoli – which covers seven square miles with every conceivable kind of edifice – displayed superb daring in their hemicycles, niches, pendentives and umbrella half-domes; while a cupola upon a curving architrave (the Piazza d'Oro) reveals a novel synthesis of vaulting and columnar methods which, like Neronian painting (p. 33), is anticipatory of seventeenth-century baroque.

Greek literature, too, produced one of its most famous figures at this time, Plutarch of Chaeronea (*c.* 46–after 120) who through North's translation taught Shakespeare so much of his classical history. Plutarch shares the claim to be founder of modern biography with the Latin author Suetonius (69– *c.* 140) whose gossipy, dead-pan studies of earlier emperors utilize the inside knowledge that he derived from his post as Hadrian's secretary.

Far more significant, however, was the historian Tacitus (*c.* AD 55–?120). Perhaps the son of a tax official in one of the Gallic provinces, he started his literary career with an acute analysis of orators and oratory, in dialogue form. Next he criticized Domitian (after that emperor's death) in a biographical sketch of his own father-in-law, Agricola, governor of Britain (p. 32). Germany, too, was another subject for a moralizing essay, of considerable historical and ethnological significance. But then Tacitus turned to his life-work, the story of Rome under the emperors. Of the *Histories* (on the years AD 68–96) only the initial part, comprising a detailed description of the civil wars, has come down to us; but the *Annals*, about Augustus' successors (AD 14–68), have for the most part survived. These obsessive, penetrating studies provide a unique source of information concerning the court. Although the author's claim to impartiality (especially in regard to Tiberius) can scarcely be supported, this abrupt, tortured narrative, ideal for conveying the malevolence of emperors and of destiny, seeks out the enduring spirit of man with an incisive eloquence which has excited many subsequent supporters of the most divergent political causes.

An even more crushing view of Rome is presented by the verse satirist Juvenal, who, while ostensibly castigating evils of the past, still sees the empire as a sick, maladjusted organism, full of ugly vicious men and even nastier women, and hard on the underdog.

Probably it was hard, in the sense that Rome's benefits did not extend to the rustic populations; yet current emperors were exceptionally enlightened, and official and private humanitarianism equipped hundreds of cities with new amenities and improved the lot even of slaves. Gaul and the Rhineland gradually replaced Italy as the workshops of the west; yet the favoured populace of Rome itself enjoyed ever-increasing distributions of wine and oil, while the annual number of festival days rose to 130 – twice the Republican total.

The government of Antoninus Pius (138–61), who had been adopted by Hadrian in his last months, was peaceful, conservative, tolerant and painstaking. Marcus Aurelius (161–80), who at Hadrian's wish became the joint (and then the sole) successor of Antoninus, was a Stoic philosopher ruling in accordance with his principles – which his Greek *Meditations* have communicated to us, revealing an introspective, melancholy, conscientious man, with a deep distaste for the fighting that occupied nearly all his reign.

For, after renewed Parthian hostilities, a more novel and ominous threat emerged from barbarian mass-movements in northern Europe. At a time when the Roman empire was devastated by plague, enormous groups of south German tribes, under pressure from other hordes behind them, broke through the frontier defences into northern Italy. Levying funds by emergency measures, Aurelius gradually repaired the breach and was indeed, at the time of his death, hoping to establish a more extended and straighter frontier line which would incorporate Bohemia. But the Column of Aurelius on which his campaigns are depicted shows how things have changed since Trajan's Column. For now there are deeply engraved shadows; a much enhanced emphasis upon emotional impact reflects the anxious spirit of the age.

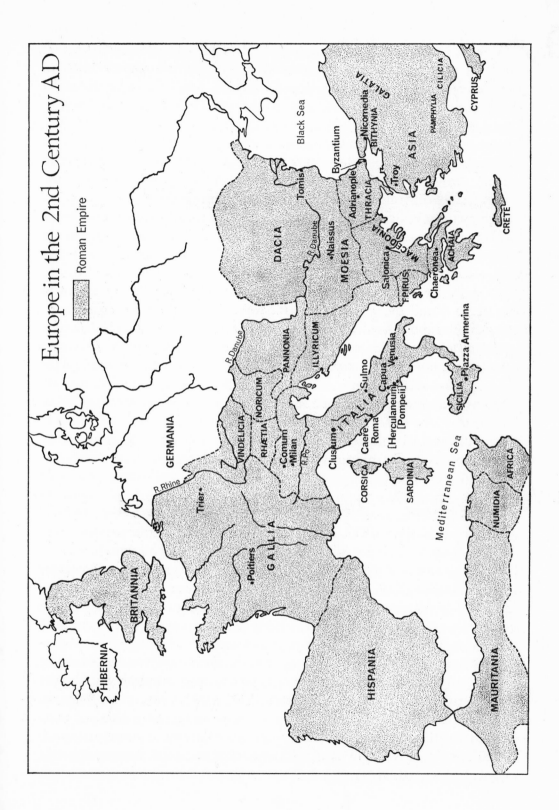

Europe in the 2nd Century AD

Roman Empire

HIBERNIA

BRITANNIA

GERMANIA

R. Rhine

Trier•

GALLIA

•Poitiers

VINDELICIA

RHAETIA NORICUM

•Comum
•Milan

R.Po

Clusium•

ITALIA

Caere•
Roma•

[Herculaneum]
[Pompeii]

Capua•

Sulmo

Venusia•

CORSICA

SARDINIA

SICILIA

•Piazza Armerina

HISPANIA

Mediterranean Sea

MAURITANIA

NUMIDIA

AFRICA

R.Danube

PANNONIA

ILLYRICUM

R.Danube

DACIA

•Naissus

MOESIA

Tomis•

Salonica•
EPIRUS

MACEDONIA

ACHAIA

Chaeronea•

Adrianople•

THRACIA

Byzantium•

Black Sea

Nicomedia•
BITHYNIA

•Troy

ASIA

GALATIA

PAMPHYLIA CILICIA

CYPRUS

CRETE

Aurelius abandoned the adoptive principle, and with it his philosophical ideals, by allowing his son Commodus to succeed him (180–92). Commodus may have been prudent in calling off his father's plans for extending the empire – since the army lacked an adequate reserve (p. 30) – but was less skilful in the succession of advisers who pandered to his degrading amusements and, finally, had him murdered. Meanwhile, however, the coin-types of Commodus, showing an overpowering Jupiter, revealed that the empire was at a turning-point of its religious experience: the victory of a new transcendental monotheism is on the way. But these coins also show Jupiter accompanied by the seven planets; for innumerable people counted upon the astrologers to liberate them from their destinies which the planets and signs of the zodiac were believed to control (p. 19). The Olympian gods, too, retain their place in official propaganda, but they are already being nonchalantly handled by the adroit and entertainingly sceptical Lucian from Samosata (born c. 120), and the versatile, fantastic writer Apuleius from Africa (born c. 123), both exponents – one in Greek and the other in Latin – of the successful latter-day 'sophistic' (p. 17) earning fortunes from their public lectures. A picaresque novelist of marvels, Apuleius jokes about Juno and the rest, yet shows passionate devotion to the Egyptian Isis: these Hellenistic mystery-religions, with their promise of a future life (p. 19), were in full flood across Europe from the east. Christianity, too, was spreading (p. 40); and the terrifying ceremonial and stern code of Mithras (p. 19) attracted many westerners, especially army officers whose tensions these orgiastic proceedings and virile ordeals relieved.

The Later Roman Emperors

Prolonged civil wars after Commodus' death resulted in the victory of the ferociously efficient Septimius Severus (193–211). He and his unbalanced son Caracalla (211–17) were guided by outstanding lawyers, such as Papinian, towards the logical and evolutionary transfer of favour, financial advantage and political supremacy from the Italians to a new privileged class of the soldiery – now mainly non-Italians – upon whom imperial success and survival depended.

However, the population of Rome still needed its rewards, and expenditure to this end (derived from vastly increased taxation) can be deduced from the towering ruins of Caracalla's Baths. They include a huge octagonal *calidarium* covered by a dome on pendentives; and the central *tepidarium* has its groined vaulting upheld by concealed interior buttresses. A somewhat later building, known wrongly as the Temple of Minerva Medica, displays an originally designed cupola upon an apsed decagon, with radiating ribs meeting in the centre, and bold new widenings and differentiations of interior spaces. Another art of the day was the relief-sculpture of sarcophagi, its themes developing from symbolism of death and rebirth (later adapted by Christianity) to crowded battle-scenes of tense, deeply undercut intricacy and vigour.

After a weird interlude under the Syrian sexual invert Elagabalus (218–32), who sought unsuccessfully to accelerate the orientalization of Roman religion, his cousin Severus Alexander (222–35) experienced a novel eastern threat from new Persian (Sassanian) monarchs who were far more dangerous than the Parthians they had superseded. Rome was ill-equipped to deal with such external menaces owing to many troubled successions, causing anarchy and disintegration; excellent coin-portraits show the careworn scowls and frowns of these hard-bitten, short-lived military emperors who, though well aware of their predecessors' fates, remained always ready to make yet another bid for the throne.

These civil wars beckoned to Rome's enemies not only in the east but beyond the Danube border. Soon after 200 the worst threat came from the Carpi beyond the century-old province of Dacia (Rumania). Gradually, however, the main role passed to the likewise non-urbanized but highly militarized Germans. Among these, the Goths became dominant from the Black Sea to the Lower Vistula, with the Baltic island of Gotland as a principal trading link between north and south. Between Upper Danube and Upper Rhine the Alamanni had formed a threatening confederacy. For the first time, also, a coalition known as the Franks surged across the Rhine. Under Valerian (253–60) these three German masses penetrated as far as Asia Minor, Spain and the Auvergne respectively.

Valerian, however, also had to move to the east against the Persians; but their king Shapur kidnapped him, and he was never seen again. Valerian's son and co-emperor Gallienus (253–68) was faced by the fragmentation of the empire into separate states including, temporarily, a union between the western provinces under Postumus. Nevertheless Roman recovery, against all odds, was achieved by the almost superhuman military exertions of three army-appointed emperors from Balkan birthplaces. One of these 'Illyrian' rulers, Claudius II, annihilated the Goths at Naissus (Niş) before dying of plague. Aurelian, 'restorer of the world', evacuated Dacia permanently, but re-established the Danube line and broke the fourth of a series of Alamannic invasions. He also suppressed the erudite, Cleopatra-like Queen Zenobia (273), who had succeeded her husband as secessionist ruler of Rome's Asian territories from her Syrian caravan-oasis of Palmyra; and in the same year Aurelian re-established control over the western provinces. Then Probus drove the Alamanni and Franks out of seventy towns they had captured.

Damage in Europe was far more severe than in the east. The area of cultivation diminished – without compensating technical advances – and urban sites, except at pampered Rome, shrank with them. Autonomous city institutions, that characteristic feature of the ancient world, could not resist the pressures of the age. While insisting that their huge taxes should be paid in pure coin, bullion, or kind, the emperors continued to depreciate the silver currency and inflate its bulk, causing a disastrous failure of confidence which brought down the whole economic system amid widespread misery and destitution (c. 260). Wealth and land became concentrated in the hands of ever fewer proprietors, whose tenants became virtually serfs on vast estates.

Amid these conditions of crisis, people turned for comfort to other-worldly beliefs. A strong attraction was exercised by Neo-Platonism, which the synthesis between various Greek philosophical schools attracted the sophisticated court of Gallienus. Plotinus (c. 205–70) saw the supreme object of human endeavour as unity with the One Good, ground of all existence and source of all values, in a supra-intellectual Love of which his exposition, a classic of introspective mysticism, was to dominate medieval theology, metaphysics, logic, idealistic moral philosophy and art.

But religions of faith exercised greater power, and Christianity in particular, with its gospel of sympathy for the poor and for women, gradually drew ahead of all the rest. Its organization and communications, too, were superior. Synods of bishops were convened, and provision made for mutual financial support. Talented Christian writers now appear not only in Greek but in Latin; notably Tertullian, overpowering in his eloquence and vindictive passion. When, therefore, with the slogan of 'back to old Roman observances', Decius (249–51) and Valerian sought a scapegoat to distract the empire from its miseries, it was the Christians whose persecution they encouraged.

Two subsequent Illyrian emperors, Diocletian (284–305) and Constantine (306–37), created a new organization for the recently re-disciplined empire, forming for its defence a permanent mobile field army with powerful cavalry.[1] But the price its peoples paid for restored frontiers was a totalitarian state in perpetual military crisis. A corrupt, extortionate, omnicompetent bureaucracy enforced oppressive taxation, and the sublime personage of the ruler was exalted by elaborate ceremonials recalling Sassanian courts.

Diocletian attempted to solve the succession problem, which had been the curse of Roman imperial history, by extending the frequently exploited idea

---

[1] The corps of heavy cavalry had been instituted by Gallienus (257) and stationed at Milan, Verona and Aquileia as the nucleus of a new system of defence in depth.

of imperial colleagues to a 'tetrarchy' of two reigning emperors (Augusti) and two emperors-designate (Caesars) who divided the empire between them. The tetrarchs' capitals Mediolanum (Milan), Augusta Trevirorum (Trier), Thessalonica (Salonica) and Nicomedia (Izmit) were now the scenes of an architectural efflorescence displayed in enormous, boldly spatial compositions. In Trier the whole north-eastern part of the city became a palace; and the wall of the basilica (p. 26), a masterpiece of brickwork, no longer exhibits a flat, blank face but is an articulated surface, with the columns reduced to niche-frames. The great Baths of Trier, too, with their running counterpoint of cubes and spheres and cross- or barrel-vaults, have window-frames which give the wall a new plastic quality; while column-capitals on the elaborate city-gate (Porta Nigra) display filigreed forms anticipatory of Byzantium (p. 51). Meanwhile recent excavations have revealed another resplendent palace at Salonica, with octagonal hall, hippodrome, mausoleum and a grandiose processional thoroughfare.

The eventual plan for the tetrarchy was that Diocletian and his colleague Maximian should abdicate (305); and Diocletian (d. 313) duly retired to another spectacular residence of which much more has survived, at Salonae (Split) in Dalmatia. With walls 60 feet high and 7 feet thick, enclosing architectural novelties such as corbelled columns and a huge mausoleum of circular plan enclosed within an octagon, this is a mighty fortress reminiscent of a legionary camp but stiffened into an intricately patterned liturgical frame for the hieratical pageantry of the day. Another palace, at Piazza Armerina in Sicily, an inorganic asymmetrical complex of restless recurrences and convolutions, may have been one of the homes to which Diocletian's colleague Maximian retired – unwillingly, and as it proved, temporarily (d. 310). At Rome, Maximian's son Maxentius (306–12) outdid Diocletian's unprecedentedly vast Baths by planning the largest hall in the ancient world, his aisled, apsed and side-chapelled basilica with three huge vault-spans of Persian aspect.

Constantine the Great forcibly made the Roman empire a single organism again. Two of his innovations heralded a new era. First, after severe persecutions of the Christians by his predecessors, he reversed their policy and accepted Christianity. Secondly, he reconstructed Byzantium as his New Rome or Constantinopolis. This was a capital which bridged Europe and Asia, Black Sea and Aegean, and was strategically placed to combat Sassanians and Goths alike.

After Constantine's death the empire was usually divided, with fateful future effects, into western and eastern halves. The latter or Byzantine half nearly succumbed, eleven hundred years before its final term (p. 155), to an unprecedentedly dangerous external threat. This was indirectly caused by the nomad Huns who, early in the fourth century, had come from the east and arrived upon the shores of the Sea of Azov. Not long afterwards they created havoc among both the main sections of the Gothic peoples (p. 39), the Ostrogothic empire which extended from the Don far into eastern Germany, and the Visigoths who had been conciliated and given army posts by Constantine. Blotting out the Ostrogothic state, the Huns pushed before them hordes of Visigoths, who crossed the Danube and overwhelmed the eastern emperor Valens at Adrianople (Edirne) (376). Soon afterwards, these Visigothic immigrants were promised land, food and markets within the Roman frontiers; and an initial 40,000 of them were to serve in the imperial armies, particularly as cavalry which now took first place in warfare. It seemed for a time, in east as well as west, that the empire could only survive with this Germanic aid (p. 44).

The Roman author of this agreement was the Spaniard Theodosius I (379–95), who for the last time reunified the whole empire (393). First, however, he had decisively rejected his predecessors' eastern, unitarian version of Christianity propounded in Alexandria by Arius (d. 356). Instead, Theodosius I required belief in the accepted interpretation of the Trinity (379), establishing this type of Christianity as the only recognized religion; though Arianism, to which Ulfilas had converted the Visigoths (c. 348), continued to prevail among the German inhabitants and neighbours of the empire.

The other principal religious movement of the age was monasticism. Fulfilling some of the same satisfactions as blood-martyrdom, which was no longer required, it originated in the ascetic tendencies of the Egyptian deserts, where St Antony (251–356) developed the eremitic tradition; but St Pachomius (292–346) and St Basil (c. 330–79) worked instead for an organized community life. Then St Athanasius (c. 298–373) introduced monks to the west, where St Martin of Tours (d. 397) evangelized Gaul, founding the country's first monastery at Ligugé near Poitiers (361). Pilgrimage, too, became fashionable, and its early development is illustrated by the *Bordeaux Pilgrim* giving the principal stages along the route.

While sculptors interpreted the growth of the personality cult by their colossal heads of Constantine and of Valens' brother and western colleague Valentinian I (364–75), contemporary architects saw extraordinary new opportunities in the transformation of pagan basilicas (p. 34) into churches. Constantine's have not survived; the first important Christian building was probably St John of the Lateran, and the largest the transepted Basilica of St Peter's, which has been the outstanding sanctuary and artistic model for western churches ever since. These buildings had wooden roofs instead of the great Roman vaults, since those seemed too worldly and overwhelming. Yet the old passive structure was tautened by every device that would turn the building into a single irresistible tide of space, with a concentrated eastward surge.

There was also an extensive development of centralized churches, baptisteries and martyrs' shrines, which adapted the designs of earlier mausoleums (p. 41) in order to mass their congregations in a central pool of space and light. In Rome, the Lateran baptistery is an octagon within an octagon; the dome of S. Costanza (c. 320–37) rests on a ring of double columns separating the central structure from a circular barrel-vaulted ambulatory. Its prototype at Jerusalem probably had a wooden roof, but S. Costanza has a stone ceiling decorated with elegant, non-representational mosaics, which have thus spread from the floors, which they had for so long adorned, to become the principal artistic medium of the Byzantine world (p. 47).[1]

Pagan Latin literature, in the fourth century, celebrated a brilliant last flowering in works such as the *Pervigilium Veneris*, a hauntingly nostalgic poem of nature and love, and in the masterly historical work by Ammianus Marcellinus, of which the final portion, dealing with his own age (AD 353–78), survives. We see that time as the beginning of an end; he rather views it as a troubled period which recourse to the old senatorial tradition could revive.

But official Christian religion also meant important Christian literature. Prudentius (AD 348–c. 408) was a Spanish lawyer who set himself to contradict the leading pagan protagonist Symmachus, but then withdrew from the troubles of contemporary life to write dedicated religious poetry that sometimes foreshadows the medieval ballad. Paulinus of Bordeaux (353–431) renounced the comforts of wealth and classical culture for a monastic Christianity expressed in moving new genres of wedding-hymn and sacred elegy. But it was another man from Gaul, Ambrose (c. 337–97), who did most to create the hymnology of the Christian west. He also set a millennial precedent by standing firm on behalf of the church against the imperial power. Incalculable influence, again, was exercised by the asceticism and scholarship of St Jerome (c. 348–420) from Stridon in Dalmatia; and especially by the Vulgate which is his translation of the Bible. The earlier works of the north African St Augustine (354–430) included, amid a gigantic output, his critical *Confessions* – one of the world's great autobiographies, re-creating successive mental states with passionate introspective skill. His *City of God* was still to come (p. 46).

[1] There was a long tradition of wall and vault mosaics too, going back at least to the first century BC.

2

FROM THE FIFTH TO THE TENTH CENTURIES

Ravenna and Italy

After the division of the empire following the death of Theodosius I (395), the western rulers grappled less and less successfully with invaders from the north, including the Visigoth Alaric, who sacked Rome in 410. The imperial troops were mostly Visigoths and Ostrogoths (p. 42) or other Germans; so were their increasingly powerful commanders, of whom the most eminent was Stilicho (d. 408). The gravest threat came from the portentously speedy and dextrous mounted commandos of the Huns (p. 42), whose terrifying monarch Attila, based on Hungary, controlled a vast confederacy stretching from far inside Russia almost to Gaul. Bought off by the eastern empire, he moved westwards, where the Romano-German armies of Valentinian III (425–55) stopped him with difficulty at a decisive battle near Troyes ('Chalons', 451). Attila then ravaged north Italy (452); but in the next year he suddenly died, and his empire disintegrated. Yet it had nearly finished off the Roman west, from which one province after another broke away; and in 476 the German commander in Italy, Odoacer, forced the last western emperor (Romulus 'Augustulus') into retirement, and asserted practical, if not theoretical, independence of Constantinople. Under his Ostrogothic successor Theoderic (493–526), Italy enjoyed unaccustomed peace and prosperity.

Pope Gelasius I, dependent on this Ostrogothic régime although it was not Catholic but Arian in religion (p. 42), wrote to the eastern emperor Anastasius I (493–518): 'The world is ruled by two things, the sacred authority of the priesthood and the kingly power.' A breach between Catholic west and Orthodox east was already foreshadowed; but then Justinian I (p. 49), through his generals Belisarius and Narses, reasserted control of Italy (535–52). Soon afterwards, however, the Lombards, a ferocious Germanic people from the lower Elbe basin, invaded and occupied north Italy (568). Becoming Catholic and gradually coalescing with the population, their commercial fortress-city Pavia dominated this whole area for two centuries; and quasi-independent Lombard duchies were established as far south as Benevento and Spoleto.

The Byzantines retained the Italian provinces of Ravenna in the north and Apulia and Calabria in the south. But the defence of Rome against the Lombard invaders fell to Pope Gregory I the Great (590–604). Haunted by the threat of barbarization, Gregory simultaneously upheld Rome's claims against Constantinople, broke Arianism in Spain and Italy, and assimilated the Celtic church (p. 74) to the Roman communion. Organizer of a novel, business-like papal government tightly controlling its bishops, Gregory filled the vacuum, left by the collapse of the western empire, with a new sort of militant Christianity.

After him many popes were Greek or Syrian appointees of eastern emperors. But Pope Leo III sought a new ally by crowning Charlemagne (800) (p. 63); and Nicholas I (858–67), determined upon papal plenitude of power, openly broke with the Byzantines. Such differences with Constantinople were heightened by a psychological contrast between the legal pragmatic attitude of the west, interested in discipline, organization and external forms, and the more subtle and metaphysical eastern approach.

By the tenth century, the efficiency and prestige of the popes had made Rome rich again. Yet their temporal authority never extended throughout the peninsula, in which the dominant power was now the German emperor (p. 66).

The fall of Byzantine Ravenna to the Lombards in 751 had meant the rise of its neighbour Venice, established for safety's sake among lagoons off the northern Adriatic mainland. During the following centuries the maritime power of Venice stamped out Dalmatian piracy in the Adriatic, and developed an important eastern trade including exports of timber, iron, salt and especially slaves, who were then exchanged at Alexandria for silk, papyrus, spices and silver. On the west coast of Italy, another commercial city which, like Venice, owed much to its landward inaccessibility was Amalfi. Genoa, whose city constitution (958) is the earliest known of such charters, had formed a fleet for defence against Moslem attacks from Spain, Provence, the Balearic Islands, Corsica and Sicily.

That island was long subject to such incursions, and early in the ninth century Ziyadatallah, the Mohammedan ruler of Tunis whose dynasty (the Aghlabids) asserted virtual independence of the central Abbasid caliphate (p. 59), had been invited to the island by a rebellious Byzantine admiral. After taking Palermo (831) the invaders were encouraged by the Lombard duke of Benevento to land in Italy itself (837), where they conducted raids up the Tiber. Although beaten off by a league of south Italian republics under Pope Leo IV (849), the Moslems continued to terrorize Latium and the Campagna – as well as establishing strategic and commercial strongholds at Bari and Taranto.

In Sicily the Aghlabids were replaced by Fatimid rulers, Shiite Moslems of Syrian origin who had seized north Africa from the Abbasids (909–10). When the Fatimids moved their capital from Tunisia to Cairo (972), Sicily's governorship became hereditary in the hands of a Yemenite dynasty, the Kalbids, under whom Palermo, city of a hundred mosques, was the most powerful Moslem base and market in the Tyrrhenian Sea. Islam brought Sicily many agricultural novelties including oranges, lemons, mulberries, sugar-cane, date-palms and the cotton-plant.

St Augustine (p. 43) had insisted upon original sin against the Briton or Irishman Pelagius (c. 360–?420), who argued that man could achieve salvation by his own actions alone. Augustine also demonstrated in his *City of God* (413–26) that external events, such as the collapse of the western empire, could not touch a true Christian.

Augustine, Boethius (c. 480–524) and Cassiodorus (c. 487–583) handed on vast portions of the ancient literary heritage to the medieval and Renaissance worlds. Condemned to death by his former friend Theoderic the Ostrogoth (p. 44), Boethius faces the fact that, although God governs the world, right does not always prevail; and yet his *Consolation*, which seemed to many the ancient world's last independent utterance, finds hope for the human race. Adept in Aristotelian logic, Boethius was second only to Cicero as a Latinizer of technical Greek terms, and second only to Augustine as forerunner of scholastic philosophy. Cassiodorus from Scyllacium (Squillace) in south Italy provides a compendium of all the worldly sciences in his encyclopaedic *Institutions*, which perpetuated the civilization of Rome. He was also more explicitly Christian than Boethius; and his foundation of monasteries, including Vivarium which was particularly active in copying manuscripts for posterity, set the pattern for a new age.

The incarnation of this movement was St Benedict of Nursia (480–547), whose perpetually binding *Rule* (c. 529), Roman in its orderly restraint, directed monks and nuns to subdue their human passions, including hysterical asceticism, and to channel them into a disciplined, balanced, communal service of Christ; St Basil (p. 42) had adapted the monastic ideal to the world, and Benedict's function was to harmonize its oriental features to Latin law and industry. His first and outstanding foundation, for which the *Rule* was drawn up, was Monte Cassino in the Duchy of Benevento (c. 529). But other houses followed, and although Benedict had no thought of an

Order, the Order which he originated became so influential (even in Celtic monasteries), and so effective a support to the papacy, that the three hundred years after 700 have been described as the 'Benedictine centuries'.

Another achievement of Italian Christianity was the ecclesiastical plain-song which, although named after Pope Gregory the Great, perhaps assumed its character a hundred years or more after his death. Even, steady and symmetrical, based upon a single and originally unaccompanied line of vocal melody in 'free' rhythm, this was for centuries the universal, official sacred music of western Europe.

The need for the last Italian emperors to watch their northern borders – and their eastern colleagues – had caused the capital to be moved from Rome to Milan and Ravenna. The latter city, a leading Adriatic sea-port for eastern trade, likewise became the capital of Justinian's Italy (p. 44). There, too, are to be found the principal surviving masterpieces of the greatest art of his day, the wall mosaic. Upon the curving interior surfaces of churches, as viewpoints change and light waxes and wanes, these patterned cubes of plaster-inserted glass, marble, silver, gold and enamel glitter in a hundred different nuances and transformations. Designed to the limits of mathematical and optical skill, such mosaics dramatically illustrated the liturgy, their multiple contrasted colours composing harmonies and unities which unveil for human eyes the transcendental world of which our own is only the shadowy counterpart.

The Ravenna mosaics, at their height, seem to bear the metropolitan hall-mark of Constantinople. Yet they stem from superb, though smaller, buildings erected at Ravenna under the western Roman emperors and their Ostrogothic successors. A domed imperial burial-place, the 'Mausoleum of Galla Placidia' (c. 450), is adorned with rich deep-blue pastoral and orna-mental compositions which may reflect the influence of Alexandria or Antioch. Another domed Ravenna building, the octagonal, niche-buttressed Baptistery of the Orthodox or Neon (451–73), shows a blaze of blues, greens and reds in which narrative is already forgotten because of the urge to communicate spiritual emotions. The reign of Theoderic (p. 44) is repre-sented by esoteric friezes in the basilica of S. Apollinare Nuovo (504), with their orientally repetitive, mesmerically rhythmical, two-dimensionally sil-houetted processions of saints and virgins, inexorably leading the eye towards the altar.

This mosaic art reaches its climax at Justinian's S. Vitale. The most com-plex creation of its time, S. Vitale's dome is related to its octagonal ground-plan by small apsidal vaults (squinches) above boldly curving arches dividing the central light from the penumbra beyond. In this church, the jewel-like colouring and dramatic texture of mosaics, replete with meanings at multiple levels, are exploited with a novel force which veers between naturalism and abstraction, and between western solidity and eastern mystery. Glowing and yet remote, ever-present and yet intermediate between God and man, the figures of Justinian and his wife Theodora stand grouped amid their courtiers with a disembodied weightlessness, unmoving or slightly swaying in a golden ambience charged with transcendental tension, and solemnly gazing with an Asian, hypnotic frontal stare which brought their powers into direct and awe-inspiring contact with the onlooker: as they offer chalice and paten to their celestial counterpart, emperor and empress are eternal participants in the daily rites of the church.

When Ravenna passed from Byzantine into Lombard hands, some of its artists migrated to Rome; others came from Constantinople, to avoid icono-clastic restrictions (p. 49), as well as from its eastern provinces which had come under Arab rule. Thus the walls of S. Maria Antiqua, built into ancient remains of the Roman Forum, were painted during the eighth century in a remarkable mixture of Byzantine, Syrian, Hellenistic and Roman techniques. The beginnings of a division between Italian and Constantinopolitan styles, already perceptible here, are again apparent in the masterly, dynamic illusionism of contemporary frescoes at Castelseprio (near Milan), a probable link in the chain of Italian and Byzantine influences upon transalpine Carolingian and Ottonian artists (p. 64), although in some parts of north Italy models were derived from Franks and Saxons rather than vice versa. These same regions, along with France and Spain, witnessed during the tenth century the beginnings of what came to be called the Romanesque architectural style. This is first discernible in small buildings which, although round-windowed like contemporary Byzantine counterparts, display a barrel-vaulted, arcaded and niched, usually domeless longitudinal structure; before long it was to evolve into the cathedrals of the west (p. 67).

Constantinople

The severest threat to the fifth-century eastern empire came from Attila's Huns. Successfully bought off, however, by Theodosius II (408–50), they turned against Gaul and Italy instead (p. 44). Under this emperor and his successors the eastern territories succeeded in avoiding both the fragmentation of the western empire and its Germanization. Soon after 500 the population of Constantinople had attained the one million mark, near which it was to remain for centuries. The city's unique wealth was based on state ownership of mines, factories, domains and cultivation, and on elaborate direct and indirect taxation.[1] The revenues from these sources, and great military strength founded on Belisarius' Asian cavalry, enabled Justinian I (527–65) to hold his own against Persia at the height of its power, and to reconquer Italy, north Africa and parts of southern Spain.

Despite the 'Nika' riots of the popular Blue and Green factions (552) and one of the severest epidemics of bubonic plague in recorded history, Justinian's indefatigable administration, controlling and consulting the church, adjusted his imperial system to the tasks of the future. The last of the Latin-speaking emperors, he instigated the compilation of a Corpus of Civil Law in which a committee of sixteen men summed up and adapted the whole legal experience of Rome, condensing three million lines of earlier law books to 150,000.

To Heraclius (610–41), founder of a new dynasty, the empire owed an efficient and flexible military organization based on army-corps districts. But Heraclius was faced with such problems that he contemplated transferring the capital to Carthage. Hordes of Slavs (p. 54) had burst into the Balkan peninsula – largely supplanting its Latin and Greek populations. Yet Heraclius launched gigantic campaigns against the Persians, and entered Jerusalem (629). Soon afterwards, however, came the meteoric rise of the Arab power under the prophet Mohammed's successors. After crushing Sassanian Persia (641), they detached Jerusalem, Alexandria and Antioch from the rule of Constantinople, which itself twice narrowly escaped capture (678, 717).

The second successful defence was conducted by the founder of a new 'Isaurian' dynasty, Leo III, who also detached the churches of southern Italy and Illyria from papal control. Leo's imposing son Constantine V (740–75), relieved by Arabic internal dislocations (p. 59), became free to deal with a new menace from the Bulgars (p. 54). An outstanding financier and administrator, Constantine V also completed his father's iconoclastic revolution – a puritan attack upon images of the divine or saintly form. This anti-idolatrous movement was closely paralleled in contemporary Islam (seen by Greek iconoclasts as the punisher, the new Assyria), and received strong support from Asia Minor where simple clear-cut rules were preferred to prolix Greek definitions. However, after official adoption, partial retraction and readoption, iconoclasm finally succumbed to the supporters of images (843).

Constantinople's magnificent ritual-laden court, showing signs of Islamic influences, was bedecked by golden mechanical devices to strike visitors with the awe-inspiring sanctity of God's vicegerent upon earth. Although the loss of Crete (823) threatened shipping, the capital, rivalled only by Baghdad as a

---

[1] The Byzantine gold monetary unit, the *solidus* established by Constantine I, dominated the European and Mediterranean markets for a millennium.

trading-centre, reached the height of its wealth and strength under Basil I (866–86) and his successors of the 'Macedonian' dynasty. Dealing with Slav, Bulgar and Italian threats, Basil also developed further the civil service which, together with the free peasantry, formed one of the bases of Byzantine success. Eunuchs were also extensively employed, in order to avoid embarrassing claims from the hereditary nobility; though the reign of Leo VI (886–912), who completed a legal recodification begun by Basil, foreshadowed encroachments upon the central government by the aristocracy.

Nevertheless Basil II (978–1025) was as powerful as any emperor during the Byzantine millennium. In the east, he followed up earlier successes by a spectacular holy war, popular because the leading families of Asia Minor wanted trade; and Kiev was converted, and linked to the imperial house by marriage (p. 56). Commercial privileges were granted to Venice (992), which before long monopolized much of Constantinople's western commerce.

A highly distinctive blend of classical and eastern, humanistic and spiritual influences, Byzantine art gave arresting expression to Christianity: as was fitting in a state which, under the guidance of its sacred ruler and the patriarch of Constantinople, was uniquely pervaded by the dominance of its church. This influence was displayed in many media under the outstanding patronage of Justinian I. His visible masterpiece is the church of the Holy Wisdom (St Sophia) at Constantinople. Its Anatolian designers Anthemius of Tralles and Isidore of Miletus, profoundly versed in the fashionable national studies of solid geometry, optical proportion, symmetry, perspective and light, synthesized two architectural formulas: the aisled and columned Hellenistic hall-basilica (p. 20), and the domed cross-shaped centralized church of which the origins are variously attributed to Syria, Persia, Armenia and Italy (p. 47). St Sophia's miraculous floating dome, adjusted to a square base by curved surfaces (pendentives) in each of the four angles, has the side-stress of its 107-foot diameter met by transepts under half-domes abutted by niches with curving open arcades. Vast yet not overbearing, subtly balanced upon the gentle flow of its gradient, this exalted design, 'describing man's course, exalting him, and returning him to earth', combines the cruciform symbol of the faith with a vision of the infinite disclosed by its ethereal cupola. Unique in spatial and spiritual conception, novel in its concentration upon interior design – reflecting Byzantine concern with the inner life – St Sophia, though final and unrepeatable, served as a model for the many peoples who were to take up this inheritance in eastern Europe.

Constantinopolitan art ranges from the classical naturalism of the palace floor mosaics with their all-over compositions based on north African models, through superb, tactile, ivory relief figures and script illuminations which colourfully blend oriental stylization with spirited humanism, to markedly eastern textile designs reflected in the lace-work 'basket' capitals of St Sophia. Moreover it was Egypt which soon afterwards provided the new Byzantine silk-weaving industry, after two monks of Khotan had, allegedly, smuggled in silkworms and mulberry leaves from central Asia (c. 552). Constantinople, under both Asian and Italian influences, produced

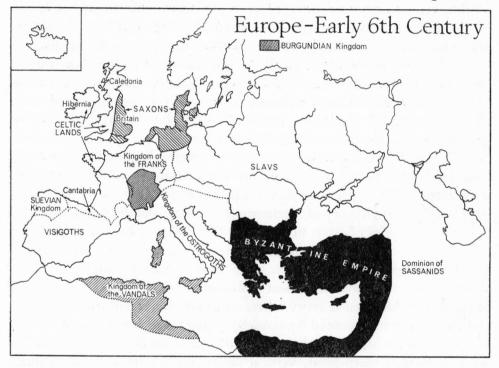

masterpieces of enamel-work such as the bejewelled reliquary-shrine presented by Justin II (565–78) to Poitiers (S. Radegonde); another collector of relics was Heraclius, who drew upon all the resources of Jerusalem. In his seventh century, although the capital produced fine secular, classicizing reliefs on silver plates, the most important surviving mosaics belong to the church of St Demetrius at Thessalonica (Salonica); following upon other work of various dates, the saint's figure, strongly personal despite its rather abstract icon-like eastern austerity, is less sophisticated and more spontaneous than its Ravenna counterparts (p. 48). Cyprus, again, contains churches with fine mosaics, for example at Kiti; after they had escaped destruction by eighth-century iconoclasts, a later Moslem ruler plastered them over.

The lifting of the ban on images was followed by an artistic renaissance.

The significant Constantinopolitan church of the Nea, built by Basil I in his enlarged palace precincts, has not survived. Adapting much smaller prototypes, it incorporated into a building of massive dimensions the simple, domed, thrust-resisting, symmetrically equal-armed 'Greek' cross (p. 50), a form which may well have originated from Armenia – a land fertile in architectural innovations.[1]

The chancel and main body of Byzantine churches are henceforward separated by a screen (*iconostasis*) which divides the spiritual and material worlds, yet links them by means of its painted icons – silent sermons, Bibles of the illiterate – that are windows from the one world to the other. Surviving ninth- and tenth-century mosaics in the two St Sophias, at Constantinople and Salonica, recall the original, dazzling inundation of all their walls with mosaics heightened by every geodetic and visual device to reflect the Byzantine idea of a church as centre of religious life, microcosm of the universe, and timeless re-enactor of Christ's life on earth, marking by its narrative succession the annual cycle of sacred events.

Brilliantly coloured miniatures illustrate increasingly sumptuous enamel-bound religious books, including, for the first time, volumes of small dimensions. On a larger scale than usual, however, are varied paintings in the *Homilies* of St Gregory of Nazianzus (c. 860–80); and the two artists who illustrate the stories of saints in Basil II's *Menologion* (c. 985) attempt novel exploitations of the permanent Byzantine tension between classicism and eastern transcendental abstraction. The new technical assurance of this wealth-inspired cultural movement shines out from the superb ivory-work of the day. While secular ivory reliefs on casket-covers still aim at the free and vivid plasticity favoured by classicizing patrons such as Constantine VII Porphyrogenitus (944–59), religious ivories (and some coins) tend towards a severely formal, sharp-lined, vertical arrangement with elongated, intricately robed, frontal figures, their aloof yet expressive features emphatic in spiritual elevation. More oriental are the lions, elephants and eagles upon silken textiles made for foreign notables by the royal looms of Constantinople.

After Theodosius II established a new university in the capital, the culmination of Byzantine education had been the quadrivium of geometry, arithmetic, astronomy and music. Yet the sixth century also produced a historical masterpiece, written in Greek by Procopius, a Constantinopolitan lawyer from Palestine who spices his vivid military narrative with embittered gossip. Moreover, although Justinian I closed down the Platonic university at Athens, an unknown Syrian monk described as 'Dionysius the Areopagite,

---

[1] The histories and cultures of Armenia and Georgia, though very remarkable, are not discussed in this book since those countries are not now, and have not generally been, regarded as parts of Europe.

Paul's convert' accepted much Neo-Platonism (p. 40) in his hierarchical theology which was to attract widespread attention in the west seven hundred years later.

The scintillating pomp of Byzantine religion was also served by a new notation for its mainly monodic music. To such accompaniment, hymnologists such as the sixth-century deacon Romanus (a converted Jew from Beirut) wrote antiphonal stanzas and refrains in a simple language which attains rich imaginative heights. Romanus may also have been the composer of the 'Acathistus-Hymn', an exalted paean of thanksgiving to the Virgin Mary, protector of Constantinople, for her preservation of the city from the barbarian Avars (p. 54).

The quadrivium fell from fashion (c. 600), and Byzantine education reverted to a purely literary system of grammar and rhetoric, which kept Greek learning alive and diffused it quite widely, although Latin gradually died out. One of the most widely read Greek books was *Barlaam and Josaphat*. This one outstanding Byzantine novel, reflecting Indian Buddhism adapted to Christian moralizing, was attributed, perhaps rightly, to John of Damascus, a mystical eighth-century poet who attacked iconoclasm from beyond the empire's eastern borders.

The victory of his followers at Constantinople brought a revival of learning, in which the outstanding names were the prodigiously learned Photius, leader of opposition to Pope Nicholas I (p. 45), and John the Grammarian. Increased subordination of Church to State led to the establishment of a new secular university of Constantinople devoted to the training of civil servants and jurists. Nevertheless, despite denunciations of monastic wealth by Nicephorus II Phocas (963–9), monks still flourished uniquely as advisers and mediators to a Byzantine society which felt that everything depended upon right belief. In 963 the Macedonian peninsula of Mount Athos was selected for the first important monastic foundation to be established with imperial support. This, the Grand Lavra, was the nucleus for a self-governing Athonite community headed by twenty 'ruling' monasteries which, at their height, contained forty thousand monks. Russians and other Slavs participated; and an influence was exerted upon their chroniclers by Leo the Deacon's modern history, which was perhaps Byzantium's best work in this field and far excelled any contemporary western production.

The Slavs

By the early sixth century the land-hungry Slavs had expanded far and wide from their earlier homelands in eastern Europe or central Asia, and were settling into their three main geographic and linguistic subdivisions (south, east, west).

The south Slavs (later Serbs, Croats, Slovenes and Bulgarians) broke across the Danube in *c.* 517, joining up with the nomad Turco-Tatar Avars, and forming a short-lived kingdom in Slovenia; before the end of the century they had penetrated far south into the Peloponnese, which they virtually controlled until after 800. The problem thus set to Constantinople became seriously accentuated as a result of the disintegration of the Turco-Tatar (and partly Hun) Great Bulgaria founded by Kubrat in the sixth century between the rivers Don and Kuban. As this state was annihilated by the Avars (*c.* 560), one part of the Bulgarian people migrated north-eastwards to the middle Volga (p. 56), but another moved south-west and assumed control of numerous Slavs, with whom they gradually became assimilated.

Conquering the Avars (803), the west Bulgar Khan Krum, with his massively fortified headquarters at Pliska (inland from Varna), established an empire which stretched from the Theiss and Save to the Black Sea, and sent armies to the walls of Constantinople (813–14). Boris I (857–88) made Bulgaria a major civilized power. After hesitating between ecclesiastical allegiance to Rome or Constantinople, he decided upon baptism under the auspices of the latter (864). Unlike Rome, which did not favour translations of the Bible, the Byzantines encouraged their autonomous Bulgarian vassals to develop their own vernacular liturgy. The promoters of this work were Cyril (d. 889) and Methodius (d. 885) from Salonica. Invited by the Moravians, these Greek missionaries moved north from Bulgaria. But the Moravian state vanished, and it was Bulgaria which adopted the alphabets (Glagolitic, superseded by Cyrillic) which Cyril and Methodius invented or diffused for Slavonic needs.

The Bulgar ruler Simeon (893–927), under artistic influences from Byzantines, Armenians, Iranians and perhaps his own eastern compatriots on the Volga, founded a magnificent new capital at Great Preslav (south of Pliska), where his colourfully encrusted and tiled Round or Golden Church is still to be seen. Conqueror of all Macedonia except Salonica, he seriously threatened Constantinople itself, but at the opposite extremity of his territories was rebuffed by the Croatians under Tomislav who, in alliance with Byzantium, had assumed the short-lived title of their king (924). Simeon's ambition was not to destroy Constantinople, but to become its ruler; but his successor Peter settled for Byzantine recognition as a Bulgarian emperor (tsar) with a Greek princess as wife, the first to be thus exported for half a millennium. His autonomous patriarchate became the first Slavonic national church and a model for others. The impetus of this civilization soon began to wane, but was momentarily revived by the tsar Samuel (980–1014), who recovered Serbia and northern Bulgaria and built a system of castles beside the Macedonian lakes. However, his empire was then obliterated by Byzantium (p. 110).

Meanwhile the Slavonic peasantry of Bulgaria had reacted against orthodox ecclesiastical teaching in favour of the Bogomil ('loved of God') heresy, a particularly persistent form of the puritanical dualist Manichaean doctrines – recognizing the evil power as well as the good – which also gained influence in Constantinople, became the state religion of Bosnia, and was subjected to a catastrophic 'crusade' in southern France (p. 116).

The eastern Slavs – later Great Russians, White Russians (Byelorussians) and Little Russians (Ukrainians) – were for a long time subject to the Khazars. Adopting not Christianity but a tolerant Judaism, this Turco-Tatar people ruled from Ityl (near Astrakhan) over an empire which linked steppe and forest all the way from the Urals to the Black Sea, bestriding the river routes that linked Baltic commerce with Byzantium, Persia and the Arab world. When, however, the Khazars became embroiled with Arabs, nomad Petchenegs blocking the Dnieper, and the Magyars whom these propelled before them into central Europe (p. 56), an opening was provided for the Scandinavians who were at the height of their Viking expansions (p. 70). Scandinavian traders and colonists moved inland from the eastern shores of the Baltic to control the Russian rivers; and Rurik (d. 879) came from south Jutland with a further body, known as Varangians or 'Rus', to seize Ladoga and Novgorod (c. 862). Far to the south, Scandinavians were already established at Tmutarakan (Taman) upon the international trade-route. According to legend, Rurik sent lieutenants who mastered Kiev and actually made an attack on Constantinople (865); Oleg then seized Novgorod and Smolensk, and made his southern outpost of Kiev the capital of 'Rus' (c. 880). At Kiev, situated near the junction of forest and steppe and with access to the river network, northern slaves, furs, honey, hides and wax were exchanged for precious metals, spices and scents, woven silks and brocades from Constantinople and Baghdad.

Oleg, and Igor or Ingvar (912–45), fought and traded with the Byzantine empire; and Igor's widow Olga, first of many Russian imperial women, went to Constantinople as a visitor (957). Her son, though blonde, blue-eyed and moustached, now bore the Slavonic name of Svyatoslav (960–72). He eliminated the Khazars and significantly chose to reside at the former West Bulgar township of Pereyaslavets (Little Preslav) on the Danube, from which he hoped to influence the Balkans; but he was repelled by the Byzantine ruler John I Zimisces (969–76).

Vladimir (980–1015), organizer of the most highly developed social services in Europe yet engaged in ceaseless northern and southern wars of conquest, sent diplomatic missions to the pope and German emperor. In order, however, to gain an ally against nomad threats to his Black Sea trade-routes, he chose Byzantine marriage and baptism (989). The first Kievan Christian art and law both came from Constantinople; and the Cyrillic alphabet was transplanted from Bulgaria (p. 54).

Farther east an important kingdom remained independent of Kiev. For when Greater Bulgaria had disintegrated (p. 54), one part of its population, moving north and assimilating Finnish and Slavonic elements, had founded Black Bulgaria on the middle Volga, with its capital Bolgar situated between Kazan and Kuibishev. After this people, no longer wholly nomadic, had been converted to Islam (922), Arab architects built them stone houses and fortresses which multiplied, as excavations have revealed, into an imposing city. Extending over several square miles, Bolgar was designed after Islamic and Hellenistic plans, with large public baths based on a municipal water supply, and a centrally heated palace. Late classical and oriental artistic styles are fused; and the Black Bulgars purchased jewellery and pottery from Byzantium and weapons from Novgorod, while also maintaining trade relations not only with Kiev but with China and Japan.

The western Slavs, later divided into Czechs, Slovaks and Poles, occupied Bohemia, lower Austria and the Drave and Save valleys in the sixth century. Against their more highly organized German neighbours (p. 65), Mojmir (d. 846) established a Moravian empire which extended from the river Theiss and Lake Balaton nearly as far as Vienna, and from the upper Oder and Vistula to the Carpathians. A high degree of prosperity and material culture is revealed by stone churches, metal-work and splendid jewellery. Massive fortresses asserted Moravia's precarious independence against Franks on the one side and West Bulgars on the other, and it was his desire to detach himself from both of these which led Rostislav (d. 870) to call in the Greek missionaries Cyril and Methodius (p. 54).

Their offer to bring these Slavs into the Catholic fold in exchange for the concession of a separate liturgy was refused by Rome, on German instigation. But in any case Moravian power disintegrated (894–906) before the incursions of the Magyars (Hungarians) whom the Petchenegs had displaced westwards (p. 55). These Magyars were horse-breeding Finno-Ugrian nomads – incorporating Hun, Khazar and Turkic elements – whose light cavalry terrorized central Europe, Lombardy, the Balkans and France before they were checked by the German emperor Otto I at Lechfeld (955). The

Hungarian ruler Stephen I (St Stephen) (997–1038) married into the German imperial house (996) and chose Roman rather than Byzantine baptism. Confined within the steppelands of the Theiss and middle Danube, the Hungarians drove a wedge between the southern and western Slavs which permanently prevented their coalescence.

The collapse of Moravia had caused its Byzantine priests to be gradually replaced by Catholic Bavarians and Saxons. Catholic, too, was neighbouring Bohemia in which a new Czech state, joined by Moravian refugees and capable of defence against its German neighbours, consolidated round the learned, trilingual court of Vaclav I (St Wenceslaus, d. 929; the builder of Prague's four-apsed circular church of St Vitus), whose martyrdom inspired the earliest important Czech literature. The establishment of a national bishopric at Prague by Boleslav II (967–99), of the same Premyslid dynasty, exercised a restraint upon German influences, which nevertheless remained strong – and in times of national weakness became paramount.

The forbears of the other principal west Slavonic people, the Poles, had reached the Oder and the Elbe by the sixth century, and before 900 built a large church at Wiślica. Their fourth duke Mieszko (Mieczyslaw) I (960–92) of the Piast dynasty, under attack from a German border knight, declared for the Roman church (966), and, although on terms of intermarriage with Scandinavia (p. 71), remained for the most part loyal to the emperor Otto II. With his capital at Gniezno (Gnesen), and a bishopric at Poznan (Posen) where he organized mass baptisms, Mieszko united the Polish tribes, organized a standing army based on strong fortresses, and extended his dominions to the Baltic. An even more powerful state existed under Otto III's close friend the soldier-statesman Boleslaw I the Brave (992–1025), conqueror of Czech Cracow (996) which became the site of a second bishopric and nucleus of the new Poland.

Spain

As the Roman hold failed in the fifth century, Spain became the battleground of invaders, especially the Germanic Visigoths, Vandals and Suebi, and the Mongol-like half-Scythian Alans. After Wallia (415–19), ruling in Aquitaine, had destroyed the Alans and excluded Germans other than his own Visigoths from most parts of Spain except Galicia, 80,000 Vandals left the country for north Africa (428–9), where they ruled for over a century until suppressed by Byzantium (534). Under Euric (466–85) and Alaric II (484–507) the power of the Visigoths, of whom perhaps 200,000 migrated into Spain, was fully established in the peninsula; and, after the collapse of the Visigothic empire north of the Pyrenees (507), it assumed a more national character.

Nevertheless, there remained a division between the Catholic south – with its Roman law and Roman, Byzantinized cities such as Seville, archbishopric of the encyclopaedist Isidore (d. 636) – and the new settlers who, with Toledo as their capital, retained their own legal codes. Nevertheless the Visigothic régime prospered, especially under Leovigild (568–86) who took Cordova from the Byzantines, annexed Galicia from the Suebi (585), and became the first monarch in a former Roman province to strike an in-dependent national coinage. Reccared turned from his Arian faith (p. 42) to the church of Rome, thus founding Iberian Catholicism and linking his government more closely with central western trends (587); a process which continued when the synodal activity of the Toledo church produced a codification of temporal and canon law (c. 654). Although possible Visigothic contributions to architecture (such as the horseshoe arch) are disputed, surviving regalia reflect the court's Romano-German grandeur and the country's increased prosperity. However, a new class of smallholders became hostile to the government, which, although Leovigild had allowed Romans and Visigoths to marry, fomented further divisions by persecuting the Jews (616) and then enslaving them (c. 694).

These Jews, accordingly, helped to betray Toledo to the Moslem Tarik, who in 711, with a small force of his fellow Berbers and Arabs and a navy of Coptic Egyptians, invaded Spain from Africa by way of Gibraltar and occupied most of the country, ruling on behalf of the governor of north Africa which Islam had conquered from Byzantium (p. 45) on behalf of the Ummayad Caliph of Damascus. Berbers won the Spanish victory and made colonization possible, but, after their revolt (741) and relegation to Castile, the Yemenite general Musa and other Arabs asserted control over Andalusia and its coastal towns. Yet Christian rule remained effective not only in Gaul, where Moslem invaders across the Pyrenees were repelled (p. 62), but also in northern Spain; so that, in spite of intermarriage between Christians and Moslems and the conversion of the former ('Mozarabs') to Islam, Spanish particularism was accentuated. Nevertheless the Moors or Saracens (as the outside world called the new rulers), while eliminating the power of Spanish nobility and clergy, allowed many towns independent councils and improved the surviving Roman agrarian organization, intro-ducing new types of fruit and horticultural methods. They also created peasant landholdings, and improved the conditions of slavery.

When the Ummayads, with the backing of their Mesopotamian army, had occupied the caliphate for nearly a century, they were supplanted by the

This Celtic shield found in the Thames at London
echoes some of the motifs of classical and Etruscan
art, yet is vehemently unclassical – closer to the
Scythian nomad tradition in its rhythmical
curvilinear patterns

After a dynasty or two of imperial courts, Roman
women had achieved a most fragrant elegance
assisted by continual fantastic innovations of
coiffure. This is a fashion of about the turn of the
first century AD

The Pantheon, as Hadrian rebuilt it (*c.* AD 115–25),
still stands, though shorn of its ornamentation.
Its concrete, stressless dome, reflecting upon earth
the majesty of heaven, is a model for all time

ABOVE: Officers and legionaries, who fittingly symbolise the sanctions and the confidence needed to rule an empire extending from the Atlantic to the Euphrates, and from the Sahara to the British Walls of Hadrian and Antoninus

RIGHT: In the chaotic crisis of the empire, brilliant attempts were made to introduce the public to the grimly militant features of short-lived emperors. Decius, fighter against Goths and persecutor of Christians, ironically celebrates the 'happiness' of a traumatic age (AD 249–51)

ABOVE LEFT: The art of the western provinces
becomes significant when it adapts rather than
imitates from Rome. This marble relief of the
second century AD, showing a girl in Celtic dress,
comes from Gurk in Carinthia (part of the
iron-bearing Roman province of Noricum)
ABOVE: When Constantine founded his new capital
and made Christianity the state religion, the
sculptors of his ten-times life-size head had
abandoned Roman realism for the transcendental,
hypnotic stare of an Asian autocrat (c. AD 313)

LEFT: The church of S. Sabina on the Roman Aventine (422–32) is descended from aisled and clerestoried Hellenistic and Roman secular basilicas, but the old passive structure is now given a powerful eastward surge – perhaps under Persian solar influences. The columns were taken from pagan buildings

ABOVE: Ravenna was the capital of Justinian I's reconquered Italian province. This is a mosaic of the Last Supper in S. Apollinare Nuovo (520–30). The fish stands for the miracle of the Five Thousand; and the letters of the Greek word for fish (*Ichthus*) stand for the names and titles of Jesus

RIGHT: The inspiration of the whole medieval millennium was Virgil; this is a fifth-century manuscript with a miniature of shepherds and animals illustrating the *Third Georgic*

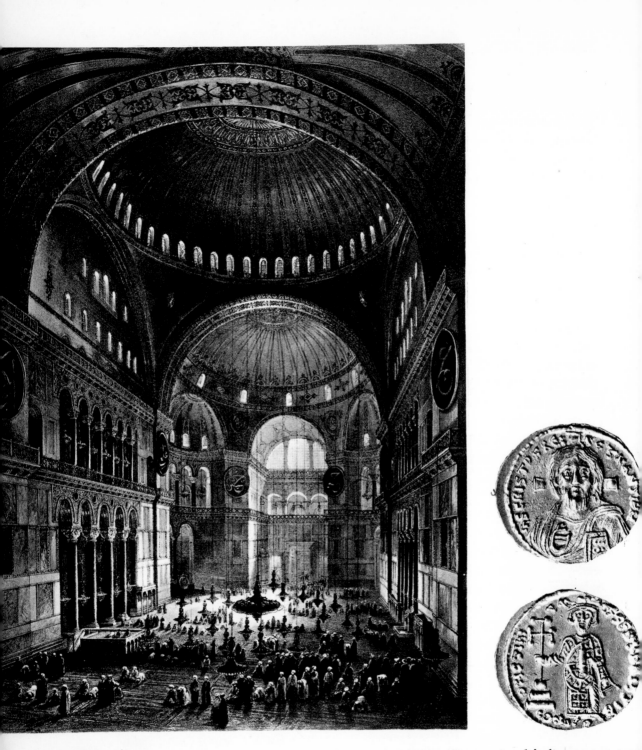

ABOVE LEFT: S. Sophia was rebuilt for Justinian (527–65) by two Anatolian masters of geometry who, blending traditions of the basilica and of cruciform domed centralization, achieved a miracle of rhythmic movement, ethereal perspective and radiant, incorporeal light. A millennium later the church inspired superlative Ottoman mosques

ABOVE RIGHT: Constantinople's disastrous eastern losses to the Moslems intensified religious forces a home. The last Heraclid emperor, the bloodthirst Justinian II Rhinotmetus (slit-nose) (d. 711), introduced the head of Jesus to the coinage. Inscriptions, still in Latin (Rex Regnantium), wer soon to give way to Greek

Abbasids based upon the resources of Khorasan. As power passed from Arab into Persian hands, oriental Baghdad replaced Hellenizing Damascus as the capital, soon attaining unprecedented heights of power and culture alike. Nevertheless, the change meant that both north Africa and Moslem Spain broke away from the central caliphate, north Africa only for a short time, but the Spanish territories permanently. They were conquered by the gigantic red-headed Abd al Rahman I, a refugee from Syria who was the son of an Ummayad by a Berber slave-girl. Assisted by a standing army of 40,000 slave mercenaries, Abd al Rahman ruled the country for thirty-two years. Conquering the market-city and river-port of Cordova, he made it his capital (756), laying the foundations of the Great Mosque (786) which was intended to remind him of Damascus.

Enlarged by his devout and scholarly son Hisham I (788–96) and doubled in size during the tenth century (p. 61), this mighty sanctuary, one of the supreme products of the 'first Islamic classicism', is the congregational building *par excellence*, a mosque amid whose two-storeyed horseshoe-arched colonnades of stone and blood-coloured brick all the world might assemble and contemplate. With no focal point or axis to fasten upon in this spatial transparency of marble, porphyry and jasper, the eye is mesmerized by the seemingly limitless, unaligned forest of twelve aisles rhythmically repeated in every direction.

Another who added to the Great Mosque was Abd al Rahman II (822–52), whose relatively peaceful reign, including a ten-year truce with the north Spanish Christians, registered cultural and economic advances reflected in magnificent luxury. Though greatly expanding his armed forces, Abd al Rahman II loved poetry and gardens; his principal advisers were a theologian, a woman, a eunuch, and the musician and arbiter of fashion Ziryab. While glassware and other products of the kingdom were exported by a trading fleet based principally on Seville, Malaga and Almeria, and relations were established with Byzantium (840) which provided mosaicists for the Great Mosque, it was Abbasid Baghdad to which the monarch looked for his organizational models, while the learned men of Cordova corresponded with Baghdad, Cairo, Bokhara and Samarkand.

Jews assimilated themselves rapidly to this culture, but as the Moslems ceased to draw strength from immigration Abd al Rahman II's good nature did not prevent the persecution of Cordovan Christianity. In the tenth century racial relations deteriorated further as the emirate came increasingly into conflict with Spaniards, Moslem and Christian alike, notably during the heroic thirty-year rebellion led by a Moslem of Visigothic origin, Umar ibn Hafsun (d. 917).

However, Abd al Rahman III el Nasir (912–61) enjoyed nearly three decades of unbroken authoritarian success, proclaiming himself as Caliph (929) in opposition to the rationalist Abbasids and heretic (Shiite) Fatimids alike (p. 46), and maintaining close relations with the Byzantine empire. At the end of his reign three, if not all four, of the Christian states of northern Spain (p. 61) were tributary to Cordova; and his navy, based on Almeria, controlled most of the Mediterranean. Great influence, however, was now in the hands of immigrants: eunuchs and foreign prisoners of war (or their descendants) procured from Verdun (p. 66) or Magdeburg (p. 67), known as 'Slavs' (slaves) but also Galician, Frankish, Lombard, and Anatolian in origin.

Moslem Spain was the most prosperous, populous, orderly and cultured country in western Europe; and Abd al Rahman III derived an annual income amounting to 6,245,000 gold pieces from import-duties and from a wide range of exports among which, as in other Islamic lands, textiles came first. In Cordova there were thirteen thousand weavers. This city of half a million inhabitants, described by a Saxon nun as the Jewel of the World, included three thousand mosques, seventy libraries, and three hundred or, according to other accounts, as many as nine hundred public baths. A few miles away, Abd al Rahman III built an unprecedentedly sumptuous combined fortress and country mansion of which little now survives, the Medina az-Zahra, extending over an area of 280 acres and housing the 6,000 women of his harem. The pink and green and translucent marble was mainly north African, but many of the artists and craftsmen who designed the abstract floral motifs, geometrical decorations and circular or oval medallions came from Constantinople.

Meanwhile the literary and scientific Moslem civilization now at its height in eastern Islam was equalled by the fruitful combination of Arabic, Hebrew and classical cultures which flourished at Cordova, especially under the sponsorship of Abd al Rahman III's Jewish chief minister Hasdai ibn Shaprut (c. 915–70), whose Talmudic school eclipsed even its Mesopotamian counterpart. Hakam II (961–76), the most learned of Cordova's rulers, invited many eastern scholars to his world-famous university, earmarked legacies for the capital's twenty-seven free schools, and merged the three royal libraries into a collection of 400,000 volumes.

Moslem Spain attained even greater power and prosperity under Hisham II (976–1009), whose minister Al Mansur (Almanzor), a fanatical mystic known as the Fox (d. 1002), was given the title of king and for twenty years exerted an effective dictatorship. He too was a phenomenal builder; and it was under his direction that the Great Mosque (p. 59), to which Hakam II had added fourteen 'transepts', was extended from twelve to fourteen aisles. Under variously ascribed north African, Persian, Mesopotamian and Byzantine influences, the building now displayed a sumptuous arrangement of cupolas and octagons in connection with the supremely rich *mihrab* (its niche indicating the position of Mecca), as well as novelties significant for the future of western architecture such as interlaced multifoil arches, and polychrome filigreed vaulting with visible intersecting ribs. Al Mansur also constructed a new town and palace east of the river, the Madinat Az-Zahira; it has now vanished, but probably displayed the influence of Fatimid Egypt which, although Cordova controlled much of north Africa, was now at its cultural height. Against the Spanish Christians he fought fifty campaigns; and although such conquests were as usual transitory, he captured both Santiago de Compostela and León.

During the eighth century Moslem invasion, a Christian, Pelayo (Pelagius) (718–37), held out in Asturias. Ruling at Oviedo, where he and his successors built a number of churches and where the cathedral contains their magnificent jewellery, Alfonso II the Chaste (792–842) introduced elements of representative government which were novel in western Europe. The most ambitious Asturian expansionist was Alfonso III (866–910); but after his abdication the kingdom was split into smaller parts. Garcia I (d. 914), whose capital León superseded Oviedo as the artistic centre, mastered Galicia, in which Santiago de Compostela was becoming an international pilgrim resort. Castile, with its capital at Burgos, asserted virtual independence under Fernan Gonzalez (d. 970).

In Catalonia, where the earliest wholly vaulted churches are to be found, the Moslems were dispossessed by Charlemagne, whose base at Barcelona (801) was maintained by autonomous counts of Visigothic origin. His invasions were made famous by the Chanson de Roland (p. 80), although at the pass of Roncesvalles (778) his successful enemies were in fact not Moslems but Basques, who then, profiting by further ambushes of the Franks (813, 824), established a kingdom of Navarre that grew in importance during the tenth century. The daughter of one of its monarchs, like the daughter of a king of León, became one of the wives of Al Mansur.

Franks and Saxons

When Rome's Rhine frontier crumbled, Visigoths ruled south-western France as well as Spain, Burgundians settled farther east, and another group of German communities, the Franks, established themselves in the north.

The Burgundians and Visigoths, being Arians (p. 42) and therefore alien to the local Catholic populations and to their bishops, were overcome by Franks, whose pagan chief and founder of the Merovingian dynasty Clovis of Tournai, on defeating the last Roman combatants at Soissons (486), had embraced Catholic Christianity with three thousand of his warriors. He was also sent the emblems of a Roman consul by the Byzantine emperor Anastasius I. Clovis and his successors extended the kingdom not only eastwards but also to the south, where Romanized southern Gaul gave them strength and civilization and was adorned with fine, octagonal Merovingian baptisteries.

St Columbanus (p. 72), crossing Gaul from west to east, established many monastic foundations, including Luxeuil (590). Although the Merovingian kings absorbed church property on a large scale, Dagobert (623–39) brought greatness to abbeys such as S. Denis, Jumièges and S. Wandrille. By now, too, there had been a revival of economic life, encouraged by watermills and by the attraction of Provençals, Italians and Spaniards to the annual fairs held at S. Denis, near the royal residences of Paris, Clichy and Chelles.

Weakened by much partitioning of their realm, the Merovingian kings gradually became puppets of their Mayors of the Palace. One of these, Charles Martel, leader of the east Franks (Austrasia) whose capital was usually at Metz, equipped his cavalry with the stirrup and enabled them to throw back a formidable Moslem invading army from Spain (732) (p. 58). This victory stimulated the Frankish kingdom and its church, and encouraged Charles' son Pepin the Short to depose his Merovingian monarch and take his place as founder of the Carolingian dynasty (751–891). Pope Stephen III, hoping for assistance against the Lombards, crowned Pepin at S. Denis (753–4). By occupying Ravenna (p. 47) and giving it to Rome – instead of to its former Byzantine owners – Pepin encouraged the idea of papal secular power.

The Carolingians reformed the Gaulish church and assumed its guidance and protection. Before his coronation Pepin was anointed at Soissons (751) by the English churchman St Boniface (Winfrith), who had spent nearly three decades converting Hesse and Thuringia (722), Bavaria and other parts of Germany. Meanwhile the Northumbrian monk Willibrord (d. 739), leaving Ripon for Utrecht, was largely responsible, in spite of many setbacks, for converting the populations at the mouth of the Rhine.

Charlemagne (772–814) broke with this policy of peaceful missionary penetration by repeated campaigns in which he forcibly converted the Saxons on the Lower Ems, Weser and Elbe. During almost every one of the forty-two years of his reign he summoned the whole Frankish nation in arms to one of his frontiers, and conducted them upon aggressive campaigns in the countries that lay beyond.

Poor in gold until conquests provided it, the Carolingians abandoned the Byzantine and Arab gold standard for a silver currency. Based, perhaps, on Persian or Spanish models, such a coinage was suitable for this mainly rural economy, as well as for the modest commercial centres in which polyglot Jewish merchants and the branches of Baghdad banks helped to maintain such external commerce as could be afforded. Guild and merchant associations revived, and a navy was organized to protect them. Ruling from the Ebro to the Oder, Charlemagne dispatched permanent inspectors to the

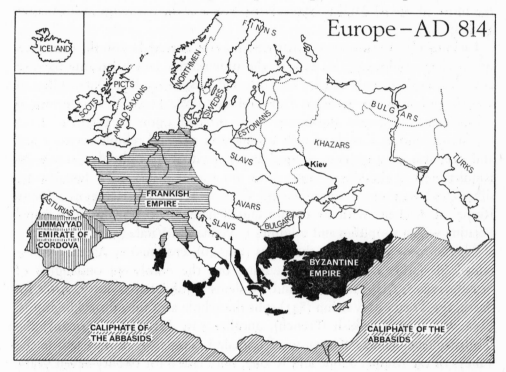

three hundred counties of his realm, and summoned legislative assemblies twice a year.

The fifth Abbasid Caliph Harun al Raschid sent him presents, and the patriarch of Jerusalem conveyed the holy city's keys. Charlemagne's coronation as 'emperor' by Pope Leo III (800), whatever its exact implications in the minds of its participants and observers, initiated the idea that imperial power could be 'renewed' and transferred from east to west. The rulers of Constantinople no doubt regarded this latter-day Constantine as a barbarous upstart; yet in 812 they accepted the implicit breach, and blockades of the Mediterranean by Islam (p. 45) meant it could not be retrieved.

Although unable to write himself, Charlemagne was almost obsessively interested in education and learning. His effort, which fertilized the whole Latin Middle Ages, aimed at the reassemblage of the ancient Roman inheritance – passed on, largely through the medium of Ravenna, from late antiquity – and its perpetuation in the malleable Carolingian minuscule script. Fostering an already existent revival of scholarship, he had his own Academy and intellectual and social round table. At the summit of a widespread though ephemeral system of general education, the palace school at Aachen flourished for fifteen years (781–96) under Alcuin of York, who transmitted the more advanced Anglo-Saxon civilization and the teachings of his master Bede (p. 74).

Lacking a lay bureaucracy, Charlemagne concentrated upon the education of his clergy, allotting this task to the monasteries which became massive complexes of cultural, social, economic and missionary life. Outstanding in wealth and learning were St Germain des Près, founded two centuries earlier near Paris, and Reichenau (724) situated upon an island in Lake Constance. Fulda, founded by St Boniface in 742 and rebuilt between 802 and 819, was an imposing physical and a spiritual stronghold. Centula (St Riquier near Abbeville, c. 790), now no more, displayed a fantastically silhouetted pattern of spired round towers. From Charlemagne's 'New Rome' at Aachen, with its Forum and Senate, there remains his Chapel Palatine which simplifies and solidifies Ravenna's S. Vitale (p. 47).

Charlemagne's son Louis the Pious (814–40), crowned at Aachen, maintained his father's cultural endeavours, but the combined onslaughts of Scandinavians, Magyars, Slavs and Moslems annihilated security. After his death, the Treaty of Verdun (843) split the whole area into three kingdoms. One was west Frankish (French), another east Frankish (German); the 'Lotharingian' Middle Kingdom of Lothair I, 'emperor' in Italy and in the valleys of the Meuse, Saone and Rhone, only lasted for twenty-seven years. At the Oaths of Strasbourg in 842, the king of the west Franks spoke to the east Frankish troops in their own language, Old German, and his eastern fellow-monarch reciprocated in Old French.

Illumination, under the influence of Constantinople, had developed an original, dramatic, northern style. The 'Ada' manuscripts (c. 800), based on Northumbrian (as well as late antique) models but technically superior to them, and the serenely Hellenistic Aachen Purple Gospels – which perhaps date from a few years later – display in their different ways fresh, vigorous Carolingian versions of Byzantine themes. Important developments also occurred at Rheims, a cultural and commercial centre which, at a safe distance from the coast and strongly linked with the past, was beginning to display urban institutions again. The Gospel of its Archbishop Ebbo (816–35) showed novel, dynamic impressionism in its nervous, explosive treatment of drapery; and the fluid energetic black-and-white sketches of a Rheims psalter, now at Utrecht (*c.* 820; the' Utrecht psalter'), boldly reinstate the classical gods in a Biblical context and echo ancient Rome by their airy landscapes. In this new confident statement of the Christian theme, reflecting a revolutionary liberation from the more formal palace-style gospel books, 'the small figures pirouette and posture, fierce and gentle, menaced in all seasons yet full of hope, their arms wildly waving in the air, their clothes vibrant with energy'.[1] A subsequent style of lavish golden magnificence can be associated with the court painters of Charles the Bald (840–77), king of the west Franks; but it is uncertain whether they should be ascribed to Rheims, Corbie, Compiègne or S. Denis, of which the king was lay abbot.

The head of Charles the Bald's palace school was the outstanding original thinker of western Christendom, Johannes Scotus (*c.* 815–77) from Ireland (Erigena). Familiar with Greek thought and particularly Neo-Platonic pantheism (p. 40), he proceeded with the demonstration, several centuries before others were to tackle it, that theology and philosophy though apparently conflicting are aspects of the same truth.

The political instability of the eighth and ninth centuries developed the feudal bonds essential to a landed society which had to fight. This institution, whether Roman or German in origin, assured a man protection in exchange for service. The monarch gave grants of land or cattle or revenue or military office (*feudum* or fief) to his vassals, who in exchange provided him with heavy-armed, well-mounted, stirruped cavalry. Lesser men, not much assisted by the royal armies which could not be everywhere at once, sought refuge in the palisaded wooden hill-top fortress built by the nearest minor potentate, and defended it for him. The aggrandizement of the aristocracy encouraged by these feudal relationships had been checked by Charlemagne's personal representatives; but in later desperate situations such arrangements revived, and in due course assumed a juridical character which formed the basis of the baronial and knightly system. This particularly flourished in northern France, which became the most highly feudalized area in Europe.

The east Franks recovered from the disturbances of the ninth century more quickly than their western neighbours. Yet the east Frankish (German) state was far from centralized, being divided into four principal tribal units or duchies – the Franks or Franconians, Saxons in the north-west, Swabians in the south-west (Suebi, Alamanni), and Bavarians. These Bavarians, who had first attracted attention in the sixth century, possessed links with southern civilization, established the first national church beyond the Rhine (*c.* 738–9),

[1] John Beckwith.

and subsequently provided the east Franks with their capital at Regensburg. The fifth duchy, lacking the tribal and geographical unity of the others, was the rump of Lotharingia (Lorraine) (p. 64), with its chief town at Metz and an important slave-trading centre at Verdun.

The dukedoms asserted an almost regal degree of independence from east Frankish monarchs. After the extinction of the Carolingians' male line (911), the duchy where their civilized tradition persisted most vigorously was Saxony, strengthened by monasteries such as Corvey (settled from Corbie), of which the western front or *Westwork* (873–85) seemed able to resist material enemies and evil spirits alike. The Saxon duke Henry I ('the Fowler') soon afterwards assumed the German kingship (919–36). Exacting subordination from other chiefs and marcher lords, Henry launched Germany upon its millennial eastward drive. He also insisted upon retaining in his own hands the nomination of bishops as well as counts – and was strong enough to have his own son Otto I the Great (936–73) 'elected' in his place.

Restless, inspiring and passionate, Otto I decisively crushed dukes, Danes, Slavs, Wends (Baltic Slavs) and Magyars (at Lechfeld, 955), defending his much-enlarged eastern and southern borders by military Marks (including Ostmark or Austria), and appointing Counts Palatine to supervise his frontiers in the west. Although their dominions were smaller than Charlemagne's, the tenth-century German rulers, collaborating with churchmen whose celibacy kept them free from hereditary ambitions, led northern Europe in power and trade alike.

Otto I's proclamation as king of Italy (951), and his coronation as emperor by the pope at Rome (962), inaugurated a new era of German involvement in Italian expansion. The Frankish claim to dominate papal Christendom was renewed: this meant rivalry with Byzantium, and Otto II (973–83) called himself *Roman* emperor to substantiate his ambitions. Otto III (983–1002) looked even more intently southwards to Rome, which he made his capital – as well as to Byzantium, which was the homeland of his Greek mother (Theophano) and his tutor and monks, in addition to providing the model for his court ceremonial. In this conception of a reborn, Christian, universal commonwealth Otto III was guided by the most learned man of the age, his friend Gerbert of Aurillac (rumoured to be a magician), who became Pope Sylvester II and gathered together a large proportion of the intellectual, artistic and spiritual leaders of the age.

The Saxon monarchs' preoccupation with Italy did not prevent an upsurge in German agricultural, economic, spiritual and artistic life. A large-scale internal colonizing programme under the auspices of the rising knightly class (p. 65) was facilitated, here as elsewhere in northern Europe, by the heavy

Opposite: Lion of St Mark, from the Echternach Gospels: 8th century AD

IMAGOLEONIS

mould-board plough (superseding the light scratch-plough), as well as by modern harness and three-field crop-rotation and cultivation. Towns, unknown to the ancient Germans, came into being. Roman foundations were revived; Mainz, Cologne and Regensburg were walled or re-walled, while Magdeburg became the centre for eastern Germanization and channel for the selling of war-prisoners to Moslem Spain (p. 60). There emerged a class of professional merchants, banded in troops for their long journeys under a Hansgraf (Doyen). Quentovic near Étaples and Duurstede (Utrecht) became shipping-centres for the export of woven clothes; and when Count Baldwin II (879–918) had expelled the Scandinavians from Flanders, Bruges, Ghent, Ypres and St Omer entered an important stage in their long commercial careers. Meanwhile the first sea-dykes had already been constructed, the heaviest of them in Zeeland where coastal contours were continually changing.

Coinage was issued by emperors, dukes and archbishops. Monasteries and abbeys were very powerful in Germany; as migration headed south and south-east, they sent Bavarian and Saxon priests to replace Byzantines in Bohemia and Moravia (p. 57). While the Hamburg-Bremen area became the headquarters of missionary work in Scandinavia (p. 71) HirsauClun (Hirschau) in Swabia, founded from Fulda in 838, enjoyed a century and a half of exceptional prosperity. Gorze in upper Lorraine (c. 933), with its movement for reforming the episcopacy, was as influential in Germany as Cluny was in France (p. 68), and more active in extra-mural teaching; under royal control of a nature which did not exist in Cluny, Gorze reformed 160 monastic houses, mostly in German lands. Low German poetry included a vigorous version of the Gospels, the alliterative *Heliand* (c. 830).

In architecture, Germany took the lead in western Christendom – or, as some would prefer to have it, profited from an imaginative forward leap by Burgundian architects – as its basilical yet cruciform churches, with imposing towers and double choirs, exceeded Carolingian dimensions in their bold lines and masses, based on geometrical and rhythmical ratios interpreting the principles of late antiquity with novel conception and precision. Magdeburg (955–) and Gernrode (c. 961), gigantically striving upwards, rooted upon earth yet mindful of heaven, heralded the Romanesque style (p. 83); and their basic nave-transept squares led towards the cross-vaults of later centuries.

The sculpture of the wooden cross of Gero, Archbishop of Cologne (969–76), is outstanding in its intense Germanic poignancy. St Gall had produced a pioneer German musical composer in Notker the Stammerer (d. 912), drawing partly upon Carolingian forbears. Mural and book painting was centred upon Trier and Reichenau (p. 93), whose school of illuminators, strengthened with Greek monks by Otto III, produced a Gospel showing the four parts of the empire – Slavinia, Germania, Gallia and Roma – paying homage to their lord; in this work Italo-Byzantine, Carolingian-Burgundian and Celtic influences meet in a novel, abbreviated fusion of naturalism with an economical idiom of incorporeal symbols. Another Gospel shows the same emperor as Christ on earth, telescoping the natural and supernatural orders in a fashion that Byzantines would have regarded as excessive.

Slower than Germany to recover from ninth-century ravages, France gradually increased in population and agricultural and technological skills. After Odo, Count of Paris, had successfully defended his city against Scandinavian invaders (885), their settlements round Rouen on either side of the lower Seine were recognized by the west Frankish (French) state as the nominally vassal, but independent, duchy of the Northmen (Normans); and their chief Rollo was baptized (911). Adopting Frankish law and speech, the settlers' descendants went through a period of anarchy before their exceptional talents for organization could take effect in the occupation of England and Sicily (pp. 94, 96), and the provision to France of its navy. Meanwhile however, in a world of ruthless and decentralized power-politics, the dukes of another region of France, Rudolph I (888–912) and II (912–37) of Burgundy, were among the most dangerous.

Yet this was also the age of one of the most far-reaching ecclesiastic reforms, initiated on the orders of pious Duke William of Aquitaine, who founded a monastery at his favourite hunting lodge of Cluny, near Macon (910). Situated in a frontier area near the Roman pilgrim route and the Rhone and Saone highways, Cluny was well placed for its drive to rejuvenate Benedictine monasticism (p. 46) and eliminate lay control. Its monks, placed under the direct orders of Rome, were allowed, by a striking innovation, to elect their own abbots, of whom the first was Bertho and the next Odo (927–41), second founder of the movement. The essentials of the Cluny method were communal worship adapted to modern needs, and organization within a disciplined hierarchy which directed its efforts towards the cessation of political violence and the maintenance of clerical celibacy. The Cluniac renaissance spread to Fleury (S. Benoit-sur-Loire) and other centres, particularly in southern France; and many of the monks from these institutions became bishops.

Cluny believed in utilizing art to the glory of God. An impressive monastic church was built, the forerunner of two more within the century; the unusually complex east end of the 981 foundation was anticipated at S.

Martin of Tours (before 918), upon the Santiago pilgrimage route (p. 61), in a series of radiating chapels which reflected the growing worship of saints and the daily masses recited by every priest.

The earliest-known form of many-voiced (polyphonic) music, the *organum*, is traditionally attributed to the Benedictine monk Hucbald (*c.* 840–930), regarded as the originator of a novel sort of vertical composition, super-imposed on the horizontal and possessing a new beauty and expressiveness. One centre of church music was the monastery of S. Martial at Limoges, but Hucbald is believed to have developed his musical activity at Rheims. Until Chartres became even more prominent as a cultural centre, people flocked to Rheims to hear Otto III's friend Gerbert (*c.* 972), later Pope Sylvester II (p. 66), teach the whole range of human learning that he had inherited from Boethius (p. 46), with special expertise in arithmetic and geometry.

Taking precedence over their colleagues elsewhere, the archbishops of Rheims, privileged to consecrate rulers of France, helped to establish the Capet dynasty (987). Son of Duke Hugh the Great (d. 956) who ruled between Seine and Loire and momentarily over Burgundy, King Hugh Capet (987–96), like his immediate successors, did little to quell his powerful independent vassals, concentrating on the consolidation of his own small royal demesne, the compact strip of fiefs round Paris and Orléans. Thus, although the Capets were as closely allied with the church as the Saxon emperors, their territorial policy was exactly opposed to the ambitious imperial view.

Scandinavia

Scandinavian territory had never come under Roman or Celtic rule, but an advanced artistic culture was revealed by the fifth-century gold horns with human and animal reliefs, signed by the artist Laegaest Holting in the Runic alphabet originating from south Jutland where the horns (now destroyed) were found.[1]

Two hundred years later a maritime Dano-Swedish empire established something of a common economic system in the Baltic, drawing revenue from trade between east and west. Out of the collapse of this union emerged two kingdoms. One was Uppland, facing east; the other was Denmark, with its centre of gravity in the extreme south of Jutland, where Hedeby on the Schlei became an important station on the new Frankish trade-route to Russia. Meanwhile in Norway King Harald I Fair-hair (Haarfager), after

[1] Jutland was probably one of the starting-points of the Anglo-Saxon-Jute invasions of England, p. 73.

suppressing an aristocratic confederacy centred upon Trondhjem, assumed undisputed rule.

All these Scandinavian peoples – as well as inhabitants of parts of Sweden who were known as Goths, and numerous hangers-on from many races – joined in the continual trading journeys, raids, colonizing expeditions and invasions which extended over huge areas, with traumatic effects, for a hundred and fifty years. Northumbria felt the first impact (793); and then the Frankish coast and most of Ireland were overrun (*c.* 834). The Seine, Loire, Tagus and Guadalquivir valleys suffered from these plundering Viking warships (840–4) which, as their radius formidably increased, had extended their purely seasonal raids in order to stay on for the winter (836). Penetrating inland, they turned from buccaneers into conquerors. Scandinavian forces pushed right through to Novgorod and Kiev and nearly to Constantinople (p. 55), and overran England and the Low Countries; French kings bought them off, first by allowing them to ravage Burgundy (886), and then by recognizing their Seine settlements as the duchy of Normandy (p. 78). Moreover between 870 and 930 15,000–20,000 Scandinavians, mainly from Norway, migrated to Iceland, replacing earlier communities of Irish monks. Among these settlers' offspring was Eric the Red, who established a colony in Greenland (985); his son Leif Ericsson landed somewhere on the American coast, at 'Vinland', an unidentifiable country of wild grapes and self-sown wheat (999–1000).

The Scandinavians, with their open-sea fleets mustering between seventy and a hundred vessels at a time, high in bow and stern, had opened up the northern world, plundering it but also reawakening its trade. Skilled in river navigation and portages, expert seamen yet unafraid of land, luxury-loving yet democratic, they provided a disconcerting blend of elemental ferocity, cunning strategy, sense of public order, legal and commercial sophistication, and advanced literary and artistic achievement. Their vast, circular, mathematically designed encampments on the Danish mainland and islands – Aggersborg, Fyrkat, Trelleborg, Nonnebakken – reveal high planning ability and technical culture. Their relief work, on ornaments and weapons, displays intricately intertwined animal ornamentation; and wooden sculpture in the round is superbly represented by the elegant logical sweep of the head from the ship found at Oseberg, in the Oslo fjord (*c.* 850).

The long-lived, highly artificial Scaldic poetry, differing in its strictly syllabic structure from the free simple variability of the Eddas (p. 131), was developed during the ninth century in western Norway. Bragi Boddason the Old, writing of battles and love and loyalty, celebrates the most famous of Viking heroes Ragnar of the Hairy Breeks, probably the same Ragnar who sacked Paris in 845. Then not only the saga (p. 93) but Scaldic poetry was developed in Iceland, particularly by Egill Skalla-Grimson (c. 910–80), a Norwegian settler's son who travelled to Norway and the British Isles. The Icelanders had established an aristocratic commonwealth which was decentralized to an unusual degree, but possessed a national parliamentary assembly of all free men, the Althing, meeting first near Reykjavik and subsequently at Thingvellir. The chieftains formed a legislature, which showed its mettle by the precise, far-sighted Grágás code. Christian missions began to come to Iceland under the guidance of Olaf I Tryggveson, king of Norway (d. 1000), apostle of the Icelanders.

Harald Blue-tooth, king of Denmark, son of Gorm who had founded a new royal line, was likewise converted to Christianity (960–5). Harald's monument near his parents' burial mounds at Jelling in north Jutland claims all Norway as well as Denmark, now mentioned by name; although perhaps the work of English artists, the artistic decoration of this monument is superior in style to its Northumbrian prototypes (p. 74). Harald Blue-tooth, however, was compelled to make peace by the Saxon emperor Otto II; and the most powerful Scandinavian monarch during the last years of the tenth century was Olof Skötkonung, who established Christianity in Sweden. The ancient trading town of Birka upon an island in Lake Mälaren, which had been visited by a missionary bishop in c. 830 but ceased to exist in c. 975, was partially replaced a few years later by Sigtuna, nearer the capital Uppsala. The leading international commercial centre, however, was Visby on the isle of Gotland, which linked the Baltic with the Black Sea and Islamic countries beyond.

The British Isles

Under the weak authority of Ireland's High Kings originating from Connaught in the west (c. 483–1002), the main principalities of the country increased from five to seven. There were also Irish settlers at many points of the western British sea-coast, including the Scots who, migrating from Dalriada (Ulster) to Argyll, gave Scotland and the Strathclyde Picts their ninth-century monarchs.

The semi-legendary fifth-century Briton St Patrick established his episcopal see at Armagh in the north of Ireland, and, farther south, St Finnian founded the monastery of Clonard (c. 515–20) which became the parent of other centres. Irish monasticism, guided by the lives and precepts of the Egyptian monks Antony and Pachomius (p. 42), was instigated initially through influences from southern Gaul. Extreme ascetics (geilt), rare elsewhere in western Europe, lived solitary lives, but the characteristic Irish monastery was a remote congregation of hermits – often on an inaccessible island such as Skellig Michael (SW Ireland) – each in his own beehive hut of clay, within a palisaded village lacking elaborate organization though under an abbot's general control.

On the isle of Iona off the west Scottish shore (c. 563–5) – already the homeland of Irish emigrants – St Columba (521–97) from north-western Ireland established the greatest of Celtic monasteries, which colonized Lindisfarne off the coast of Northumberland (635; p. 74) and organized the conversion of northern Scotland. St Columbanus (543–615) of Leinster spread Irish missionary activity over much of western Europe, from Brittany to Burgundy (p. 62), and finally in Italy where he died at one of his leading foundations, Bobbio north of Genoa.

In Ireland itself, this Age of the Saints comprised not only ascetics and missionaries but a remarkable literary output, committed to writing in the Irish majuscule script. Although this literature – the oldest north of the Alps in a vernacular tongue – has mainly come down to us in later Middle Irish versions, it culminated as early as the seventh century AD in the Law Tracts; in the Ulster cycle of prose sagas and hero tales of prehistoric origin such as the *Cattle Raid of Cooley*, describing a way of life similar to that of the Gauls and Britains before the Roman occupation; and above all in the nature poetry of hermit life. Poems of this kind, such as the dialogue between King Gúaire of Connaught (d. 663) and his half-brother Marbán the Hermit, reveal an unparalleled fusion of religious feeling, sensitiveness to beauty, and self-mocking adventurous fantasy.

Irish visual art, too, now found its finest expression. Drawing upon Egyptian (Coptic) and Syrian models – possibly with Galicia as an intermediary – and displaying Scythian (p. 13) and kindred influences in its fondness for interlaced, stylized animal motifs, this is the first basically non-representational Christian art. Its complicated spiral rhythms are like the overlapping verse structure of the early Irish lyrics; there is an explosive dynamism and an inexhaustibly imaginative elegance in the unerring complexity of these curvilinear, geometric, never repetitious patterns. In the eighth century, large ornate stone crosses rose at Ahenny (Ossory) and elsewhere, and startling effects of restrained sumptuousness were produced by the golden, bejewelled, filigree surfaces of the Tara brooch (c. 720) and Ardagh chalice, in which the contrast between massive full lines and microscopic virtuosity of detail achieves a satisfying balance.

The Book of Kells, perhaps made at Iona and brought to Kells (SE Ireland) after Iona had been destroyed by the Scandinavians (c. 800), is a book of Gospels upon thick glazed vellum, in the usual fine round script. It contains a wondrous proliferation of illuminated capital letters by various artists, some of whom were familiar with Gaulish and Northumbrian work (p. 74). Tumbling into an avalanche of richly patterned, tightly interwoven foliage and animals and stylized human figures – certain of which reflect Carolingian associations – the turbulent, ever-changing rhythm of these designs displays a serpentine profusion far removed from classical traditions of equilibrium.

The Scandinavian invaders dominated the country from the sea-port towns, notably Thorgil's capital at Dublin (841). The tide turned when their descendants first at Limerick (968) and then at Dublin (999) were defeated by Mathgamain and his brother Brian Boru from the south west. In the intervening period, though monastic communities often had to seek refuge in their circular bell-towers, and the country's outstanding philosophical thinker Johannes Scotus migrated to the Frankish court (p. 65), Irish art had developed a new and more monumental 'Hiberno-Viking' style displayed in High Crosses such as Muiredach's at Monasterboice (923). Associated with austerely mystical, anchorite movements emanating from the influential south-eastern monastery of Lismore, these crosses eliminate the traditional semi-pagan sculptural ornament, leaving more space for sacred narrative which anticipates later Romanesque designs (p. 85).

Across the water Germanic invasions of Gaul during the fifth century AD had cut Britain off from Rome, which ceased to send officials and troops. Already increasingly vulnerable to raids from beyond Hadrian's Wall, England was invaded and largely occupied, in about 450, by massive incursions of a number of German peoples – perhaps the relatively civilized Jutes (from Jutland) in the south-east, Saxons elsewhere in the south, and Angli (from Schleswig) in Norfolk, Suffolk and their hinterland. The descendants of these invaders expanded their separate territories, clearing the forests and bringing the heavier valley soils under cultivation. For a short time Kent under King Ethelbert, who was married to a Frankish princess and converted to Christianity by Gregory I's delegate the second St Augustine (597), was the political as well as the economic centre of the country. Soon after 600, however, leadership passed to the east Anglian monarchs, whose flamboyant sumptuousness is displayed in the Sutton Hoo treasure of gold and polychrome jewellery with its ornate elongated animal art blending English, Frankish and Swedish influences.

Meanwhile, however, King Edwin of Northumbria was converted to the Roman church by Paulinus (626). Subsequent members of his house, Oswald and Oswy, became overlords of nearly all England. Under the latter, the fundamental clash between St Colman (d. 676) with his Celtic disciples of Columba (p. 72) and the Rome-based followers of Augustine led by Wilfrid (d. 709) came to a head at the Synod of Whitby (664), where the church of Rome won a victory which, during the following century, extended to Scotland and Wales. The English church, exceptionally devoted to Rome, showed a taste for intellectual and proselytizing activity that made it for a time the focus of west European Christendom.

Pre-eminent among leaders of this church was Theodore of Tarsus, Archbishop of Canterbury (669–90) which became a place of advanced education and letters. But the principal artistic centres were in Northumbria. The Book of Durrow, which is written in the 'Irish' script but may well be Northumbrian work of the later seventh century, displays a blend of Celtic exuberance and continental economy of design; and there are reminiscences, also, of Romano-British mosaic pavements, of the metal and enamelwork for which Anglo-Saxon craftsmen were renowned, and of various eastern schools. Then the Gospel of half-Irish half-Northumbrian Lindisfarne (698–740, p. 72) introduces a version of Italo-Byzantine humanism which recalls that Theodore had originated from Asia Minor, that the great builder Wilfrid (above) used foreign craftsmen at Hexham (671–4), and that Benedict Biscop, founder of Wearmouth and Jarrow (682), came back from Rome with between two and three hundred books. Yet such classical trends are only one element in the Lindisfarne Gospel's novel brew of tightly woven, kaleidoscopic, audaciously dismembered animal forms; something new is emerging in western art. The crosses of Bewcastle and particularly of Ruthwell tilt the balance towards Mediterranean naturalism. Dateable to the period when Ceolfrid, Abbot of Wearmouth, went to Rome (701), the Ruthwell reliefs echo both Ravenna and Egypt as well as local Roman remains. Supplemented by a running spiral of scroll-ornament and by lines of an Anglo-Saxon poem (*The Dream of the Rood*) in which Irish techniques still survive, the English classical tradition displays itself here with a highly distinctive self-conscious emphasis.

The Northumbrian cultural efflorescence reached its literary climax in Bede (*c.* 672–735). This encyclopaedically learned, universally read monk of Jarrow, with his calmly unobtrusive and sober humanity, spent forty years teaching and writing scriptural commentaries. In his *Ecclesiastical History of the English People* (731) he looked back across the chasm of the past to unite the Anglo-Saxon and Celtic components of his newly emerging nation with central Christian traditions of classical learning.

By this time, however, Northumbria's strength had been weakened by the Picts (685), and the inland extension of more advanced economic conditions

After St Boniface had organized Bavaria's church, its expansionist Duke Tassilo III founded Benedictine Kremsmünster (777), to which he and his wife presented this copper and silver chalice with linear, English-inspired ornamentation

ABOVE: Carolingian Rheims assimilated but
transformed classical and Byzantine styles of
illumination, for example in the dynamic spiritual
intensity of this figure of St Matthew in the Testament of Archbishop Ebbo (816–35)
RIGHT: Offa of Mercia (757–96), succeeding to
Northumbria's power, claimed to be king of all
England. The heads on his Canterbury silver
pennies were more imaginative, varied and skilful
in detail than any other European coin portraits
for centuries to come

A Viking's head from the waggon on the Oseberg
burial-ship, Norway (c. 850). Exploring thousands
of miles to east, west, north and south, the
Scandinavians united elemental ferocity, sense of
public order, legal and commercial sophistication,
and advanced artistic culture

ABOVE LEFT: A favoured medium of the second Byzantine Renaissance under the twelfth-century Comnene emperors is the ivory panel, stylised, elegant, severe, with intricately folded formal sharp lines: art of the spirit not the flesh. Here are John the Baptist, Philip, Andrew and Thomas

ABOVE: Croatia has stood throughout history on the borders of east and west, Slavonic but Catholic. This relief of a Croatian king's coronation (tenth or eleventh century) is in the Baptistery of St John at Split, formerly the Temple of Jupiter in Diocletian's palace

LEFT: The Virgin from the Crucifixion mosaic at Daphni near Athens (c. 1100). Wall-mosaics, infinitely varying in optical effects at different hours and seasons, are the supreme Byzantine art: bringing to worshippers with stupendous impact the religious events of the calendar – and the transcendental order of the Universe

RIGHT: Great free-standing tenth-century Hiberno-Viking High Crosses; such as 'Muiredach's' at Monasterboice, anticipate Romanesque with their reliefs of sacred narrative: Bibles for the unlettered. The summit is fashioned as a contemporary shingle-roofed church

ABOVE: Built at their capital of Cordova by Abd al Rahman I (786) and his successors, the Great Mosque, a seemingly limitless forest of marble, peorphyry and jasper aisles, is one of the supreme masterpieces of Europe and Islam

BELOW: Winchester 'Troper', eleventh century. Troping was a type of musical interpolation into traditional liturgical plainsong (the last syllable of *Alleluia* is elaborately decorated), which later, when words were added, helped to create religious drama

At Kiev, Novgorod, Pskov, Vladimir and Moscow, the Byzantine cultural heritage superimposed upon Russia's Slav and Viking origins assumed brilliantly original forms. Characteristic of Novgorod is the buoyant, forcefully vertical brick and stone plainness of St Sophia (1045–52)

Durham cathedral (1093–1130), with probably the
earliest rib-vaults in Europe. The creative
Romanesque drive, structural and monumental,
expands into a revolutionary control of mighty
rhythmical masses

now brought power to the kingdom of Mercia which had expanded from its origins round the upper basin of the Trent. Offa of Mercia (757–96), who claimed to be king of all England, is depicted on his silver pennies with a royal portrait which was not to be surpassed in quality for hundreds of years. But the Mercians, in their turn, were superseded by their south-western neighbour Wessex under Charlemagne's pupil Egbert (802–39), whose effic-ient rule was backed by clerical support. Egbert's far-sighted and culturally enlightened grandson Alfred (871–99) had to grapple with large-scale incur-sions by the Scandinavians who, migrating to the Orkneys and Shetlands towards the end of the previous century, had also raided Northumbria, Ire-land and the Isle of Man. Maintaining a unity of command that was unique among contemporary Germanic states, Alfred won a victory at Edington (878) which kept the Danes north of a line running from London to Chester, and resulted in the baptism of their king Guthrum. Thus Alfred made pos-sible the national unification achieved by Edward the Elder (899–924) and Athelstan (924–39). These two kings strengthened their positions by marriage alliances with the western Franks and Germans; Athelstan also secured tribute from Wales, and crushed King Constantine III of Scotland and his Scandi-navian allies from Dublin at the unidentifiable site of Brunanburh (937). Chieftains of Wales, Scotland and Strathclyde submitted in 973 to Edgar (959–78), whose highly organized government extended from the Channel to the Clyde, lavishly patronizing the church under Archbishop Dunstan of Can-terbury. But the impetus was lost when Ethelred 'the Unready' (978–1016) failed to deal effectively with renewed Danish raids.

Meanwhile there had been an important revival of Anglo-Saxon art, not-ably at Ely and Winchester which produced its resplendent episcopal Stole and Maniple (909–16) and the Benedictional of St Ethelwold (975–80). There also flourished a vernacular literary culture exemplified by the only complete early Teutonic narrative epic, the poem of Beowulf (c. 1000). Incorporating material of various dates back to the sixth century, it blends a historic Beo-wulf, king of 'Geatas' (Goths), with a mythical Beaw: strangely combining, in many gnomic and moral passages, the Christianity which England had championed and the old heroic pagan virtues of courageous endurance.

In the fifth century, large areas of Wales had been occupied by Irish-speak-ing settlers, whose kingdom in the north-west, Gwynned, dominated the country. Within another hundred years, these princes had been converted to Christianity by monks including Dewi (St David). The Celtic rulers of Wales were first separated from their kinsmen in south-west England by the victorious progress of Wessex; then, within the next two centuries, they were thrown back within the present Welsh borders both by Northumbria and by Offa of Mercia (p. 75), who demarcated the frontier by his earth-work or dyke. Next, Wales was violently and frequently attacked by the Scandinavians, to the particular detriment of its coastal monasteries, although St David's in the far south-west kept learning alive.

But Scandinavians and English alike were resisted by Rhodri the Great (844–77), founder of Welsh princely houses, who controlled most of the country; and it is to the Welsh struggle against the English that 'Llywarch Hen', the anonymous storyteller of Powys, devotes his hauntingly sad poetry combining incantatory repetition with a compact verbal economy. This last quality was again manifested, with precision, subtlety and clear technical expression, in the outstanding intellectual achievement of early Wales, the legal reform of Howel the Good (Hywell Da) (910–50); coming from south Wales, he absorbed the northern branch of his ancestor Rhodri's line and, calling himself 'King of all the Welsh', summoned an assembly at Whitland in Carmarthenshire to receive the new code.

3

THE ELEVENTH AND
TWELFTH CENTURIES

France

The Duchy of Paris, based on the Ile de France, was the natural nucleus of the French kingdom because of its central and dominant position in relation to the valleys of the Seine and Loire, the main arteries of trade. The Capet kings Robert the Pious (996–1031) and Philip I (1060–1108) both succeeded their fathers peacefully. In 1023 the German emperor Henry II had a meeting with King Robert, the only European ruler with whom he would confer on equal terms. Philip I, though fat and greedy, took action to make the turbulent aristocracy submit. The old feudalisms were giving way to centralized control, as French monarchs asserted the Frankish tradition of a sacred Christian sovereignty; though Philip missed the First Crusade (1096) (which many of his noblemen joined) because the pope excommunicated him for a bigamous and adulterous marriage.

Louis VI (1108–37), advised by Suger Abbot of S. Denis (d. 1151), eliminated brigandage and strengthened the administration of the Ile de France and Orléanais. Furthermore by marrying his son Louis VII (1137–80) to Eleanor of Guienne, the richest heiress in western Christendom, he added Aquitaine to his possessions, increasing them fivefold in size. But the annulment of this marriage, followed by Eleanor's marriage to Henry II of England and Anjou (p. 95), heralded a period of Anglo-French strife in which the French kingdom, now established at Paris – the first fixed capital in the west – was overshadowed by the extensive Angevin possessions. Eleanor's heritage was centred upon Bordeaux, but she set up her court at Angers, and later (after estrangement from Henry II) at Poitiers; from these centres chivalry and culture radiated to northern France and Spain.

The successor to Louis VII on the French throne was the greatest of his dynasty, Philip II Augustus (1180–1223), who exploited the political unwisdom of Richard I of England and acquired vast territories. The French nobility was now a fully developed and differentiated social class; the earliest written rule of knighthood dates from 1128, and three decades later it had become a religious dedication. But there was also an unprecedentedly effective administrative class to support the authority erected by the kings upon Roman law. Towns were growing rapidly, and so were municipal institutions and guilds. Marseille benefited from the Italian commercial revival, the Laws of Oléron were accepted as the common maritime law of the North Sea and the Atlantic, and until the end of the thirteenth century the fairs at Troyes and other towns of Champagne upon the main Italy-Flanders land routes, with safe conduct guaranteed by its counts, were well placed to act as central clearing-houses for European trade and finance. The sale of textiles, the first important western industry, was in their hands; so was the marketing of France's richest commercial product, its wine, already favoured by those able to afford it in many neighbouring countries.

The independent, though nominally vassal, Viking state of Normandy went through startling transformations during the eleventh century. Although after a serious peasant revolt the duchy for a time remained in a chaotic condition, its ancient and new nobilities alike adventurously staked their fortunes in support of Robert Guiscard, his brother Roger, and William I, conquerors of south Italy (1046–71), Sicily (1060–91) and England (1066) respectively; and Robert's son Bohemund was the effective military leader of the First Crusade (p. 98). William I ruled Normandy along with his English possessions; but Philip II Augustus reasserted French authority.

The many endowments and reconstitutions of monasteries in eleventh-century Normandy bear witness to the strength of ducal control and the ambitions of the new nobility. One of the new foundations was at Bec, where Lanfranc (d. 1089), learned in the Roman, canon and Lombard law of his native Pavia, founded an important school (1045) attended by pupils from many western countries. There Lanfranc and his compatriot Anselm of Aosta (1033–1109), who succeeded him as Archbishop of Canterbury, made a heroic attempt to settle the conflict between reason and faith to which Johannes Scotus had addressed himself earlier (p. 65). 'Last of the Fathers and first of the scholastics', Anselm achieved considerable originality in his confident, argumentative explorations.

Normandy received its intellectual stimulus from the Italians, but its religious vigour, displayed in keen worship of the Virgin Mary (who was associated with chivalry) and in works of devotion by Norman pilgrims, was largely derived from Burgundy. There the Cistercian order, founded in 1086 at Citeaux near Dijon, played from the mid-twelfth century onwards a dominant part in the land clearance and colonization which was bringing about the largest increase in cultivable areas since prehistoric times. The Carthusians, established at Grande Chartreuse (Grenoble) since 1084, laid special stress upon austerity and renunciation: in Burgundy, as in western France and Lorraine and elsewhere, this was a time of recluses, hermits and self-chastising ascetics. Launched amid a mystic enthusiasm due largely to the spirit of Cluny, the First Crusade (1096) was accompanied, under pressure of famine and of inflammatory wandering preachers like Peter the Hermit, by the massive parallel surge of the People's Crusade, an extraordinary manifestation of supra-national devotion, propaganda and restlessness. After suffering huge losses en route, and causing consternation upon their approach to Constantinople, these hordes of ravaging travellers from France and many other countries were exterminated in Asia Minor by the Seljuk Turks (p. 101). Burgundian knights, on the other hand, were the founders of the Templars (1119), dedicated (often with Moslem goodwill) to the protection of pilgrims – and later to the extension of their own power.

In an age when cathedral schools were eclipsing their monastic counterparts, Fulbert (*c.* 960–1028) made Chartres the most vigorous centre of learning in western Europe, in which philosophy, theology and mathematics were enriched by a humanism surviving from the classical tradition. At Chartres, too, Bishop Ivo (St Yves) (*c.* 1040–1116), born near Beauvais, devoted his realistic brain to the study of canon law and the adaptation of papal principles to governmental tasks.

Then, however, to the regret of contemporary humanists, the classical renaissance of Chartres was cut short by the logical scholarship of the rising school at Paris. This walled and partially paved town, the most important in transalpine Europe, became the nucleus, not only of contemporary music under Léonin of Notre Dame, but of a great outburst of dialectical and theological speculation centred upon the new university. Junior to the eleventh-century Moslem foundations, but the model for all west Christian universities of masters as Bologna was the model for universities of students (p. 101), Paris already possessed an important Masters' Guild by 1170. Its reputation was built upon two generations of teachers in the institutions which preceded its foundation. Peter Abelard (1079–1142), a daringly original and versatile logician and religious poet from Le Pallet in Brittany, sought in the Paris cathedral school to systematize Lanfranc's and Anselm's reconciliation of reason with faith; he has been regarded as the founder both of theology in the modern sense, and of scholastic philosophy. Then a bishop of Paris, Peter the Lombard (d. 1160) from Novara, gave influential voice in his *Books of the Sentences* to the new comprehensive and conciliatory spirit. Other cathedral schools, too, were extremely active, Men went for philosophy to Rheims and Laon, which had a brief period of theological brilliance; for medicine and law to Montpellier; and for literature to Orléans as well as Chartres.

From 1179 every diocese began to be required by Church law to provide a free schoolmaster. The initiative was passing from monks to secular clergy, and for the first time since antiquity a distinctively lay civilization was taking shape. There was a brilliant revival of Latin verse, especially in the Loire valley – it dates back to Hildebert of Lavardin (c. 1055–1133/4) – and the oral tradition of vernacular French was committed to writing. Between 1120 and 1160 the *chansons de geste*, verse chronicles set to music, enjoyed their fullest flowering; their inspirations were the courts of Louis VI and VII and the cult of Charlemagne, fostered at S. Denis and pilgrim centres along the route to Santiago de Compostela (p. 61).

The *Chanson de Roland* symbolizes this stream of pilgrims, and the warriors who, in anticipation of the eastern crusaders, had broken across the Pyrenees (p. 61). Outstanding both in literary merit and in historical importance, ancestral to all western vernacular poetry, the *Chanson* tells of the unalterable resolution of a few doomed men, under a feudal order whose rough, grim, physical prowess is mitigated by sacrifice and patriotic idealism.

Far different was the erotic poetry of the more southern regions whose rulers were not subject to Paris. These included rich Provence with its classical, eastern and Jewish links and century-long political affiliation to the counts of Barcelona and kings of Aragon (1112); the polyglot region of Languedoc, where at the end of the eleventh century the county of Toulouse maintained its resplendent court under Raymond of St Gilles; and its rivals the dukes of Aquitaine, crowned at Limoges (Limousin). In a number of French dialects, and in tones adapted from Byzantine, Spanish–Moslem and other models, the *troubadours* of these regions created the European lyric, and gave poetry a social function for the first time for five centuries. Their songs of stylized courtly love echoed the novel feminine sympathies of the age – for the knight is a humble servant whose adventurous quests are in his Lady's honour – and reflected with sparkling, exuberant virtuosity the current ostentatious expenditure on fine clothes, armour and poetry. Two thousand six hundred songs and 250 melodies by 400 troubadours have been collected; the first known exponent of the genre was William IX, Duke of Aquitaine and Count of Poitou (d. 1126), and the most sensitive is Bernart de Ventadour. Troubadours from the south, and corresponding *trouvères* from the north, were brought together at Eleanor's court – the principal home of the fashionable chivalrous tendencies which, partly under Cluny's influence, were debrutalizing the feudal aristocracy.

But it was the counts and countesses of Champagne and Flanders who patronized the master of another form of literature, the new *roman courtois*. This was Chrétien of Troyes, whose *Lancelot* (1172–5) intermingles southern French eroticism, in which love can take precedence over honour, with Anglo-Saxon romancing and Celtic Arthurianism. Chrétien dislikes Paris, and makes fun of the outmoded *chansons de geste*; nor does he favour either Rome or the German empire. Another product of this period was the *chante-fable*, sung in alternating prose and verse. An example admired today

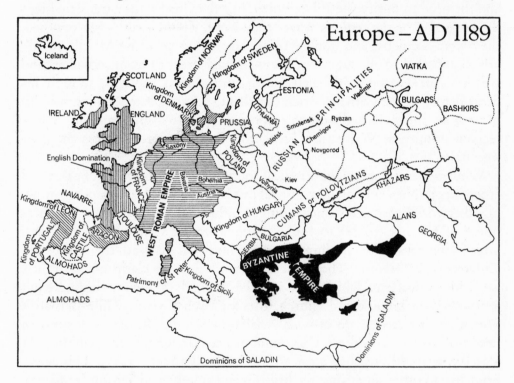

is *Aucassin et Nicolette*, telling of two young lovers who refuse to be separated; the story is of Moorish origin, the setting is Provençal, but the skilful author, whose name is unknown, comes from northern France.

This age of lay emancipation, intellectual activity and unprecedented wealth was also an epoch in which religious deviation became a leading issue. King Robert the Pious seems to have been the first to burn heretics (1022). During the next century various heretical creeds began to appear, and in about 1140 there arrived in southern France, apparently from Constantinople and Lombardy, missionaries of the dualist Manichaean doctrine of eastern origin and strong Bulgarian (Bogomil) associations, according to which (in one of its forms) the world originated not only from God but also from Satan (p. 55): equally alarming was their disregard and distaste for the hierarchy on earth. This was the first time for a millennium that an eastern religion had attempted to take over the west. Within two years subversive dualist doctrine spread from the Pyrenees to the Rhine and beyond; its base, however, was in Languedoc where its bishopric at Albi earned converts the name of 'Albigensians'. They were also called 'Cathars' ('pure', or puritan), since they stressed the purity of the soul – as against the evil of the world – and the need to purify the Bible which, like the Greeks, they translated into the languages of the regions where they lived. Though ruthlessly opposed, they were a quietist and non-revolutionary 'Church of the Middle Road', which appealed to all classes but drew especial strength from scriveners and weavers. In keeping with such ascetic anti-clerical thought, though independently of the Cathars, a rich merchant of Lyon, Peter Valdes, sold his possessions and preached voluntary poverty (c. 1161–80), founding a persecuted primitivist Waldensian brotherhood which spread across the Alps into Italy.

While reformers set up these radical counterpoises to authority, St Bernard (1090–1153), born at Fontaines, instead cast its aegis over his own programme of otherworldliness. This outstandingly influential monk left the mother-house of Citeaux (p. 78) to found a monastery at Clairvaux in the Jura, which soon became the leading Cistercian house; at his death there were 343 Cistercian communities. Their practical novelty was the compactness of their great monastic farms which they worked themselves, living within a day's journey of their house and church. But for twenty years, while Bernard's preaching attracted huge crowds, Clairvaux outdid Rome as a spiritual headquarters and as western Christendom's censor against free-thinking. At Vézelay, Bernard preached a call to the Second Crusade (1145). This enterprise, like its successor against the brilliant and enlightened Saladin (1189–92), ended in disaster and recrimination for the western invaders. Those of them who returned brought back leprosy; but they also brought commercial and cultural contacts, superior materials, better cooking and improved ideas of personal hygiene.

The century's most important secular artistic monument, unique for its depiction of recent history, is the Bayeux tapestry (c. 1073–83), of which William the Conqueror's half-brother, Bishop Odo of Bayeux, has been regarded as the guiding spirit. In a fluent and skilful arrangement of contrasted scenes this strip of embroidery, worked upon coarse linen in woollen thread, emphasizes the obligations of the English Harold II to William of Normandy and depicts Harold's downfall (p. 94), giving a flattering picture of the skill shown by the Normans in capturing fortresses, and of the agility of their cavalry.

Normandy again, along with variant styles in Auvergne, Burgundy and classical Languedoc, was in the forefront of the Romanesque architecture which now proliferated in western Europe. Ancient Roman in its round arches which spring, however, not from entablatures but (as in later antiquity) straight from massive piers (p. 33), this style also borrows from both Germanic and Celtic motifs of all degrees of sophistication, as well as from recent and even ancient developments in the east. Yet in spite of all these traditional elements Romanesque churches are essentially forward-looking; more spacious, lofty and varied than any Carolingian or Ottonian achievements (p. 67), this is an art of novel mass and volume – 'no longer crustacean, but vertebrate'. With their tunnel-vaults replacing timber roofs, their bays articulated by tall shafts from floor to ceiling, and their internal proportions based on a crystalline three-dimensional language of horizontals and verticals, prisms and pyramids harmonizing with vividly abstract stylized decoration, these huge edifices are fortresses of God, strongholds on earth to serve His glory against evil. It is also their purpose, beneath the shadow of the temporal power, to curb and frighten the faithful while offering them shelter and protection as well.

Rebuilt Jumièges and S. Etienne at Caen date from 1037–66 and 1067–8. But the grandest of all exteriors was the boldly monumental S. Sernin at Toulouse (1077–1119), one of a series of tall dark churches, perhaps modelled after Tours, upon the pilgrim route to Santiago. Another imposing achievement of the style – symbolic of the spirit of the First Crusaders – was the new abbey at Cluny (p. 68), reconstructed from 1089–1121 onwards and now, since 1810, demolished. With two pairs of aisles, two apsed transepts, many semicircular eastern chapels and a polygonal spired bell-tower, this church, standing for the marriage between stupendous architecture and lavish ornament, was for centuries one of the largest and most imitated ecclesiastical buildings in the world. But meanwhile French Romanesque architecture continued to develop in majesty and balance, with a tendency in the south for architects to show the materials for what they were and fix them with classical simplicity to the earth, while northerners aimed rather at dividing and articulating their components.

However, in the early 1140's Abbot Suger, minister of the kings of France, instigated one of the most revolutionary steps in the artistic history of Europe, by stimulating the combination of certain recent architectural developments in order to create the Gothic style. Under his direction were merged the pointed arch which had evolved from Roman roundness, the flying buttress which took the weight off sideways stresses, and the intersecting crosswise rib-vaults which concentrated the roof-load at four corners, thus making large windows possible. Vault and side-walls lost their inertia, and the solid masonry quickened its rhythm, springing alive with dramatic poise and balance: muscular, energetic, vertically concentrated curves, penetrating instead of compassing space, framed the free circulation of light and air in a luminous transparency which elevated men's minds to the transcendental contemplation of the Christian God.

The spiritual experience was sensuous, and yet the miracle was achieved by the mathematical linear precision of thrust and counter-thrust. This was a hard-headed, cerebral, organizational art – the characteristic achievement of the Ile de France, not hitherto in the forefront of the visual arts. At S. Denis the only parts of Suger's foundation to survive are the crypt, the façade (restored), a little vaulting, and the choir chapel. But the next products of this first wave of Gothicism were none of them far away. They were at Chartres, where only the west portals of this date (c. 1145) remain; at Noyon (c. 1150–70), where the addition of a triforium between gallery and clerestory combined horizontal continuity with emphasis on shadowy depth; at Senlis (from 1155); and at Notre Dame in Paris (1163), where the glory of God and the king are proclaimed by forcible internal rhythms and a façade of weightless perfection.

Suger invited craftsmen from all lands, for a cathedral was the mother of diverse achievement. Notable among them were the metal-workers for which Limoges and Verdun were famed. But the outstanding medium, vital also in its relation to the architecture, was stained glass. This art, probably adapted from simpler models at Constantinople (of which only fragments have survived), combines supreme technical skill with an emotional effect of broken, vibrating colours and light effects changing from hour to hour even more vividly, owing to their transparency, than the mosaics of eastern Europe (p. 47). The finest twelfth-century glass is at Chartres, with its Virgin and Child (La Belle Verrière), and its great innovation the western rose window on which the Tree of Jesse is displayed. Elsewhere in the country, as chemical experiments made the fresco technique better understood, dramatic mural paintings exploit the symbolic and sacramental use of colour – particularly in central France, for example at S. Savin near Poitiers, and at Berzé-la-Ville where Christ reigns in His majesty.

St Bernard deplored figurative sculpture, at least in monastic churches; though he might have agreed that different considerations applied to churches intended to lead laymen to the truth. In any case, the later Romanesque architecture was also accompanied by the deliberately alarming, demoniac early twelfth-century sculpture whose rippling motions form an integral part of its tunnel-vaulted churches. One of the main themes is the Last Judgment. It is intended to terrify and yet also, in response to current waves of apocalyptic fear, to exorcize: to assert the authority of the church on whose pleadings the people's salvation depends. A technical leap has been taken by the vivid, almost hallucinatory representation of man – in the grip of passion and horror. At Moissac in Languedoc, on the west gate of the Church of S. Pierre (*c.* 1120), Jesus is revealed at his Second Coming, accompanied by two mighty angels in a central area of calmness amid responding lines of violent, twisting movement. At Souillac there is an even intenser grotesqueness, instability and shock; while on the narthex door at Vézelay in Burgundy, the ghost-like cadaverous forms, in the swirling quiver of their drapery, are blasted and distorted by the Holy Spirit's descent.

And then, as Gothic overtakes Romanesque, there is a gradual change: technically, as a new naturalism turns all the relief figures into freely moving statues – the change is apparent on the portal at Senlis (*c.* 1185) – and spiritually because, as love begins to replace fear, the church becomes a picture of heaven on earth, and the implacable wheel of fate is transformed into a radiant sun.

Spain

In Moslem Spain, victories against the Christians were won by Hisham II's regents and military dictators Al Mansur and Muzaffar (1002–8). But then the 'Slavs' (powerful descendants of prisoners, p. 60), together with Berber elements, broke up the state; Cordova was destroyed, the Ummayad caliphate collapsed (1031), and there followed an era of small republics (*taifas*) anticipatory of Renaissance Italy. In the south, Berbers ruled; Cordova, under a triumvirate, recovered and created an outstanding university; Granada, breaking away from Malaga, was ruled by the bloodthirsty Berber Badis who, advised by his Jewish chief minister Samuel ibn Naghzala, added to his dynasty's sumptuous buildings.

In the east, Slavs were in control. Mojehid, prince of the Balearic Islands, was a patron of letters and the most dangerous pirate of the day. Almeria became, after Constantinople, one of the wealthiest cities in Europe, with its large navy, iron foundries, potteries, public baths, inns and hotels – one thousand in number – and its enormous trade, including the products of 3,000 looms which supplied Europe and Africa with rich silken stuffs. Saragossa, before falling to the Christians (1118), reached its peak under Moctadir and Mutamin, who encouraged philosophy and mathematics and largely contributed to a resplendent palace-citadel and mosque, the Aljaferia, with its sumptuous, minutely interlaced decoration.

But as this new art developed in isolation from the rest of Islam, the cultural capital, as well as the most powerful political centre, was Seville, still under Arab rulers – Yemenites of the Abbadid dynasty. Outstanding among these was Mutadid (d. 1069) who, in opposition to Granada, greatly extended Sevillian rule; erudite, poetical, drunken and ruthless, he possessed diplomatic and strategic gifts, a harem of eight hundred women, and a macabre sense of humour. His son Mutamid temporarily, and by treacherous means, gained possession of Cordova; yet he was also a sensitive poet who made Seville a city of music and festivals.

But he and other Moslem princes, hard pressed in their disunity by King Alfonso VI of Castile and León (p. 61), fatally called in the fanatical Berber Almoravids ('Frontier Warriors for the Faith') (1086), who had formed an African empire from Algiers to Senegal. Mutamid was deported, to become legendary for his chivalrous brilliance and romantic misfortunes. The Almoravid Yusuf ibn Tashfin (d. 1106) reunited Spanish Islam as far as the Tagus and the Ebro mouth; and his son Ali (1106–43) added to these dominions Madrid, Saragossa, Lisbon and Oporto. A man of devout, hermit-like character, he allowed the theologians (Fakihs) of his court to stimulate persecutions of Christians and Jews. But then the Almoravids, in both Morocco (1147) and Spain, were overthrown by the dynasty of Almohads ('Unitarians') founded by Mohammed ibn Tumart (d. 1130), a Berber from the Atlas mountains who denounced anthropomorphism and spiritualized the conception of God. After the Almohad conquest of Spain, Abd al Mumin (1145–63) united the whole coast from Egypt to the Atlantic, maintaining close contact with Italian merchants.

At Seville was the great seventeen-naved mosque of Abu Yacub Yusuf (p. 87), constructed under Egyptian influences transmitted through Morocco, and intended to rival Cordova (p. 61). The main building has vanished, but its tower, the Giralda (1184), has survived as an example of the new monumental, restrained grandeur of Almohad architecture in which structure was more important than decoration.

But above all, this was an age of literary and philosophical output in Moslem Spain almost as distinguished as the contemporary Mohammedan culture of Khorasan and Bokhara. As the Ummayad caliphate in Spain was collapsing, the seven-week monarch Abd al Rahman V had entrusted the premiership to Ibn Hazim (994–1063), the most learned man of his age and the most fertile writer Spain ever produced. His demonstrations of the logical superiority of Islam (written by a man whose family had formerly been Christian) were accompanied by criticisms of tyrants which caused his works to be burnt by Mutadid of Seville. Avempace (Ibn Bajja) of Saragossa (d. 1138) was the first outstanding Spanish representative of the Aristotelian (p. 17) and Neo-Platonic (p. 40) philosophies, concerned with a thinker's freedom to express himself in a world under unsympathetic control. The geographer from Malaga, Idrisi (*c.* 1099–1154), studied at Cordova before undertaking his extensive travels, which included prolonged residence at the Norman-Sicilian court (p. 97). By the middle of the twelfth century, the manufacture of paper was established at Xativa, Valencia and Toledo.

The scholars who enjoyed the favour of the Almohad ruler Abu Yacub Yusuf (1163–84), under an austere régime by which intellectual pursuits were more highly valued than in the Latin world, included Averroes (Ibn Raschid) of Cordova (1126–1198). The last important Arab philosopher, Averroes – who gained vast posthumous influence (partly through mis-translations), not least among the heterodox and in Paris (p. 117) – summed up the work of two centuries. A vigorous defender of Aristotelianism,[1] he even implied the denial of individual immortality. Yet his aim was to reconcile religion with philosophy: this was based on the argument that religion is true because it is divine revelation, philosophy because it depends on the thought of the human mind which also comes from God.

Cordova and Seville were the fountain-heads of the vernacular poetry, drawn from Arabia and Persia, which was to flow on from Andalusia to Languedec (p. 80). The Cordovan minister Ibn Hazim's poems on the psychology of love were particularly influential, and the poet-ruler Mutamid of Seville employed in a similar ministerial capacity (until their friendship was fatally broken) his fellow-poet Ibn Ammar. From Cordova, in a later generation, came Ibn Guzman (*c.* 1078–1160), whose popular short poems (*muwassahas*, *zéjels*) were adaptations of the Mediterranean folk-song tradition. But under the Almohads who (unlike the Almoravids) favoured their activities, the outstanding circle of poets was now at Seville.

These centuries also witnessed, in Spain, a renaissance of Jewish poetry and philosophy unequalled elsewhere in the world. The outstanding Hebrew poet of the Middle Ages was Judah ben Samuel Halevi (*c.* 1055–*c.* 1140), a doctor by profession, born at Toledo when it was still Christian; he was particularly noted for his liturgical hymns and Odes to Zion, which gained the admiration of Heine (p. 260). The only Spaniard (though he emigrated from Spain) ever to produce a complete philosophical system was the Jew Maimonides (1135–1204). He, like Averroes, saw no quarrel between religion and scholarship.

---

[1] Logic, metaphysics and natural science. Averroes' belief in the eternity of the universe contradicted the Moslem, Christian and Jewish view of creation.

Yet his synthesis was much more favourable to religion than Averroes', blending religious conviction with a serene Graeco-Roman intellectualism which, although it offended orthodox Jewry, profoundly affected Christian mystics including Meister Eckhart (p. 129); while his idea of God as the Supreme Artist was adopted by St Thomas Aquinas (p. 112).

In Christian Spain, Sancho III the Great (1000–35) briefly made Navarre the dominant power. Extending his empire to León, where he declared himself emperor, Sancho III also ruled Castile and was suzerain of Barcelona. But he himself presided over the break-up of his kingdom by arranging that after his death it should be divided among his sons. Under his second son Ferdinand I (1033–65), Castile emerged as a state with a personality of its own. The brilliant Alfonso VI (1065–1109), succeeding to the thrones of Castile, León and Galicia, married Constance of Burgundy. Under her influence, the monastic movement of Cluny (p. 68) organized hostels en route to the rebuilt shrine of Santiago de Compostela. There, French, Burgundian and Norman pilgrims flocked in even greater numbers than before, to the advantage of the Castilian exchequer.

Alfonso VI, conqueror of Toledo from Islam (1085), called himself 'emperor of the two religions', and included Moslems and Jews in the charters granted to colonists in the border areas. Meanwhile the semi-legendary Cid (Sidi) Campeador, Rodrigo Diaz de Vivar, employed intrigue, violence, chivalric prowess and Moslem alliances to conquer Valencia and carve himself out a principality there.

Sancho III's fourth son Ramiro I (1035–65) created the kingdom of Aragon – looking east and south – and resided at Jaca, where the cathedral (1063) is probably the oldest in Spain. This Aragonese state rose in importance under Alfonso I (1104–34) who conquered Saragossa from the Moslems (1118) and made it his capital, repopulating his kingdom with 14,000 Christians (Mozarabs) transported from the south.

However, Alfonso VII of Castile and León (1126–57) became suzerain not only of south-western France but of Aragon as well, declaring himself at León, in the presence of Moorish as well as Christian vassals, to be 'emperor of all Spain' (1135); but his dominions broke up again after his death. Even in his lifetime his cousin Afonso I Henriques had assumed the kingship of Portugal at Oporto (1140), to which, with the help of crusaders on their way to the Holy Land, he added Lisbon also (1147).

Although the Spanish nobility strengthened itself by the establishment of military Orders, parliamentary institutions displayed a degree of development unparalleled elsewhere in Europe. A democratic spirit was abroad in

Castile; the Aragonese *Cortes* met in 1162–3; and Alfonso IX of León (1188–1230) swore to the *Cortes* there – including municipal representatives whose help he needed against the nobles – that he would not act against the person or property of a subject except by process of law.

Alfonso VI's conquest of cosmopolitan Toledo, its culture enriched by Jewish refugees from Almohad persecution, opened up new horizons to Christian men of learning from numerous countries. Archbishop Raymond I (1126–51) established a school of translators who Latinized the scholarship of the Arabs, including their versions of Aristotle – far more complete than those hitherto known – and Galen and Ptolemy, recently translated in Norman Sicily (p. 97) and now rendered in a much more influential version by Gerard of Cremona (1175). A new Euclid emerged, and a new algebra, and treatises on perspective; and, during widespread travels extending over a quarter of a century, the Toledan Jew Abraham ibn Ezra (*c.* 1093–1167) diffused a knowledge of his own scriptural, philosophical and mathematical erudition and poetic gifts.

Toledo was now producing famous Hispano-Mauresque lustre pottery, and churches with 'Mudejar' brick decoration, the work of Moslem artists under Christian rule. In Catalonian churches, the mural frescoes display dramatic adaptations of Byzantine styles. But the masterpieces of the age are found farther to the north-west, in the precociously brilliant sculpture of the Cámara Santa at Oviedo, and the Pórtico de la Gloria at Santiago de Compostela (1183) with its arresting figure of the laughing Daniel.

It was a Christian from Medinaceli on the Moslem side of the frontier who wrote *El Cantar de Mio Cid* (*c.* 1140), some forty years after the death of its warrior hero (p. 88). This sober, realistic, terse dry epic – independent of French models – celebrates in no crusading tones, but in a comparatively humane and law-abiding spirit which has done much to shape the character of Castile, the worldly success of a self-reliant man.

Germany and Central Europe

In AD 1000 Germany, despite all disruptive influences, was the most powerful kingdom in western Europe. Under the last of the Saxon house Henry II (1002–24) and the first two Salian (Franconian) rulers Conrad II (1024–39) and Henry III (1039–56), imperial relations with ecclesiastics and lesser princes had developed promisingly. Henry II, founder of the bishopric of Bamberg, achieved an excellent understanding with the church. Conrad II could not abolish the power of the German duchies, but he stabilized the imperial territories as a territorial bloc 'the Roman Empire', as well as gaining the overlordship of Burgundy and reviving German authority in Italy. Henry III, the most powerful of these rulers and suzerain for a time of Poland and Hungary, was a friend of Abbot Hugh of Cluny and a champion of reform. Sweeping away three contesting popes and replacing them by a series of four German reformers, he declared the papacy to be a mere annex of his national church; though before long this papacy was raising anti-kings in Germany as the empire had put up anti-popes.

The central chapter of the Middle Ages began with the trouble between Henry IV (1053–1106) and Pope Gregory VII (Hildebrand). Their dispute was a conflict between two violently opposed conceptions of European society. This took the shape of an argument about simony (temporal gain from spiritualities) and clerical marriage, followed before long by the Investiture Contest relating to the form in which episcopal appointments should be made. Gregory's humiliation of the emperor, whom he kept shivering outside Canossa (1077), was spectacular but far from final (p. 98); profound political, spiritual, cultural and artistic forces were involved.

Although these quarrels retarded political development, the country was displaying rapid economic progress. The leading centres of trade were at episcopal and other cities such as Hamburg, Cologne, Würzburg, Mainz, Nuremberg, Magdeburg and Trier; whereas Worms became the first self-governing city by driving out its bishop in 1073. The Jewish community at Worms (like its city hall) claimed to be the oldest in Germany, but the largest was at Mainz. The episcopal Rhineland cities were the worst sufferers in the first great massacre of Jews (alleged to be in league with Islam) which accompanied the First Crusade and originated their dispersal throughout central and eastern Europe.

The German emperors, hostile to the pope, did not take part in the Crusade. Yet there were important religious developments. The founder of the Carthusian Order, Bruno, had been born (c. 1030) and ordained at Cologne, and the belatedly Cluny-inspired congregation of Hirsau in Swabia (Württemberg) became the first German religious movement. The training of lay brothers and itinerant preachers by its Abbot William (1069–91), an active controversialist and friend of Pope Gregory VII (p. 98) and Anselm (p. 94), militated against the noblemen whom the Investiture Contest was encouraging to seek wider powers.

Under Henry V of Germany (1106–25), this imperial conflict with the papacy shrank into a legalistic dispute, for which a solution was sought at the Concordat of Worms (1122). This more or less preserved the canonical structure of episcopal elections, while allowing the emperor the right of

Jeremiah: beside the door of Moissac's monastery church in Languedoc (c. 1115), which displays Islamic decorative motifs. These figures of nervous, febrile sinuosity reach their climax in demoniac Last Judgments, charged with terror for the humble congregation

ABOVE: This Danish crucifix (*c.* 1140) has the rugged, elemental power characteristic of the country's Romanesque sculpture. A Danish national archbishop under the influence of Hamburg had been established at Lund (Sweden)

LEFT: A 'bracteate' coin of Margrave Otto I (1170–84) of sparsely populated, backward Brandenburg, perpetually fluctuating on the eastern frontier of the explosive German expansion, colonised with settlers from the Lower Rhine

RIGHT ABOVE: St Vincent and his brothers being led to punishment; from the Basilica of St Vincent at Avila. Spanish Romanesque reliefs already display the tortured tension of the peninsula's later religious sculpture

RIGHT BELOW: Relief (shortly before 1200) of Bishop Adalbert receiving his crozier from the German emperor. From the cathedral door at Gniezno (Gnesen), home of Poland's independent church. Strengthened under Boleslaw III (1102–38) the country sometimes accepted German suzerainty

ABOVE: Relief by Giovanni Pisano at S. Andrea, Pistoia. Working with French stonemasons, he broke with the formalism of the past, displaying turbulent staccato emotions and rhythms unequalled until Bernini. Byzantines were breaking away too; but Giovanni was in closer touch with Roman antiquity

LEFT: Fresco of the Scribes, Boiana, Bulgaria. In this country which led the way in Slavonic power and culture, the thirteenth-century artist infuses Byzantine traditions with a highly individual plastic vitality

ABOVE: Harlech castle in Merionethshire (Wales). These great fortified keeps were the principal means by which medieval rulers guarded their frontiers and kept down subject peoples

LEFT: The facade of the abbey of Ják in Hungary (1256). Its decorative sculptures are now performing the architectural functions already introduced, under Italian influences, to Bohemia and Moravia (Záboří, Tišnov)

ABOVE: Monkish meditation with heaven was
all-important to Byzantium, and Mount Athos is
still Christendom's largest monastic complex.
This is the church at Chilandari, founded by
Stephen Nemanya who created the first Serbian
empire (1197, rebuilt 1290)
RIGHT: The best preserved of Norway's 'stave'
churches: twelfth-century Borgund (Laerdal), with
its gables, dragon-headed carvings and Runic
inscriptions. Pope Eugene II had sent the English
Cardinal Nicholas Breakespeare to found a new
Norwegian archbishopric

At Granada's Alhambra (Red Palace), European
Islam achieved this unsurpassably seductive Patio
de los Leones, built by Mohammed V (1354-91)
on a cloister-like pattern attributed to his contacts
with Pedro I the Cruel, 'the Christian Sultan of
Seville'

veto; but the effect tended to be that the pope retained the last word in Italy, and the emperor in Germany.

However, during the decades which followed – including the débacle of the Second Crusade (1145) – there was violent rivalry between the Dukes of Saxony and Bavaria (Guelphs) and the Hohenstaufen Dukes of Swabia (Ghibellines). The latter gained the imperial throne under Frederick I Barbarossa (1152–90), but at the price of division, since the Guelph Henry the Lion (1142–95) gained the suzerainty of the Baltic bishoprics and of recently founded Lübeck with its incomparable trading position; while Henry's rival the Margrave of Austria was compensated by promotion to a hereditary dukedom.

The new ways of thought which were taking shape under southern and western influences included the rise of an articulate national German feeling, expressed, for example, in rivalry with France. Moreover, although the 300 states of the empire were largely Germanic, its rulers, in their diplomatic conflicts with the papacy and Byzantium, mobilized universalist ideas of world-dominion which gave birth, under the winning knightly personality of Frederick Barbarossa, to the phrase the 'Holy Empire' (1157).

Under the impulse of the more progressive personalities of this empire an administrative class of knights (*ministeriales*), roughly corresponding to Serjeants in England and France, had come into being; and Frederick designated the Jews of Regensburg as members of his civil staff. Unlike Italy, Germany was a country where the rising cities helped the crown against the nobles: and, at the height of his power, Frederick broke Henry the Lion – in the first political high court action (1180) – and made peace both with his other rebellious vassals and with the pope.

After Germany, early in the eleventh century, had vindicated its control of the Thuringian marches against Polish invaders, there followed a time of extraordinarily rapid expansion, not necessarily guided by imperial policies and often in opposition to them. Princes and knights (particularly restless younger sons) were to the fore; and churchmen, especially Cistercians and Premonstratensians;[1] and peasants from the west whom they recruited as colonists. These drives nearly doubled German territory, pushing the frontier forward as far as Breslau. Not only Holstein and Mecklenburg but large areas beyond the Oder were gradually Germanized, and Leipzig became the trade junction for these vast eastern lands. Although Slav landlords as well as Germans joined in the colonization, there was also constant, inhumanly savage warfare between the two races. A German gathering at Merseburg in 1108 proclaimed that warriors against the Slavs would ensure 'salvation for your souls and settlement on the best lands'.

[1] The Augustinian White Canons, an Order founded by St Norbert (c. 1120).

Yet, even before that, some of the frontiers of Germanism to east and south had, on more or less fluctuating lines, begun to take shape. In 1000 Boleslaw I of Poland (p. 57) reached an agreement with Otto III which gave the Poles an independent church at Gniezno (Gnesen) and the control of large areas of central Europe; while, after a period of vassalage to Henry III, Boleslaw III the Crooked Mouthed (1102–38) successfully asserted (for his lifetime) Polish independence, culture and unity against Henry V (1109). Hungary, too, had profited by the friendship of Otto III to enter the western orbit as an independent power. Stephen (997–1038) was baptized and received a crown sent by the pope, and Koloman (1094–114) joined Croatia to Hungary (1102), with which it remained for eight centuries. Bohemia, too, stabilized its boundaries under Bretyslav I (1037) of the Premyslid dynasty, and his successor Ottakar I (1197–1230) secured the royal title for himself and his descendants.

German Romanesque architecture reflected the regional diversity of the country. Hirsau introduced the style of Cluny's reconstruction (p. 83), with transept chapels and complex east ends. In Lower Saxony, where these influences were added to the Ottonian monumental tradition (p. 67), Hildesheim was fortified by its Bishop St Bernward (993–1022), who also erected the church of St Michael (1001–) with a complex, rhythmical, architectural design. In Westphalia the usual steeply rising basilica pattern is varied by earth-bound, hall-like buildings in which nave and aisles are of the same level. Rhineland churches display fantastic groupings of as many as six cylindrical towers. Speyer, with its novel, dynamic clusters of columns, is also perhaps the earliest of Romanesque edifices in which nave and aisles were all vaulted (or intended to be vaulted) from the first (c. 1100). Other great imperial cathedrals, at Worms and Mainz, have double choirs, for the bishop at the east end, and for abbot and monks at the west.

The doors made under Bernward's direction for Hildesheim cathedral (1015), each cast as a whole in bronze according to antique precedents, show reliefs of the Creation, Fall and Redemption: their tense, twisted, un-classical figures make a poignant emotional impact. At the end of the eleventh century Saxon sculpture achieved a further triumph in the crucifix at Werden abbey (Westphalia), in which geometrical emphasis, and distortion for the sake of emotional forcibility, look ahead towards modern expressionism (p. 287).

Fine church murals appeared in Bohemia, and early stained glass at Augsburg; important book illuminations were produced at Salzburg, an outpost of Byzantine influence, and at Regensburg where the chief stimulus was the abbey of Reichenau (p. 67). One of Reichenau's monks was the outstanding universal scholar Hermann the Lame (1013–54), a Swabian count's son who devoted himself to mathematics and astronomy, made watches and astrolabes, and expressed in his musical compositions the new spirit of the Virgin Mary's worship (p. 78). South of the lake was St Gall, where Notker Labeo (d. 1022) had made the basic cultural material of the day available in German. At the other end of the country, Adam of Bremen (d. 1076) was a historian and geographer acquainted with Scandinavian discoveries in the north (p. 70).

Scandinavia, England and the Low Countries

The principal masterpieces of Germanic literature in this epoch were written in Iceland, where the old ninth-century settlers' commonwealth (p. 70) was developing an oligarchic concentration of power which was to lead in the thirteenth century to struggles resulting in submission to Norway. Ari Thorgilsson (c. 1067–1148) was the pioneer of vernacular Icelandic history. The written sagas, based on oral traditions (four to eight hundred years old) relating to kings of Norway or legendary German heroes, begin, as far as we know, with the *First Saga of St Olaf* (Olaf II Haraldsson of Norway, 995–1030). This was composed in c. 1180, probably at the Benedictine monastery of Thingeyrar which had been founded half a century earlier. Another of the monastery's inmates, Odd Snorrason, wrote a life of the Norwegian king Olaf I Tryggveson (969–1000) who was regarded as Iceland's apostle (p. 71).

In Norway itself the first and second Olafs, their country's traditional heroes, were among the leaders of two linked movements: towards a united national kingdom of Norway, with the rudiments of a parliamentary government (*Thing*), and towards the establishment of Christianity. Olaf II was the first to rule all Norway from his capital at Trondhjem, and both Olafs were active in Christianization. This did not, however, prevent the continued violent attacks by Danes and Norwegians against Christians of other lands, along the coasts and up the river valleys, over a huge area from the Baltic to the Bay of Biscay.

With the assistance of disaffected Anglo-Saxons, the Danish king Svein (Sweyn) I Forkbeard (c. 986–1014) continually ravaged England, and under his son Cnut (Canute) (1014–35) Danish expansion was at its height. Cnut's sway extended over England, Denmark, Norway (1028), part of Sweden, and the Hebrides. The most powerful ruler in north Europe, he showed a new beneficence and statesmanship by his multi-racial policy and subsidies to abbeys; but in spite of sea-power, and of diplomatic links exemplified by a visit to Rome (1027), the connexion between his territories remained purely personal and ephemeral.

In England, after Cnut had permitted land and authority to be concentrated in the hands of a few great earls, the crown returned to the house of Alfred under Edward the Confessor (1042–66). Though conceding internal power to the Saxon earl Godwin and his son Harold, Edward orientated the court of his increasingly prosperous country towards Normandy where he had grown up, rather than towards Scandinavia. Upon Edward's death Harold had to fight for his throne simultaneously against Harald III Sigurdson (Hardraade, 'the hard ruler') of Norway (1046–66), whom he defeated and killed at Stamford Bridge, and William of Normandy (1035–87) – bastard son of Duke Robert the Devil – who, by Frankish cavalry shock-tactics and Norse-style archery, defeated and slew Harold at Battle (Hastings). The result of William's conquest of England was to turn the country permanently away from Scandinavia and ultimately (after the initial erection of barriers against reformed monasticism) towards its closer neighbours in France. Hundreds of years of Norse invasion had come to an end; but four centuries of immersion in French feudal conflicts were to follow – with a profitable Flemish trade link as compensation (p. 123).

Meanwhile William, replacing 20,000 leading Anglo-Saxons by as many Normans, introduced an efficiently centralized régime exemplified by his exhaustive Domesday Survey (1086). Although he confirmed the customary law of the Anglo-Saxons and stressed his continuity with their state, William possessed a far more thoroughgoing monarchical power than French or German rulers – based on an exalted personal conception of his role, suggestive of Byzantine ideas absorbed by his fellow-Normans who were conquering south Italy (p. 96).

Henry I of England (1100–35) compromised successfully with the pope and Archbishop Anselm of Aosta (1033–1109) over the investiture of bishops (p. 90) – surrendering the right, but retaining control over 'free' elections; he also established a finance department which was to make the Anglo-Norman monarchy a major economic power. After prolonged civil wars, Henry II (1154–89) greatly increased English authority both in Britain and France. Scotland, brought into the modern world by Malcolm's wife the cosmopolitan St Margaret (d. 1093) and their cultivated son David I (1123–53), came temporarily under English suzerainty. So did Wales, after a period of great bards, and princes such as Gruffydd ap Llewellyn (1039–63); and in Ireland, whose people – now distinguishable from the Scots and, since the battle of Clontarf (1014), free of the Scandinavians – had achieved transient unity,

Henry II established a foothold after being called in against one of the national High Kings by a deposed ruler of Leinster.

In France Henry II controlled a Norman-Angevin realm – including his wife Eleanor's Aquitaine (1152) – far stronger than the French kingdom of her former husband Louis VII (p. 77). Governed by exceptional ministers and buttressed by castles, this empire, until the irresponsibilities of Henry's son Richard I Coeur de Lion (1189–90), was the most powerful in western Christendom. The restless, passionate, untiring Henry II adapted the Frankish jury system to English common law, and dispensed from Westminster and Caen an efficient and polyglot government which was the admiration of Europe: to whose rulers (of Saxony, Sicily and Castile) he married his daughters. His desire to keep the church in order culminated in a quarrel with Archbishop Thomas à Becket which resulted in the latter's death – martyr of the current European struggle between popes and secular authorities (p. 90).

Henry II, like Eleanor his wife, was a versatile patron of the arts. By the end of the century Oxford, with its central position and stone bridge over the Thames, had a concourse of scholars not much inferior to Paris. John of Salisbury (Old Sarum), bishop of Chartres (d. 1180), was one of the best educated men of his time. No philosopher or theologian, but sane, cautious, critical and observant, he concentrated, according to the classical tradition, upon the true development of individuality which was the main problem of contemporary humanist intellectuals.

Durham cathedral (1093–1135), while remaining a thoroughly massive and Romanesque 'mixture of Norman savagery and sophistication', anticipates Gothic with its early rib vaults, pointed arches and decorative motifs, though these are still abstract in form. The specific 'Early English' form of Gothic, with its abandonment (for decorative purposes) of the Anglo-Norman thick wall, its narrow single or grouped windows, and clusters of linear, detached pipe-like columns, was gradually introduced later in the century. Canterbury (1174) shows French influence, but Wells (c. 1180) and Lincoln (1192) display signs of a comfortable lack of spatial tautness which was to be characteristic of English Gothic (p. 125).

An English monk at this time described the merchants as 'a bloated swelling of the people, a terror of the kingdom, a wet blanket on the church'. England now supplied part of the wool woven in the Low Countries, the Meuse towns, Champagne and Paris. Flemings had helped William I to conquer England, and their trade greatly benefited from the connexion, prospering under the Baldwin counts who had defended the line of the Scheldt against the Northmen and incorporated the rich Walloon and Artois church possessions. Flanders was a land of weavers, fullers and assertive municipal and guild institutions, with liquid capital already available. At the Flemish capital of Bruges (then an inland port), and at Ghent which temporarily out-shone it (*c.* 1180), the specialized techniques of weaving and marketing cloth interested merchants as far afield as Italy and Russia. A monument to the advanced civilization of the region is the five-towered, multiple-arcaded cathedral built in the eleventh and twelfth centuries at the wealthy trading and quarrying town of Tournai.

As in many parts of Europe, agriculture was expanding in correspondence with steady increases of population. In the Low Countries this pressure led to the reclamation of fallow sea-board marshes by dams, dykes and sluices; and modified versions of the Persian institution of windmills were introduced. Meanwhile the independent districts and villages of Friesland, as well as Hollanders and Zeelanders, were evolving a maritime commerce and fishing industry.

Sicily and Italy

After the invading Normans had gained a foothold in south Italy and established a principality under Rainulf at Aversa behind Naples (1030), Robert Guiscard ('the resourceful') of Hauteville (d. 1085) conquered south Italy (1046–71), making Pope Leo IX his prisoner and then submitting to him. Robert declared himself Duke of Apulia, Calabria and 'hereafter Sicily' (1059). That island, where the Kalbite Arab state (p. 46) had split up, was occupied during the next thirty-two years by Robert's brother and vassal Roger I (d. 1101), founder of the Normans' Sicilian state. Roger II united the island to the Duchy of Apulia (1127) as 'the two Sicilies', and obtaining the consent of the pope – whose power he rivalled – assumed the royal title (1130–54). With his army of Norman knights and Moslem mercenaries, and his Greek-officered navy second only to Byzantium, for a time he even controlled the coasts of north Africa, from Tunis to Tripoli.

Before passing by marriage to the German emperor Henry VI in 1196, the two Sicilies enjoyed a brilliant century under Norman rule. Roger II's wealth, the most extensive of any ruler in western Europe, was based upon state monopolies and upon the suzerainty, mainly taken over from Byzantium, of the south Italian trading cities of Gaeta, Naples, Salerno, Bari (1071) and Amalfi (1073). The feudal Norman nobility, sharing the royal talent for organization, resembled its Anglo-Norman relatives (p. 94) in efficient subordination to the crown, which was also served by Mohammedan financial advisers as well as by Greeks; a trilingual secretariat enabled the government to attain unprecedented standards of efficiency. Polyglot, again, was the judiciary which at the Assizes of Ariano (1140) brought into force a co-ordinated system of Roman, Byzantine and canon law.

Presiding over a court comparable to Cordova and Toledo in cosmopolitan learning, Roger II, known as 'the pagan' for his favour to the Moslems, employed the Malagan geographer Idrisi (c. 1099–1154) – who made him a silver celestial sphere and disc representing the known world of the day – and was patron to the greatest of Sicilian Arabic poets Ibn Hamdis (d. 1132), whose verse has come down to us in Spanish and Syrian versions. Roger's successor William I (1154–66) had works of Plato and the geographer and astronomer Ptolemy (long studied by Moslem scholars) translated into Latin. Under William II (1166–89), who himself read and wrote Arabic, Christians now looked and dressed like followers of Islam, and the favourite royal residence at Palermo was surrounded by palaces of colonnades and fountained gardens like those at Granada – the Favara (or Maredolce) and domed Cuba, both on artificial islets, and Ziza and Menani amid their lush parklands.

Yet, in this Moorish ambience, the coronation mantle of King Roger II reminds us that weavers had been brought to Sicily from Thebes and Corinth, and that – although political policy towards Byzantium was frequently hostile and acquisitive – the conception of the Sicilian monarchy and the ceremonial of its court were derived from that quarter; indeed Roger I had so favoured the eastern church that his eighteen monastic foundations included four Benedictine establishments but as many as fourteen Greek.

The Royal Chapel of the Palace at Palermo (1130's and '40's) is entirely covered by mosaics designed by several schools of Greek artists. These display – together with Arab decorative detail and architectural motifs – a fully patterned Byzantine interior, ranging from the starry heavens of the ceiling and flowering meadows of the pavement to a vigorously impressionistic scene of the *Entry to Jerusalem*. And yet this chapel is of western, apsidal design. Cefalù, again, is no Greek cross but a lofty, three-aisled, longitudinal Italian church. Its mosaics, the finest in the island, are primarily decorative, but the contemporary image of godhead is imposingly conveyed by the majestic tranquil rhythms of Jesus as Pantocrator, the ruler of all, glorious amid the great empty spaces of the apse. At Monreale, the mosaics designed under the patronage of William II are cruder than those at Cefalù, but they present the completest surviving liturgical cycle in the whole of Byzantine art; and they reflect the emergence of a local Sicilian tradition, inspired by the new human intensity and mobility that were influencing contemporary Byzantine styles at so many of its far-flung centres (p. 104).

In Italy, where tensions were high between nobles and bishops and between higher and lower nobles, there were risings against the dominant German emperors in 1004, 1024 and 1026. Henry III, however, eliminated no less than three popes, replacing them by nominees of his own race and restoring spirit. One of these, the tireless Leo IX (1049–54), was the first occupant of the papacy to wage war in person in the name of the Church (though this led to his capture by the Normans). The Tuscan Hildebrand (Gregory VII, 1073–85) counter-attacked against the empire, which he defined with revolutionary vigour as merely the secular arm of a centralized, omnipotent, territorial master-Church. The result was the half-century long Investiture Contest which shattered western Europe into two, and raised Gregory to his triumph over Henry IV at Canossa (p. 90) but brought him down to death in exile. By insisting on priests' celibacy, Gregory had bound them more closely to Rome and raised their moral standards, while setting them above and apart from the lay community.

As the strife between pope and emperor unleashed unprecedented torrents of argument and propaganda, Gregory, ready to use excommunication as a weapon against individuals and whole societies, became the most powerful promoter of the popular religious emotions of his time. These emotions were canalized by the French Pope Urban II, preaching at Clermont (1095), into the First Crusade against the Moslem occupants of Palestine. The difficulties of western pilgrims and trading visitors to the holy places were not new – Pisans and Genoese had been fighting Islam since early in the century. But this communications problem had become more serious because of the weakening of Byzantium by its eastern neighbours (p. 101). Though not unsympathetic to the Byzantines, the pope also saw the crusade as opening up possibilities of their assimilation with the Roman church. Moreover, the support which he could whip up for a crusade would consolidate resistance to his principal enemies the German emperors.

The First Crusade showed the papacy at the height of its power, with the chivalry of many countries beneath its banner. This massive expedition was one part, as the German eastward drive was another, of the first important process of European expansion and colonization since the Vikings. Neither Urban nor the kings (though they scarcely participated themselves) were reluctant to see the backs of unruly superfluous noblemen and younger sons. Though it achieved no permanent results, the First Crusade was spectacular in its immediate, temporary conquests (Antioch, Edessa and above all Jerusalem), thus encouraging further efforts of the same kind.

In the eleventh century there was a very rapid expansion of urban and commercial life in Italy, where privileges were granted to Lucca by the

German emperor Henry IV in order to spite Matilda, the powerful margrave of Tuscany who resided in that city. The pattern was soon repeated at Pisa, at Milan (1094) – now outdistancing Pavia, against which it had revolted (1057) – and at Genoa (1099). The most prosperous Italian towns were those which benefited from the revival of eastern trade, and diverted it from Byzantium. Amalfi, at its height in the mid-eleventh century, declined after submitting to the Normans (p. 96); Venice profited from a treaty exempting it from Byzantine duties. The capture of the Levant by the First Crusaders was a godsend to Italian businessmen, who exported slaves and iron and timber to the east in exchange for silk, spices and drugs. They were therefore willing enough to transport, finance and exploit the waves of crusaders who were still to come.

After the death of Matilda (1115), her extensive Tuscan domains became a new source of conflict between the empire and the papacy, whose supporters in the various Italian cities became known as Ghibellines and Guelphs respectively (p. 111). In spite of Frederick Barbarossa's reinforcement of the imperial position in Italy, city communes continued to extend their power and autonomy, especially after the Guelph Lombard League's victory over Frederick at Legnano (1176) had secured them from serious imperial encroachment. The cities of Lombardy were particularly conscious of their new or recovered political freedom, and their financiers were known throughout Europe. South of the Po, the Garisenda and Asinelli towers are spectacular emblems of Bologna's municipal pride; and Florence, freed from Matilda, developed its textile industry as well as the banks that had grown out of money-changing along the business-routes.

For it was from Italy that the revival of Europe's trade began. With the help of the crusades, the whole Mediterranean was re-opened to Italian merchants, accompanied overseas by consuls with powers of jurisdiction. Venice, though engaged in twenty-one wars for Dalmatia within three centuries (from 1115), assumed the maritime and commercial lead,[1] issuing its own government stock at least as early as 1171. And the Venetian constitution, which was to fascinate American and French revolutionaries, took shape when the Doges became subject to the Greater and Smaller Councils of 180 and 60 members respectively.

Venice reflected its central cultural position in St Mark's (1063–95), the most important surviving example of the domed Greek cross, with auxiliary cupolas. Here the decorative façade and mosaics of various epochs blend Latin with Greek traditions; and in the magically elegant Virgin at the

---

[1] But much of its trade passed before long to Pisa and particularly Genoa.

neighbouring island of Torcello, older styles, as well as current occidental influences, are combined with the latest metropolitan spirit of Byzantium (p. 104).

In other parts of north and south Italy alike, vigorous versions of Romanesque architecture were to be seen. A Lombard speciality is the brick tower, each storey with more windows than the one below. The church of St Ambrose at Milan, with its high four-part cross-vaulting anticipatory of Gothic, strikes an original, northern, Hohenstaufen note. Pisa, at the time of its maritime importance, established new fashions with its cathedral's rhythmical, airy gallery-façades (1063–1118), scaling down the Orders of the Colosseum into festive wall decoration; while at Florence the delicate, civilized, parti-coloured west front of S. Miniato al Monte provides a new synthesis – which was to be acceptable to the Renaissance – between Roman or Romanesque simplicity and the rising intellectualism of the Tuscans. Mural paintings also emerge, and sculpture: in the statues and reliefs made by Benedetto Antelami for the octagonal Baptistery believed to be designed by himself at Parma (1196), classical traditions are enriched by contact with France by way of Provence.

The early years of the eleventh century had witnessed decisive steps in musical theory and notation prompted by Guido of Arezzo (c. 990–1050), protégé and instructor of Pope John XIX (c. 1030). His innovations include the introduction of the first six notes of the scale, *ut re mi fa sol la*, still basically employed in many countries. Guido was a young monk and later abbot of Pomposa, near Ferrara. At the time of his death, a more southerly monastery was becoming pre-eminent for learning. This was Monte Cassino (p. 47), whose abbot Desiderius (Pope Victor III, 1086–7) supervised both the construction of a great basilica and the reduplication of ancient books which played a leading part in the conservation of classical learning. Meanwhile, Salerno was at the height of its fame as the chief medical centre of Europe. Its political relation to the Normans placed it at the meeting point of Arabic, Jewish and Latin influences, and its scientific study of Hippocrates and Galen was encouraged by frequent communication with Constantinople.

But the finest intellectual talent of the day gravitated to the study of civil and canon law, from which so many of the world's political and social developments have stemmed. At the culmination of this legal revival, which he extended by his own commentary, was Irnerius. Regarded as symbolic of the outstanding school of law at Bologna (c. 1116–40), he was probably the first to utilize for his teachings the whole rediscovered corpus of Justinian (p. 49), which now became the *lingua franca* of jurisprudence.

There also Gratian, a monk from Camaldoli, published his *Decretum* (c.

1151) which cleared the canon law of contradictions and contaminations, forging it into a powerful, systematic instrument for the training of popes – while experts in civil law simultaneously produced arguments for emperors against the papacy. Lay Roman law schools and monastic schools of canon law flourished alike at Bologna; and so did episcopal and municipal schools of letters. Not long after 1150, the city possessed an institution which became the model for universities based on guilds of students, just as guilds of masters looked to Paris (p. 79). But above all, in this most legal of centuries, Bologna was world-centre of law, owing its pre-eminence to its central position and hospitality; to the fame of Irnerius, Gratian and others who attracted lawyers from Rome; to its meticulously regulated Latin style (*dictamen*); and to its flexible modern formulations for the novel requirements of business life, prominent among the factors in contemporary society which stimulated this whole process of legal revival and innovation.

Constantinople, Serbia and Bulgaria

The Byzantine emperor Basil II 'the Bulgar-slayer', in the latter part of his long reign (p. 50), ruthlessly eliminated the Bulgarian state (996–1018) and re-established control of the Balkan peninsula. The empire was larger that it had been for four centuries and, owing to his austere thrift, enjoyed unparalleled prosperity.

The half-century which followed Basil's death was a period of huge wealth and strong economic efflorescence. But now the central administration was weakening, and the metropolitan civil aristocracy (in opposition to the military nobles of the provinces) filled the vacuum. These years also witnessed a further and spectacular deterioration in the religious relations between east and west. The schism, dramatically symbolized by quarrels between the Patriarch Michael Cerularius and Cardinal Humbert (1054), was due ostensibly and in part to theological terminology, but also to practical events, including the Norman conquest of south Italy and Sicily and the loss of Constantinople's trade to Italian maritime cities.

The last Byzantine strong-point in the west, Bari, fell to the Normans in 1071; and in the same year the emperor Romanus IV was shatteringly defeated and captured at Manzikert by the Seljuk Turks, invaders from the Lake Baikal area who, adopting Islam in the tenth century, had occupied large parts of Asia Minor and finally Baghdad (1055). The debacle of Manzikert, from which the empire never wholly recovered, greatly diminished Byzantine contact with the Anatolian territories that had traditionally supplied military recruits and provided access for pilgrims to the Holy Land.

Among many enemies, these Moslems were now the most dangerous. To deal with them, much larger mercenary forces were needed; and these were only obtainable from the west. Reinforcements from this source, as well as a personal guard now largely consisting of Anglo-Saxon refugees from England, were employed by the founder of a new dynasty, Alexius I Comnenus (1081–1118). By hard work, financial reform and diplomacy, he staved off collapse for a century. But the price paid was a feudal decentralization in which the great military landed noblemen took over power from the civil aristocracy of the capital. Although Alexius' appeal to the pope for mercenaries helped to bring about the First Crusade (p. 98) and landed upon him an unexpectedly vast horde of crusaders – whose barbarism was denounced by his literary daughter Anna Comnena (d. 1148) – he efficiently accommodated them, avoided too much damage at their hands, and shepherded them across to Asia Minor (1096). But the future pattern was plainly revealed, not only by the Norman Bohemund's suggestion to the pope that the crusaders should seize Constantinople, but by their appropriation of territories – Jerusalem, Antioch, Edessa – which had formerly been in Byzantine hands and could have helped the empire to recover not only religious prestige throughout Europe but also the far eastern trade it had lost to Cairo.

The last twenty years of Alexius' reign were occupied with the persecution of heretics, wars against the Seljuk Turks, and intrigues about the imperial succession. John II Comnenus (1118–43), whose principal threat came from Norman Sicily, controlled the situation with prudent perseverance. But the most remarkable of these three able Comnene rulers was Manuel I (1143–80). Though he was fully conversant with the culture of the west (which provided him with two successive wives), his profound belief in Byzantine universal sovereignty led him to keep western statesmen at arm's length; and he allowed many of the Second Crusaders to be killed by the Turks (1147). A thirty-year truce was signed with William I of Sicily (1158). But the real threat now came from the German emperor Frederick I Barbarossa, who incited the Seljuk Turks of Iconium (Rum) and, when they had overwhelmed a Byzantine army at Myriocephalum (1179), claimed that his own empire included east as well as west.

An earlier German emperor, Conrad III, had been looked after personally by Manuel when he fell ill on his way to the Second Crusade (1147). Byzantine medical treatment was as sensible as anything known until recently, and its social services, both state-provided and voluntary, were the best in any Christian country. The business activity of the capital too, was enormous. But it received a setback when the last Comnene ruler Andronicus

I (1183–5) allowed or encouraged a massacre of westerners in Constantinople and throughout the empire.

The dynasty of the Angeli which briefly followed was threatened on all sides by Serbian, Bulgarian and Cypriot separatism, by Hungarian and Norman-Sicilian invasions, and by the Third Crusade led in person not only by Frederick Barbarossa but also by Philip Augustus and Richard I, kings of France and England. As all these descended upon the Byzantine empire, its end seemed to have come. But temporary breathing-spaces were provided, first by the bad relations between the crusading monarchs, next by the accidental drowning of Frederick in Asia Minor (1190), and then by the death of his son Henry VI (1197) while he was planning a further crusade specifically intended to include the conquest of Constantinople.

In the eleventh century there had been marked literary and philosophical activity in the Byzantine capital. While Constantine IX Monomachus (1042–55) founded a chair of philosophy (including theology) and a school of law, one of the literary leaders of the movement was Michael Psellus (1018–78), an amusing cynic who was perhaps the most distinguished author Byzantium ever produced. In a pronounced revival of classicism (or rather Hellenism, since he did not know the difference between Cicero and Caesar), Psellus studied Plato, Aristotle and especially the Neo-Platonists (p. 40); while simultaneously indulging to the full his talent for political intrigue.

One of the most significant literary productions of the following century was of a very different character. This was the earliest-known version of the romantic epic of Digenis Akritas, a marcher-lord of mixed Christian and Moslem origin who had lived some two hundred years earlier. This poem, the most popular ever to come from these lands, survives in a number of versions, Russian as well as Greek; and scenes from its adventures appear on domestic pottery found at Athens.

In the visual arts of mosaic and painting, there are clear signs of opposition between the classically based traditions of the court and an entirely different, powerful narrative expressionism of which the inspiration is sometimes ascribed to the monastic schools of Constantinople – which perhaps in their turn owed something to Mesopotamia and Syria, or to the Armenians who were prominent at the capital. Constantine IX (above) prompted the foundation of a monastery on the island of Chios, the Nea Moni, in which the church mosaics tell their story with the strongly austere, stiffly geometrical lines, the forcible colour contrasts, and the heavy vivid shading of that 'monastic' tradition. Similar tendencies are apparent in the rather cruder mosaics at St Luke in Phocis with their brilliantly glowing hues, sharp-edged planes and linear distorted contours. At the end of the eleventh century, the climax of this sort of style is attained by a great artist in the mosaic of the all-powerful Saviour (Pantocrator) on the dome of a little church at Daphni near Athens. In supreme contrast to 'gentle Jesus meek and mild', these dusky features display a terrifying scowl highlighted to a violent magical intensity. Yet elsewhere in the decorative scheme of the church – and perhaps later in date, since artists very often worked from the top downwards – are mosaics expressing entirely different courtly, antique traditions. The Nativity is a gracious academic work, there is pathos in the Crucifixion's peaceful, symmetrical rhythm. An outstanding metropolitan exemplar of this courtly style (c. 1200?) is the nobly formal, rhythmical mosaic of the Intercession of the Virgin and St John before Christ (*Deesis*) in the south gallery of St Sophia.

In the twelfth century, a period which favoured development in many fields of art, panel painting came to assume great importance – especially as the medium for a new expression of love and gentleness, in which Byzantium anticipated Franciscan ideas (p. 112). 'Our Lady of Vladimir', preserved by the Russians yet painted at Constantinople in c. 1100–25, combines austere restraint with deep and tender feeling. But the metropolitan painting of the period is best exemplified in the miniature art of manuscript illumination, which reached fresh heights of vivid, creative fantasy in the novel designs and clashing reds and blues of an anonymous artist's illustrations for the sermons of a monastic preacher, James of Kokkinobaphos. Recent finds of coloured, leaded window glass at the Pantocrator church in the capital suggest that the figured stained glass of French and German cathedrals was anticipated by Constantinople. Byzantine enamelled objects also – now larger, and based on colour-schemes in which white and turquoise-blue predominate – were exported and imitated in many countries from Kiev and Georgia to Italy and the Rhine. Ivory-work also reached a remarkable standard under the Comnene emperors; its masterpieces are stylized, elegant, severe and slightly dry.

The crusades and Byzantine-Turkish wars endowed the outlying island of Cyprus with strategic importance, and for a time its cultural as well as military links with Constantinople were strengthened. Early in the twelfth century there are church paintings which display impressive rhythmical groupings; and the finest of all Byzantine frescoes of the island, completed in 1192 at Panaghia Arakiotissa near Lagoudera, combine inherited liveliness with a metropolitan courtly note.

Cypriot styles show analogies both with Kiev and with Macedonia, where outstanding frescoes were likewise produced at this period. The third ruler of an independent Macedonian dynasty, Samuel (980–1014), formed a West Bulgarian empire extending over a large part of the Balkans. Samuel's capital was at Ochrida which, after his elimination by the Byzantine emperor Basil II (p. 101), came back with the rest of his territories under the control of Constantinople. Shortly before 1150 Ochrida's church of St Sophia, whether at the hands of native or Greek artists, produced major masterpieces at a time when in Constantinople itself the best surviving work is on a much smaller scale. These deep-green, purple and blue portrayals of Christ and of the Dormition of the Virgin are unsurpassed for the balance of their accomplished composition, and for a dignified and somewhat abstract style which nevertheless show signs of a sympathetic and psychological approach.

To the north of Macedonia, the Serbs had centred round two rudimentary states, one on the Montenegrin sea-coast (Zeta), and the other (Rashka) in the mountainous interior between Belgrade and Skoplje. But it was the removal of the Macedonian-Bulgarian Tsar Samuel which gave Serbian independence its chance, and within another century and a half Stephen Nemanya of Rashka (1159–96) combined all the Serbian and Macedonian territories, up to the Bosnian border, into a powerful independent state. Meanwhile, it was again Macedonia that best illustrated the intimate and tender humanism of the mature Byzantine Renaissance (p. 104). Near Skoplje, the church of St Panteleimon founded by a member of the Byzantine imperial house at Nerezi (1164) displays paintings of metropolitan, classical delicacy and skill which nevertheless make a new and profound emotional impact through their personal, compassionate depiction of human agony at the moment of supreme dramatic tension. Later, Kurbinovo, although indebted to Nerezi, departs further from Byzantine models towards a native Macedonian style of violent storm-tossed robes and angular linearity (1191); while in the Greek-speaking area of Kastoria similar developments occurred. The monasteries of Rashka, too, were now commissioning paintings which, although at first derivative, hint at a more specifically Serbian school (p. 135).

But now the political centre of the Balkans was passing to northern Bulgaria, where a rising of Vlachs and Bulgars under the brothers Ivan and Peter Asen of Trnovo reasserted independence of Byzantium (1185); and Ivan, backed by the Cuman nomads occupying the steppes north of the Danube (p. 106), indicated his ambitious designs by assuming the title 'tsar of the Bulgars and Greeks'.

Russia

Kiev enjoyed great splendour under St Vladimir's son, Yaroslav (d. 1054), of Viking stock which had gradually become assimilated with Slavism

(p. 55). Already elective prince of Novgorod, Yaroslav reunited extensive territories under the grand duchy of Kiev, and promulgated new laws for their government. More interested in chivalrous, occidental knight-errant traditions than in the east, he married his sons to a Pole, a Greek and a German, and his daughters to a Norwegian, a Hungarian and a Frenchman. The importance of Kiev was founded partly on extensive agriculture and partly on trade, though southern commercial links were broken by an influx of Cuman (Polovtzy) nomads (1054).

At the great Monastery of Caves, Russian chronicles had grown into a fresh and fluent *genre* of historical narratives, systematically designed within a religious framework. Byzantine models were utilised. They were blended with pagan traditions and folk poetry images in an outstanding panegyric of the Kievan royal house; this is the *Tale of Prince Igor's Raid* of 1185, written in rhythmical prose which contrives a highly original blend of heroic spirit and historical truth.

Larger than any contemporary western city, Kiev included among its four hundred churches the spectacular St Sophia, designed by Greeks but departing from Byzantine precedent and looking forward to future Russian complexities by its galaxy of thirteen cupolas – low domes on high narrow drums. The main building was flanked by a three-sided, oval-alcoved peristyle reaching into the city's main square. St Sophia's mosaics and frescoes (1017–37), although the latter portray the Kievan royal family, are of purest Byzantine work. They also include, on a staircase (situated in church precincts), the secular scenes that have so rarely survived in Byzantine art – representations of one hundred and thirty wrestlers, animal tamers, musicians and other performers who had participated in Games held for Russian visitors at Constantinople.

Because of danger from Kiev's neighbours and the consequent diversion of east-west trade, Andrey Bogolyoubsky, of a cadet branch of the ruling house, moved north to a new capital Vladimir in the poorer but safer woodland areas of Suzdal and Rostov (1151), earlier the home of Finnish tribes. His subsequent storming of Kiev itself (1169) marked the end of Russian unity and the decline of the southern state, in favour of Vladimir which became the grand princes' coronation city. It was a meeting place for Kievan, Romanesque, Byzantine and Caucasian architectural themes. Their fusion created lofty, cubic buildings of white sandstone, round-headed windows, blind wall-arcading that suggests Italian influences, and elongated cupola drums; the Church of the Intercession of the Virgin on the Nerl (1166) already has a dome of snow-resisting 'onion' form. An unprecedented feature of these buildings was their external relief sculpture, going back to wooden models. This is to be seen at Vladimir in the church of St Dimitri, which also has important frescoes (*c.* 1198). A large panel of about the same date from Yaroslavl depicts the praying Virgin with luminous hues and restrained, sensitive feelings; some of the work of this school displays analogies with contemporary work in France.

Meanwhile, three hundred miles to the north-west, Novgorod had become a centre of the fur-trade, owing prosperity to the hunting and trapping of sable, beaver, marten, polar fox and fox. Fur had magical and prestige powers – even squirrel skins served as small change – and Novgorod, virtually independent of Kiev, already controlled a commercial empire extending to the White Sea and Arctic Ocean, and beyond the Urals. The city's princes, the forty most prominent families of Boyars, were checked by Councils and the mass-meetings of popular assemblies; although, in the absence of corporate merchant organizations, no city bourgeoisie developed as in the west.

An independent, distinctive school of architecture, rather remote from Byzantine models and derived from native wooden styles, began at Novgorod and its autonomous south-western satellite Pskov. A characteristic feature was the pointed 'helmet' dome; six of these clustered upon the cathedral of St Sophia at Novgorod (1045–52), a small-windowed forthright edifice of perpendicular lines which reflects the city's international role by the German affinities of its bronze doors. A later stage is represented by the Church of St George in the same city's Yuriev Monastery (1119), with its three asymmetrically arranged cupolas. This building was erected by the princes in rivalry of St Sophia, after their supersession by a Republican form of government had caused them to migrate to the lower town.

Novgorod was also the centre of a rich national school of painters. Starting as a provincial variant of Kievan Byzantine, this school modified the styles of Constantinople owing to Novgorod's greater proximity to western artistic developments. The extensive frescoes at Nereditsa, painted by at least seven different artists combining astonishing varieties of technique (1198), were destroyed in the Second World War; but in those at the Mirozkhsk Monastery at Pskov (1156) a powerful, sombre, monumental intensity and originality can still be seen.

4

THE THIRTEENTH AND
FOURTEENTH CENTURIES

Sicily and Italy

The outstanding figure of the age was the Hohenstaufen, half-Norman emperor Frederick II (1212–50). Born at Iesi near Ancona, brought up at Palermo, he disliked Germany, devoting his principal attention partly to the reconquest of Jerusalem which he fleetingly achieved, and partly to the modern organization of his government in Sicily and Italy. This centralized, all-powerful, resplendent monarchy, which for all its dependence on tradition anticipated future nation-states, derived its vast wealth from wheat-production and a vital geographical position upon the east-west sea-routes.

Questioner of many of the church's traditions, Frederick claimed to be king without clerical mediation. The common man, too, he suggested, could make his own peace with God. The scandal of the age was his quarrel with the papacy; but the Guelph factions which popes commanded in the cities were too strong for him to master. Yet Frederick was '*stupor mundi*', the wizard who staggered and shocked the world. He was in many ways a man of his time: the end of a tradition as well as a beginning. Yet he was also unprejudicedly interested in any and every question, replete with scientific curiosity, at home in Latin, Byzantine, Arabic, Norman, French and Lombard culture, the dazzling, dynamic pioneer of every creative intellectual movement.

Palermo, headquarters of his rule and his harem, was a magnificent city, and more comfortable to live in than any western city since classical times. With a population of five hundred thousand, it was half as large as Constantinople, twice the size of Paris, and five times larger than any town of the Italian mainland. Cross-fertilized by many influences, this Sicilian culture was conspicuous for a novel preoccupation with man and the world around him. Major Italian poetry came to life when poems approaching the sonnet-form were written at Frederick's court, perhaps by his own chancellor Piero delle Vigne (d. 1249); their intimate love of nature, characteristic of the

Sicilian school, seems to draw upon Moslem and Provençal models. Himself one of the first to write Italian verse (as well as a book on falconry), Frederick, after a second papal excommunication, addressed a questionnaire on religious and philosophical themes (the Sicilian Questions) to some half-dozen leading scholars of the Islamic world.

In his sponsorship of numerous translations of Arabic philosophical treatises (particularly those going back to Aristotle), he was advised by the wandering scholar, astrologer and supposed magician Michael the Scot (*c.* 1175–1232). Mathematical treatises, also, were translated; Frederick introduced Christian students to Arabic numerals and algebra, and engaged the greatest of medieval mathematicians, Leonardo (Fibonacci) of Pisa (*c.* 1170–1230), to solve problems publicly at a tournament. Medical works too were published, and Frederick enlarged Salerno's medical school, as well as establishing a zoological collection. But his principal learned foundation was the University of Naples (1224), the first state university in Christian Europe, to which he entrusted a virtual monopoly of learning in many fields. A few years earlier, he had produced a legal code, the Constitutions of Melfi (1221), which rivalled the Codex of Justinian itself – and asserted that all are equal before the law.

Melfi, in Lucania, was an administrative centre where the emperor enlarged the castle to provide a royal residence. But the strategic territory of Apulia was the principal region, apart from Sicily itself, of the bizarre polygonal, moated and turreted castles and machicolated lodges which he constructed in abundance. Foggia was a pleasure-house, Gioia del Colle a comfortable mansion, Bari and Trani maritime defence posts, Lucera the centre of the imperial army (mainly consisting of Mohammedans), and Castel del Monte – the best preserved of these buildings – an octagonal hunting box partly oriental in design, and partly Gothic and French. It was classical Italian tradition, on the other hand, which dominated a vigorous new school of art exemplified by portrait-busts, by an equally superb head on his golden *Augustalis* (1231) which was the finest of all medieval coins, and by the Roman-inspired, sculpturally adorned Capua Gate (1235–9) of the emperor's own design which, now demolished, was an important influence upon Renaissance artists.

After Frederick's death, the young emperor Conradin's defeat at Tagliacozzo and public execution (1268) indicated the final removal of the Hohenstaufens from Italy. The popes had achieved this by bringing in the French, under Louis IX's brother Charles I, Count of Anjou and Provence, who also assumed the titles of King of Sicily and Jerusalem (1246–85). But Charles' formidable design of a Mediterranean empire, based on the reconquest of Constantinople itself, was ruined by the Sicilian Vespers (1282). The result of this revolt by the natives of the island was to introduce another great power and initiate a long period of Spanish intervention; for at the wish of the parliament of Palermo the island was transferred to King Peter II of Aragon (I of Sicily) (p. 121).

Yet the dominant factor on the South Italian mainland was still France; and the principal protector and leader of the pro-papal Guelphs (p. 99), as well as a generous patron of literature, was Charles' grandson Robert of Anjou and Naples (1309–43). However, even before his death Naples had drawn in its horns, and for the rest of the century its influence was weak.

Innocent III (1198–1216) raised papal authority to its zenith; supported by an impressive financial organization, the pope defied kings of France, influenced the election of German emperors, and rebuked England, Aragon and Portugal. For the time being the papacy could still compete with the rising nation states, and the identity of Europe with western Christendom did not seem an entirely intangible conception. The Fourth Crusade, though it got out of control, was the product of Innocent's idea that this conception could be realized by a church purged of corruption and of heretics. Against these, Gregory IX, friend and patron of St Francis, developed the papal Inquisition (1230–3), entrusting special powers to the Spanish Dominicans (p. 121) who were furnished by the recodified canon law with powers of judicial torture new to Europe.

Frederick II's enemy, the learned Innocent IV (1234–54), formalized the doctrine that the pope was superior to all lay rulers. This deadly struggle between popes and Hohenstaufens was ruinous to both alike: the former seemed to prevail, but then the defeat of Charles I of Anjou at the Sicilian Vespers (p. 109) meant the decline of papal power. The last and loftiest attempt to insist upon global obedience to the papacy was made by Boniface VIII (1294–1303), with the help of his English, Italian and Spanish lawyers. The dream was extinguished when, at Boniface's home-town of Anagni (1303), a French commander seized his sacred person.

The next seven occupants of his throne (1305–78) mostly resided at Avignon. There, although the town belonged to the counts of Provence and then to the popes themselves (1348), this 'Babylonish Captivity' brought them somewhat under the influence of the French monarchy. Even if the universality of the western church was not seriously affected, their loss of Italian influence and revenues caused them to impose severer taxes, collected by an imposing administrative machinery which John XXII (1316–34) elevated into the world's leading financial institution, a position reflected in the pomp and luxury of his court.

'Captivity' was followed by the far greater scandal of Schism (1378–1417), during which – amid fanatical hatreds anticipatory of Reformation times – the emperors, the English and most northern nations generally supported the nominees of Rome, while the French, Spanish, Scots and some Germans favoured the Avignon candidates.

Such quarrels were reflected in Italian states, of which the populations had, for a hundred and fifty years, been torn between their (originally) pro-imperial and pro-papal factions, the Ghibellines and Guelphs respectively. From the early thirteenth century onwards, as Guelph business interests in many a town confronted Ghibelline nobles, the primitive local parliamentary democracies tended to succumb to rigorous dictatorial governments, which often became hereditary. Thus the insatiably ambitious Gian Galeazzo Visconti added Milan to Pavia, was invested with the dukedom by the emperor Wenceslaus (p. 127), and narrowly failed, owing to his death (1402), to create a great north Italian kingdom which would have broken the uneasy equilibrium between the leading northern states Milan, Venice and Florence.

Venice alone escaped from serious involvement in these fights. Thus it retained freedom not only to form a north Italian land-power – nourished by the opening of the St Gotthard pass – but to concentrate upon its maritime trade. Venice was both the largest Italian grain market and the main supplier of salt; its international commerce was stimulated by its share in the conquest of Constantinople (1204). Merchants and missionaries alike followed the eastern routes made famous by the travels of Marco Polo and his uncles (1260, 1271), and, by the fourteenth century, Venetian galleys were appearing in north-western Europe. The city contained 290 merchant families with Levantine 'empires'. But the state determined a wide range of policy, and from 1297 a limited oligarchy was given shape by the 'Closing of the Grand Council' to all but high nobility, with its executive vested in an annually elected Council of Ten. This system, self-perpetuating for half a millennium, spared Venice the suicidal class warfare of its maritime rival Genoa, whose great financial families, advisers at many courts, displayed an excessive individualism that caused the loss of Genoese independence to the French in 1396.

In the disturbed history of Florence, faction warfare was given pause by the city's first middle-class democracy the Primo Popolo (1250), which, however, soon gave way to a coalition of hereditary and financial noblemen under the pro-papal (Guelph) auspices of the invading Charles I of Anjou (p. 109). The craft guilds, which had lived their greatest days early in the century, were now being diversified and supplemented, in an explosively expanding money economy, by more formidable financial forces such as the great banking combines. Pioneered by Siena, and prominent in the cities of Lombardy as well as in Florence, these lent money at heavy rates all over western Europe, and issued bills of exchange. But the stakes were high, and bankruptcies frequent because of defaulting clients such as the English king Edward III (p. 123; 1346).

In many areas the population was halved by the Black Death, which first came to Italy at Genoa from its Crimean outpost Caffa – and brought alcoholism in its train. Nevertheless, the Florentine cloth-weaving industry, which was the most important European capitalistic enterprise of the day, continued to expand, punctuated by numerous political disturbances including the revolt of the Ciompi (wool-carders) (1378). This rising resulted in a brief period of dominance by organized textile-workers, after which, however, Guelph power was partially restored.

Against this background of rising wealth, urbanism and disorder, St Francis (1182–1226) of the small city-state of Assisi had preached humility, charity, close contact with nature, and total renunciation. In his supreme open-hearted challenge to social ills, he took poverty to be his bride, and called for a joy born of perfect explicit surrender to the bitterest of the world's fruits. The Grey Friars whom he founded with papal approval (1209) lived, unlike monks, among the poor, and unlike ascetics and dualists (p. 82) accepted the world as essentially good. The overwhelming success of the early Franciscan movement shows how exactly it suited the inarticulate yearnings and tensions of the age. Alien to the disputes which rent his order, Francis had wanted no Houses, preferring a defenceless exposed brotherhood. Yet by 1282 there were 1,583 Franciscan foundations in Europe; and their members, like those of the other great Mendicant Order the Dominicans (p. 110), had become not only – as their founders would have wished – the chief instruments of the church in bridging the gulf between clergy and laity, but the bulwarks and ambassadors of Catholicism.

The Franciscan St Bonaventure (1221–74), the equal of Anselm (p. 78) in intellectual stature, achieved a new cohesion between doctrine and rationality. Bonaventure was born at Bagnorea near Viterbo; whereas his contemporary the Dominican 'Angelic Doctor' St Thomas Aquinas (1226–74) was of Lombard-Norman family from Roccasecca, though he travelled to Cologne and Paris. The sober, patient argumentation of Thomas was a triumph for the synthetic power of reason. In the most thoroughgoing of all endeavours to blend the Hellenic philosophies with Christianity, he made his resultant amalgam the supreme integrated sum of a whole, closed symmetrical universe. In this all-embracing 'theologically founded worldliness', theology treats of God's supernatural word while philosophy (of no less divine origin) rationally examines the natural order and its consequences in human action. But this 'middle way' earned him the criticism of the Right for too sharp an enlightenment, and of the Left for a too conventional divine superstructure.

While the Mendicant Orders were building throughout Tuscany and Umbria, the first native Gothic style appears in the church of St Francis at Assisi (1228–53), a spacious, aisleless hall for popular sermons, with no eastern chapels since the Franciscans were friars and not priests. Based on the designs (later much modified) of Arnolfo di Cambio (1296), the Duomo at Florence is a proclamation of sturdy local spirit, with its arches (though pointed) looking backwards to Romanesque and forward to the Renaissance. Planned deliberately to surpass the best classical models – and the cathedrals of Florence's rivals Pisa and Siena – it displays a festally colourful exterior and a serene, unmysterious, firmly articulated interior in which the upward thrust is soberly halted by horizontal lines. As the fourteenth century developed, there was a great deal of communal building activity at Florence, with the various guilds and corporations forming commissions to deal with each project; while the Loggia dei Lanzi (1376–92) was an *open* Gothic hall, democratically designed so that the public could watch state ceremonies. More imposing were the Palazzo della Ragione at Padua (1306–), unparalleled for size, and the resplendent Doge's Palace at Venice (*c.* 1345).

Although on the one hand the inspirational, unearthly side of the Franciscans' teaching influenced sensuously vivacious schools of music (willing to pass on their mysteries rather than restrict them to a select group) and Tuscan art-cycles of dreams and of visions, their concern for nature and reality stimulated a practically minded middle class to encourage new naturalistic schools of sculptors. Their pioneer was Niccolò Pisano (*c.* 1220/5–84). Born probably in Apulia – where he may have encountered Frederick II's French architects (p. 109), and studied late Roman sarcophagi and other ancient sculpture – he displays in his Pisa Baptistery pulpit (1260) a blend of formal Gothicism with a novel substantiality, freedom of movement and respect for classical proportion and for the human figure. The turbulent and independent talent of his son Giovanni Pisano (*c.* 1245–after 1314) employs staccato rhythms more dramatic than those of any sculptor in marble before Bernini. His standing statues of the Madonna were a Gothic innovation that broke decisively with Byzantine styles (p. 134).

In painting, eastern and western styles had begun to diverge several centuries earlier (p. 48). Now, the artists of Siena and Florence developed methods which breathed a new and ultimately transforming life into Byzantine forms, though in exceedingly different ways. While the Florentines, under Roman influence, are intellectual, massive and geometric, the more conservative art of Siena reflects the delicate, mercurial lyricism and self-conscious refinement of its poets and mystics. Duccio (*c.* 1255–1319), though akin to the contemporary neo-Hellenic tendencies of Constantinople (p. 134), mirrors not only Franciscan tenderness but the advanced Gothicism of the north in his linear narrative rhythms, organized within windows of 'picture space'. In the decades following Duccio's death, this Sienese taste for spatially arranged illustration was developed by the Lorenzetti brothers into illusionistic landscapes and town-panoramas. Simone Martini (*c.* 1285–1344), who visited the papal palace at Avignon and greatly influenced the new courtly 'international style' (p. 148), interpreted heavenly beauty in sensuous terms; his feeling for magnificence and grace, evident also in contemporary Sienese gold-work, is displayed in swirling silhouettes and sophisticated harmonies of colour.

The first decisive steps, however, towards a truly individual western style had been taken at Rome, where Pietro Cavallini (*c.* 1250–1330) designed frescoes (*c.* 1293, 1296) and mosaics which show him to be an outstanding innovator in the handling of three-dimensional forms, and particularly of human forms, within the framework of their environment. His tranquil heavens, and the tangibility of his toga-like robes, fuse Byzantine and Romano-papal traditions. It is usual to interpret him as a reviver of antique styles; and yet he can also be regarded as one of those who for the first time begin to leave late antiquity and early Christendom behind. Further steps towards the plastic enlivement of Gothic stiffness were taken by the unknown 'Isaac Master', perhaps a Roman pupil of Cavallini, who introduced new psychological poignancy into his Assisi rendering of Isaac, with a crisp and shimering beard.

Italy had at last taken the artistic lead again; and with these Sienese and Roman masters the centre of the movement is shifting from sculpture to painting. The Florentine Cimabue (*c.* 1240–1302) visited Rome (1272), but the extent, if any, to which he was influenced by Cavallini rather than by native idioms remains doubtful; he seems to have infused a similar solid, classical naturalism into the Byzantine and Gothic styles current at Florence. Giotto (*c.* 1266–1337) was the Florentine painter of passionate imagination and epic power who, fired by these trends, and possibly by current developments at Constantinople (p. 134), and by Franciscan humanism, inspired his figures with an enhanced and unprecedented reality. Upon the walls of the Arena Chapel at Padua, within severely composed landscapes which have rediscovered the illusion of depth, there are hosts of live individuals, gesturing with a vigorous economy, and reacting forcibly upon one another. As though a friar is exhorting us to visualize the Bible tales, we sense the sacred

Opposite: Icon of the Annunciation from the church of St Clement, Ochrida: 14th century

story happening, in all its awe and grief. A universal artist of murals, panels and mosaics, Giotto, with his large workshop, was probably the only Florentine of his day and profession to earn large sums from his city, and from its ruling middle class for whose realism he catered; and he was honoured with unprecedented numbers of imitators.

His contemporary Dante Alighieri (1265–1321) met his love Beatrice at their native Florence when they were both nine years old. After her death in 1290, he took an active part in politics which resulted in his exile by the Guelph supporters of Pope Boniface VIII; after much travelling he died at Ravenna. His *Commedia* is the product of poetic genius, a profoundly original brain, and acute theological, philosophical and political learning and insight. Medieval in much of his thought – replete as it is with Arab, dualist and Jewish as well as west European cosmology – Dante heralds the Renaissance in his respect for human achievement: he mirrors all of the soaring aspirations of his age. Noblest exponent of love earthly and divine, yet scathing in hatred and satire, he lavishes upon his fellow-journeyers through hell, purgatory, and heaven all his angry grief for the world, and all his ecstasy. Hating Florence and loving it, he looked far beyond its confines. An admirer of St Francis, he also reveres the papacy as a potential puritan moral force – and yet in his *De Monarchia*, the forerunner of revived political science, he attacks papal claims to overlordship, and the canon lawyers who assisted in their formulation, as responsible for Italy's disunity and shame. The German empire, too, had been brought down by imperial as well as papal ambition, although he vainly hoped for its revival as the apocalyptic medium of a redemption. For him, this was indeed the Holy Roman Empire – the same as ancient Rome, cradle of his spiritual guide Virgil who bridged the gap between paganism and Christianity as Dante himself desired to link the ancient world with his own.

Petrarch (1304–74), likewise a Florentine, insisted still more strongly on the significance of the classical writers, yet viewed them in a historical perspective which showed new consciousness of his own position in time. To him, Virgil is not so much supernatural as a friend. But his greatest admiration was for Cicero, as paragon of eloquence and stimulating moral thinker. For Petrarch, forerunner or instigator of many a Renaissance idea, preferred ethics to theology, and displayed Ciceronian respect for human worth and dignity (p. 28) and for the justification of men's lives by their actions. He could not accept the philosophical, scholastic arguments of preceding centuries as leading to any final solution – and one of his works is entitled *On His Own Ignorance and That of Others*. Born in exile at Arezzo, Petrarch was one of the earliest Italians to offer patriotism to country rather than city.[1] Yet he

[1] But he thought Cicero's political activity was excessive.

also travelled restlessly through western lands, a world-citizen who often writes of 'Europe'.

Boccaccio (1313–75) was illegitimately born at Paris to a Frenchwoman; his father was a Florentine of the merchant class, from which authors were now beginning to come. He was also the first leading author to be familiar with the Greek language. Worldly and sensual yet romantic, the *Decameron* is an infinitely varied passing show of stories old and new – including many caricatures, with a sting in their tail, of both the simple and the sly.

France and Flanders

The rapidly rising power of Philip Augustus (p. 77) was contested by a coalition that included King John of England, Henry the Lion's son Otto IV, and the rulers of Flanders and Lorraine. The victory of the French at Bouvines (1214) set the seal upon their country's unification, and caused the prestige of Philip to rise throughout Europe; more than any other single man, he was creator of the French monarchy. Louis IX (1226–70), surrounded by Franciscans and Dominicans and later canonized, became the continent's political and moral arbiter and most fervent crusader. More successful, however, against deviants from Catholic orthodoxy than against Moslems, he completed a ferocious 'crusade' against the dualist Cathars or Albigensians (p. 82), destroying the rich vernacular civilization of Languedoc (1209–29).

He also secured Sicily and South Italy for his brother Charles I of Anjou (1263); and when the island was lost to the Aragonese (p. 110), Philip III the Bold (1270–85) retaliated by an invasion of Catalonia which, though unsuccessful, set a precedent for foreign aggressions. Philip IV the Fair (1285–1314) got the better of Pope Boniface VIII and, relying on an enhanced concept of the state and of sovereignty provided by the Orléans laws school, moved towards a centralized modern state; in which the French king, according to his adviser Pierre Dubois (1306), could become leader of a federated Europe as a prerequisite for further crusades. Within France however, as elsewhere, a universal failure of crops (1315) caused chaos, cannibalism, and apocalyptic frenzies – which recurred amid the devastations of the Black Death (p. 123).

England's French possessions, and the contested riches of Flemish trade, made the two countries fight their Hundred Years War (1337), which created Anglo-French nationalist and territorial hatred. In its early stages, France suffered heavy defeats culminating in the capture of King John II the Good (1350–64), whose endeavours to finance his war-effort had been unsuccessful. However, after a revolution led by the Paris merchant Etienne Marcel (1357–

8), Charles V (1364–80) and the mercenary companies of his Breton commander Du Guesclin hit back against England until it only retained five towns. But the century closed in prolonged civil strife between Frenchmen themselves.

The *Roman de la Rose* – the rose is the symbol of love's success – is the first of the great allegorical poems, written in an age that was ready for them. It consists of two very different parts. The first 4,000 lines (*c.* 1235), by Guillaume de Lorris of Orleans, are a tender, lyrical, late-flowering bloom of courtly poetry that reflected and guided current aristocratic conceptions of love. The remaining 18,000 lines (*c.* 1270), the work of Jean de Meun, subject courtly ethics to a cold, bitter, un-idealistic attack – seeing love as a force of nature to be endured because it cannot be avoided. This is a middle-class rather than an aristocratic attitude; and another contrast to chivalrous romance was the *Roman de Renard*, which combined animal-fable with mocking and racy narrative.

French intellectualism was supreme in western Christendom. Paris University, incorporating Franciscan (1218) and Dominican teachers (1219) (soon at odds with one another), became the arena of combat for the ablest philosophers and theologians, into whose midst the whole body of tradition – Aristotelian, Neo-Platonist, Arabic, Jewish – had now been decanted (*c.* 1260). One powerful and fashionable product was a cold, penetrating, barely Christian 'Averroist' rationalism – a radical, earth-bound interpretation of Aristotle through the Arab Averroes (p. 87), which, to the point of incurring an official ban (1277), virtually denied divine creation and guidance, and the individuality (and so immortality) of the soul. Such doctrines – like mysticism on the opposite, non-rational side – meant an end of the prolonged medieval attempts to reconcile faith and reason, theology and philosophy.

Meanwhile it was in Paris again, at its Cathedral of Notre Dame, that a new phase of important musical development began under Pérotin, who, in the style later known as 'Ars Antiqua', composed rhythmical, monumentally logical polyphonic motets. Although Pope John XXII denounced modern music (1324), it flourished at papal Avignon, and a subsequent style departed farther from tradition by novel ideas of tempo and a more imaginative scoring of vocal parts. This 'Ars Nova' reached its climax in the secular songs (and pamphlet on motet composition) of Philippe de Vitry (1291–1361), whose pastorals also led a movement of contempt for the courtier's life; and in the composer, statesman, priest, lyric poet and mathematician Guillaume de Machaut from Champagne (*c.* 1300–77). Invited to the courts of Bohemia and Normandy as well as France, Machaut displayed supreme ability and taste in his mass for four voices – almost the earliest surviving polyphonic mass – and in his instrumentally accompanied dance-songs and ballad-motets, more sensuous now than spiritual, which led the way to secular themes. There were signs that the barrier between popular and 'higher' music, so thoroughly re-erected before our own time, was being removed or blurred.

The Gothic principles of ecclesiastical architecture devised in the twelfth century (p. 84) were given ever more lucid and uncompromising expression. French cathedrals leapt and soared, vehemently striving for the unattainable in eastward and upward drives, balanced one against the other in extreme tension and suspense: Amiens (1220–) with its severely vertical nave, emphatic and orderly Rheims, the airy lines of rebuilt Chartres and St Denis, Beauvais (after initial collapse) with the loftiest choir, and Notre Dame with its spires which supremely express the heavenward urge.

The seas of light that flood such buildings, so different from the sombre fortress-like Romanesque, are reflected through jewel-like incandescent glass surfaces enlarged to fill whole walls. Foremost among these unprecedentedly brittle and slender mid-thirteenth century churches is the Sainte Chapelle of Paris (1243–8), designed by the logical intellect of Pierre Montereau to house the relics amassed by Louis IX. The same extremity of light and colour is transmuted into larger dimensions at St Urbain of Troyes (c. 1261–77), with its intricate lacework of slender window tracery anticipating the 'flamboyant' later Gothic style (p. 146).

Reflecting St Thomas Aquinas' insistence upon total unification of detail, reflecting also St Francis' praises of the Creation, the transcendental urge of the church planners was accompanied by an acute consciousness of the beauty inherent in particular objects, and of their significance within the Christian scheme. Already at the beginning of the thirteenth century the slender statue of St Anne at Chartres had shown a happy and almost mystic compromise between Gothic spirituality and a new naturalistic observation of the realities of motherhood. At Notre Dame in Paris, the work of the Mary portal (1210–20) is tranquil and pure. And so the full picture of humanity redeemed and set free is attained in the sculptures of Bourges, capital of Berry, and in the magnificently profiled grave-portraits and Virgin's portal with Annunciation and Visitation (c. 1240) at Rheims – classically inspired, as is this whole Gothic conception of three-dimensional figures in the round – and at Amiens in its serene and idealized *Beau Dieu* and elegantly swaying Golden Virgin (c. 1280): influential symbols of a taste which in that prosperous town had prompted its master-craftsmen, now of independent status, to a dexterous, cheerful, fastidious refinement.

Such tendencies are again mirrored in naturalistic frescoes at Avignon, and in the tapestries of Paris and Arras. French miniature paintings from Berry such as Jean Pucelle's Belleville Breviary (1352) became the norm of perfection everywhere north of the Alps. A duke of Berry, too, commissioned the gold and enamelled 'cup of the Kings of France and England' (1380), work of the professional goldsmiths' guilds who also chased the handles of swords exported from Lyon.

Flanders, centre of a textile industry scarcely smaller than that of Florence (p. 96), was ruled for most of the thirteenth century (1214–80) by Joanna of Constantinople and her sister Margaret, both of whom maintained good relations with the cities. Although they adopted French as their official language (1221), this was also the time of Dutch-Flemish writers including the famous and learned poet Jacob van Maerlant (c. 1235–1300).

Philip IV of France recovered from the defeat of his heavily armed knights by Flemish burghers at Courtrai (1302), but failed to annex the region; and the French-backed Counts met with strikes and lock-outs and democratic, anti-clerical rebellions. At Liège the thirty-two craft guilds won an outright victory with the acceptance of their representation upon the city council; and Duke John III (1312–55) granted his territory of Brabant its charter entitled 'La Joyeuse Entrée'.

The Hundred Years' War was partly fought for the Flemish wool-market, and at first fought in Flanders itself. For Ghent with its 4,000 weavers, and sea-linked Bruges symbolizing by its town hall (1376) the rich inheritance of Champagne's trade (p. 78), looked towards England. But in spite of successes by Philip van Artevelde, the war led to decisive French victory at Roosebeke (1382). Flemish weavers fled to England, where their skill became a vital national asset; but Flanders passed to the Burgundians. Handed over to the French king's brother Philip the Bold (1363–1404), Burgundy, like Brittany, enjoyed virtual independence, maintaining at Dijon a resplendent court which professes the meticulous, archaic, decadent chivalry celebrated in the *Chronicles* of Jean Froissart (c. 1337–1405) (p. 147).

Financed by Fleming wealth, this Burgundian court stimulated outstanding artists from the Low Countries, such as the panel-painter Melchior Broederlam from Ypres. Sculptors, too, from Tournai, Courtrai, Bruges and Brabant assembled at Dijon. But outstanding among them was Claus Sluter (c. 1350–1406) – perhaps from Haarlem – whose figures outrun the formula of Gothic with their savage contorted energy and massed swirling draperies. On the gate of the ducal chapel at the Chartreuse de Champmol, the statues of Philip the Bold and his duchess show a physical and psychological realism unequalled until Rembrandt; and at the nearby Well of Moses the Crucifixion group startles and shocks by its revelation of spiritual experience.

Spain

The five principal Christian rulers of Spain momentarily united to defeat the Almohad caliph Mohammed al Nasir at Las Navas de Tolosa near Jaen (1212); and by 1230 the Almohad empire in Spain (p. 86) had disintegrated. Yet Christian unification of the peninsula did not follow, because most of Andalusia (from Almeria to Gibraltar) was annexed instead by Ibn al Ahmar of Arjona, prince of Jaen, whose Arab dynasty now supplanted Berber rule at Granada (1238). King Ferdinand III the Saint of Castile and León (1217–52) took Cordova and Seville (1236, 1248), but acquiesced in the Moslem régime at Granada because of the large annual tribute that it paid him.

This obligation helped to prompt a high degree of productivity at Granada, which derived its wealth not only from the most fertile and cultivated agriculture in Spain but from many other industries, particularly weaving and cloth-making. A paternalistic ruler who subsidized the poor and sick and encouraged education, Ibn al Ahmar was also the real creator of the Alhambra (Red Palace): it was by his almost obsessive hydraulic activities that its unequalled harmony of buildings and gardens was made possible. Then, in the age of Yusuf I (c. 1333) and Mohammed V, and outstanding scholars such as the polymath vizier Ibn al Kharib (1313–74), these columned pavilions assumed their final slender seductive outlines, covered with a silken filigreed Arabesque calligraphy of dexterous design which their physical environment and local traditions, and echoes of African and eastern Islamic styles, combined to inspire. In the 'silver chalice encrusted with emeralds and jacinths' that was Yusuf's Granada, the Alhambra was surmounted by the palace and gardens of the Generalife, a hidden, peaceful foretaste of Islamic paradise, with its intimate textile-like fantasies of secluded foliage amid fountains and rivulets.

The Moslem world was beginning to replace Byzantium as the home of sumptuous objects, such as the interlaced gold-lustre Alhambra vase (c. 1380–1400). This is probably an example of the recorded 'golden pottery' of Malaga, Almeria and Murcia, which later in the century, however, were succeeded by Paterna (Valencia) and other centres in Christian Spain (p. 157).

But the outstanding instances of Mudejar architecture (p. 89) are found at Toledo, Saragossa and Seville. The oldest parts of the Seville Alcazar, sponsored by Peter the Cruel (1350–69), display beneath complex ornamentation of brick, wood and plaster a structural firmness that owes something to Romanesque and Gothic sources as well as to the Almohad tradition (p. 86).

The complete Christian reconquest of Spain was postponed not only by

Castile's desire that Granadan tribute should continue but also by rebellions among its new Moslem subjects (1263). Nor was there unity among the portions of the peninsula already under Christian rule. These coagulated into three main blocks: Castile (now joined with León), possessing democratically elected town councils (*c.* 1220) but so poor that its political predominance caused the ultimate economic defeat of Spain (p. 168); Portugal, of which the expansion was still to come (p. 158); and Aragon, whose warrior-legislator and art-patron James I (1213–76), ruling also over maritime Catalonia with its professional school of hydrographers, seized the Balearics (1229–35) and Valencia (1238). But Aragon, which had already abandoned its trans-Pyrenean interests, now had to meet aggression from France (1284) (p. 116); this was however successfully resisted.

Meanwhile Dominic de Guzman (1170–1221) from Calaroga in Castile had founded his intellectual, combative Order of Preachers, the Black Friars. Their primary purpose was to fight and convert heretics, especially the dualist Albigensians of southern France (p. 82). His followers, the 'Hounds of God (*Domini Canes*), also became the popes' surest henchmen and principal weapons of their Inquisition. Dominican preachers gravitated to theological contests at universities in Spain (Palencia *c.* 1212, Salamanca *c.* 1243) and elsewhere, and their missionaries spread along the North African coasts.

But the revival of Spanish learning that followed under Alfonso X of Castile and León (1257–84) owed much to the Jews, and to other polyglot scholars under whom the translation from Arabic and Hebrew at Toledo reached its zenith; the church of S. Maria la Blanca in that city was used for worship by Christians, Jews and Moslems alike. Called 'the Wise' for his erudition – though he was incapable as a statesman – Alfonso X encouraged astronomy and produced a legal code. He also wrote four hundred songs on the miracle of the Virgin. For these he chose the softer Galician tongue, while employing Castilian in his important national history which exercised much influence upon Spanish epic and drama.

What Alfonso X had done for the language of Castile, Ramon Llull (1233–1315) of Majorca achieved for his native Catalan. Restlessly mystical, more at home in Arabic than in Latin, Llull in his search to discover arguments for converting the Moslem arrived in his prose and poems at an all-embracing vision in which science, theology and state affairs were fused and at one.

Among Castilians of the next generation Juan Ruiz, the Archpriest of Hita (*c.* 1280–1351) from Alcalá, infused into his gay yet touching, ironically mock-pastoral *Libro de Buen Amor* an ultra-Chaucerian vigour, a new human warmth, and a novel autobiographical self-awareness; the work is a 'Comédie

Humaine' reflecting the mature alertness of the society for which it was written.

As Castile and Aragon-Catalonia increased in strength, their rulers, both absolutist in tendency, came to blows. The Castilian king was Alfonso XI (1312–50), victor over Moroccan invaders at Salado (1340). His opponent Peter the Ceremonious (1336–87) not only took the lead in Spanish ecclesiastical and civil architecture but, with Barcelona at its mercantile height and Sicily and Athens under his relatives and viceroys, was for a time dominant in the Mediterranean. However, the strain caused by this widespread dispersal of effort was too much for Aragon, which came under the influence, first of France, and later of the Castilian kingdom.

The Portuguese, on the other hand, with the support of English archers at Aljubarrota (1386), reasserted their independence of Castile. The poverty and, smallness of Portugal caused it to seek a living from the ocean; and the sailors of Lisbon, assisted by Italian merchants and by Jewish map-makers in flight from Majorca (1391), fished and whaled in the Atlantic and carried salt to northern Europe. The Aviz dynasty occupied the Portuguese throne, but their sea-faring merchants played a large part in the management of the country.

England

King John of England (1199–1216), the only western monarch to have a navy of his own, reacted to the loss of most of his French possessions by founding a naval dockyard at Portsmouth (1204); while his Welsh and Irish projects were provided for by the creation of a port at Liverpool (1207).

The country was entering an age of baronial estates and demesne farming; and these barons, the first Europeans to turn agriculture into an industry, compelled John to sign Magna Carta (1215). Although intended to safeguard baronial privileges, the charter was significant because of its definition of feudal rights and duties, because of the practical remedies it assigned to current ills, and because its principle that the king's authority was subject to the Law implied an assertion of national rights.

Under Henry III (1216–72) full-scale war with France temporarily came to an end. His government was noteworthy not only for the numerous efficient foreign functionaries whom it employed, but for the simultaneous development of parliament as a primarily political assembly. Its meeting of 1258 was perhaps the first which was something more than an informal feudal Council; and when Simon de Montfort obtained dictatorial powers – in the interests of a wider society than the barons – his Commons of 1265 convened both the nominees of the boroughs and the knights of the shires.

ABOVE: One of the outstanding silhouettes of Christendom: the conical cupola and Byzantine spherical domes of the church over St Anthony's tomb at Padua, begun (1231) shortly before Frederick II established Ezzolino da Romano as governor

LEFT: A gold 'Augustalis' of Frederick II, issued probably at Brindisi (*c.* 1231) and suggesting by its classical name and style one aspect of this startlingly talented emperor, *stupor mundi*, ruling a multi-racial, anti-papal German–Italian state

LEFT: Like its Gothic forerunner at Amiens, Cologne cathedral rebuilt from 1248 vehemently strove for the unattainable in furious opposite eastward and upward drives, balanced one against the other in extreme tension and suspense. Meanwhile archbishop and merchants fought for the city's control

ABOVE: English Gothic diverges and expands from French spatial concentration into intricate decorative effects and transverse movements, luring the eye into diagonal viewpoints. This is the enormous arch or strut between the nave and crossing of Wells Cathedral (1338)

ABOVE LEFT: Bishop Wolfhard von Rot (d. 1302),
buried at Augsburg, lived in an age of asceticism
and licence, mass burnings, pogroms and
flagellant neuroses, passionate denunciations of
heresy and sorcery, the Dance of Death, and the
new mysticism of Meister Eckhart

ABOVE RIGHT: Uta, from the series of Founders in
the choir of Naumburg cathedral in Saxony
(c. 1250–60), shows a new and extraordinarily
expressive approach to the ideal by German
sculptors through three-dimensional humanity

ABOVE: The Kiss of Judas: in Giotto's frescoes
covering the Arena (Scrovegni) Chapel at Padua
(c. 1305) Roman moderation, Gothic emotion
and Franciscan humanism are fused by the epic
passion and imagination of this Florentine into
a living plastic reality

RIGHT: Panel-painting of St Elizabeth feeding a
beggar, by Master Theodoric, founder of the
Prague corporation of painters established in 1348 –
the year in which Central Europe's first University
was created in the same city, capital of the
Empire under Charles IV

ABOVE: Plato and Socrates on a thirteenth-century
manuscript. Through many intermediaries Plato
dominated medieval thought; but meanwhile
Aristotle was becoming known from Arabs, Jews
and Persians

RIGHT: Jean Fouquet from Tours combined
classicism with Flemish precision in his easel
portraits and exquisitely complex miniatures that
adumbrate a French school: this (Gothicized)
Building of the Temple at Jerusalem (c. 1475) is an
illustration for Josephus' *Jewish Antiquities*

Ainst en ainsi de quan
tes uertus et de quants
biens il a este aucteur
a ceulx de sa lignee. et
combien plain de grant aige il est
mort nous lauons declarie ou li

ure deuant dit. Quand salomo
son fil: ancores ieune enfant eut
pzins le royaume de son pere. et fa
assis ou siege royal. tout le peuple
solennelement saueur. comme on
seult saire a un roy au commence

Artists from the dependent Low Countries,
attracted to the grandiose protocolaire Burgundian
court, included Claus Sluter, whose Moses and the

Five Prophets at the Abbey of Champmol near
Dijon exhibit a violent naturalistic energy
(1395–1402)

The parliaments of Edward I (1272–1307), notably the 'Model' gathering of 1295, were more representative still, resolving conflicts by legal means and reflecting by their membership the gentry's unique role in English constitutional development. These eruptions of parliamentary government were isolated outcrops in the path towards the present forms of parliament, which followed a tortuous route, influenced by many political and economic factors.

An important and farsighted legislator, Edward I increased both material prosperity and national feeling – as befitted the first monarch since 1066 to bear an Anglo-Saxon name. However, he persecuted the Jews, citing usury and coin-clipping as pretexts for their expulsion (1290). Ordering universal military training, Edward also struck at the Scots, who under Alexander II and III had been enjoying a golden age of peace; and at the Welsh whose nationalism had been given impetus by Llewellyn the Great (1195–1240). South Welsh longbowmen and north Welsh spearmen now joined Edward's army – leaving Wales (pinned down by great castles) weaker and quieter without their presence. After setbacks, the Scottish guerrilla chief William Wallace was defeated at Falkirk (1298). But Robert Bruce's reversal of this result at Bannockburn (1314), followed by a Franco-Scottish alliance, postponed the unification of England and Scotland for three centuries.

Edward III (1327–77), a charming, impulsive soldier and huntsman, whose court displayed much chivalrous ceremonial but little statesmanship, obtained financial help from numerous parliaments (as well as from unfortunate Italian creditors, p. 112) in order to launch the Hundred Years War with France. Despite the devastating casualties of the Black Death (p. 112), his bloodthirsty son the Black Prince won spectacular victories – representing a military superiority unparalleled in English history – but these were followed by expulsion from every occupied territory in France except Calais and a strip of Gascony.

The subsequent reign of Richard II (1377–99) witnessed a dangerous peasants' revolt (1381) due to pressure from royal tax-collectors. However, as the richer merchants joined the ruling class, feudal methods of production based on a serfdom more emancipated than elsewhere in Europe were being transformed by the rise of towns (of which London was far the greatest) to political and economic autonomy. Moreover, the multiplication of sheep, in pasture-land vacated through the Black Death, enabled England to become a large-scale producer of woollen cloth for export to Flanders and north Italy. But the Black Death had another effect also: by increasing the market value of labour and thus weakening the bargaining power of employers, it created a rural middle class which fundamentally modified the social structure.

Pioneer of the Oxford Franciscans, who equalled or led Paris in scientific learning, Roger Grosseteste (*c.* 1170–1253) was the first to give Europe a complete translation of Aristotle's *Ethics*. Claiming the supremacy of mathematics (chiefly geometry), he also outlined an English philosophical method based on experience and empirical verification of facts. Even greater stress was laid on experiment by Roger Bacon (*c.* 1210/20–93), a thinker of intuitive and also vituperative power whose 'four causes of error', seeking to relate thought to life, mark an epoch in the progress towards scientific scepticism.

Duns Scotus (*c.* 1270–1308), too, displayed a scholarly reluctance to accept uncertain 'proofs'. Yet his bold theological speculations were conservative, being directed towards the defence of faith against Aquinas' emphasis on reason (p. 112). To Duns Scotus the great gulf between God on the one hand – arbitrary and incomprehensible – and his creations and their speculations on the other, seemed to be bridged by the Virgin Mary. To William of Ockham (*c.* 1295–1349), the divine power seemed no more easily understandable; but he accepted the gulf. In English fashion, this mordant, deeply influential thinker founded 'nominalism' – refusing all real existence to general concepts and universals, and thus denying that man's perception has the powers which had been ascribed to it. William's limitation of these powers to demonstrable facts suggested that most institutions are not natural but artificial – and that states should therefore come to sensible agreements. Such conclusions, leading ultimately to doctrines of human rights, gained the immediate support of northern Universities and northern students at Paris, but also earned him exile and excommunication. Likewise condemned (1382), after a period of support by a political group, was the Yorkshireman John Wycliffe (1320–84). His fault, however, lay not so much in metaphysics as in two other contributions to the current breakdown of the church's universalist claims: his attacks on papal hierarchies and institutions, and his insistence on the Bible as sole rule of faith.

By now a distinct English nationality was arising, more mixed and richer than the earlier Anglo-Saxon civilization. The new culture was endowed with two universities, Oxford and now Cambridge (1209), both of which developed as their most distinctive feature the multiplication, within their single institution, of separate, self-governing colleges. A native tongue of novel suppleness found its pioneer exponent in Geoffrey Chaucer (*c.* 1340–1400), scholar, soldier, diplomat and traveller in Italy and France. French courtly love, in its earnest and satirical forms alike, reappears in his vigorous poetic novel *Troilus and Criseyde* (1385–7), and in the unfinished *Canterbury Tales*. A unique picture of the age is presented by these realistic, vivid *fabliaux* told by pilgrims on their way to Canterbury; the Wife of Bath is conspicuous for her caustic comments on men. In Wales a contemporary of Chaucer, who like him sought to nationalize European themes, was Dafydd ap Gwilym (born *c.* 1320), a poet of love and nature and pioneer of Welsh poetic diction.

The thirteenth-century Gothic cathedrals of England developed elements far removed in character from France. One of these features is the soaring spire of Salisbury (1220–65). The interiors of these massive buildings, however, lack the extreme spatial concentration of their French counterparts, developing more comfortable, relaxed proportions in which (as in the great monastic complexes of which they formed part) the French insistence on a comprehensive view is replaced by a series of detailed, gorgeously intricate decorative patterns. Typical of this art – to be seen, for example, in the rebuilt Westminster Abbey (*c.* 1245), the most important church of the time – is the Chapter House, 'of sunny breadth . . . in which generous tracery circles give safe and happy contact with the ground'. So, too, in the ornate Angel Choir at Lincoln (1256–80) – erected while Simon de Montfort was asserting the national cause – the tracery flows in luxuriant foliage, and Exeter (1280–) displays a complex ornamentation of close-meshed vaults.

Architecture was the leading art of the English, but other arts in which they played a significant role were gold and silver work (including splendid coins), painting on wood and glass, and particularly the embroidery (Opus Anglicanum) which reflects and adapts the advances in those techniques. More famous abroad than any other English artistic product has ever been, these silken, silver-gilt-threaded priestly vestments and other robes and stuffs were financed by large-scale investors in professional workshops mainly located within the City of London.

In the fourteenth century, sweetness comes into English art, as sculptural detail reflects its tender perception of intimate and natural objects. Meanwhile the 'Decorated' style, in which the Gothic windows are adorned by a light network of curving traceries, provides varied and alluring developments at Bristol and Wells cathedrals (1338), where the eye is tempted by diagonal glimpses and intricately unfunctional vaults. At Ely (1323–30) the transept crossing is crowned by a sophisticated octagon, beyond which appears the rippling lights and shadows of the Lady Chapel.

But now began the most original of all English architectural styles, the 'Perpendicular'. The south transept and choir at Gloucester (1331–), and the naves of Winchester and Canterbury display slender repetitive vertical and horizontal window-ribs and vaults in the form of star-shaped unstructural patterned 'lids' – the abstract and angular, cerebral creation of a few strong-minded, perspective-conscious architects reacting against soft, 'Decorated' undulations. In this age of a rising, vigorous merchant class, many of the finest Perpendicular achievements are to be seen in the parish churches, with their fantastic wooden screens reminiscent of shipbuilding; and in great manor-houses such as Penshurst (1341–) and Kenilworth.

Germany and Its Eastern Neighbours

Ascending the throne immediately after a decisive German defeat by the French at Bouvines (1214), Frederick II Hohenstaufen (1215–50) (p. 108) maintained the link between his empire and its south Italian and Sicilian domains in which he dwelt. Yet because of his preoccupations with these, and his struggles with popes, he left Germans a chaotic heritage resulting in the Great Interregnum (1254–73). The full title 'Holy Roman Empire' had begun to replace earlier definitions (pp. 90, 91) at a time immediately preceding the unthinkable humiliation of its emperor Conradin's public execution in Italy (p. 109).

The electors chosen to appoint emperors – four secular and three ecclesiastical princes – partially filled the power-vacuum. But no less significant was the rise of the Hanseatic League. At first an association between the aristocratic merchants who ruled Lübeck and its allied cities, this soon became a trading union of ninety towns with a maritime and riverain commercial traffic equalling the trade of Mediterranean ports. The League had long since colonized as far afield as Riga, Dorpat and Reval (Tallinn); and it possessed its own imposing buildings at Novgorod. Its members joined the Prussian Teutonic knights and other militant monastic orders, especially the Cistercian Grey Monks, in the colonial drive which advanced Germanism from the Oder to the Dvina and the Vistula. As the heavy German iron plough superseded the wooden implement of the Slavs, hundreds of new villages were founded in Silesia, Pomerania and Brandenburg. The period of maximum expansion was the early and mid-thirteenth century, as colonists poured into areas devastated by the Mongols (p. 131); and Germans even joined up with the Black Bulgars as far away as the middle reaches of the Volga (p. 56).

From the headwaters of the Rhine came a business-like knight with a sense of humour, Rudolf of Hapsburg, who transferred his activities to Germany's south-east bastion Austria and halted disintegration by establishing himself as the founder of a new imperial dynasty (1273–91).

After Rudolf had checked one of Bohemia's most formidable and acquisitive rulers, Premysl Ottakar II (1278), the emperor Henry VII (1308–13) seized Bohemia for his own son John; but Henry's ambitions to restore German rule in Italy, which attracted Dante's hopes (p. 115), were destined to remain unfulfilled. In opposition to the Hapsburgs, Ludwig IV Wittelsbach (1314–47) of Bavaria, with his capital at Munich, gained the imperial throne; and he too, with the aid of the learned Marsiglio of Padua, found arguments for the supremacy of the Holy Roman Empire and its independence of the popes. But Charles IV of Luxemburg (1347–78), one of the cleverest of the emperors, abandoned the endeavour to win back untenable positions in Italy and Burgundy alike. Ruling in Prague, he strengthened the Bohemian crown at the expense of German territories such as Bavaria and Austria, and founded the first German and Czech university (1347), endowing an influential school of jurisprudence. After Charles IV had confirmed the electoral system of succession by his Golden Bull (1356), his son Wenceslaus (Wenzel, Vaclav IV of Bohemia; 1378–1419), though opposed by the Czech national saint John of Nepomuk (1393), was the first emperor to succeed peacefully for two centuries.

Nevertheless, German order and security deteriorated, as the knights declined into an impoverished and lawless class. This was the doing of the towns which, under the vigorous influence of their guilds, combined with one another in strong associations such as the Swabian League (1376). The Hanseatic League (p. 126), too, was now at the peak of its power, with a membership which increased to 160 towns, capable of dictating terms to Scandinavian monarchies – until their Union of Kalmar (1397) called a halt. During these two centuries Hungary, Poland and Lithuania, with their capitals at Buda, Cracow (a university town since 1364) and Vilnius respectively, all had periods of weakness and strength involving varied relationships with Germany.

Meanwhile the economic situation of German lands had presented a varied picture. In spite of peasant wars, revolts and economic recessions, there had been important technical developments, such as the Rhenish discovery of the smith's bellows (c. 1300) which was to stimulate cast-iron production. While the large-scale growth of cereals (and to a lesser extent cattle) was deliberately increased over north-central Europe, a cotton industry developed in Swabia, linen was exported by south Germans and Westphalians, and the coats of mail and blades of Nuremberg were famous. Like other countries, too, Germany continued to produce earthenware peasant pottery of superb rhythmical line.

The early thirteenth century witnessed an efflorescence of German poetry, in which court epics and popular epics of the south-eastern areas, after centuries of submerged existence, assumed their final shape. The *Nibelungenlied*, cast into definitive form by an Austrian knight (*c.* 1200), reproduces in the story of Siegfried and Brunhilde all the subjects of Teutonic epic poetry – the magic, mythical, partially Christianized lays of a lost people, plunged into the depths by a woman's hatred, amid uncontrollable passion, anger, and treachery. Yet these themes, although they retain all the tragic frenzy of the sixth or seventh century frontier community from which they originate, are reshaped to the taste of a courtly society.

Gottfried von Strassburg's *Tristan*, written mainly in 1211–15, is based on Celtic themes sung by the French *trouvères* (p. 80); yet it tells of love with Germanic psychological profundity. All the formal arts of courtly literature are employed to unveil, in original and daringly beautiful rhythms, the lies and delusions of the courtly world. The empire is praised; but the new sacrament of love undermines all hierarchies.

At the same period the Landgrave Hermann of Thuringia gathered round himself at the Wartburg a group of the Minnesingers – aristocratic minstrels who Germanized *amour courtois* (*Minne*) (p. 81), often in religious terms reflecting contemporary adoration of the Virgin Mary. This group included the enigmatic genius Wolfram von Eschenbach, whose fame however rests less upon *Minnesang* than upon the epic *Parzifal* which he wrote in about 1200. Parzifal was a young knight taught to 'keep his spirit pledged to God, without losing his hold on the world': his loyalties win God's approval, and he recovers his lost faith and family and wins the Grail. In this pilgrimage of the soul, obscure yet full of hope and sanity, one of the principal themes is unbelief; while the central subject of his other vernacular romance *Willehalm* is tolerance, including a spirit of co-existence with the pagan who is no longer merely an object of slaughter, since his destiny is of value to God.

The most famous of the Minnesingers was Walter von der Vogelweide (*c.* 1170–1230), a wandering minstrel (perhaps from the south Tyrol) who in Bavarian dialect sang poems set to his own music. His patrons included three Babenberger dukes of Austria, at whose cultured cosmopolitan court western, Byzantine and Russian influences met; and he also enjoyed the support of Frederick II. Supreme among secular German lyricists before Goethe, von der Vogelweide blended artistic *Minnesang* with folk-themes in which courtly love is transformed with charm and wit into human *Liebe*. He is also the first patriotic, political poet, attacking Roman avarice, revealing his own experience of a landless man's hardships, and foreseeing world-wide catastrophe. 'Injustice stalks the high road', and salvation was to be found in simple faith.

But faith took varied forms. One of the two Children's Crusades started in the Rhineland (1212), where the ten-year-old Nicholas of Cologne collected

20,000 boy and girl recruits who were kidnapped by Italian slave-dealers and sold to Egypt. The chief inquisitor Conrad of Marburg (assassinated in 1233) had many people burnt to death, and by his sadism touched off latent mass neuroses. Ferocious, again, in his denunciations of heresy was Berthold of Regensburg (c. 1220–72), the outstanding preacher of his day. Yet in the same century the charitable Hungarian St Elizabeth of Marburg (1207–31) had set a new example of humble service to the poor.

The only German at the height of the new learning was Albertus Magnus (c. 1200–80), from Lauingen in Swabia. His massive encyclopaedic output, mainly produced at Cologne and Paris, embraced the entire knowledge of the day, exercising particular influence through his understanding of Aristotelian natural science, enriched by Oxford studies and by his own observations. His grasp of Neo-Platonic speculation too (p. 40) stimulated the mystics of the following century. Meister Eckhart (1260–1327) from Erfurt resisted the spiritual collapse of church and empire and shored up the inadequacies of scholasticism by encouraging devout men and women to seek direct, individual communion with an almost pantheistic God. But this was a time both of extravagant saintliness and of every hysterical religious aberration, of fierce asceticism and equally unrestrained licence. Occultism, sorcery and anti-Semitic pogroms abounded; the Black Death (p. 112) was one of the origins of the flagellant Brethren of Cross, who spread from Hungary to become a messianic mass-movement throughout German lands. The same ungovernable tensions produced a central artistic, literary and dramatic theme of the time, the macabre and fantastic charnel-house Dance of Death.

To the secular pietism of Gerhard Groot (Geert Groet) (1340–84) from Deventer (Utrecht), the solution to current evils was a pure and simple life. His attacks on the sins of clergy and others were followed by the establishment of lay communities dedicated to primitive piety and poverty. The Brothers of the Common Life (c. 1380), the principal organized group of this 'Devotio Moderna', spread rapidly in the Low Countries and north and central Germany.

Ambitious German secular buildings appear at the Wartburg, at Goslar, and at Henry the Lion's capital of Brunswick. Ecclesiastical Gothic, too, assumed magnificent shape both at Cologne (1248–) and Strasbourg (1250–). National specialities included the open pierced spire, and light and airy Westphalian 'hall' churches, with short naves equal to the aisles in height (p. 152). German thirteenth-century church sculpture displays a new approach to the ideal through a vigorous realism expressed in novel three-dimensional form. The Bamberg Rider embodies aristocratic attitudes; and Founders' statues at Naumburg, paragons of chivalry yet flesh and blood, include the 'most beautiful young women ever carved'. Yet Naumburg (*c.* 1260) also shows a wide range of more earth-bound individuals, and the tense figures of the Bamberg choir (1220–30) seem to reflect the bitter conflicts of the new learning. Man has been rediscovered as a complete, living blend of body and mind.

As the Virgin Mary's life-cycle became a favourite theme of mural painting, there also evolved the sculptural concept of the Mother of Sorrows, exemplified in the poignant Bonn *Pietà* (the scene of grief after the Deposition from the Cross) and adapted in late thirteenth-century Bohemia, under Franco-Italian influences, to the profound pathos of the 'Beautiful Madonnas'. This is also an age of north Hungarian, Bohemian and Moravian mural painting, and of Bohemian portrait sculpture – for example, the royal busts by the Swabian Parler in St Vitus' Cathedral at Prague (1370–80); while the altar-piece reliefs at Vyšši Brod (*c.* 1350) and Třeboň (*c.* 1380) in southern Bohemia use light to break up colour, and employ deep shadows to heighten the pathos of their themes.

Scandinavia

Sweden, with its island Hanse outpost Visby – an immensely prosperous link with Novgorod, until superseded by Lübeck (p. 126) – was taking a shape in which the peasantry played a larger political part than in other countries. The later thirteenth century witnessed the establishment of the Västergötland and Uppland political laws, providing for the possibility that the monarchs, being elected, could be deposed. A new cathedral was founded at the ecclesiastical capital of Uppsala (1273–); and there followed the missionary activity of St Birgitta (*c.* 1302–76).

Valdemar II (1202–41) of Denmark had established a large ephemeral empire over north-eastern German-Slav lands and Estonia. Then Norway, at the height of its sea-power and colonial empire, became one of the best organized states of Europe, especially under King Haakon IV Haakonson the Old (1217–63), who was crowned at Bergen by the papal legate in 1247.

The Hanseatic League, however, was often capable of dictating terms to all three Scandinavian countries, until they more than counterbalanced its power by joining together in Eric of Pomerania's Union of Kalmar (1397), which formed close relations with Poland-Lithuania (p. 153). This triple unification was short-lived, but the union of Denmark and Norway – whose joint queen Margaret was the guiding force – lasted for four hundred years.

Under the patronage of Haakon IV many prose sagas, based on foreign romances, were written in Norway. But this was also the epoch when Icelandic scholars and poets committed earlier sagas (p. 93) to writing, collected

Opposite: St Michael, from a triptych (*c.* 1319–20) by Simone Martini

the Eddic poems and compiled summaries of Scandinavian and Germanic mythology, genealogy and law. This extraordinary output presents the harsh, pessimistic world of the Teutonic peoples at many stages from the migrations of much earlier centuries until the authors' own day.

While a new critical sort of history emerged in the Bishops' sagas of Skálaholt (S. Iceland), the western Icelandic chieftain Snorri Sturluson (1179, 1241) displayed artistry of a high order in his terse, vivid sagas of the Norwegian kings (*Heimskringla: Orb of the World*), and his great *Prose (Younger) Edda* with its almost Christ-like presentation of leading Germanic mythological figures.

Also committed to writing, at this time, were antiquarian 'family' sagas about Icelandic heroes ascribed to the tenth and eleventh centuries. Excelling in vivid, sympathetic characterization, these works attain their climax in the tragic and deeply moving prose of *Njáls Saga*, written shortly before 1300. The *Poetic (Elder) Edda*, copied, perhaps a little earlier, from originals which in turn were the products of prolonged oral transmission, comprises lays of the pagan gods and poems based on heroic German, Norwegian, Swedish and Danish legends. The lays begin with the *Sibyl's Prophecy*, a superb wide-ranging story of the world and the gods, culminating in their final death. The legends that follow go back as far as Ermanaric (d. 375), the Ostrogothic ruler overwhelmed by the Huns (p. 42): another of their heroes is Attila, who had hurled the Hunnish power against Rome and Byzantium in the following century (p. 44).

Russia

The last great migration from the central Asian plains was heralded by the armies of Genghiz Khan, not mere nomads but possessing an organization based on the existing Kidan state of Mongolia. Better in strategy, movement and intelligence than anything the west could offer, these Mongols penetrated far into Europe (1237), inflicting ravages only excelled by their appalling holocausts in Islamic Asia, where one and a half million people were massacred at Herat alone. They soon withdrew from central Europe. But the Russian states (p. 106) were rapidly reduced to various degrees of subordination, excluded from the steppe, and confined for two centuries to the forest. Their overlord was Batu who, as first Khan of the Golden Horde (Kipchak), established the west Mongol capital near the mouth of the Volga at Saray; and popes and western monarchs soon began to send their envoys there.

Pagan animists, and later Moslems – with their women mostly Nestorian Christians – the Mongols were tolerant about religion and had no objection to coexistence. They allowed an Orthodox bishop at Saray, and invested a Metropolitan of 'Kiev and all Russia'. But they required vassalage and stiff tax-payments.

When the Mongols had sacked Kiev, Novgorod was left relatively undisturbed under the guidance of its warrior-saint Alexander Nevsky (d. 1263). Defeating the Swedes (1240) who had conquered Finland, and the Germans (1242) who had conquered Estonia, Livonia and East Prussia, Alexander paid homage to the Mongols and obtained from them the Grand Ducal title (1252), now associated with Vladimir (p. 106) instead of ruined Kiev. Novgorod continued to build, with sloping roofs suited to the climate and with original versions of the cupola; while the peculiarities of its enterprising and turbulent 'younger brother' Pskov (p. 107) were the detached bell-towers of its churches and their porch-like western extremities.

In the mid-fourteenth century there was an impressive revival of Novgorod fresco-painting. The murals at Volotovo (1360–80) are intense, lightly sketched scenes of zigzag, energetic, colourful compositions; and the white, red and green icons of the same school which now appear – often on the recently introduced chancel screens (p. 52) – are notable for their emotional poignancy and rhythm. The most remarkable practitioner of both these branches of painting was the Greek immigrant Theophanes. The rapid nervous strokes of his violet, blue and silver wall-paintings in the Church of the Transfiguration at Novgorod display an impressionistic distribution of profuse highlights that look ahead to the unearthly esoteric wisdom of El Greco (p. 170). In the 1380's Theophanes left for Moscow where, although his murals have not survived, icons of a profoundly emotional ascetic severity are attributed to him.

A trading-centre far from the ravaged southern area, Moscow showed diplomatic patience in its vassalage to the Mongol power, whose chief tax collectors its dukes became; and before long they took over from Vladimir the title of grand dukes of all Russia. Ivan I Kalita (Money-bag) (1328–41) extended his power throughout the Moscow province, and much of the upper Volga region and other areas were added by Dmitri Donskoy (1362–89), with the blessing of the national saint Sergius of Radonezh (c. 1314–92) – one of the leaders of a huge expansion of Russian monasticism in desert regions. Dmitri also defeated the Mongols at Kulikovo (1380). Their Khan of the Crimea and later of the Golden Horde itself, Toktamish, was preoccupied by vast and prolonged hostilities against the only comparable cavalry power in the world, led by Timur (Tamerlane; d. 1405), Turkish successor to the heritage and destructiveness of Genghiz Khan (p. 131), and the greatest conqueror in world history. Both Toktamish and Timur briefly occupied Moscow; but Timur's capital was far away in Samarkand, and Mongol rule continued in Russia for another century – though it henceforward assumed less stringent forms. Meanwhile, backed by increasing financial, industrial and agricultural strength, Moscow firmly continued to display a rich architectural development, utilizing shapes and techniques derived from tents and wooden buildings.

The Balkans

Scarcely any crisis in European history has made a more shattering impact on the development of events than the sack of Constantinople by the Fourth Crusade (1204) – ostensibly on its way to Egypt – and the establishment there of a principality under Baldwin I of Flanders (d. 1205). Allotting three-eighths of its territory to the Venetian traders who were its principal beneficiaries, this precarious state, described by Pope Honorius III as 'almost a new France', perpetuated the split between the churches of east and west (p. 101). Its weakness, inadequately shored up by other crusading principalities in Athens, the Peloponnese or Morea (Mistra, c. 1246) and the Archipelago, shifted the balance of power to west European rulers, and deprived the Balkans and central Europe of their bastion against oriental invaders.

However, Greek monarchs remained in office, and established their own states, in north-west Greece (Epirus) and Asia Minor (Nicaea, Trebizond). In 1261 Michael VIII Palaeologus (1259–82) of Nicaea, with the help of the Genoese who were now challenging the Venetians as the principal trading power (p. 99), recaptured Constantinople from Baldwin II, and re-established the Byzantine empire.

Surviving on a limited scale for nearly two centuries, this Palaeologue régime was under the control of the great Greek families and church foundations; it depended upon Genoa for its fleet, and upon the rising Ottoman Turks (p. 136) for its very survival. However, imperial attempts at union with the Roman church, aimed at mobilizing western political support, were regularly resisted by the patriarchs of Constantinople. Another ecclesiastical manifestation of the time was the quietist movement of the Hesychasts with their mystic vision of the Divine and Uncreated Light. This movement, closely linked with Mount Athos and first fully articulate under Gregory Palamas, gave rise to important writings. In other respects, too, this was an epoch of strong, if nostalgic, literary revival, including history, philosophy and poetry of love.

In spite of political difficulties the revived Byzantine empire was far from poor; for the Genoese, in particular, provided links with the west and also, through their Crimean colony Caffa, with the Mongols whose conquest of Russia meant that much eastern trade passed through Constantinople instead. Churches – many of them now built by rich private patrons – still abounded with precious materials. At Constantinople and Thessalonica (Salonica), which was now almost as important as the capital, these buildings tend to be smaller and higher, with central and lateral narrow domes upon tall drums. There is much ornamental brick-work, and elaborate arcading which recalls the somewhat feminine charm of contemporary late Gothic (p. 118).

Byzantine painting on walls and in illuminated books, and on the wooden panels which had now become more widely available, now enters a new and glorious period, in which light modelling and delicate colouring reflect an intimate humanity. The outstanding Constantinopolitan frescoes in this Third Renaissance, as well as its best surviving mosaics, are in the church of the Chora (Kahriye) monastery (1305–15). In particular the elongated, high-lighted figures of the Descent into Limbo, with their elliptical or transverse draperies, are agitated by violent cross-currents that reflect a novel, stressful freedom.

This last fresh flowering of Constantinopolitan culture, with its subtly experimental or sometimes neo-classical rhythms, is an art of rarefied blues, greens and golds. It is closer to Siena than to Giotto, though perhaps it influenced both (p. 114); and it has turned a little away from the earlier Byzantine spiritual intensity towards the individualism of convincing, anecdotal gesture and human pathos; only occasionally does a fierce mysticism show through. At Athos, too, there are important paintings – with profuse, colourful, meticulous ornamentation – attributed to Manuel Panselenos, under the patronage of the emperor Andronicus II (1282–1318).

While Athens did not return to Byzantium, passing from French dukes to Aragonese (1312) and then to Florentine businessmen (1388), Mistra (p. 133) was ceded back by the Latins to the Greeks (1259). At this Peloponnesian capital, there are paintings of exceptional quality in the Peribleptos church; brilliant in their lustrous decorative richness, they have abandoned monu-mental styles for an almost abstract icon-technique, in which attenuated, strangely costumed figures are illuminated by sharp yet dream-like contrasts of darkness and light.

The first Latin emperor of Constantinople, Baldwin I, was captured by the Bulgarian Tsar Kaloyan (1205) – encouraged to assert himself by the collapse of Byzantine power. Outstanding among these Bulgar monarchs (p. 105) both as conqueror and patron of learning was John Asen II (1218–41) who, ruling over most of the Balkans, developed his capital Trnovo as a cultural centre. Its churches possess widely varied plans diversified by skilful external decorations of brick. Among them St Peter and St Paul, after the middle of the century, have paintings of depth and plasticity. But the best work is at Boiana near Sofia, where the warm and simple frescoes, inscribed in the Slavonic script but still Byzantine in their emotional expression, mingle spiritual strength with a sense of individual human personality. After the Asen dynasty became extinct (1280), anarchy and Mongol invasion followed, and then Bulgaria came under Serbian control (1330).

The fall on Constantinople (1204), which had enabled Bulgaria to revive its power, also gave Serbia (p. 105) the chance to achieve true independence, with its new archbishopric of which Stephen Nemanya's son St Sava was the first occupant. Stephen Uros I (1243–76), who married the daughter of Baldwin II of Constantinople (p. 133), maintained friendly relations with France in the hope of partitioning the Byzantine empire. The austere Stephen Dushan (1331–53), crowned tsar 'of the Greeks and Serbs' at Skoplje (Üsküb; 1345), conquered most of the Balkans, and gravely threatened Constantinople; though Byzantine influences are apparent in his Book of Laws (1349), which are also abreast of western developments.

The earliest of the purely Serbian frescoes known to us, though they show certain Italian analogies, are those of Studenica (1209, 1233); and the earliest of three churches at Péc shows a severe and sombre but moving and effective style. A fully developed humanism, with a solid plasticity that again owes something to west as well as east, appears in the paintings of the monastery church at Mileševa (c. 1235), built and decorated by the Serbian king Vladislav whose portrait one of the Greek-named but perhaps Slav artists includes among his designs. The work done for Stephen Uros I at Sopocani (c. 1260) continues this tradition of robust forms and stable poises, but in a less classical and more experimental fashion, and with closer links to nature; richer and subtler and more varied techniques and colour schemes entitle these paintings to be regarded as the first mature masterpieces of the Serbian school. In about c. 1300 comes a second flowering of the art, both in Serbia and in an accentuated, dramatic Macedonian style. The principal painters are identified as Astrapas, and his less conservative pupil Eutychius; perhaps the fresh, brilliant painting in the Church of the Mother of God at Prizren (1309) in southwestern Serbia is attributable to Astrapas, and Staro Nagoricino (c. 1317) may be Eutychius' work. A special interest in narrative themes, reflecting an excellent relationship between decoration and architecture, becomes accentuated in the rich, restrained work of the Church of the Annunciation at Gracanica (c. 1321), with its many narrow arches and small vaults.

After the death of Stephen Dushan, the Serbian conquests were taken over, at first momentarily by Stephen Kotromanic (St Tvrtko) of Bosnia (1376–91), and then by the Ottoman Turks, central Asian immigrant conquerors of north-western Anatolia whose Sultan Murat I (1359–89) overwhelmed an army of 10,000 Serbs, Hungarians, Moldavians, Wallachians and others at Kossovo, though he himself lost his life in the battle.

Murat's predecessor Orhan (1326–59), who drove the Byzantines out of most of Asia Minor, had been allowed by Emperor John VI to garrison Gallipoli across the straits (1352). From there Murat I had captured Adrianople (Edirne), where he established his capital, and Philippopolis (Plovdiv); he also perfected the irresistible, multi-racial force of the Janissaries, the most dreaded troops in Europe. After Kossovo, Bayazit I (1389–1403), a soldier of enormous strength and orgiastic power, suppressed the Bulgarians (1393) and put an end to western interference (instigated by Pope Boniface IX) by annihilating or ransoming an army of French, Hungarian, German and other crusaders at Nicopolis (1396). It was now inevitable that Constantinople should fall to the Turks (p. 155). A conspicuous figure in their culture during this century was Yunus Emre, whose superb folk-poetry blends a spontaneous, genuine concern for humanity with a mystic search for eternal bliss in union with God.

The northern extremities of the Balkans were still outside the Turkish sphere of influence. Here both the principal components of modern Rumania, the Moldavians and Wallachians, in spite of their participation in the Kossovo disaster created important states which penetrated as far as the Black Sea during the course of the fourteenth century. The Moldavian kingdom was founded by Bogdan in c. 1350; a Wallachian state had been established at Campulung for several generations, and extended its power under Mircea the Old (1386–1418) of the Basarab dynasty.

The masterpiece of Wallachian art at this period is the Prince's Church (Biserica Domneasca) of Curtea de Arges (c. 1350–80), which reflects Greek influences in its paintings, whereas its architectural design fuses the styles of Constantinople and Bulgaria.

5

THE FIFTEENTH CENTURY

Italy

Fifteenth-century Italy was still divided between small governments, among which Naples, Venice, Florence, Milan and the Papal States were the strongest. Their interaction provided a microcosm of inter-state conditions foreshadowing the European system that was soon to destroy them. Early in the century there were violent dislocations and upheavals, crises of plague and finance and recurrent war. The years 1454 to 1494 brought something like equilibrium, an early example of balance of power. Florence, Milan and Naples were mostly friends; Florence and Milan initiated the modern custom of exchanging resident embassies (*c.* 1448), and Venice laid down rules governing ambassadorial procedure. But the return of instability to the peninsula invited invasion by Charles VIII of France (1494). Although after initial victories this aggressive action remained fruitless, it ominously taught other great powers, Spain and the German empire, to take the same view of Italy as a field for conquerors.

An early unifier of Italy might have been Gian Galeazzo Visconti of Milan, from whom Florence was only saved by his timely death (1402). In Florence this narrow escape, identified as a triumph for the ancient Roman Republican virtues, introduced a period of patriotic euphoria. The city was at the height of its prosperity, exporting 16,000 pieces of cloth to Venice in each year, and operating a profitable silk industry. Devotees of ruthlessly competitive commercialism, the relatively small Florentine upper-middle class controlled production, trade and money-lending alike, and for a time exercised a banking stranglehold over the Papal States.

In the forefront at Florence were the Medici family, lesser nobles in origin (*nobili populari*), channelling their influence through city-state institutions. Cosimo de Medici, son of the first millionaire of his family, was a crafty politician who, although titular 'gonfalier' for short periods only, in effect ruled the city, with armed force at his disposal, for thirty years (1434–64).

Remaining in touch with his own class, he accommodated himself unobtrusively to the strong men of Milan and Naples, and brought Florence unprecedented decades of peace at home and abroad. His son Lorenzo the Magnificent (d. 1491), though again basically a financier, ran into insolvency, succeeding more conspicuously as a patron of that culture which was, however, temporarily swept away – as French invasion threatened – by the pro-French, anti-Papal, militia-enforced dictatorship of the fanatically ascetic demagogue Savonarola (1494-8).

While it lasted, the achievements of this civilization had been dazzling. Its unequalled Renaissance was the creation of many artists stimulated by Italy's economic and social leadership of the west, and by its creation of an emancipated urban class (p. 115) which, taking advantage of these various conditions, adorned its homes with works of art. This Renaissance was the combined product of genius, environment, evolution and a new way of illuminating contemporary feelings and tendencies from the remains of antiquity which were visible on every side.

This was particularly the method of the restless insubordinate Florentines, who, curiously searching in an era of economic, political, artistic and intellectual unheaval, exploited classical models not for imitation but in order to give movement, narrative and colour to their own ideas of the revival or rebirth for which they longed. Antiquity had, in the past, been invoked primarily by ecclesiastical interests; but now, as they formed a historical sense of perspective about the fashionable ancients, artists also turned from an introvert metaphysics to the empirical world. Gradually, therefore, naturalism adopted its own grammar of visual expression, and assumed the scientific methodical character which, until the present century (p. 287), remained the basis of western art.

As Florence pulled out of depression and crisis into spectacular self-confidence, there seemed nothing that men could not do. Patronage was one of the principal instruments of Medici policy, and Cosimo took the lead in encouraging the fruitful craze for the antique which spread rapidly from literature to art. Rich merchants such as the Rucellai not only erected important buildings – and a large proportion of such expenditure now went to secular construction (p. 139) – but collected expensive panel-pictures for their furniture (*cassoni*). Artists, gradually breaking out of their medieval guild organizations, were becoming masters in their own right, with the feeling that they could not only receive favours but confer them.

Yet the most imposing artistic developments preceded the full expansion of this patronage, and were the product of societies which, while confident, were often fighting for their lives. There was an early sculptural revival under Jacopo della Quercia (c. 1374–1438), perhaps a Sienese, whose solid, expressive human figures display an ambivalent originality that looks forward as well as back, to the Gothic north of Sluter (p. 119) as well as to the classical south. In the 1401 competition for the second Baptistery doors at Florence, he was defeated by the goldsmith and autobiographer Lorenzo Ghiberti (1378–1455), a man who in spirit still belonged to the old world, but whose (limited) mathematical grasp of perspective – derived from Donatello (p. 140) – makes him a vital link between old and new. In painting, the same dual role is played by the Dominican Fra Angelico (c. 1387/1400–1455). His linear rhythm is conservatively Gothic, his radiantly serene colour recalls the illuminators, his purpose is mystic, reverent and didactic; and yet the clarity and sureness of his forms herald a different epoch.

In the vanguard of this Florentine movement which, for all its dependence on what had gone before, possessed a truly revolutionary character, were Brunelleschi in architecture, Donatello in sculpture, and Masaccio in painting. F. Brunelleschi (1377–1446), the first artist to have his life written by a contemporary, utilized the themes of antiquity to produce quite new effects. There are classical Orders exploited to provide masterly non-functional syntheses, with arches springing from capitals in the later classical and Romanesque fashion (p. 33), and with an emphasis on dark structural features against light walls. But above all Brunelleschi, in his determination to master and organize space and achieve 'ideal' proportions, called upon his profound geometrical studies to create principles of regular optical recession which painters might follow. The Old Sacristy at the church of S. Lorenzo (1421–8) and the Pazzi chapel (1429–) – perhaps the first ecclesiastical buildings in the Renaissance style – are stated with the Platonic, elemental integrity of a theorem, in black on white; and the grave perfection of his cathedral dome (1420–36) and of S. Spirito superimpose these novel ideas on the study of antiquity and on Florence's Romanesque past, with a confidence which suggests how the leaders of this movement felt themselves to be on the verge of deciphering the innermost structural secrets of the universe.

Alberti (1404–72) was one of the architects who built forbiddingly massive, rusticated, corniced, hollow-square Florentine palaces with Romanesque window divisions. His Rucellai palace, with the classical Orders reduced to superficiality, faces the problem of handling column against wall. But he also devised means, particularly by adaptations of the ancient Roman triumphal arch, to create west fronts of churches so as to project their tall nave and lower aisles externally without abandoning the Orders: a heritage which remained dominant in church architecture for three centuries and more. To Alberti, a great theoretician who saw mathematics as the common ground of art and science, the essence of beauty lay no longer in the organic growth character-istic of Gothicism, but in the calculated determination of a total plan so that nothing could be added or taken away or altered without impairing the whole design.

The achievements of Brunelleschi and then Alberti, in drawing upon the past and yet decisively breaking with its traditions, were paralleled by the no less startling statues and reliefs of Donatello (c. 1386–1466). Their multiple conflicts between Gothic decorative formal ideas, the new geometrical real-ism, and antique classical styles – which he understood better than any other Florentine – intrigue the brain and penetrate the emotions. Many of our ideas of this fifteenth century are foreshadowed by the heroic St John the Evangelist (1409–11), a three-dimensional unity embodying his enthusiastic innovating spirit in features and naked form of the tautest energy and con-centration. Donatello's marble and bronze Davids (1408–16 and early 1430's) are independent studies of actual human bodies, the first real nudes for a mil-lennium, all expressive contour and tense drama. But the drama can be trans-posed to uncanny chaos in his Mary Magdalene (perhaps after 1460), or in the disturbing terror of the Risen Christ still encumbered with the dissolution of the grave.

In painting, the same creative role of gathering up the past and forging a revolution from it was fulfilled by the short-lived Masaccio (1401–c. 1428). Like Cavallini and Giotto (p. 114), he gave each figure its proper weight, with the dense plain strength of a peasant, but now also with an original in-sight into the body's objective structure. Masaccio's Florentine frescoes in the Brancacci Chapel (S. Maria in Carmine) reveal figures that are novel in their nakedness or solidity – and in the palpable air that surrounds them. Here is a completely articulated world of logical space-construction and atmospheric perspective, brought about by a new, scientifically precise observation that adapts from the later work of Giotto a light and shade restrainedly expressed in characteristically Florentine rusts, greys and sepias. Despite all debts to the past, there is towering innovation in the massive volume of these uncom-promisingly square, robustly grouped figures, and in the sober flash of the highly charged gestures which reveal their firmly differentiated nervous lives. A shivering boy, a cripple, St Peter, tormented Adam, reveal a personal, pioneering mixture of clinical realism, abstract power and human warmth.

His pupil Filippo Lippi (c. 1406–69) developed a more dramatic presenta-tion of the beauty for which Florentine fashionable taste had become insati-able. Paolo Uccello (c. 1397–1475), an early example of the modern eccen-tric artist, took a conscious delight in the potentialities of perspective as a framework for pattern and design. Antonio Pisanello (c. 1395–1455/6) turned his gift for observant painting to the production of incomparable portrait-medals; and Luca della Robbia (1400–82), the most human of contemporary artists and founder of a flourishing family business, attained world fame as a sculptor in white and pale-blue ceramics. Domenico Veneziano (d. 1461) was deeply concerned with the transmutation of colours into a rich, enchanting poetry of light – the guiding element to a later generation of the Venetians (p. 145) who were perhaps, as his name suggests, Domenico's compatriots.

One of his assistants was Piero della Francesca (1410/20–92), from Borgo S. Sepolcro in E. Tuscany. Piero's stay in Florence with Domenico (1439) added a hitherto unimaginable dimension to the art of central Italy, sensationally displayed in his frescoes of the True Cross in S. Francesco at Arezzo (c. 1452–66) and then in the baffling imperturbable solemnity of the Resurrection, which in turn was followed by paintings showing Flemish influences (p. 149). The perfection of his human, natural and architectonic forms, and of the intervals that separate them, reveals an exceptional control of linear relations; as in his written studies on the same subject, Piero fully exploits current discoveries in perspective. The almost cubist ordering of these geometrical structures systematically solves the fundamental question of all representational art: how to convert the real world's three dimensions into the ideal world's two. But this Cézanne-like appeal to intellectual rigour, and to the illusion of depth, is augmented by Piero's adaptation from Domenico Veneziano of the immense new possibilities of light, which models his ceremonious yet unconstricted forms and melodious, significantly interrelated structures in a clear, fresh and pervasively serene ashen purity.

Painting at the same time as Piero, or in some respects anticipating him, Andrea del Castagno (c. 1423–57), reputedly an uncouth villager, imbued these same new solidities with a mood of stark dramatic realism; and Antonio Pollaiuolo (c. 1432–98), working with his brother, achieved an intensified potency of fluid line and a new precision of anatomical insight in the furiously active nudes of his bronze statuettes and groups. Luca Signorelli (c. 1441–1523) of Cortona, trained by Piero, carried still further this cult of exaggerated muscular action, anticipating Michelangelo in his grandiose illusionistic foreshortenings, and pouring his whole violent sense of human vitality into passionate pictorial sermons on sin and salvation.

Sandro Botticelli (c. 1445–1510), too, is concerned with the stresses of the soul, but this preoccupation is tempered by an almost morbid hunger for physical beauty, expressed in a languid, decorative delicacy that tinges spring's promise with the pale subdued colours of a lyrical, diaphanous twilight wistfulness. The forest meadows glimpsed in his backgrounds are not tangible like Piero's Tuscan farmlands, but fragile and fanciful. All the longings of this age for renewal are implicit in those bowers of bliss, the great allegorical Spring and the Birth of Venus. Rapturous and buoyant, heart-breaking in her evanescent voluptuousness, the goddess Venus has the un-antique curve of a Gothic ivory; yet she is also one of the pioneer mythological creations of a Renaissance poet-painter. These subtly sophisticated archaisms, blending psychological insight with detailed descriptions and borrowings from the antique, were painted for Medici halls and for the second generation of a society which, under Lorenzo, had become less obviously mercantile and more leisured and precious and fastidious.

Towards the end of his life, Botticelli adopted new contortions of style and feeling which may reflect a mystic asceticism attributable to Savonarola (p. 138). Yet the sources of his earlier allegories had been drawn rather from the Neo-Platonic ideas (p. 40) revived by the informal Platonic Academy at Florence (1462) which under the guidance of Marsiglio Ficino sought to bridge the gulfs between classical and Christian thought. Another of its members was the tasteful but waspish and anti-clerical Politian (1454–94), whose graceful language, in his Latin and Italian poems, recalls the serene remoteness of Botticelli.

This detachment from life, fostered by the Academy, was probably not unwelcome to its sponsors the Medicis, since it conveyed the implication that practical things are best left to the rulers. Yet civic responsibility was coming into fashion, since Cicero was no longer censured, as by Petrarch (p. 115), for his political activities, but praised by the Florentines as a model of citizenly conduct in the city of pure reason to which they aspired. But what above all still appealed to them was Cicero's conviction that man and his successful activities are of some value in themselves, a doctrine which was attractive to the broadening circle of educated people.

The pervasive classicality of the period was of mixed origin. With this Ciceronian humanism was combined not only a native Italian tradition of rhetoric, but debts from French medieval Latinity, as well as echoes of Plato, of Aristotle (whom he had not yet by any means superseded), and of other Greek writers introduced or reintroduced to the west by emissaries and refugees from contemporary Constantinople. Thus, although Greek studies were regarded by Florentines as less important than Latin, Giovanni Aurispa brought many Greek manuscripts west in 1413 and 1423. Even before the elimination of the Byzantine empire by the Turks, westerners were claiming superiority to the Greeks in scholarship (1438).

In the second generation of the Renaissance, new artistic currents entered Florentine life through the almost incredible versatility of Leonardo da Vinci. His teacher Andrea del Verrochio (1435–88) was a typical early

Renaissance craftsman, skilful at handling any material, and exemplifying the new liberation of figure-sculpture and painting from architecture. Born at Anchiano (near Vinci) in Tuscany, Leonardo (1452–1519) spent thirty years at Florence, nearly twenty at Milan, and nineteen in further wanderings which ended in France. His range of interests and talents was so gigantic, and his phenomenal inventiveness so evenly matched by a dilatory streak, that few of his major enterprises were completed. Combining mystic romanticism with an extreme inquisitiveness – excluding the humanistic and Platonic sides of the Renaissance, yet ranging from anatomy, geology and astronomy to projects for aircraft, helicopters, submarines and tanks – in all these activities Leonardo sought a single truth. He saw his art as a problem soluble by going direct to nature with an exact eye, and by representing all that he had discovered about light, perspective and the human form. In the Renaissance, as manifested in him, the aspect of revival had been wholly superseded by discovery.

The artist, he claimed with a novel and effective urgency, is as good as the poet or philosopher. His own legacy consists of drawings ranging from incomparable beauty to fantastic experimental distortion, and a small number of paintings which locate humanity within its surrounding universe amid a unique aura of mystery and romance. This magical flavour, by means of which his paintings of the 1480's far outshone other contemporary work in visual plasticity, is owed to a new dynamic, luminous fusion and flux of outlines and atmospheric tones (*sfumato*) that led to the romantic shadowing of so much subsequent European art. The specific flavour of Leonardo is also owed to a method of composition which carefully balances one form or gesture against another (*contrapposto*). His St Jerome (*c.* 1483), for example, although like his other works greatly faded from its original condition and colouring, displays in the saint's magnificent gesture a grandiose continuity of interlocking rhythms, thrown into dramatic relief by the rockbound aquatic gloom of the cavern beyond. And then a new era, the eve of the High Renaissance, is ushered in by Leonardo's Last Supper (1495–7), with its unprecedentedly subtle stress on instantaneous psychological tension, and its dynamic, fugue-like contrasts of movement.

While Florentines were thus launching the Renaissance, and transforming it into the High Renaissance, their ideas spread gradually to the papal court at Rome. But during the century's earlier years, the popes had rather been pre-occupied with theocratic politics and organization. The church's great Councils – Pisa (1409), Constance (1414–18), Basel (1431–8) – represent the religious side of the current European trend towards more broadly based government. Constance, the first great international congress of Europe, marked a new scale of political conflict and a new attempt to reform the Church, by applying parliamentarianism to its organization. The failure of the congress struck a decisive blow against European unity through papal universalism, and the divisions of the Reformation (p. 178) were among its fruits. Nevertheless, Constance achieved an immediate result when it terminated the Schism (p. 110) by the agreed elevation of Martin V (1417–31) to the papacy. Nicholas V (1447–55) sent to Florence for the planners of a vast new Rome, and he and Sixtus IV – who reigned respectively before and after the eloquent humanist Pius II – founded the Vatican library, the greatest in the western world. The sensational Alexander VI Borgia (1492–1503) extended energetic management and patronage to new fields and dimensions including not only the arts but the ambitions of his son Cesare to build up a central Italian kingdom; and one of the last acts of Rome as mistress of the world was Alexander's division of all America between the Spanish and Portuguese (p. 158).

North Italy was not far behind Florence, and well ahead of Rome, in the adoption of Renaissance ideas by its absolutist secular rulers. Milan, formidable under the Viscontis (until 1447) and then the Sforzas, built near its flourishing dependent university town of Pavia a Carthusian monastery (Certosa) of elaborate and harmonious magnificence (1396–1465). The Gonzagas of Mantua sponsored the most influential educational establishment of all time, precursor of modern systems, the Casa Gioiosa of Vittorino da Feltre (1423–96) – aiming, under Platonic influence, at the creation of the Renaissance 'universal man', and stressing science and gymnastics, individual personality and instruction of the poor. Andrea Mantegna (c. 1431–1506), after experiencing the strong influence of Donatello (p. 140) and then painting at Padua under the Carrara dynasty, was given a home at Mantua by the enlightened prince-patron Lodovico Gonzaga, who also employed Alberti. In his introduction both of the bourgeois and of the courtly Renaissance to these cities, Mantegna combined expert knowledge of Roman antiquity with a northern awareness of nature, devoting to both a highly personal metallic technique and the complex *trompe l'oeil* perspective illusionism of a theatrical producer. But the principal centre of dramatic production was at Ferrara, whose masters the Estes patronized the first permanent theatre in modern Europe, producing *masques* and subsidizing romantic poets.

The smaller the state, the more generous tended to be the patronage; art increased a ruler's fame and helped to prop his power. Thus Faenza and Orvieto produced the finest European pottery, and a leading cultural centre was the little hill town of Urbino, where both Piero della Francesca and Uccello worked. Urbino's creator was Federico da Montefeltro (1444–82), a former mercenary commander who tripled the size of his state, successfully playing off potential aggressors at a time when defence was still easier than attack. Alberti was employed at Rimini by Sigismondo Malatesta, a byword for enlightened cultural patronage and criminal brutality. At Perugia too there was horrifying bloodshed, in addition to eight epidemics of plague – sufferings which made its people responsive towards the emphasis placed by S. Bernardino of Siena (1380–1444) upon the greater importance of spiritual values.

Venice, on the other hand, was remarkably stable, under a hatchet-faced oligarchy of merchants who satisfied the populace with prosperity and carnival and did not tolerate dictators; the Council of Ten reached the height of its power when it forced the Doge Foscari to abdicate after a long reign in 1457. In addition to its repeated attempts to expand on the eastern Adriatic shores, Venice had absorbed most of north Italy. Its arsenal, with rapid galley-production and standard spare parts available everywhere, was the wonder of Europe; and Venetian trade extended to every civilized land. Welcoming all manner of expatriates, it also superseded Syria (whose glass-workers Timur (p. 132) had deported) as the world's largest producer and exporter of glass.

The luminosities of Venice and its lagoons, together with its artistic traditions exemplified by St Mark's (p. 99), combined with Florentine and Flemish influences (p. 149) to create a Venetian school of painting, which produced a supreme poetical artist in Giovanni Bellini (*c.* 1430–1516). He carried further the colour-experiments of Domenico Veneziano (perhaps his compatriot, p. 141) and Piero della Francesca, and softened them into the glowing sensuous hues of radiant light, blurring sharp contours yet possessing its own direct and concentrated pureness – a chromatic unity of supernatural golds and ultra-marines.

Meanwhile, bringing to his native Sicily the secrets of technique which he had learnt in Flanders, Antoniello da Messina (1430–79) painted spacious panoramas in which light, volume and realistic detail are handled with powerful vitality. Sicily and Naples at this time belonged to half-brothers of Aragon (p. 110), sons of the resplendent Alfonso V, conqueror of Naples from another great art-patron, René of Anjou (1442): of whom something will now be said.

France, Burgundy and the Low Countries

The symbol of romantic and tragic inconstant fortune, René, first at his brilliant court at Angers and then at Aix in Provence, stimulated not only pastoral drama and poetry but sculpture, gold-work, tapestry and painting, such as the sumptuous miniatures of his *Livres des Tournois* and the *Cuer d'Amours*

Épris (1460–70), in, which enchantment and domesticity are mingled. Meanwhile, at René's residence Aix, painting on a larger scale had achieved the loftiest standards in an unknown painter's *Annunciation* (*c.* 1442–5), which bathes Flemish realism in a luminous Burgundian-Provençal light. Nearby Avignon too, still a papal possession after the popes had departed, maintains its artistic role with the penetratingly modelled, emaciated figures by which the *Pietà* of Villeneuve-lès-Avignon ennobles, with a harsh pathos, the sorrow of death and bereavement.

The influence of Avignon, as well as of Florence and other Italian cities, is apparent in Jean Fouquet (*c.* 1420–81), born at Tours where the French kings frequently resided. Fouquet's combination of classicism, warm feeling, experimentation (especially with backgrounds), and Flemish traditions of portraiture derived from van Eyck (p. 148), brought France ahead of the world in this branch of art; his *Madonna and Child* possess a strange, softly rounded, geometrical serenity and charm that gives the painting an almost hallucinatory appeal. Although there were many French artistic centres, still reminiscent in various degrees of the schools of Flanders, Burgundy and Italy, Fouquet contributed a note of that specific individuality which was to become characteristic of his country's art. In the field of architecture, however, it was Normandy, and especially its capital Rouen, which led the free and robust late Gothic 'flamboyant' style, its basic form the ogee with curve answering curve.

Meanwhile Paris, at the outset of the century, had asserted its intellectual leadership of the west through its university. This, under the outstanding churchman Jean Gerson, led the conciliar movement to constitutionalize the papacy (p. 143) – and indeed aspired to judge popes and anti-popes.

It was however the city's drinking houses, rather than the university, which knew François Villon (*c.* 1430–63) – one of the truest and most spontaneous French lyrical poets, half vagabond-crook and half moralist-clown; whose *Ballade de Notre Dame*, with its vivid realization of death, plangently reflects his own life of turbulent hardship, and the sorrows of his times.

For these were the years when the Hundred Years War against England had entered its second phase. After the French feudal nobles, compelled to fight on foot, had been defeated by English infantry and archers at Agincourt (1415), the astonishing leadership of Joan of Arc – with her faith and peasant commonsense – enabled Charles VII to be crowned at Rheims (1429). Although she was captured and executed (1431), French armies exploited the use of cannon to win victories at Formigny (1450) and Castillon (1453) which led to the expulsion of the English from all France except Calais. The beneficiaries of the war were nationalism, the middle class which superseded the discredited ranks of chivalry, and the French monarchy. Charles VII would not allow his compatriots to appeal to Rome, and Louis XI (1461–83) developed a towering concept of royal authority which made wealthy, solid France the prototype of absolutist continental power-states. Its sixteen million inhabitants were more than one quarter of the total population of Europe; though the backbone of its infantry were Swiss (p. 150), and Albanians were the nucleus of its light cavalry.

Burgundy and Flanders formed the southern and northern cores respectively of a vast, rich and virtually independent state extending from the Somme to Friesland, and from Jura and Alps to the North Sea. This federation, although uncohesive and at times dependent on French support, had become the most considerable political force in Europe, drawing wealth from its Flemish resources, hoping for more from Alsace, and remembering the short-lived pretensions of Lotharingia as a Third Force between France and Germany (p. 64). Violent revenge, pursued amid an arrogant bravura of hatred and covetousness, was a sacred task of Burgundian dukes such as Philip the Good (1419–67). The other occupation of their fantastically luxurious court was an over-ripe chivalry, devoting passionate attention to precedence, etiquette and ceremonial, and minutely regulating the politeness of social intercourse.

Court extravagance reached its height at the fêtes of Lille (where Philip resided) and of Bruges (1454–68). For the centre of the kingdom was shifting from Dijon (Burgundy) to these rich Flemish centres, anticipating modern capitalism; and the grand belfry at Bruges (1482) indicated its continued position as the principal money-market of Europe. But cities in other parts of the Low Countries also were now coming forward. Brussels, where the dukes founded a great library and town hall, was beginning to look like the capital of the southern Netherlands. Antwerp, too, where half-finished English woollen goods were given their final form, began to overshadow Bruges as a commercial force; home of the first European exchange (c. 1460), it was the most cosmopolitan city in any northern country.

Meanwhile Holland, with something like a monopoly of North Sea fisheries, was showing signs of a new national sentiment; and Amsterdam had become the shipping centre for Norway and for Baltic grain. Such cities retained a large measure of municipal freedom and regional control.

Yet, in this age of formidable contrasts, Netherland cities and the Burgundian royal house, for all their materialism, were influenced by the mystic visionary Denys le Chartreux, alternating violent ecstasies with forty-five theological publications compiled at his Ruremonde cell. A widespread reaction towards mysticism, based on a distrust of learned speculation, reached its climax in Thomas à Kempis (1380–1471), born at Kempen but trained at Deventer (centre of Groot's Brethren of the Common Life, p. 129), and for seventy-two years a monk at nearby Zwolle (Overijssel). His *Imitation of Christ* was translated into more languages than any book except the Bible itself.

Meantime in the extreme south-west of the Netherlands, the spiritual aspirations of the age received their finest expression in the sphere of music. Cambrai was the city where the leading composer of the day, Guillaume Dufay (before 1400–74), was trained and died. Born probably at Chimay in Hainault, Dufay reconciled late Gothic and English elements with Italian styles he had learnt in the papal choir at Rome: the sensuousness of his music is restrained by a mellow, autumnal intimacy. Joannes Okeghem (*c.* 1430–95), an outstanding musical teacher at Tours, was born at Termonde in east Flanders, and received his training at Antwerp. As accompanied song gave way to a choral idiom distributed among parts, Okeghem converted the simpler Dufay style into a freely and richly unfolding flow of the larger polyphonic forms in which this 'prince of music' particularly excelled. Jacob Obrecht (*c.* 1430/52–1500/5) probably came from Utrecht, and after travelling in Italy worked mainly at Cambrai and Antwerp. His masses and motets display a majestic sonority, and a well defined Renaissance construction in which vertical harmony overshadows counterpoint.

The secular songs in which Obrecht transcribes Netherlands folk-tunes show signs of a tendency, growing from the 1460's as in other arts, towards picturesqueness and the expression of feeling. These features were accentuated in the music of Okeghem's pupil Josquin des Prés (*c.* 1450–1521). Born in north France or Hainault, des Prés, 'the painter of music', was deemed by Luther and others to be the master of his age. His new forms of mass, motet and *chanson*, with their deeply expressive simplicity and disciplined balance modified by mystic undercurrents, strongly influenced Italian composers – and were influenced by them. Des Prés himself went to Rome; his journey symbolizes the transfer of western Europe's musical centre from the Low Countries to Italy (p. 167).

The musical pre-eminence of the Netherlands during the fifteenth century went hand in hand with a Renaissance of its painting, which in originality, enriched and stimulated by traditions of the past, was the equal of Florence (p. 140). A masterpiece of the Burgundians' luxurious courtly Franco-Flemish art is the splendidly illuminated Calendar *Les Très Riches Heures du Duc de Berri* (1413–16) by the 'Limburg brothers', probably from Limbricht in Gelderland. In such work – the climax of the International style (p. 146) – glamorous ducal formality is already modified by a precocious factual approach which shows peasants, children and sheep in their daily lives, anticipating the bourgeois picture of manners. For great changes were at work. As artistic as well as political pre-eminence (p. 147) migrated from feudal Burgundy to the Flemish merchant capitals, new schools of painting developed from the work of northern miniaturists enriched by Italian influences. Roger van der Weyden (c. 1399–1464) visited both Rome and Ferrara. The brilliant heraldic simplicity of his reds and blues, reminiscent of stained glass and miniatures,

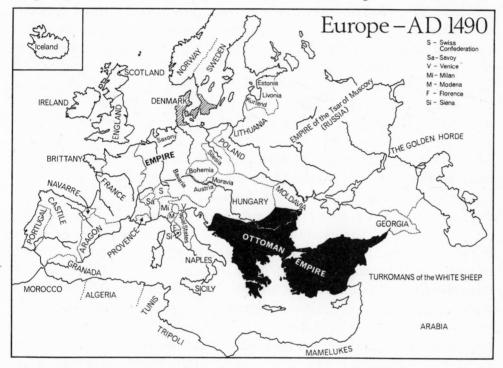

appealed to many tastes; for no one had ever exceeded his power to convey emotions and sensations, warm and spiritually intense and bitter-sweet.

Although van der Weyden's Brussels studio was the most important in the Netherlands, the outstanding personality of the Flemish Renaissance was Jan van Eyck from Maaseyck (Maastricht) (c. 1390–1441), court painter and 'valet de chambre' to Philip the Good, of whose colourful court he missed nothing. In about 1420, collaborating with his brother Hubert, he developed the panel-paintings which gradually superseded frescoes and miniatures alike. He also improved, or perfected, the use of pigments mixed with oil (instead of egg), a technique perhaps of Italian discovery which had hitherto been utilized only for special effects. Enabling van Eyck to move beyond the comparative flatness of the International medium, and perpetuating his brilliant colours, this enamel-like medium was also fluid enough to let him render his minute, characteristically Flemish details with a serious yet delighted, adventurous acceptance of the whole intricate visible world. His astonishingly sensitive analysis of surfaces enshrines Masaccio's and Brunelleschi's mathematical concept of linear perspective (p. 139) in outlines as bold and forms as solid as sculpture. By such explorations of light and space, van Eyck contrived his hypnotic, magical illusions, reconciling a detached materialistic inventory of infinitely small earthly experiences with the totality of the universe which embraces them all. The result might be the paradise-garden of the *Adoration of the Lamb* at Ghent – a new sort of convincing landscape, though not of this earth – or a portrait of unprecedented objectivity, or descriptive scenes which combine the mystic splendour of God's purpose with a very present and truthful and intimate world. Hugo van der Goes of Ghent, who died of religious melancholia (1482), changes the serenity of van Eyck into a new guilt-laden strain and exaltation, evident, for example, in his *Death of the Virgin* amid the dramatically contrasted reaction of the twelve Apostles. Hans Memling (*c.* 1433–94) was born at Seligenstadt near Frankfurt-am-Main, but spent his life at Bruges which, like Antwerp, attracted artistic work from farther east, for export to Paris and elsewhere. Memling may have been a pupil of van der Weyden: his strength lies in repose, and in the childlike innocence of his soft modelling which, while dwelling upon the actual, never lost sight of the underlying spiritual idea. Hieronymus Bosch (*c.* 1450–1516), named after 's Hertogenbosch in north Brabant, devoted his unequalled powers of fantasy to endowing the nightmarish chaotic horrors of hell's flames with every anarchic perversion of organic form. At a time when old ideas were still rampant but new methods of depicting them were available, he gave painful and macabre shape to the diabolical fears, denying human reason and natural order, which haunted the minds of man. Popular folk-lore, echoing book illuminations, is present in his phantasmagoric images, but so perhaps is the distorted symbolism of esoteric religious beliefs foreshadowing Reformation ideas.

When Bosch was still a young man the Burgundian state, in which these various painters worked, came to a sudden end. Outwitted by the far cleverer Louis XI of France (p. 147), Charles the Bold (1467–77), planning to link his northern and southern territories by the conquest of Alsace, was killed when his unwieldy army of knights succumbed at Nancy to Alsatians, Lorrainers and the Swiss pikeman who served many countries as mercenaries and were now Europe's leading military force.

The dream of a great state separating France from Germany was at an end. Burgundy and Flanders were sundered. The Duchy of Burgundy became one of Louis XI's many important acquisitions; and the marriage of Charles the Bold's daughter Mary to the future Holy Roman Emperor Maximilian, son of Frederick III (below), brought her inheritance of Flanders under Hapsburg control. The result of this latter arrangement was a conflict between France and the Hapsburgs which lasted for three centuries.

Germany and Its Eastern and Northern Neighbours

Albert II (1438–9) was the first Hapsburg to occupy the throne of the Holy Roman Empire. The second emperor of his house, Frederick III (1440–93), was the last to be crowned at Rome. Though he was a man of peace, ominous fissures in the imperial structure deepened during his reign. In spite of the notions concerning divine right of kings that were abroad, the German emperor's position progressively weakened in relation to territorial princes. The Elector of Saxony was the most important of these; but it was significant for the future that the Hohenzollern margrave and Grand Master amalgamated the Prussian Order of Teutonic Knights (p. 126) with the backward Electorate of Brandenburg, incorporating under his dictatorial rule large regions beyond the imperial frontiers.

The cities, too, suffered from princely encroachment. Even before Atlantic exploration, the Hanseatic towns (p. 126) were declining; and the southern cities, commanding the Alps–Rhine routes, were weakened by the diversion of the spice-trade to Antwerp and Lisbon. Yet at Augsburg the banker Jakob Fugger (d. 1469) was the richest man in Europe, owing his wealth to the control and revival of silver mines in Bohemian and Hungarian as well as German territory.

Another unique figure, though in a different way, was Cusanus (from Kues on the Moselle) (1401–64), whom Leonardo da Vinci greatly admired. Influenced by the Brethren of the Common Life at Deventer (p. 129), he can equally be described as the acutest medieval thinker or as the outstanding name in the northern Renaissance before Erasmus (p. 171). Writing in 1440 amid blindest credulity, resigned defeatism and terrors of the devil, Cusanus, though at times preserving orthodoxy at the expense of logic, believed with dynamic progressive optimism in mathematics and physical experimentation, and partially foreshadowed Copernicus by appreciating the involvement of the earth – a star among other stars – in a movement of universal scope.

German arts displayed masterly technique; but, until Dürer began to work late in the century (p. 177), no exceptional talent emerged to accelerate the gradual breach with earlier ways of thought. Stephan Lochner (c. 1400–51) painted sweet and gentle pictures, of infinite naturalistic observation, characteristic of Cologne to which he migrated, by way of the Netherlands, from his home at Meersburg on Lake Constance. Michael Pacher (d. 1498), at Bruneck in the Tyrol, showed a robust nervous originality in his fusion of violent, fleshy German realism with the classical balance he had learnt at Padua. The country's late Gothic architecture likewise blended mystical piety and sound practical sense in the undulating forest-like interiors of its wide, airy, star-vaulted 'Hall' churches (p. 129), filled – especially in southern Germany – with colourful carvings by Veit Stoss in wood and Adam Krafft in stone. Krafft's home was at Nuremberg which also, in the later part of the century, witnessed the apogee of the armourer's craft.

Martin Schongauer (1453?–91) of Colmar in Alsace was a master of copperplate engraving, an improvement on the woodcut owing to its greater capacity for detail. Printing, the creator of lay cultures and national languages, ancestress of modern industrial inventions, 'unmasker of priests and dethroner of kings', attained decisive developments at Mainz, a Rhenish ecclesiastic capital with a rich economic and social life and craft tradition. Block-printing had already been in existence for some decades, and in c. 1454–6 John Gutenberg, a Mainz goldsmith, placed metal letters together within a frame for the printing of his Bible, the first major book in the west made from movable type. Coster of Haarlem reached the same stage at almost the same time; and with the aid of machinery, capital and rag-paper (available since the invention of the spinning-wheel [c. 1300] popularized linen shirts), printing spread rapidly, first through Germany and Italy – where there were fifty-one and seventy-three presses respectively by 1500 – and then in other western countries.

The emperor Albert II (p. 151) was king not only of Germany but of Bohemia and Hungary also. Bohemia had become one of the leading exponents of the International Gothic style of sculpture, continuing to produce a series of poignantly beautiful statues of the Virgin Mary (p. 130).

But although Bohemian peasants had formerly been the most prosperous in central Europe, the same years witnessed internal wars – conducted with a violence that announced the death of chivalry – between the imperial authority and a native rebel leader of genius, Ziska. The revolts were in posthumous support of John Hus. Influenced by Wycliffe (p. 124) but more moderate, Hus had wanted the church to rely upon the Bible and St Augustine as its sources, and to avoid the temptations of wealth. Leader of the Slav party in the empire, he was executed for defiance of the ecclesiastical power (1415) – leaving behind him the first national schismatic church. Sensing the precarious isolation of Bohemia, one of its later kings, George of

Podebrad, sponsored a scheme for European union against the Turks (1462).

But the main power in central Europe, although ephemerally, was Hungary. The exploits of John Hunyadi, its most praised statesman and knightly hero, put a stop to Turkish aggressions (1442–4, 1456) for nearly a century. With Jajce, capital of semi-dependent Bosnia, as his outpost against the Turks, John's son Matthias I Corvinus (1458–98) established a strong and equitable central government which almost – but as always not quite – realized plans for a powerful central European state. Matthias' court was a focus of learning, with its Corvina Library, its first Hungarian press, and an outstanding Hungarian humanist Janus Pannonius – though the language in which he wrote was Latin.

To the south and east were three other monarchs of momentarily powerful kingdoms. George Castrioti (Skanderberg) (d. 1467) for a brief period united Albania. Vlad IV 'the Impaler', nominated by John Hunyadi as ruler of Wallachia (1456–62, 1476–7), combined exceptional sadism with able defiance of the Turks. Stephen IV the Great of Moldavia (1457–1504), ruling at Suceava, defended his country against Turks, Hungarians and Poles alike. He was also Moldavia's greatest builder, founding the monastery at Putna (where he is buried) and endowing his forty new stone churches with an original mixture of eastern and western elements which include elongated narthexes and distinctive two-storeyed cupolas.

Under Casimir IV Jagiello the Great (1447–92), whose father had amalgamated the country with Lithuania, Poland aspired to become a modern nation and leader of the eastern states. Extending for a time from the Baltic to the Black Sea, and reducing Prussia and the Teutonic Knights to subordination, it was by far the largest kingdom in Europe.[1] But its permanent retention of this status was prevented by the decay of trans-continental trade, the intractable temperament of the Polish nobility, and the failure of schemes to relieve peasant serfdom.

Nor did the Union of Kalmar, in which Eric of Pomerania (Eric VII of Denmark) had sought to unify the three Scandinavian kingdoms (p. 130), remain effective. In Sweden, after a peasant rising under Engelbrekt Engelbrektsson from Bergslagen – who called the first representative parliament (*riksdag*) at Arboga (1435) – there followed rivalries between pro-Danish and patriotically minded noblemen. Moreover, before 1500, Sweden had begun its three-century embroilment with Russia. In Denmark, the political situation was dominated by tension between the king on the one hand and noble landowners and bishops on the other, and by deepening gulfs of class.

[1] Polish paintings, under Italian then Flemish influences, developed masterly originality.

Russia

Neither Scandinavia nor Poland-Lithuania could command sufficient unity to counterbalance the rapid growth of Moscow, at the centre of Russia's river-system. A Great Prince with a novel nationalistic spirit, Basil I (1389–1425) incorporated Vladimir (p. 106) and the remaining portions of Suzdal into the Moscow Grand Duchy, and Basil II the Blind (1425–62) added further territories to north and south.

This was a golden age of Russian icons, combining simple intense feeling with adventurous, colourful experiments involving subtle repetitions and oppositions of line. To the conservative Novgorod icon of clear-cut, rhythmical, black and white design the Greek Theophanes, when he moved on to Moscow (p. 132), added settings that are symbolic and esoteric, and distortions of form pervaded by unearthly colour-schemes. His pupil and collaborator was Russia's most gifted painter (and the first known to have been born in the country), Andrew Rublev (c. 1370–1430). But the wall-paintings of Rublev, and especially the panels and icons in which his more developed style appears, abandon his master's impressionist broken outlines in favour of a more continuous technique closer to the traditionalist precision of Novgorod. In the lyrical innocence, compassion and fervour of his Old Testament Trinity (c. 1410) from S. Sergius' monastery at Radonezh, Rublev sums up and transforms the whole Byzantine experience in a Russian and personal idiom of delicate tints, and subtly swaying unearthly figures which subordinate every inessential to a unified composition of serene yet forceful spiritual intensity.

As in the west, though with differing emphases, Russian artists were seeking various unions between abstraction and naturalism. The last great attempt to bridge the gap between them came from Dionysius (Denys) (d. 1505), whose murals at Borovsk (1470) and subsequent icons adventurously explored the potentialities of new rhythmical combinations and formulas of light and shade. His refined and dematerialized yet ardent figures, with their swirling high-lighted drapery, contrast strangely with the virile ferocity of contemporary public life.

The architects of Moscow recreated and interpreted the styles of Vladimir and Suzdal in the exhilaratingly domed, ornately pyramidal cathedrals of the Assumption, Annunciation and Ordination. The Assumption church was designed by an Italian, Fioravanti; and the cathedral of the Ordination in the Kremlin was constructed by masons from Pskov who, in their own city, were innovating with several-storeyed balconies and dome-drums upon corbelled arches, in some cases thrown laterally across the nave.

These Moscow cathedrals date from the reign of Ivan III (1462–1505). Pro-

Roger van der Weyden (Rogier de la Pasture),
who with the Van Eycks and others introduced an
epoch of Flemish painting comparable in
significance to the contemporary Italian

Renaissance, depicts this reading figure of St
Barbara with a revolutionary and deeply touching
human intimacy

ABOVE: The Old Sacristy at the church of St Lorenzo by Brunelleschi (1429). Embroidering freely upon Florence's Romanesque heritage and current ideas of classical rebirth, his mathematical and optical genius set the fashion for half a millennium

LEFT: What Brunelleschi did for architecture Donatello's emotional power, and innovating scientific enthusiasm, achieved for sculpture. As terrifying as his *Mary Magdalen*, this Risen Christ on an unfinished bronze pulpit for S. Lorenzo, is still heavy with the disintegration of the tomb

A few years after Donatello's Resurrection,
Piero della Francesca painted his own version,
hallucinatory yet palpable, exploiting with
mathematical rigour the possibilities of light

Leonardo da Vinci's versatile, inquisitive,
romantic inventiveness endows his St Jerome
(*c.* 1483), nobly posed against a dramatic cavernous
background, with a grandiose continuity of interlocking rhythms

Grammatica Noua

ABOVE: Self-portrait of the young
Albrecht Dürer; painter, draughtsman,
engraver, mathematician, engineer,
admirer of Luther and Erasmus, who
combined Renaissance and Gothic
techniques into unprecedented
rhythms mirroring his tormented age
BELOW: The title page of Nicolaus
Perrottus, *Grammatica Nova;* Heinrich
Gran, Hagenau, *c.* 1491. More than
two-thirds of the 30,000 books
printed in Europe before 1500
('incunabula') came from German-
speaking centres, which also introduced printing and publishing into
Italy

ABOVE: Turkish tiles of the sixteenth century. Such superb faience from Iznik, with which the new buildings of Constantinople (Istanbul) were filled, displays a wide range of lush yellows, blues, greens and reds

LEFT: The conqueror of Constantinople: a medallion by Costanzo da Ferrara. Product of many races, tolerant in religion, a Renaissance empire-builder and tourist, Mehmet II (1451–81) was the greatest administrator of his age, with a unitary world state as his dream

ABOVE: An icon by Andrew Rublev, in whose delicate unearthly lines culminate the religious profundity and superlative technique of the diverse Byzantine-inspired Russian schools. It is a sad commentary on the parochiality of art-historical studies that he is not habitually mentioned (in the west) as one of the supreme European masters

RIGHT: The great age of Portuguese exploration is reflected by these knights represented on the St Vincent polyptych of Nuño Gonçalves (*c.* 1470), who became court painter to Afonso V at about the time of Prince Henry the Navigator's death. His work shows Flemish influence

The Selimiye, built for Sultan Selim II at Edirne
(Adrianople) – formerly the Ottoman capital –
was the supreme triumph of Sinan, an ex-Janissary
who interpreted and outdid his Byzantine models
without abandoning Turkish traditions (1569–75)

fiting from the break-up of the Golden Horde (p. 131) so as to cease the pay-ment of tribute, Ivan brought Novgorod, Tver (Kalinin) and Yaroslavl under his control. This spectacular trebling of his lands ensured complete security from the north; and by the end of the century the Russian state of his creation extended as far as the Arctic Ocean. Tsarism took shape, amid an increased regimentation owing debts both to his Mongol predecessors and to the Byzan-tines from whom so many elements of Russian culture had been derived and adapted. For the tsar had inherited from Constantinople not only a Palaeo-logue wife but the sanctity of his position and its accompanying ceremonial, as well as a conscious heirship of the Christian legacy enunciated in the unofficial doctrine that Russia was now the permanent 'Third Rome' (p. 184).

This doctrine carried repudiation of the Roman church. Yet Ivan III was now inescapably linked to western state-systems, with which his centralized régime began to have something in common. His war with Sweden was the first of nine such wars in three centuries; and contacts with the west were multiplied, as he called in not only Italian architects to embellish Moscow, but Italian engineers to undertake its fortification.

Constantinople and the Turks

The Second Rome, Constantinople, was no more. It had fallen to Mehmet II in 1453, after a siege which had reverberated round Europe. In the years pre-ceding its catastrophe, the Byzantine empire, though still producing fine tex-tiles, had been reduced to the control of little more than the city – and the single, semi-independent province of the Morea (p. 134), usually ruled by the younger son of the Paleologue emperor. The Morean capital Mistra, which remained in Greek hands for ten years after the fall of Constantinople, became an interesting cultural centre, and the home of a philosopher who was per-haps the most original of Byzantine thinkers, George Gemistus Plethon (c. 1355–1452). The last important Platonist, Plethon conceived an original dream of a new polytheism that would supersede both Christianity and Islam in a classic Peloponnesian commonwealth. His passion for the ancient glory of Greece exercised influence among the Italians, from whom Mistra's rulers often took their wives; Cardinal Bessarion came to visit him, and Plethon's lectures at Florence (1439) helped to inspire the Platonic Academy in that city (p. 142).

Conversely, there are Florentine features in the gay arcades and built-in ceramic decoration of the Pantanassa church at Mistra. In its frescoes, too, there is a final synthesis of Byzantine and Renaissance attitudes. The *Raising of*

Lazarus (1428), with which the style culminates, fuses religious emotion and realism in strongly modelled shades of yellow, pink, green and purple that anticipate El Greco or Gauguin. Excellent fresco work also continued in other areas momentarily free of Turkish invasion, such as Cyprus and the Morava valley of northern Serbia.

The Turks would have taken Constantinople much earlier had their distant relative Timur, successor to the Mongol inheritance, not beaten Bayazit I at Ankara in 1402. Even so, it was not possible for the Byzantines to stand up for long against efficient Ottoman unity, backed by powerful financial resources and the superior military skill of the Janissaries, the first standing army since Roman times. Mehmet I (1413-21) was a cautious, benevolent man of psychological insight, devoted to learning and poetry; Murat II (1421-51) a Marcus Aurelius who was formidable in war but loved contemplative retirement. During his Sultanate, a school for princes was established at the capital Edirne (Adrianople) – which also has his Muradiye mosque with richly varied early Ottoman tiles – and Mehmet II (1451-81) provided the same facilities for civil servants. These were now of Christian origin, the products of a tribute of children which, augmented by the offspring of renegades and prisoners of war, gave the Turks, for centuries, their best officials.

A warlike, secretive, calculatingly intellectual Renaissance empire-builder and tourist, Mehmet II was not only the conqueror of Constantinople, henceforward to be called Istanbul, but pre-eminent among the administrators of his age, with a unitary world-state as his dream. His portrait appears on Italian medals and a miniature painting by Nakkas Sinan, who had visited Venice. Of mixed blood like all his house, Mehmet showed religious tolerance after the conquest of Constantinople. Its patriarch was granted the civil headship of the empire's Greek inhabitants or 'nation'; and a nominee was selected who had no love for Rome.

Imperial still, Istanbul now displayed not only religious but secular buildings – such as the Çinili Kiosk with its striking new sense of strong colours – and inaugurated a classical age of Turkish literature, including poetry which assimilated Persian and Arabic traditions and adapted these to its own quite distinct linguistic medium. In particular Necati (d. 1509) was an inspired and refined lyricist and elegist, from whom later poets found much to learn.

Mehmet II's quiet and austere successor Bayazit II (1481-1512) disliked war but, as part of a programme of internal reorganization, substantially increased the Turkish fleet, so that by the turn of the century it was in a position to compete with even the strongest enemies from the west.

Spain and Portugal

The historic Moslem conquest of Constantinople was to some extent counter-balanced at the other end of the Mediterranean, twenty-nine years later, by the Christian conquest of the last Islamic state in Spain, the kingdom of Granada (1492). The centuries of hostility that preceded this event had created Spain's military tradition and given its monarchs the finest infantry in Europe. The same wars had also helped to unify its heterogeneous lands; the most important merger was the union between Aragon-Catalonia, ruled by the illiterate but diplomatic Ferdinand II (1479–1516), and Castile under its outstanding ruler, the blunt and tenacious Isabella I (1474–1504).

The combination of these two states rapidly made Spain an important power. It is true that the kingdoms each remained sovereign, with Castile strongly preponderant in strength as in population, though Catalonia was politically and commercially more mature. Nevertheless the joint monarchs regulated their feudal nobilities with lasting success; and ideas of divine right, enforced by the police powers of the Santa Hermandad, reflected the growth of centralized authority.

But the chequered history of the country had created seven distinct groupings of race and religion. Their unification was forcibly attempted by the Grand Inquisition (1480), initially introduced – under royal far more than papal control – to examine the sincerity of Jewish converts, but under the Grand Inquisitor Torquemada (1483–98) extending its activities in order to burn two thousand insufficiently right-minded persons. Feelings ran high against the financially successful Jews; and some 165,000 of them went into exile rather than renounce their religion, thus depriving Spain of much-needed expertise.

Seville Cathedral (1402–) was the largest medieval church in the world – and Gerona (1417), with its bare and powerful aisleless nave, one of the widest of vaulted cathedrals. But more typical of Spanish Late Gothic is an extreme, almost Islamic passion for unbroken surfaces crammed with close-knit two-dimensional ornament, such as the façade of St Paul's at Valladolid (1480's). There was also a special predilection for enormous, elaborately carved altar-screens (*retablos*) of wood. The green-enamelled glass-work of Barcelona achieved especial fame, and the softly glowing, golden or purplish armorial lustre dishes of Valencia (*c.* 1425) were supreme in European ceramics, until Spain's Italian pupils superseded them (p. 144).

Valencia was also the literary capital of *Lemosi*, an adaptation of the Limousin Provençal dialect which was the vehicle of Auziàs March (1397–1459) from Gandia, a tortured, analytical yet sensual poet agonizedly searching for true love and obsessed by death. In the Marques de Santillana (1398–1458), Castile produced a masterly lyricist and generous patron of letters; and his nephew Jorge Manrique (1440–79) was moved by his father's death to write a poem which sums up the accumulated feelings of an age. One of the first and most individual European novels was *La Celestina* (1499), probably the work of a converted Jew, Fernando de Rojas; a lover's tale in which, despite its tragic theme, the fantastic bawd of the book's title is a figure of the raciest actuality.

The very date of Granada's fall and of the anti-Jewish edicts (1492) was also the year when Christopher Columbus, a Genoese in Spanish service, sailed to the Caribbean and landed there. Two journeys later (1498), in the belief that he had reached the Indies, he set foot on the American mainland in Venezuela. The history of Spain was never to be the same again; and indeed the whole horizon of Europe was explosively enlarged. It stood at the beginning of four centuries of world-domination shared among a few of its most powerful states. It stood also at the outset of an equally violent enlargement of its mental horizons: for exploration, the most empirical of all sorts of enquiry, proved a powerful solvent of established ideas.

But already earlier in the century this transitional phase from a medieval and European outlook to a modern and global one had been created and entered by Portugal, the only western kingdom where nationalism was facilitated by homogeneity of language. Prince Henry the Navigator (d. 1460), working at Sagres in the Algarve, was the catalyst who launched the repeated expeditions that extended European influence into the Atlantic and its African coasts. Mastering Moslem navigating skills and employing new three-masted light manoeuvrable *caravels*, the Portuguese established Europe's first permanent African foothold when they occupied Ceuta (1415). Madeira (1420), the Canaries and the Azores were then reached, and at Arguim island, behind Cape Branco on the west coast of Africa, the Portuguese established the first trade and slave centre overseas (1448). The motives for this astonishing activity include the desire to increase the home-country's strength – in the directions which most readily lay open to it – and to provide fresh trade for its rapidly increasing population. Other driving forces were the crusading urge to confine Islam and to convert (as well as to deport) the Africans; and a strong scientific curiosity.

With the aid of the first general treatise on navigation (*c.* 1480), renewed Portuguese expeditions followed, culminating in the rounding of the Cape of Good Hope by Bartholomeu Diaz (1488) and in Vasco da Gama's discovery of the sea-route to India, where he landed at the spice-port of Calicut (1498). Portugal was now the most prosperous nation in Europe, owning a line of forts and factories ten thousand miles long. Some hint of its formidable personalities is apparent in their portraits by Nuño Gonçalves (*c.* 1470), on his polyptych of the Adoration of St Vincent at Lisbon. The Portuguese king Edward (Duarte) I had also possessed a royal chronicler, Fernan Lopes (*c.* 1380–1460), who was outstanding among European historians of the day.

England

England, though like Portugal an Atlantic bastion of Europe, was not yet an exploring country; its defeat in the Hundred Years War (1453) compelled it, instead, to concentrate upon internal economic development. After the turbulent knights and archers flocking back from France had rallied to the Houses of Lancaster (1399–1461) or York (1461–85) in the prolonged civil Wars of the Roses, a resolutely protectionist and mercantilist policy was introduced by Henry VII, founder of the Tudor dynasty (1485–1509). Far the best business-man who has ever been king of England, he employed arbitrary but popular law courts and military commissions to instal the monarchy in the strongest position it has ever occupied. Although the formerly vigorous House of Commons was eclipsed, there was a new alliance of crown and commerce; and the Fellowship of Merchant Adventurers of London (1486) became a bulwark of the cloth trade with Antwerp (p. 147).

William Caxton's printing press (1476) helped to standardize the anarchy of dialects, of which Scots was at present producing the richest literary results. But the principal artistic achievements of England were in music and architecture. Before Burgundy and Flanders took the lead (p. 148), English harmonies began to influence continental composers (*c.* 1400), and John Dunstable (d. 1453) led Gothic music to an impressive and original culmination in the sonorous contrapuntal inventiveness and sensuous advanced harmonies of his motets and secular part songs.

At the same time English architects, especially in the west with its wealth from wool, were now developing to its logical extremes the national, Perpendicular version of the late Gothic style (p.125). In the chapels of Eton, King's College at Cambridge (1446), and St George's at Windsor Castle – all begun in this century, but completed in the next (p. 173) – wall surface has become smaller as window area increases. A geometrical network of vertical lines dominates window tracery and wall panelling alike; construction is simple and sober, yet in these rationalist box-like edifices there is an exuberant proliferation of decorative vaulting.

THE SIXTEENTH CENTURY

Italy

Now began the first of the major struggles for European hegemony, which have lasted until today. The power which dominated the north Italian plain controlled Europe – or could prevent another from doing so. After the French invasions which started in 1494, the European giants of the time, France and the united Hapsburg empire of Germany the Netherlands and Spain, fought with each other for two generations to conquer this area and with it the whole of Italy. Four devastating wars (1521–44) between François I of France and the emperor Charles V reached new depths of butchery and atrocity, since aggression had now become more effective than defence: castles and heavy cavalry gave way to more flexible combined tactics, supported by increasingly effective firearms.

For the small Italian principalities, the superiority of these new attacking weapons meant ruin, which a growing desire for Balance of Power – formulated by the Florentine historian Guicciardini (1483–1540) – could do nothing to avert. The final victors of the wars were the Hapsburgs, who took control of Naples, Milan, Genoa (1528) and Florence (1537), retaining local princes as their puppets. The Treaty of Cateau-Cambrèsis (1559) between new rulers, Philip II of Spain (now separated from Hapsburg central Europe) and Henri II of France (torn by religious dissensions), marked the final renunciation of French claims upon Italian territory. But any such understanding between the two greatest powers was perhaps even more ominous to a small state than their disagreements, since it boded ill for unorthodoxy and independence.

Until the Medicis definitively returned, with Hapsburg help, as lords of Tuscany (1531), Florence was the scene of continuous *coups d'état*, disturbances and invasions. When the Medicis had temporarily revived their power on an earlier occasion (1512–27), Machiavelli (1469–1527) wrote his little pamphlet *The Prince*, which left contemporaries in no doubt concerning the dual morality in current use. For since men are bad and foolish, suggested

Machiavelli, rulers must act as though they are in a jungle; the subordination of political to ethical or religious considerations would be hypocrisy. From his pages there emerges an autocratic ruler new not so much in ruthlessness as in the coldly explicit, dramatic skill with which he is recognized and defined. Subordination to such princes, with special reference to the ruler of Urbino (p. 144), is inculcated by Castiglione's international best-seller *The Courtier* (1528). But the main purpose of the work is to outline the virtues of un-ruffled, mannered elegance, respectful towards fighting and learning alike, which set the pattern of gentlemanly west European conduct for centuries to come.

At Ferrara, Lodovico Ariosto (1474–1533) from nearby Reggio had mod-ernized the ancient epic genre in his *Orlando Furioso* (1503–16), written in a magnificent style compounded of dignity, pathos and a decorative, fantastical nostalgia for old times. Torquato Tasso (1544–95), a southerner from Sor-rento who likewise resided at Ferrara, devotes his richly complex, lyrical epic *Gerusalemme Liberata* (1593) to showing how Renaissance love of life could be linked with the crusading spirit of the Counter-Reformation (p. 165).

A traumatic event of the century's earlier years had been the sack of Rome in 1527 by a mutinous, starving, leaderless German and Spanish horde. This greatly reduced Rome's population (some fifty thousand before), and dis-persed the painters who had been making the city into the world's artistic centre.

Pope Julius II (1503–13), a tough organizer whose aim was temporal in-dependence, had laid the first stone for the new St Peter's (1506) which for more than a century was to be the majestic workshop of Europe's principal artistic innovations. Lavish court life and patronage reached their zenith under the subtle Medici Pope Leo X (1513–21), to whom Rome's reassertion of western cultural leadership was largely due.

Then came the disaster, and after it – as the northern Reformation spread from country to country (p. 179) – the launching by Paul III Farnese of the ascetic Counter-Reformation. When attempts to reconcile Protestantism had failed (1541), the Council of Trent (1545–63) strengthened the pope's theoretical and practical autocracy, bringing it into line with the new stature of secular monarchs in other lands. The papacy could now put an end to campaigns for oligarchic control; and it laid down for the Church a clearly defined, compact, dogmatically exclusive body of doctrine. Summed up in the sainted Pius V (1566–72), this Counter-Reformation was a time of sadness, gravity and contrition. Yet the pictorial and musical arts were enlisted for carefully chosen religious themes, designed for a wider public.

Raphael of Urbino (1483–1520) was a pupil of the quiet and religious Perugino (c. 1445/50–1523) – the principal painter of the Umbrian school – and spent some time in Florence (he was certainly there in 1508) where he assimilated all there was to learn. Raphael then became established in the Vatican, where he and the staff of his novel, rationally organized studio painted a series of rooms (1509–) in a fashion that symbolizes the short-lived High Renaissance. This has generally been regarded as having at last achieved parity with the artistic achievements of the ancients; and it points ahead to every European style until the nineteenth century. Nature is faithfully observed, but transmuted into a pure and classical equipoise of figures disposed with supremely harmonious sanity and freedom. Such radiant power to grasp the ideal through the senses, and to bring this amalgam to life by the masterly elimination of inessentials, is most clearly seen in the melodious golden serenity of his Madonnas who, while enshrining a tender and glamorous conception of Christian faith, nevertheless reflect a confidence in humanity that had not been felt or seen since antique times. Founded on a visual imagination of exceptional range, Raphael's sensitive-ness to his artistic environment was unusually acute. No one has ever responded more whole-heartedly to the influences round about him. And yet each successive new impact brought out something fresh and decisive in himself – leading him first to ever more vivid and sensual portraits, richer colours, and more spacious monumental conceptions, such as are embodied in the transformation of his Virgins from simple naturalism to a different simplicity that is no longer mortal; while the serenely classical poise and balance of the *School of Athens* (1509–11) gives place to the *Transfiguration*. Designed just before his death, this shows a new violent tension that has caused some to call its painter the first of the mannerists (p. 164). For Raphael, despite his conservatively decorous acceptance of current aristo-cratic ideals, was an untiring experimentalist, whose apparently tranquil, timeless balance was only attained, precariously, after agonies of struggle.

Michelangelo Buonarroti was born at Caprese, south-east of Arezzo, in 1475 and died at Rome in 1564. After serving as apprentice to the Florentine painter Domenico Ghirlandaio, he went in 1496 to Rome where, after returning to Florence and making his gigantic statue of David (1501–4), he decorated the ceiling of the Sistine chapel (1508–12). The tomb of Julius II, however, he left unfinished, with his statue of Moses as its principal master-piece. In Florence, between 1516 and 1534, Michelangelo designed the Medici tombs, and thereafter spent the rest of his life in Rome where he painted the Last Judgment of the Sistine Chapel (1536–41) and the frescoes in the Cappella Paolina (1542–9), carved the Florence and Rondanini *Pietàs* (be-

Opposite: Polychrome bust of Charles V
(1516–66) by Conrad Meit

low) (1550–64) – more than half a century later than his rendering of the same theme for St Peter's, of which he also now designed the dome, as well as the Piazza del Campidoglio.

Greatest of all sculptors, painters and draughtsmen, outstanding also as an architect, Michelangelo with his unequalled emotional intensity, his simple yet awesome *terribiltà*, is undeviatingly absorbed with the tragic struggles of man. His finest poem – for he was also a poet of considerable stature – reflects an inward struggle between the Platonic ideal of beauty and a fervent faith in Christ. Twisting the antique sculptural forms to match the spiritual turmoil of his soul and his age and the effervescence of his Tuscan nervous strength, Michelangelo poured himself into the active, moving, male human body as the vessel to contain his ideal. Its first heroic assertion was his David, violently posed yet reflecting in its lucid design the shape of the block of stone from which it was cut away.

But soon Michelangelo moved beyond the confident and humanist clarity of the short-lived High Renaissance, anticipating and embracing in his own single life-span all extremities of the artistic styles which the next century was to produce. Already in his Medici tombs (1520–34) there is a declension from bodily power towards a strangely lethargic emotional exhaustion, reflecting the futility of human endeavour. The sublime fusion of Gothic and classic art in the St Peter's *Pièta* (1498–1501) gives place to the angular, desperate pathos and collapse of the Florence version (1550–5) and finally, at the very end of his life, to the tremendous vision of its Rondanini counterpart (*c.* 1556–64) – almost amorphous and unarticulated, yet unbearably poignant in the hang and turn, the agonized weight, of the lifeless Christ. The criss-cross spiral of the Florence group is replaced by a stark up-and-down movement, with strangely contrasting areas of high finish and rough incompleteness. Forcibly wresting his miracle from the inchoate material in a metaphorical repetition of the primal chaos-shaping act, Michelangelo has almost broken with his medium; as he could break with every convention that other men needed and he did not.

His painting *The Last Judgment*, commissioned for the Sistine Chapel by Clement VII because he thought the end of the world was at hand, is created of mighty dominant curves and discontinuous spaces, which have abandoned Renaissance harmony and beauty in favour of an expressiveness replete with the profoundest human feelings. Above all, in these times of destruction, menace and religious rebellion, the vast picture is a cry of personal pessimistic despondency and spiritual suffering. Perhaps also it reflects the Oratory of Divine Love, a religious society with which at this time Michelangelo sought to console his intolerable tensions.

Then, eventually, these tensions found a bewildered and incoherent expression in his Conversion of St Paul and Crucifixion of St Peter for the Cappella Paolina. In such conflicts between tormenting, foreboding doubts and icy frozen self-discipline, in which Michelangelo's puritanical spirit accentuates its endeavour to purge the weight of guilt, perspectives become ever wider and more abstract, and the importance of the individual dwindles; between the work of art and its viewer there are the signs of a disturbing breach.

The same conflicts gave birth to the illogical architectural frustrations of the Laurentian Library anteroom (1524–59), theoretically justifiable in terms of the building's function, yet anticipating, in their torture of classical themes, the mannerism that was to be developed by his successors (below). Michelangelo turned architecture into individual expression; and he did so again in a very different spirit when these paralysed designs were followed by the dome of St Peter's: an excelsior of ethereally soaring, mass-dominating force to which baroque architects were to return in admiration.[1]

Unsociable, distrustful, unwashed, insensitive to details and to the outer world, tormenting himself and others, Michelangelo was essentially a timid man who suffered, despite his efforts to co-operate, from patrons who – as in the case of Julius II's tomb – changed their minds. Nevertheless his claim to shape his own work himself, as his own intellectual property, was an important step towards obtaining recognition that artists were more important than craftsmen – and that they needed larger fees. The Renaissance notion of genius transcending rules, as a gift of God, was coming to be accepted.

Meanwhile a master of illusionism, Antonio Correggio (1489/94–1534), festooned the domed ceilings of his native Parma with paintings – as if the domes did not exist but were the very heavens into which he transmuted their surfaces. His figures are delicacy itself, yet he was far more than, say, an illustrator of Castiglione's contemporary Courtier. For Correggio was also an exciting innovator and master of light-effects who added to Leonardo's tender voluptuous softness (p. 143) a delicately flowing human warmth. Painter-poet of pagan physical love, with unique insight into femininity, he drew in these anxious years a delicately equivocal line between sacred love and profane.

Carrying further the illusionism which Correggio had explored, and eagerly pursuing Michelangelo's inventive caprices and restless searches, the 'mannerist' artists and architects from the late 1510's onwards infuse new interest and spirituality into the classical Renaissance motifs by livening them with a newly elaborated ideal of elegance, and deliberately contorting them into ambiguous discrepancies of scale, elongations of form, and dissonant figure-groupings which reflect the agonized crises of the times. This is a mod-

[1] The present height and spring of the dome owe something to Giacomo della Porta (1588–90).

ern art, for it lacks any common denominator that would be comprehensible to most of its contemporaries; its esoteric purpose demands a special vision, an act of willed understanding.

Thus the architects of the Uffizi palace at Florence, or of Peruzzi's Palazzo Massimi alle Colonne at Rome, supplement classical horizontality by curves and chiaroscuro and long narrow vistas towards distant pinpoints. They leave out parts of cornices and arches, and remove the loads from beneath columns, which are bunched or rusticated or disconcertingly supported upon brackets. A sophisticated familiarity with the rules is expected of the viewer – so that he can see how they have been turned upside down.

Contemporary painters too, often men of extreme personal eccentricity, introduce difficult intertwined compositions, unresolved conflicts, and oblique deflected angles of vision casting cold harsh lights upon attenuated, sinuous, spectral figures. Under strained classical forms are revived the yearnings and allegories of Gothicism; optimistic Renaissance objectivity is supplanted by individual anxieties and morbid preoccupations with the grave. The Florentine Giovanni Battista Rosso (1494–1540), in his *Deposition from the Cross* at Volterra, conveys the grotesque horror of the scene with a sharply outlined, restless garishness approaching hysteria. Pontormo, born near Empoli (1494–1557), converts the same subject into a pent-up, melancholy fantasy of exquisite azure and violet tints and bizarrely contorted papery forms; and the figures portrayed by his pupil Bronzino of Monticelli (1507–72) achieve startling extremes of alabaster serpentine nudity. Giulio Romano (1492/9–1546), in his *Fall of the Giants* painted from floor to ceiling at Mantua, creates an overwhelming feat of illusionism and *trompe l'oeil*; while Francesco Parmigianino (1503–40) from Parma, who appears to have disliked monumental paintings of this type, advances far beyond his teacher Correggio to ecstatic swooning figures neurotically attenuated, yet compulsive in their subtle contradictions.

The only Italian state to benefit from the French invasion was Venice. After resisting a dangerous coalition in 1508–10, it now rose to greater strength than any other government in the peninsula, proud bastion, in its own eyes, of Republicanism as Florence once had been – with the outstanding secularist university of Padua not far away. A greatly expanded silk and glass production, and the quadrupling of fine woollen output within fifty years, helped Venice to counterbalance Turkish threats and French competition in the Levant.

Such hazards, as well as serious diminutions of Venetian popular freedom, were hidden beneath a lavish, long-lasting, artistic climax, revealing itself above all in the pupils of Giovanni Bellini (p. 145). Outstanding in the generation after him, and an inheritor of his tradition of harmonious colours, is Giorgione (c. 1476/8–1510). Easel-paintings were a feature of this century, and Giorgione seems to have been Venice's first exponent of the small picture in oils, intended for rich and leisured private collectors; their existence enabled him to create an art possessing its own secret laws and devices, with no purpose but sheer private enjoyment and the supreme expression of a precious moment or mood. Introducing a new poetic depth of tone and a vital, colourful sensuousness that was a deliberate change from the austerity or elevation of the Florentines, Giorgione's mysterious evocations of nature such as his *Tempest* reveal magical, hallucinatory landscapes immersed, for all their sensitive musical harmonies, in the spell of a disturbing, thundery atmosphere. There is a hypnotic stillness: something frightening is about to happen.

A Venetian who learned much from Giorgione, though Giovanni Bellini had been his formal teacher, was Titian (c. 1487/90–1576). A provincial from Pieve di Cadore who became a world figure loved by popes and emperors – when Titian dropped a brush, Charles V picked it up – he revolutionized the whole artistic tradition by his lavish textures of pervasive light, extending over the whole surface of the canvas. These effects foreshadow Impressionism; and the Ellesmere Venus, a female nude for its own sake, leads on to Renoir (p. 246). Disregarding time-honoured rules of composition, Titian relied on colour to restore the unities thus broken; and he relied on movement, since he possessed a novel power of depicting moving forms.

In his last pictures the paint seems to vibrate and smoulder and burst into flame, enveloping the beholder by a process of instinctive communication that was something new. Titian's ardent Christianity, shining through his *St Jerome Penitent* and *Crowning of Thorns*, is matched by complete confidence in the physical world – and in Venice. For his fresh and living portraits, with their immediate and apparently effortless grasp of solid and practical life, gave the Venetians (whom they represent) the same heroic assurance of power and position that were conveyed by the cool silvery brilliance and gorgeous painted pageantry of Paolo Veronese (c. 1528–88), the splendours of Sansovino's Library of S. Marco, and the happy, serene palaces, theatres and villas of the surrounding countryside in which Andrea Palladio (1508–80) adapts classical motifs to secular residences and blends landscapes and buildings into a single theatrical setting.

It was also in Venice that mannerist painting (p. 164) reached its height under Jacopo Tintoretto (1518–94). Responding deeply to the religious rebirth but finding that even Titian's forms and colours could not adequately convey his excited feelings, Tintoretto sought instead to rack the emotions by weird flickering lights and broken shadows, rushing diagona fore-shortenings and suctions, oblique perspectives and violently receding vor-tices. His inventiveness dramatizes optical experience to a point where Renaissance symmetry and frontality dissolve in a dynamic balance between nature, caught up in his whirlwinds, and a startling vision of the supernatural.

In architecture, the leading mannerist city was Rome, where Vignola and Della Porta created the façade and chapelled, dome-lit interior of the Gesù that influenced their successors for centuries. In music, supremacy was shared between Rome and Venice. Giovanni da Palestrina (1526–94), appointed to the Vatican by Julius III (1551), wrote masses, motets and religious madrigals which enriched the texture and meaning of Christian ritual and transfigured the older school of pure counterpoint into a more than human serenity of meditation, awe and the soft but colourful elation of strong-willed faith. Meanwhile at Venice the Fleming Willaert had made in the 1530's a new type of secular madrigal, contrapuntally composed for several voices, which is one of the most significant expressions of Renaissance humanism. Willaert's pupil Andrea Gabrieli (c. 1510–86) developed a Titianesque Venetian style of ecstatic passion and mystic fervour, massing multiple choirs with a monumental, dramatic instrumentalization which paved the way to modern orchestras.

Portugal and Spain

The first Portuguese viceroys of India, Almeida (d. 1510) and Albuquerque (d. 1515), were leading advocates of sea-power and land-power respectively. The richest harbour in the world was Lisbon, from which they established a quasi-monopoly of the vast eastern trade in spices.

Under Manuel I (1495–1521), this prosperity is reflected in the spectacular exuberance of his late Gothic ('Manueline') buildings. Architect-sculptors such as the southern Frenchman Diogo Boytac (Boutaca) working at Batalha, and the brothers Francisco and Diogo Arruda, embody imperial experiences of Portugal in an opulent tropical wealth of eastern and maritime motifs, lace-like marine branches and foliage, crustaceans and other creatures of the sea, and billowing rope-lashed sails. In 1572 Luis de Camoẽs glorified the same overseas explosion in his epic Os Lusiadas, exhilarated, liberty-loving, assailing corruption, yet fraught with the nostalgic loneliness of his national temperament. This is the first epic poem to contain that specific note of universalized suffering which speaks to the modern world; and speaks with a grandeur on equal terms with antiquity, proclaiming that the deeds of old have been rivalled, if not surpassed.

Yet before the century was over Portugal, with its annual rate of between 2,000 and 4,000 emigrants to India, had been first overtaken and then absorbed by its Spanish neighbours. Along with his other vast imperial heritages (p. 171), now including not only Germany but the Netherlands which provided his retinue, the young French-speaking Burgundian Charles V (1516–56) became the first foreign king of Spain. Hampered by the communications difficulties of his heterogeneous territories, he struggled ceaselessly to maintain his European empire against the French and their Turkish allies (p. 180) from without, and against Lutherans who helped them from within.

Meanwhile Magellan had circumnavigated the globe for him, and Cortes and Pizarro had conquered Mexico and Peru. Charles V was ruler of half the globe, world-sovereign as none before or since; and yet the immense quantities of American silver pouring in through Seville never stayed inside Spain but flowed on to its creditors in the Netherlands and Italy. Spanish prices rose threefold during the century; the years 1557–8 witnessed the first great inflation of modern times. There were also acute enmities between city and country, between Castile's Atlantic and Aragon's Mediterranean interests, and between both or either of them and their emperor's more European conception of Spanish destiny. Yet the soldiers of Spain, organized in regiments (*tercios*) of arquebusiers and pikemen by the Great Captain Gonzalo de Córdoba, had now replaced the Swiss as best in the world. Victorious over the French after their long Italian struggle (p. 160), they maintained in the Netherlands the earliest standing army in the history of western Europe – though while its officers were Spaniards, most of the soldiers were Italians, Germans and Walloons.

When Charles' son Philip II (1557–98) became king, not indeed of the empire's German territories, but of Spain and subsequently Portugal (1580), he controlled Europe's every overseas colony and foothold from China to Peru. Earlier, as husband of Queen Mary I Tudor he had been king of England too, but his subsequent endeavour to subordinate that country by invasion (p. 174) proved unsuccessful. Philip was a capable, conscientious administrator with a strong sense of justice, but too conservative to remedy his antiquated, unproductive system by anything but unremitting, partly unavailing work and by the elaborate bureaucracy which was his bequest to later Europeans. The country was bankrupt in 1596.

Meanwhile, however, De Las Casas (1474–1566) was saying most of what has been said in later centuries about the evils of immoral colonization; and a world lead was taken in international law under Francisco Vitoria (1480–1546) of Salamanca, a Dominican who presented a broad list of international duties in which he allowed neither emperors nor popes their claim to rule the world. In the religious field – and under Philip one-quarter of the adult population were clerical – the Counter-Reformation's spearpoint was the Jesuit Order established by St Ignatius of Loyola (1491–1556). His *Spiritual Exercises* (1548) were written less to convince men's intellects than to toughen and subdue their whole personalities by soldierly, precise and detailed instructions. Outstanding missionaries and pre-eminent confessors, the Jesuits made it their special task to fight Protestantism, whose rise they checked in many countries. Yet they were the most secular among men of religion, their aim being not contemplation, but action in the life here below; they produced the best schoolmasters in Europe. Though they were formally constituted in Rome (1541), the foundation, spirit and personnel of the Order, as of the Dominican Order before it, were largely due to Spain, which dominated also the Council of Trent (p. 161).

A more secular note appears in the technical mastery and musical ear of Garcilaso de la Vega (1503–36), who adapted Italian versification to his own gravely sober Spanish diction, reflecting the Erasmian restraint of the courts of Charles V and Naples. His poems were carried to the far corners of the earth by Spanish soldiers; among them are verses expressing war-weary, pessimistic horror at the endless strife and the ruin it brought to human lives. In the next generation the forceful, rhetorical poetry of the Sevillian Fernando de Herrera 'el Divino' (1534–94) won great admiration both during and after his lifetime. But even more far-reaching in its success was the first Spanish picaresque novel *Lazarillo de Tormes*, published anonymously in 1534. This long-short story of a poor boy's adventures at Salamanca perfectly displays in its vivid, unsophisticated, underwritten prose the Spanish power of observation, tinged with melancholy.

Lazarillo de Tormes satirized the pride, idealism and romantic chivalry of Spaniards, and even their Church. Yet the literature of Spain, which now dominated Europe, was chiefly stimulated by what was also the guide of Spanish life itself: religion, with all the problems that the national history had imposed upon it. S. Teresa of Avila (1515–82) and her Spanish fellow-mystics, lovingly atoning in the cloister for the sins of the world, explored the deeper levels of human personality. With a passionate faith equalled by her administrative gifts – devoted to reorganizing the Carmelites – S. Teresa in her compulsively flowing *Castillo Interior* (1577) reflects the acutest tension between spirit and senses, and the most exacting spiritual exercises of which the human mind and frame are capable.

Fray Luis de León (1527–91), from Belmonte de Cuenca, was a leading Augustinian at world-famous Salamanca: a restless pugnacious master of

prose and poetry who sought peace in the Christian faith, Platonic humanism, the countryside, and a mystic vision of music. At a less recondite level,
though with a soaring, ecstatic lyricism, St John of the Cross (1542–91)
allegorizes the mystic experience in his *Search of the Beloved (Soul) for the
Lover* (1577–8). St John was a Carmelite, but an opponent of St Teresa's reforms. Like Luis de León, he was no stranger to persecution.

The counterparts of this mysticism in the visual arts are the emotionally
charged, agonizedly gesturing figures of his fellow-Castilian Alonso Berru-
guete (c. 1488–1561), a sculptor of revolutionary power who converted Italian influences into the fervent intensities of Spain.

All these tendencies, perhaps blended with some apprenticeship in
Byzantine anti-naturalism, combine in El Greco (c. 1541–1614) (Domenicos
Theotocopoulos), who was born in Crete, trained in Venice, and spent the
last forty years of his life at Toledo, the Spanish city next in importance to
Madrid and Seville and the centre of the country's ecclesiastical life. El Greco
combined the intellectual realism and visionary mysticism which are the twin
poles of Spanish culture. But his passionate idiosyncrasies outran the taste of
his former admirer, Philip II; for El Greco's style became ever more asy-
metrical and violent, transfiguring the mannerist tendencies of the age in the
phantasmagoric urgency of its fantastically elongated human forms and slant-
ing, diagonal vistas. The acid, icy greens and greys of these vertical rippling
compositions, his cadaverous inward-looking men tormented by the sadness
of life and dazzled by the glory of God, underline an intense preoccupation
with inner meanings: never again, until Picasso (from this same country),
did a major artist depart so far from the substantiality of the visible
world.

The flamboyant late Gothic Plateresque (silversmiths') architecture of
Spain, mingling Gothic, Islamic and Renaissance motifs in closely packed,
intricate tapestry-like patterns, reflected the desire of the world's dominant
nation to display its magnificence. Yet music designed for such churches, such
as the stupendous counterpoint composed by Cristobal Morales (c. 1500–53)
as he restlessly wandered through Spain and Italy, was a model of austere
though lyrical clarity; and in architecture too this same strictly articulated
severity, accompanied by a grandiose interplay of silhouettes and masses, is
the keynote of the Escorial (1563–84), the first architectural composition on a
palatial scale. It was designed by Juan Bautista de Holanda (d. 1567) – an encyclopaedic scholar, probably from Toledo, who had worked with Michelangelo at Rome – and by his pupil Juan de Herrera (1530–97), to give expression to Renaissance and antique ideals and to mirror the unfrivolous
personality of Philip II; and it was located near, though not too near, the

ABOVE: The Episcopal church founded by Neagu Basarab (1512–21) at the ancient Wallachian capital of Curtea de Arges. Byzantine and Moslem themes are blended in a brilliant style in which the helicoidal turrets are particularly effective
RIGHT: The Byzantine domed church and Russian tent-shaped building merge with fantastic originality at St Basil the Blessed in Moscow's Red Square, built by Postnik and Barma (1555–60) to commemorate Ivan the Terrible's conquest of Kazan

LEFT: The lace-work radiation of King's College Chapel's fan vaulting, at Cambridge (1512–18), is the climax of England's original version of late Gothic; it is reminiscent of the linear, curved extravagances of Celtic and Northumbrian illuminations

RIGHT: The final haunting miracle in which Michelangelo almost breaks with his medium: the unfinished Rondanini Pieta (1564), almost amorphous and unarticulated, yet unbearably poignant in the hang and turn, the agonised weight, of the lifeless figure of Jesus

LEFT: Raphael's untiring, keenly observant experiments transmute nature into a melodious serenity. His tenderly conceived Madonnas reflect a greater confidence in humanity than had been seen since classical times

BELOW: Giulio Romano's *Fall of the Giants*, painted from floor to ceiling at Mantua, is a feat of *trompe l'oeil* which typifies an anxious epoch's Mannerist reaction from Renaissance certainties towards restless, tortuous forms and garish conflicts

Titian's ardent religious belief, which shines
through his *Ecce Homo* (Milan), is expressed by
rich harmonies of sensuous texture and pervasive
light and marked by complete confidence in the
physical as well as the spiritual world

LEFT: The Adoration of the Magi by Pieter
Brueghel. His philosophical, occasionally macabre,
comprehension embraced human and inanimate
nature alike. He was the first northerner to paint
easel pictures for private use

ABOVE: Supported (like Luther!) by Frederick
the Wise of Saxony, the elder Cranach turned from
Teutonic forests and religion to his exquisite
Venuses, emblematic of the Renaissance's
rediscovery of nudity and myth

ABOVE LEFT: The founder of Presbyterianism
John Calvin (1509–64), a northern Frenchman who
imposed his logical clarity and discipline upon
Geneva and much of the north: 'the most
determined and consistent man ever to found a
church'

ABOVE RIGHT: The widely travelled Lassus
(1530–94), the outstanding composer of an age in
which Flemish music took the lead, conducting
his choir under the patronage of the Bavarian
court at Munich

LEFT: The Teatro Olimpico at Vicenza, Palladio's
last work (1580) finished by Scamozzi, is a wood
and stucco reconstruction of an ancient theatre
imbued with receding vistas and other Mannerist
optical devices. Palladio's published designs gained
him fame, especially (much later) in England

new federal capital which, owing to its central position and healthy climate, had been arbitrarily located at Madrid.

The Low Countries

Erasmus (c. 1466–1536) from Rotterdam or Gouda, throughout the wide range of countries in which he travelled before settling at Basel (1521), brought into existence the northern literary Renaissance. Gently devout but with a sceptical irony, strong in mind and weak in body, learned and popular, meticulous yet careless, Erasmus has left as the most durable of his numerous religious, educational and literary works the Greek Testament (1516) by which he showed that the Latin Vulgate of the Church was second-hand and, in parts, erroneous.

Erasmus and his creation blend many streams, flowing out of – rather than in opposition to – traditional idea; the classical element is milder than in Italy, and the religious and medieval component stronger. Midway between the scholasticism of Aquinas and the agnosticism of Voltaire, Erasmus reconciled the proud new spread of education – which he wrongly saw as heralding a golden age of concord – with a very human, practical form of late medieval Christian fervour.

Born and brought up in the Netherlands, where national feeling was growing, Charles V (p. 168) was personally popular there. But owing to the vastness of his empire he could give them little attention, delegating viceregal powers to his aunt Margaret of Austria and then to his sister Mary, who were unable to check the rapid spread of Protestantism. Moreover, owing to his numerous wars, he compelled these rich Low Countries to pay heavy taxes; his birthplace Ghent resisted, incurring a crushing fine and the loss of its liberties (1540).

The middle years of the century were the great age of Antwerp which, superseding Bruges and Ghent, not only handled eighty-five per cent of all Netherlands commerce, but increasingly concentrated the trade of every important commercial nation. With its population of 200,000 and two annual fairs, Antwerp possessed the first international stock exchange (1531). This handled many deals and speculations, including those relating to Spanish requirements of German capital, and all the tempting but dangerous business of state-loans. Profiting from the ocean routes which had broken Venice's eastern monopoly, the city also developed and exported a famous brand of porcelain, and multiplied no less than tenfold, in less than two decades, its trading in English cloth. Often, at a single time, 2,500 ships were loading and unloading along the quays of the Scheldt.

Antwerp also became the artistic headquarters of the Low Countries, organizing annual contests of morality and mystery plays, as well as housing three hundred painters and exporting their pictures. Its visitors included Cranach, Dürer and Holbein;[1] and it became the home for some years of Pieter Brueghel (*c.* 1530–69), who was born near Breda in North Brabant, travelled in France and Italy, and spent the last part of his life at Brussels. Brueghel made easel pictures for private use, choosing his own methods, and to some extent his own subjects – painting, in revolutionary fashion, 'as I see it': and what he saw was a human condition which, unlike the wonders of uncorrupted nature, had fallen into disorder. Among the outrages of the times, Brueghel, for all his satire, gusto, and recurrent horrors as unnerving as those of Bosch (p. 150), is as deeply sympathetic with suffering, labouring man as with other facets of the world around him. The most comprehensive and humane of painters, Brueghel increasingly identified himself with peasant life, not because he was a peasant or working for peasants – his Spanish and other clients were men of discriminating taste – but in order to display the unity of man with his surroundings; and to show, like Shakespeare, the foolish tragedy of mankind.

While Josquin des Prés continued to produce superb music (p. 148), another Fleming, Adriaan Willaert (*c.* 1490–1562) of Bruges, not only extended the musical traditions of his own country, but founded and developed the Venetian school of madrigals (p. 167). The climax of Flemish music is reached with Roland de Lassus (1530–94) of Mons, the most versatile and universal composer of this golden age of counterpoint and polyphony. Working at Antwerp and Munich on two thousand compositions – including a new sort of spiritual madrigal (1585) – de Lassus, with the help of the developing harpsichord and clavichord, devoted his exceptional virtuosity of technique to achieving a remarkable blend of Flemish depth, French wit and the secular trends of the Italians.

Antwerp lost its position for ever during the long wars of revolt against the modern centralized absolutism and budgetary planning of Philip II and his regents Margaret of Parma (1559–67) and the Duke of Alva (1567–73), whose Council of Troubles condemned 13,300 people of the Netherlands. The revolt was initiated by the high aristocracy, in defence of old regional ideas, but it developed into an anti-Spanish and anti-clerical movement among gentry and burghers. The outcome was a general rebellion joined by all elements of religious, political or social discontent.

But from now on the destinies of the two parts of the Low Countries

---

[1] Joachim Patinir from Dinant (*c.* 1475-1524), painter of fantastic hallucinatory landscapes, also lived there.

stood apart; for in the ten southern provinces the rebellion failed, whereas the independence of the northern territories was successfully asserted (1576–81) by the Calvinist convert and guerrilla leader William the Silent of Orange-Nassau. Sponsored by William's novel faith in rule through consent, there came into being the first federal government in modern history, delicately balanced on an equilibrium between the Stadholders (successors of the old royal lieutenants), the Council of State, and the States-General of the constituent United Provinces (1579). The independent nationhood achieved by crowded experiences almost overnight, when other countries had taken centuries to reach the same stage, was confirmed by the victories of Maurice of Nassau's small and elastic tactical units (1590–4).

As Spain became insolvent in 1596 (p. 168) and the ruin of its Italian and German bankers followed, Antwerp – weakened by the expulsion of its Calvinists – was superseded by Amsterdam as the focal point of the European money-market. Amsterdam was also the headquarters of fisheries, and of river and Baltic trade; and in the last two years of the century sixty-two Dutch ships set sail for the Indies.

England

The revolt of the Netherlands found support across the Channel, where a leading power was now taking shape in England. Although Henry VIII (1509–47) spent the huge treasure left by his father (p. 159) on a pretentious foreign policy in aid of the European balance of power, his State Secretary Wolsey, who was Britain's first significant foreign minister, saw that he paid for these operations by doubling the country's export of cloth, autocratically managing its parliaments, and absorbing the wealth of the monasteries. These were taken over when, in order to divorce Catherine of Aragon and remarry, the king broke with Rome and created a national (though not in other respects reformist) church.

Henry's advisers equipped his warships with novel rows of cannon which could fire broadsides from portholes; and the fleet which he thus armed was the first built by an English monarch to repel invasion.

The reign of Henry VIII saw the climax of English Late Gothic in John Wastall's fan-vaulting, 'perpendicular' window tracery, stained glass and rood screen at King's College chapel in Cambridge (1512–31). While English learning and art owed Renaissance ideas to visits from Erasmus and Holbein, Tyndale's and Coverdale's translations of the Bible (1525, 1535) moulded English character and stimulated the rising Puritans – believers in Calvin's predestination (p. 179), in the uniquely exclusive authority of the

Scriptures, and in the sanctity of the human conscience regarding that interpretation. The Puritans gained in power when Henry's son Edward VI (1547–53) added to his father's political reformation a doctrinal one. This was sharply reversed when Catholicism was reintroduced by his sister Mary I (1553–8), wife of Philip II of Spain, who thus became king of England also. But Mary's policy was abandoned for a middle-of-the-road Anglican Protestantism by Elizabeth I (1558–1603), a superb operator of intuitive diplomacy, prevarication, calculated inaction and espionage.

Henry VIII had united and welded Wales. Elizabeth achieved a reconciliation with Scotland, and put down Ireland; while the English north, discredited by revolts, became finally subordinated to the south, and in particular to London with its rapid growth in population and foreign commerce. Fortunes were made in farming and the wool trade; the men who mattered in the '50's and '60's were monetary and commercial experts such as Sir Thomas Gresham who represented the English monarch at Antwerp and, on Antwerp's model, founded the Royal Exchange (1556). While price-rises created a city proletariat, new industries and inventions were capitalized by joint-stock trading enterprises granted state-monopolies – the Muscovy Company in 1555, followed by the Eastland (Baltic), Levant and East India Companies (1600).

Although Elizabeth was not interested in colonizing the new world, England's Merchant Adventurers (p. 159) were in the forefront of the maritime movement. Hostilities with Spain, including the spectacular rebuff of the Armada (1588) which excluded Philip from northern waters, were the first important naval war, the first in which England owed its survival to its navy, and the first modern coalition of smaller powers against a leading aggressor: England's friendship with the Dutch (1581), to which Philip objected, having been discovered as a first principle of British foreign policy. The rule of the seas was passing from the Mediterranean to northern states. But as the queen accordingly sought to tighten her central controls, including mobilization of manpower, she paid an increasing price in strained relations with the country gentlemen who formed the backbone of her parliament.

In the 1560's and '70's began a reconstruction and modernization of England, in which were erected gigantic, boastful, picturesquely mullioned mansions of overwhelming vitality such as Burghley House, Hardwick (1590–7) and Longleat, many of them with stucco-ceilinged long galleries and an unfamiliar profusion of household furnishings. Such huge residences, many of them 'Prodigy Houses' built to accommodate Queen Elizabeth I on her travels, represent an extraordinary composite flowering of Italian, Flemish and native elements.

In music, the most imposing figure of the English Renaissance is the Catholic William Byrd (1543–1623), organist of Lincoln Cathedral and then the Chapel Royal, and joint monopolist of music-printing from the Queen. His sombre, noble and human style, including original descriptive elements, gave the traditional forms of his masses and motets a new strength and poetry, which contributed largely to the English creation of harpsichord music taking full advantage of the keyboard.

Meanwhile English literature received its second foundation in the colourful, rhythmical verse of Spenser (c. 1552–99), whose *Faerie Queene* unites with the earthy speech of the countryside a mixture of Platonic ideals, knightly courtesy, the Italian neo-classical pastoral, and Calvinistic Puritanism. A novel balance is being forged, in fitting style and language, between tradition and the demonstrative individualism of the times. The prolific, semi-delinquent Robert Greene (1558–92) was perhaps the earliest English prose-writer and dramatist to seek a living from the entertainment of a broad reading public. But it is above all Christopher Marlowe (1564–93), obsessed in his *Dr Faustus* by the tragedy of humanism and in *Tamburlaine* by ruthless brute force, whose colourful images and daring extravagances gave English tragedy its true metre and diction, capable of enshrining Renaissance aspirations towards knowledge and beauty and power.

Further developments of extraordinary scope and profusion became gradually apparent in the early plays of William Shakespeare (1564–1616). *Love's Labour Lost* (1594–5) displays a new supple coherence, skilfulness and wit; and the historical plays leading to *Henry IV* (Parts I and II) and *Henry V* represent a first climax of his achievement, appealing to Protestant middle-class nationalism in their studies of the ideal nature and divine ordination of kingship, the politics of naked power, the ethics of treason, and the heaven-sent deliverance provided by the Tudors. Falstaff is a supreme comic character whose delineation evolves sharply from play to play; the coldness of his final casting-off prepares us for the tragic masterpieces that were to follow (p. 204).

Germany and Its Southern and Eastern Neighbours

In 1500 there were about twenty million Low and High Germans – the latter including two millions in the five Hapsburg duchies – compared with sixteen, eleven and seven million in France, Poland and Spain respectively. These Germans, forming the nucleus of the hugely extended Holy Roman Empire and its dependencies, were coming back into the main stream of western Europe. The rakish, intelligent knight errant Maximilian I (d. 1519) endowed the empire with an Imperial Court of Justice, an improved Diet, and a Privy

Council. But far more vital developments were the awakening of north European humanism under Erasmus (p. 171), and the beginnings of the Reformation against which thereafter, as also against French and Turks, Charles V fought throughout his long reign.

After the abdication of Charles (1555–8), Spain and the Netherlands went to Philip II (p. 168), but German territories to Ferdinand I (d. 1564) – ruler of Hungary and Bohemia since 1526 – whose anti-Turkish preoccupation made him the first Hapsburg with a specifically Austrian point of view. Maximilian II (1564–76), the only member of his family to have some personal understanding of Protestantism, was over-optimistic about the chances of a religious settlement; and the literary and artistic Renaissance established by Rudolph II (1576–1612) at his capital in Prague was accompanied, in this most economically advanced imperial state of Bohemia, by simultaneous, combustible movements both of Protestant (Hussite as well as Lutheran) inspiration and of Catholic revival: a combination which, in the following century, was to lead to the far-reaching Thirty Years War (p. 207). Meanwhile however the Turkish invasions, during which most of Hungary succumbed but Vienna was saved (1529), had helped to create a new heroic conception of the Holy Roman Empire as a multinational, universal Christian bulwark, centred upon Germany and Austria.

Yet the emperors were limited not only by princes and cities, but by their dependence on tycoons such as Jakob Fugger's sons Ulrich, Georg and Jakob, who multiplied their mining production (p. 151) fivefold, and financed Charles V's claim to the imperial throne. Farming Spanish trade and dominating Antwerp, the Fuggers agreed with the Hochstetters how to divide the spoils between the Netherlands and Italy, and operated a merger with the mine-owning Thurzos in Hungary, where the Welsers – investors in the East Indies and Venezuela – also had shares. But the unadaptability of local rulers and landowners, in changing economic conditions, brought about revolts, first among the declining Imperial Knights and then (far more dangerously) among peasants in Baden (1522–5) and other areas. Nationalism, too, was on the rise among the Germans: Johannes Nauclerus now described them as the original European race (*Urvolk*) which had, throughout the Middle Ages, invigorated all the others.

German in many of its fertilizing processes and in a certain national romantic flavour, yet also international to an extent that has never subsequently been recaptured, was the Renaissance humanism which now spread north of the Alps. The transition is apparent in the paintings of Lucas Cranach (1472–1553) from Franconia, Luther's friend and fellow-protégé of the Elector Frederick the Wise at Wittenberg (p. 178). In middle age, supposedly under the influence of Giorgione's Venus, Cranach turned from mysterious deer-haunted thickets and tragic violent passions to a series of *chic* female nudes, successful expressions of eroticism which reflect the cultured self-confidence of German courts despite all surrounding tensions.

Two of Cranach's contemporaries from Bavaria, where reformers and Jesuits were at war, brought far more formidable idiosyncrasies to bear upon their fusions of medieval and Renaissance attitudes. The hysterical, hallucinatory vision of Matthias Grünewald (*c.* 1455/70–1528) from Würzburg depicts an unspeakable greenish lacerated image of Christ. Such a mystical, revivalist attack on the emotions in the cause of sacred truth echoes the choking dramas and fervent faiths and wild despairs of an earlier age. Yet Grünewald was also a supporter of the new Reformation, and his individual interpretation of Italian researches in perspective and space (p. 139) looks forward both to baroque and to modern expressionism. Affected by Grünewald was another Danubian introvert, Albrecht Altdorfer (*c.* 1480–1538) from Regensburg, a spontaneous lyrical illustrator of religious passion and pathos and eccentric secular delights, whose penetrating eye, attracted to the novel idea of a landscape without happenings, creates magic from the twisting, menacing, organic forest growths of Germany.

Nuremberg in the same region – the first imperial city to adhere to the Reformation – housed the Meistersingers, lyric poets of artisan and trading background including the prolific Lutheran song-writer and dramatist Hans Sachs (1494–1576). An outstanding centre of goldsmiths, medallists and bronze-casters (such as the Vischers), Nuremberg was also the home and birthplace of the painter, draughtsman, engraver, mathematician and engineer Albrecht Dürer (1471–1528). Dürer was a devotee of medieval art; yet his first visit to Italy (1494) inspired him to a unique supplementation and enrichment of Germany's northern heritage by his theoretical and practical knowledge of the Renaissance. Although displaying this knowledge in forms acceptable to contemporary German aristocratic society, he was an admirer of Luther (as well as Erasmus) who superimposed his own expression of the desperate, tormented insecurity of the age. His experience of Christ's suffering is conveyed with a vividness as apocalyptic as if this had been a frightful daily renewed occurrence in his own life. Dürer also elevated drawing into a separate art in its own right. The sweeping lines of his designs, imitating nature with unprecedented concentration, dexterously gather up all the Gothic details, romantically ideal and earthily real alike, and transmute them into a grave and compassionate unity of original rhythms and imaginative relationships. Portrait painting continued to attain fresh achievements in the next generation, when Hans Holbein of Augsburg

(1497/8–1543), a Lutheran working in Basel and London, created the most penetrating portrayals of the human face that northern countries have ever produced.

In addition to discontents among knights and peasants, and the stirrings of national sentiment and unprecedented intellectual forces, Germany was full of religious unrest, especially in urban areas where unfamiliar capitalist techniques were breaking up old traditions. An answer was universally wanted to the typical medieval question: how can I be saved? – and this answer was not provided by the Renaissance, which had little to offer the miserable poor. Mystical movements, quietists and clandestine radical Anabaptists provided responses regarded as anti-social: witch-burnings, in terror of sorcery, were at their height.

The moral reform of society was a general aspiration – and Germany was full of princes who saw religious war as a chance to increase their powers at the emperor's expense. Others were equally ready to make trouble, not against the emperors, but against the Italian pope and his ecclesiastical representatives, who were criticized for their fund-raising institutions such as Indulgences – rewards for good works which by contrast inspired the Reformers to argue for justification by faith alone.

Martin Luther (1483–1546), a Thuringian (partly Slav) born at Eisleben, posted on the door of the castle church at Wittenberg his protest against the Indulgences by which the Archbishop of Mainz hoped to repay a debt to the Fuggers (p. 176). Protected by Frederick the Wise, greatest among powerful Saxony's Electors (1486–1525), Luther reiterated that he had not started a new organization but was seeking to re-establish original Christianity. However, his refusal to retract criticisms of the pope's divine right brought him excommunication (1521) – as well as the disapproval of Erasmus (p. 171), whose adverse comments on existing institutions did not go to the length of conceiving western Christendom as divisible.

Nevertheless, Luther judged the prospects of peasant revolts to be bad, and stirred up the state rulers against them. In spite of break-away movements from Luther, the religious Peace of Nuremberg (1532) ensured the German survival of his doctrines, backed now by a league of princes; and after Luther's death the Peace of Augsburg (1555) accepted and finalized the split between Catholics and Protestants according to the faith of each local ruler, into whose power the churches within their territories were thus finally placed.

The jovial, brave, coarse Luther was at one and the same time a self-confident religious prophet, a destructive individualist, and a scholarly, musically minded theologian of original methods and views. His unrivalled conviction and power of appeal secured his acceptance by millions as their champion. He led them to his Bible, which sprang direct from the Hebrew and Greek and is written in epoch-making language upon which modern German rests. Turning the mystical tradition into an ethical challenge, Luther believed that the essence of religion lies in spiritual experience – not in will-power or good works or juridical systems, but in the divine grace by which alone these could be justified.

Huldreich Zwingli (1484–1531), born at Wildhaus (St Gall) but invited by local notables to the free city of Zürich, broke with Luther in 1529, and broke also more thoroughly than he did with the medieval church, insisting that the Scriptures alone possessed authority. Zwingli was a pupil of Erasmus in his sense of practical Christian charity. Accepting the support of the secular power, he conceived a noble vision of a scriptural commonwealth.

France

The strength, on the other hand, of John Calvin (1509–64) from Noyon in Picardy lay rather in the French lawyer's logical clarity with which, in excellent and influential French prose, he presented his theology; and in the gifts for disciplinary organization imposed on Geneva. After expulsion from France, this became his adoptive city, and the acknowledged stronghold of the Calvinist version of Protestantism.

The most determined and consistent man ever to found a church, Calvin taught in his *Institutes* (1536) a doctrine of predestination owing much to Augustine, to Luther and to the contemporary Strasburg theologian Martin Bucer (1491–1551). According to this belief, all man's promptings lead him to evil, but God has foreordained some to eternal life, others to eternal damnation. Calvinists confronted this appeal to the individual soul by seeking to demonstrate, through the manner of their lives, that they were the elect – founders and leaders of a new kind of church for a new kind of world, of which the advancing political and capitalistic conditions did not escape their notice.

Calvinism spread in France, where it eventually extended to about ten per cent of the population – especially urban artisans, professional men and bankrupt 'hedge squires' west of the Rhone and south of the Loire.

The first half of the sixteenth century, before this happened, had witnessed a French Renaissance; the second half was an age of political, economic and cultural set-backs owing to religious wars.

The architect of the French Renaissance had been François I (1515–47), residing at Paris which, with its population of 400,000, was the largest city in western Europe. Despite the relative failure of his imperialist policy in Italy (p. 160), François was a magnificent autocrat; and for all his growing dependence upon financial aid from the increasingly prosperous middle class, he allowed parliamentarianism no voice. Political theory was now thoroughly secularized in France, with sovereignty vested absolutely and perpetually in the monarch, who was soon surrounded by the secretaries of state, governors and 'nobility of the robe' characteristic of *ancien régime* society. His emancipation from traditional ideas was displayed by an anti-Hapsburg alliance not only with the Lutheran princes of Germany but with the Turks (1536) – which made havoc of the crusading identification of Christendom with Europe, but gained the French long-lasting dominance in the Levant (p. 182).

Henri II (1547–59) abandoned France's Italian claims, but strengthened its position along the north-eastern border. However, disastrous splits between parties, grouped round the over-powerful families of Bourbon, Guise and Montmorency, took the shape of internal warfare against the Calvinists (Huguenots). These, with their crowning horror, the massacre of some hundreds of Protestants at Paris on St Bartholomew's Eve (1572), cost the regency of Catherine de Médicis (1560–89) loss of influence in the old and new worlds alike.

Henri IV of Navarre (1589–1610), the first Bourbon monarch and one of the few really effective occupants of the French throne, was also one of the earliest rulers in western Europe to propose that competing religious ideas should be tolerated: his Edict of Nantes (1598) to this effect secured acceptance, at the price of his own abandonment of Protestantism (1593). Since this new unity of France was supported by the popes, these could no longer wholeheartedly back the Hapsburgs in the onslaught against Spanish supremacy which the French were soon to renew.

Although a peacemaker rather than a reformer, Henri IV founded the four oldest infantry regiments in France. He also employed as his adviser the economic expert Sully, who particularly sought to enrich France by the encouragement of agriculture. French linen was now competing with Dutch in the Spanish market, the pottery of Bernard Palissey (1510–89) was the best in Europe, French silk-weaving challenged the Italian monopoly, and Marseille had supplanted the commerce of Genoa, Livorno and Venice with Islamic North Africa and the Levant.

French invaders returning from Italy brought artistic ideas back with them; and in 1530 Rosso (p. 165) came north to lead the stuccoists and mural painters decorating François I's gallery at the royal palace of Fontainebleau. Rosso's mannerism, the first international style since Gothic, was especially sympathetic to the French courtiers because of its *chic* devotion to the eternal feminine which formed the reverse side of the more grotesque and garish elements of mannerism.

In a wing of the Chateau of Blois (1515–25) François I had built a spiral staircase, and included north Italian motifs which showed that architectural innovations were on their way. He also began to reconstruct the Chateau at Chambord with its fairytale silhouette of dormers, chimneys and cupolas. As the architectural centre of the country moved from Loire to Seine, Pierre Lescot (*c.* 1510–78) designed his façade of the Louvre (1546), French as well as classical in its alert polish and ostentatious rhetoric; while the vanished Tuileries, the Anet gateway (1552) and Chenonceaux's bridge-castle (1557) reflected a specific French Renaissance under the brilliant guidance of Philibert de l'Orme.

France now led western Europe in scholarship, especially at the Collège de France (1530) where the new learning could not be stifled. But the most exuberant reaction against medieval formalism was provided by the *Pantagruel* and *Gargantua* (1533–5) of François Rabelais. There are Gothic gargoyles in this inexhaustible flow of mirth, but there is also all the Renaissance appetite for erudition as well as enjoyment – spiced with a Gallic defiance of proprieties, and with Rabelais' own experienced understanding of human nature.

A conscious refinement on the other hand, and a sly terse elegance, are apparent in the poetry and translated psalms of Clément Marot (1496–1544). But above all it was a movement opposed to Marot, the Pléiade, which brought French verse closer to humanistic trends, guided by the poet of love and nature Pierre de Ronsard (1524/5–85) and by Joachim Du Bellay (1522–60), first master of the sonnet. The Pléiade's aim was to apply to the vernacular the principles of criticism they had learnt from the classics; but its exponents also created the modern personal lyric, which provided a medium for the romantics of the future (p. 241).

The capital innovations of Michel de Montaigne (1533–92) were the Essay, and the full portrait of himself which his compositions thus entitled present (1572–88). The most human of thinkers, a desultory personal writer of witty imaginative irony, Montaigne launched himself upon self-descriptions and analyses of the sub-conscious which prefigure the psychological preoccupations of the twentieth century, and the autobiographic concerns of Proust (p. 276).

These generations also witnessed the climax of the elegant *chanson* (1530–60), one of the outstanding French contributions to music; and Italian ballet, now evolving into a recognized art-form, became established at Catherine de Médicis' court, where its starting point is often located at the wedding festivities of Margaret of Lorraine (1581).

Turkey and Rumania

Turkey's alliance with France in 1536 (p. 180) made it the arbiter of Europe, able to trim the balance of power; and its strength was now at its height.

Following upon Selim I the Grim (1512–20), who had concentrated on the eastern front and gained vast conquests in Asia and Africa, Suleiman I the Lawgiver or the Magnificent (1520–66) not only caused widespread Christian distress by his capture of Rhodes (1522), but broke explosively out of the historic Orthodox domain towards the west. His superbly disciplined and equipped field force of 150,000 regulars (including 20,000 Janissaries) and 50,000 irregulars overwhelmed Hungary (1526), and narrowly failed to take Vienna (1529). Meanwhile the newly created first-class Turkish sea-power welded together the north African Islamic states and put to flight imperial, papal and Venetian forces off Preveza in Epirus (1538).

The Ottoman empire, extending from the Danube to the Persian gulf and from the Sea of Azov to Aden, was the strongest in the world; its fifty million inhabitants nearly equalled the population of the four other largest European nations combined (p. 175). The Sultan Suleiman, poet and art-patron as well as statesman and soldier, was the most enlightened and tolerant European monarch of his day. He delegated a good deal of his enormous powers, not so much to his Council (Divan) as to his friends, whom he selected with wisdom and from many parts of the empire; himself, like all Sultans, of mixed racial origins, he was markedly cosmopolitan in his choice of advisers. His leading admiral Barbaros Hayrettin was the son of a Macedonian and a Mitylenian; Albanians were to the fore; and his witty and influential wife Hurrem (Roxelana) was the daughter of a Ukrainian priest, and favoured Serbs and Montenegrins. Indeed, Serbo-Croat was the lingua franca of the Sultan's household, and the most eminent of his Grand Viziers, Sokollu Mehmet, came from Herzegovina. Subsequent Sultans relied on the advice of Joseph Nasi, a Jewish refugee from Portugal who was made duke of Naxos, and of the Sultan Safiye (Baffo) who was from Venice.

Under Suleiman, although appointments could now be bought and although unconverted Christians and Jews experienced financial disabilities, the reasonable living conditions which generally prevailed had not yet been lowered by petty oppression; excellent roads were constructed, and the national income doubled during the reign. Against the Hapsburg enemy, defeated at Djerba (1559) but victorious with its Italian allies at Lepanto (1571), Murat III (1574–95) was prepared to renew the concessions ('capitulations') already granted to France and Venice, and to sign similar agreements with Tuscany (1578) and England (1580).

The Turkish poet Fuzuli (d. 1556), who struck a classic balance between emotional and intellectual processes, never came to Europe, remaining in Iraq. But the outstanding architect Sinan, though again from Asia (Kayseri), left his unique stamp upon the cities of Ottoman Europe. His imaginative blend between eastern designs – recalling the Prophet's courtyard at Medina – and the cupolas and half-cupolas of S. Sophia (p. 50) contributed to the conception of the imperial mosques, with the orderly complexity of their domes and minarets and majestically centralized or polygonal interiors – vast restful auditoriums avoiding the Christian conceptions of crisis or gradation or mystery. Sinan's Şehzade (1548), with its four semi-domes, is a triumph of audacious logic. His Suleimaniye (1550–7), a solemn sanctuary with four gigantic piers, stalactite niches and pendentives, and jewelled translucent windows, is reminiscent of Cairo; while the Sokollu Mehmet (1571) and Rustem Pasha mosques are unequalled for the lushly realistic yellow, blue, pistachio-green and coral-red tulip-patterned tiles of Iznik faience, which were an integral part of their design and reappear in pavilions of Murat III (1574–95) in the Topkapi Palace. But Sinan's masterpiece is his mosque at the former Ottoman capital of Edirne (Adrianople). This Selimiye (named after Selim II, 1566–74) is a simple two-storeyed hall; its low-hanging dome displays an admirable clarity of internal line, in keeping with the harmonious exterior which achieves a new perfect relationship between its buttressed semi-domes and four tapering, fluted minarets. This was also the age of the outstanding Ottoman miniature painters, Osman and Haydar Reis (Nigari) (b. 1494), portraitist of Suleiman and Barbaros Hayrettin.

Before the thrones of the princes (Hospodars) of Moldavia and Wallachia became readily purchasable from the Turkish government by Greek or Rumanian nobles, independent or semi-independent native rulers continued at times to exercise authority. In Moldavia Stephen the Great's bastard son Peter Rares (1527–46) played off the German and Turkish emperors against one another. His reign witnessed the climax of Moldavian painting, a vibrant art with Serbian, Bulgarian, Russian and Italian analogies which revived and extended an earlier Byzantine tradition by providing a unique range of painted church exteriors, protected from the weather by overhanging roofs. A favourite artistic theme is the Virgin Mary's intervention against the Turkish besiegers of Constantinople.

In Wallachia the slightly earlier Voivode Neagu Basarab (1512–21) had built a cathedral at his capital Târgovişte. But it is his small episcopal church at Curtea de Arges which achieves the most distinguished originality in the fusion of Byzantine and Moslem themes displayed by its blue, green and gold external decoration, and above all by the two elegant spiral, helicoidal turrets in front of the building's principal cupola.

At the end of the century a powerful Wallachian Hospodar emerged in Michael the Brave of Craiova (1593–1601) who, ruling at Bucharest and Jassy as vassal of the Hapsburgs instead of the Turks, united Wallachia, Moldavia and Transylvania – detached from the Polish-Lithuanian empire of Stephen Bathory (p. 185) – into an imposing but ephemeral 'Greater Dacia'.

Russia, Poland and Scandinavia

Believing that nemesis had fallen upon Constantinople because some of its emperors had tried to barter Orthodoxy for western help (p. 133), the monk Philotheus of Pskov wrote to the Muscovite Grand Prince Basil III (1510): 'Two Romes have fallen, but the third stands, and a fourth there shall not be.' This lofty claim for Moscow was given reality by Ivan IV the Terrible (1533–84); for a new epoch in European history was inaugurated when, after the first conflicts between Turks (Tatars) and Russians on the Volga and the Don, the Muscovites occupied Kazan (1552) and Astrakhan (1556) and gained possession of the Volga basin.

The first ruler of Moscow to be crowned Tsar of All the Russias (1547), Ivan IV established with the help of his secret police (oprichnina) an effective autocracy founded upon serfdom, and upon a four-way defence system relying on western Europe for its fire-arms, mercenaries and technicians. Russia now had an outlet to the White Sea, and an important trade with Persia. Its territory was also enormously extended into north-eastern Russia and Siberia, where the family of the Stroganovs from Novgorod lent support to the conquering soldier of fortune Yermak (d. 1585), and employed many thousands of workers in their private commercial empire based upon the exploitation of metals, sulphur, salt, timber and furs. The Stroganov headquarters at Solvychegodsk (Perm) became a place of churches and palaces and of a harsh, exotically brilliant school of icon-painters.

At Moscow, now a city of 200,000 inhabitants, the outstanding art was architecture. Perfecting a system of wooden prefabrication far in advance of western Europe, the Russians translated its effects into harder media. Ivan III's and Basil III's five-domed Kremlin cathedral of St Michael the Archangel was rebuilt (1505–9) in brick by the Milanese Alevisio Novi, with stone Renaissance cornices and capitals. Ivan IV's superbly bizarre church of St Basil the Blessed proliferates with prodigally lavish colours, textile-like patternings and swollen twisted forms, surmounted by a mass of round or octagonal cupolas which – recalling simultaneously the Byzantine dome and the Russian tent-shaped turret – rise in spiky bulbous curves above the pitched roofs of eleven chapels.

But this was also the 'golden century' of the neighbouring kingdom of Poland, not yet weakened by the difficulty of controlling an active and intelligent, but violent and change-resisting, nobility. Poles and Russians between them colonized the Ukraine with Cossacks – runaway serfs, adventurers and outcasts who organized themselves into two democratic military republics on the Dnieper and the Don. Meanwhile Sigismund I (1506–48) organized Polish border defences with new efficiency and, married to a Sforza, deepened the western-looking Latin trend of Polish culture. In his reign, too, Copernicus (1473–1543), born at Torun (Thorn) and trained at Cracow, Bologna and Padua, concluded that the earth is spherical and revolves round the sun; so that God's creation of man is less significant than had appeared.

For nearly two centuries Lithuania, of which the official language was now White Russian (Byelorussian), had with occasional lapses been attached to Poland in a personal union; and in 1569, after a war between Lithuania and Russia, a joint Polish–Lithuanian parliament at Lublin sought a more organic unification under Sigismund II Augustus (1548–72). Stephen Bathory (1576–86) combined these territories with his native Transylvania and achieved further unsurpassed foreign and domestic successes, including the annexation of Danzig (Gdansk) and the recovery of nearly all Livonia from Ivan the Terrible of Russia (p. 184).

Although the Jesuits, arriving in 1565, reasserted Catholicism with the support of Stephen Bathory, the Compact of Warsaw (1573) granted an exceptional degree of religious tolerance; and the literary Renaissance was led not only by Catholics but by the Protestants whose faith had temporarily made progress here. The 'father of Polish literature' and its bridge between Middle Ages and Renaissance was Mikolaj Rej of Naglowice (1505–68), writer of rich, vigorous Calvinist sermons and of *The Life of an Honest Man* (1568). The leading literary personality, however, was the brilliant Catholic poet and humanist Jan Kochanowski (1530–84), a lyrical, heroical and satiric writer who had studied in Padua and met Ronsard in Paris; his *Treny* (Laments) (1580) are of classic European stature.

The kings still resided in the Wawel castle at Cracow, one of the grandest Renaissance cities north of the Alps. But in 1596 Sigismund III (1587–1632) moved the capital to Warsaw, an important centre of Polish-Lithuanian trade where the first permanent bridge had been built across the Vistula (1568). However, the election of this king, son of John III of Sweden, saw the rise of grave problems for Poland, since the Hapsburgs had designs upon its areas of Cossack colonization in the Ukraine (p. 185); while Sigismund aspired to the Swedish throne. Gustavus I Vasa (1523–60) had created a unified Swedish nation with a state-controlled Lutheran church and the first national army of modern times (1544), further developed by his son Eric XIV. After the latter's dethronement for insanity and replacement by John III (1568–92), the Polish king Sigismund III's Catholicism lost him the Swedish crown to Charles IX (1594–1611), although the latter too experienced religious difficulties since his Calvinist ideas conflicted with the increasingly evangelical tendencies of the clergy and people.

Gustavus I of Sweden cherished a life-long distrust for the Danes, whose power was based on the control, unwelcome to the Swedes, of both shores of the Baltic-North Sea passage. Under Christian III (1534–59), the Danish state church became Lutheran (1536), and the royal power increased at the expense of business men and peasantry. From c. 1560 the landowners of Denmark, too, profited increasingly from their agricultural enterprises, especially the export of corn via Amsterdam to southern Europe. Fine buildings were constructed in Dutch style by Christian IV (1588–1648); and, in a period of active intellectual advance the astronomer Tycho Brahe (1546–1601), established by the king on Hven Island, was the real founder of the techniques and precision standards of his science.

7

THE SEVENTEENTH CENTURY

Italy

Although individual popes might pursue independent policies – their might increased, rather than diminished, by wars between the Catholic great powers (p. 196) – Italy was now for the most part subordinate to Spain. The secular state which retained the greatest measure of independence was Venice. Resisting the papacy, it counteracted international setbacks, such as its loss of Crete to the Turks (1645–68), by diplomatic activity organized through an ambassadorial network which was a model for all Europe. The export production of Venetian glass at Murano and elsewhere, improved by a new jewel-cutting technique, helped Venice to compensate for its super-session by the new Ocean routes.

Venice was also the scene of a musical revolution. Earlier types of enter-tainment, combining a few songs with recitative and a short ballet, were welded into the new major art-form of opera. Its pioneer was Claudio Monteverdi (1567–1643). Born at Cremona, he produced the very individual *Orfeo* at Mantua (1607), and then moved to Venice where he entertained an unprecedentedly large public with his voluptuous, melodious masterpiece *L'Incoronazione di Poppea* (1642); its ardent drama was accentuated by every baroque device that the stage machinery of the new opera-house could provide. With his grandiose colourful imagination, Monteverdi reversed the relation of language and music, intensifying the significance of his libretto by inexhaustibly inventive, freely flowing harmonies.

Instrumental music began to vie with polyphonic compositions in popu-larity; and the increasing numbers of instrumentalists were on the way to becoming a modern orchestra. In this new world, solo instruments and voices could convey ineffable agonies, passions and delights. And this was also the age of massive double Venetian choirs, introducing every refinement of dramatic light and shade into their resplendently festive accompanied masses and oratorios.

To house such triumphs, Baldassare Longhena gave the domed, octagonal church of S. Maria della Salute (1632) its incomparable setting; the nobility of Venetian architecture is enriched by a complex vigour and elegance, compounded of ingenious and subtle effects analogous to those of the contemporary theatre.

Anticipations of the operatic movement had been devised in Tuscany, where Giulio Caccini, a Roman in the Grand Duke's service, collaborated with Peri to produce an early version of *Euridice* (1600), and suggested in his *Nuove Musiche* (1602) how the new daring expressiveness could be reflected in madrigals and canzonets.

Although losing its civic liberties to the Grand Ducal government, Florence, where these developments took place, was well ruled and enriched by Ferdinand I (1587–1609) – pro-French unlike his pro-Spanish predecessors – but degenerated under the rulers who followed. Yet under them the Pisan Galileo Galilei (1564–1642), who transformed physics into an exact science and dethroned immutability, made Florence his home.

At Rome the century opened with a sensation caused by the pictures of Michelangelo Caravaggio (1573–1610). Variously known as inventor of modern painting, prototype of rejected artists, pioneer of social realism, and rebel against the counter-Reformation, Caravaggio does not seem to owe much to his Brescian origin and Milanese training; distinctive characteristics animate his religious naturalism, in which starkly realistic contemporary personalities and environments, often from the semi-delinquent underworld, strike the viewer with an intense visionary vividness. The poignant glare of these scenes is infused with a humble, classless sympathy towards human fallibility; and the painter, though never short of clients, has some awareness of an isolating destiny. Wanted by the police for murder, he was still at Rome when Clement VIII Aldobrandini (1592–1605) and his Cardinals were reviving their capital's position as centre of European culture.

The determined and erudite Urban VIII (1623–44), though his Inquisition disciplined Galileo, was one of a series of popes who employed architects and sculptors of innovating genius. Pre-eminent in both these arts was Gianlorenzo Bernini (1598–1680), a dramatic Neapolitan whose bronze canopy in St Peter's (1624–33), with its four gigantic twisted columns, is the first baroque masterpiece and herald of a new age in which the frustrations of mannerism (p. 164) are past. Classical horizontality is remembered and still employed for un-classical purposes, yet now no longer to stimulate tortured perversities but as the life-giving framework for an unrestrained luxuriance of movement and curve corresponding with the grandiose rituals of the day. The *Cathedra* in the apse of St Peter's, commissioned by Alexander

VII (1655–67), is the culmination of the new artistic epoch in which Bernini merges building and statuary into a single complex fabric to be grasped by the spectator in an instant; a mighty emotional and spiritual rush of energy with nothing defined or explained.

His group of St Teresa and the angel, in the church of S. Maria della Vittoria (1645–52), is a most individual unification of painting and stucco with architecture, some of which is real and some fictitiously added. Marble spectators, in an open box at the side of the chapel, enhance the technique of daring illusion up to the very effacement of the frontier between the artist's space and our own. In the figure of St Teresa appears all Bernini's virtuoso mastery of sensuous drapery folds and supple rippling human flesh. At the moment of her penetration by the divine shaft, her abandoned limbs and features tell of a transfiguration which her own writings had described (p. 169) but which only Bernini could translate into marble: 'the fleeting and agonizing fusion of living matter with Divine Spirit – the final end of carnal love, but also the almost deathlike ecstasy of spiritual union.'[1]

Francesco Borromini (1599–1667), an introspective celibate mason from Bissone in Lombardy, conveyed a highly personal version of the same revolutionary *brio* in the ovals and rotatory spirals of his Roman churches. Jettisoning classical logic and rules – which survive only in superficial decoration – he manipulates the solid masonry, like clay, into a voluptuously swaying and undulating, rhythmically intertwined counterpoint – a jubilant rhetoric both cerebral and deeply pious. The triumphal upsurge of S. Carlo alle Quattro Fontane (1638–42; façade 1665–7) shows how even in a diminutive interior and façade the fullest play can still be given to massive dynamic tensions; and these erupt with equal force in the soaring rotatory momentum and fantasy of star-shaped S. Ivo, the rocking swerves and perspectives of S. Agnese. By such shock-treatment the supernatural traditions of Gothic, sensuous Renaissance realism, and the intensity of the counter-Reformation, are gathered up and transformed into something excitingly original, giving voice to the age's unquenchable aspirations towards infinity, and grasping together every extreme of human feeling between yearning mysticism and rationalist intoxication with human power. Baroque was the manifestation of a society which expressed itself by display. Yet for all its adaptation to the theatrical grandeur of mighty patrons, this art struck wide-spreading popular roots. When the counter-Reformation sought to mobilize culture to spread its ideals among the masses (p. 161), mannerism possessed far too limited an appeal; but Bernini and Borromini had found the answer. Painters, too, could readily adapt these ideas; and Roman baroque continued in a riot of

[1] V. L. Tapié.

illusionistic ceilings indissolubly linked with the structures which they adorn. Deriving certain of their ingenious lighting effects from Correggio (p. 164), Pietro Cortona (1596–1669) and many another depicted great sweeping, curving masses of figures; in their midst appears a momentary glimpse of the luminous fleecy clouds of Paradise itself.

These Roman ideas of architecture, and the ornamentation which was now inseparable from it, were adapted and modified to suit the circumstances of other parts of Italy. Naples, the third largest city in Europe, had a baroque of its own under Cosimo Fanzago (1591–1678), who covered the surfaces of his vertically soaring arcades and vaults with a kaleidoscopic wealth of colourful incrustations. In Apulia, under the influences of its Neapolitan rulers' Spanish culture, the soft honey-coloured façades of Lecce's churches (1644–1720) were likewise embossed by Francesco Zimbalo, Giuseppe Cino and others with an extravagant plethora of spiritedly writhing harmonies.

In the north, there was a more direct development of Roman ideas at Turin. When Italian Piedmont superseded French Savoy, Turin replaced Chambèry as the capital of this still rather remote border court and its increasingly rich, display-loving aristocracy. Under Emmanuel I (1580–1630) and II (1637–75) the continuation of this Italianizing tendency caused the city to be adorned with palatial operatic edifices by Guarino Guarini from Modena (1624–83). A versatile, widely travelled architect who excelled even Borromini in breath-taking experimentation, Guarini lavished his taste for geometry upon unprecedented groupings of shapes and volumes; square designs concealed beneath convex surfaces, and many another eye-catching mathematical device, are combined to produce *tours de force* such as the ribbed, light-filled cupola of S. Lorenzo (1667–87).

And then, from Turin, baroque made its way across the Alps (p. 222). Counter-Reformation severity was ended; the Jesuits were less stringent, and popular saints of the day were figures of mercy and charity such as St Francis of Sales (p. 198), who had been the adviser to Charles Emmanuel I of Savoy (1580–1630).

Spain

Although the century's first two generations felt no loss of martial glory, the reign of Philip III (1598–1621) suffered not only from plagues but from the expulsion of hundreds of thousands of former Moslems (Moriscos), whose departure stripped many regions of their skilled workmen and labourers (1609–14). The trebled expenses of the court – arbiter of European fashion until superseded by Louis XIV – were defrayed by debasements of the coinage which contributed further to the economic decline of Castile.

Moreover, doctrines of royal absolutism made no provision for the royal incompetence of Philip III and IV (1621–65); and Olivares, upon whom this absolutism depended, proved unable to knit the peninsula's divergent territories together into a European nation-state.

The secession of the northern Netherlands (p. 173) became an accomplished fact, and disastrous fighting with France continued during and after the Thirty Years' War (1635–59). Not only did Portugal break away (1640), moving towards an era of enrichment by Brazilian gold, but the revolt of Catalonia made it virtually a French province for sixteen years; and the battle of Rocroi (1643) showed that the Spanish infantry had lost its invincibility to France. In the reign of the cretinous Charles II (1665–1700), Spain sank to political and financial collapse, and artistic barrenness.

Under Philip III had been written the only Spanish work to attain a fully international reputation, *Don Quixote* (1605–15) by Cervantes (1547–1616). This masterpiece of the ridiculous and the sublime, of the fantastic and drily matter-of-fact, sums up in its ironical psychology of the conscious and unconscious mind the two basic opposing forces of Spanish life. Sancho Panza is the simple yet shrewd exploited under-dog; but the knightly Don Quixote protests against the limitations of worldly existence. He lives nobly in mental illusions, and to us, as to him, their disappearance brings deprivation. The tragedy of the romantic in an unromantic age was the fate of the chivalrous Spanish nobles in a century when chivalry was no longer enough.

For all the royal failures, Philip IV was unprecedently munificent in his support of drama and painting. His theatre *Buen Retiro* (1633) was the most splendidly equipped in Europe, and his patronage extended to a group of leading writers from La Montaña, cradle of Castile. The play was the most typical literary form of the age, and Lope de Vega (1562–1635) its most prolific exponent. His vividly staged, eventful three-act works incorporated a spacious optimism. Respectful of church and crown, he is also attentive to human personality, mirrored in sharp and rapid delineations of character. *Fuenteovejuna* is the unforgettable depiction of a community's corporate ways.

Pedro Calderón (1600–81), writing for the court rather than the public, was less creative than Lope de Vega, but had a keener sense of the stage; *La Vida es Sueño* (1635) is a rich poetical depiction of human life, viewed with an exhilarating philosophical intensity. Francisco de Quevedo (1580–1645) came from the same Castilian region as Vega and Calderón, but lived at Valladolid. His feverishly gloomy, satirical *Sueños* dwell with prodigious imagination upon macabre visions of hell and of death. Cynically contemptuous of all values, he made many enemies. One of them was Luis de Góngora from Cordova (1561–1627), the most notable wit of his time, whose complex and stylized poetic romances (*Soledades*) caused a controversial sensation by the contorted yet luminous imagery of their nostalgic Arcadian world. At Toledo a different note of contemporary extremism was struck by Tirso de Molina (*c.* 1584–1648), whose dynamic Don Juan, *El Burlador de Sevilla,* is the superman breaking loose from the social framework into self-destruction.

The current tension between spirit and senses is given a religious context in precocious examples of Spanish baroque architecture such as the Cartuja façade at Jerez de la Frontera (1667), contrasting classic lines with encrusted ornamentation; and above all in the anguished wood-carvings through which sculptors of Andalusia and Valladolid gave three-dimensional expression to their passionate ascetic ideal. While the Sevillian J. M. Montañés (1568–1649) is comparatively calm and classical, Gregorio Hernández of Valladolid, supreme exponent of naturalism, plunges his polychrome figures and groups into the last extremities of sacred grief and passion.

Painting developed along parallel lines. José Ribera (1591–1652), who left Valencia to become court painter at Naples, depicted saints emaciated by fasting and bloodstained in martyrdom. Francesco de Zurbarán (1598–1664), from near Badajoz, settled at Seville and filled the monasteries of southern Spain with studies of white-robed monks, who by more sober and subtly emotional means expound and exemplify their duty to bridge the gulf between this world and the life of God.

Born at Seville of Portuguese origin, Diego Velasquez (1559–1660), court painter to his admirer Philip IV, broadened and disciplined his Andalusian visual imagination by two years in Italy. At a time of profound national disillusionment when Spanish imperial splendour no longer seemed so meaningful, his steady imperturbable eye, uniquely perceptive of human character, saw the subjects of his portraiture in a detached, disinterested light. The uncompromising objective truthfulness of tone with which these grave, aloof men and women are painted, alone or in strangely significant rhythmical groupings such as the *Meniñas* (1656), stems from a spectroscopically precise and minute power of scrutiny, and from a new inventive command of light, depth and space. This unmatched amalgam of gifts is translated, by a rich *impasto* technique, into a sweeping impressionism which profoundly intensifies the moment and the visible world.

The Low Countries

Peter Paul Rubens (1577–1640) travelled widely preceding his appointment as hugely famous and successful court painter to the Governors of the

Spanish Netherlands. This territory, now reduced approximately to Belgium, contained an extravagant aristocracy unaffected by surrounding economic decline. The Jesuit clergy also fulfilled a powerful role – though Cornelius Jansen Bishop of Ypres (d. 1638) struck a different note, later to re-emerge in the Jansenism of Port Royal (p. 198), by his Puritanical preoccupation with predestination and sin.

Rubens' religious feeling, though devout, was too full-blooded for such sympathies. Born at Siegen in Westphalia of an Antwerp family, he studied with Flemish painters. Then, during eight years spent mainly in the household of Vincenzo Gonzaga duke of Mantua (1600–8), he embarked upon the most energetic and fruitful career in the history of art – the last outstanding master to found his work upon the human figure. His unprecedented concern with the texture of flesh and skin created a new, happy type of female nude, as Michelangelo had created a new type of male. The luxuriant massive forms of Rubens' women give an exciting lustre to his exuberant compositions of furiously curving spirals and diagonals crammed with the movement which he had the gift of impetuously seizing upon the wing. The organization of these buoyant canvases, as well as of his warmly glittering portraits and of crucifixions that poignantly contrast life and death, combine a very full and admiring knowledge of the Venetians – as well as of the whole range of earlier Italian Renaissance painting – with the enthusiastic northern belief that painters must paint the world around them.

The breakaway of the northern Netherlands from Spain (p. 173), during a struggle that was the testing ground of modern weapons, had been practically recognized in 1609 and was confirmed at the end of the Thirty Years' War (1648). In this young nation, the first federal experiment of the modern world, one-third of the population was dominated by a strict Calvinist church which, with the support of Maurice of Nassau (d. 1628), executed his fellow-liberator Oldenbarnevelt (1547–1619) for adhering to a moderate and anti-Calvinist (Arminian) wing of the reformation; rather as a later leader De Witt (1625–72) succumbed to the popular demand for an Orange restoration, while his own oligarchical party favoured instead the rights of individual states.

The treaty of 1648 confirmed the primacy of Holland over other provinces; and within Holland the Bank (1609), Bourse (1611) and splendid town hall (1648–55) of Amsterdam symbolized its supreme position as the world's largest business centre and money market, with unequalled stocks of precious metals and capacity to provide loans. Only two million strong, poised between sandbanks and sea, the Dutch were also the fishermen, shipbuilders, carriers and hygienic pioneers of Europe. They had become a major imperial power; and so they clashed with their former British allies early in the century, and then again in a series of mid-century naval wars.

The study *On the Laws of War and Peace* (1634-4), by Hugo Grotius (1583-1645) from Delft, embodies a new rational, tolerant principle insisting that states should negotiate, and that those who wage aggressive war should be punished. Grotius, convicted with Oldenbarnevelt and forced into exile, wrote his book for Louis XIII of France. To the same court, at Colbert's invitation, went Christiaan Huygens of the Hague (1629-95), inventor of the pendulum clock (1656) which helped to give Europeans the sense of time that is one of their distinguishing characteristics. Conversely, Holland itself attracted many refugees from elsewhere. Amsterdam became the home of Vondel (1587-1679) – born at Cologne of parents exiled from Antwerp – a poet and dramatist of sparkling, majestic felicities, whose masterpiece *Lucifer* (1654) on the Fall of the Angels is a literary counterpart of Rubens' majestic flamboyance.

Spinoza (1632-77), a Portuguese Jew born at Amsterdam, accepted Descartes' mechanistic rationalism (p. 198) but not his ambiguous dualism, which he replaced by a unity of God and man, a fusion of mind and matter, in a Universe pantheistic in name but seeming to many atheistic in its application of human mathematical reason to divine affairs. An early theoretician of liberty, Spinoza invested the state with the functions, not of a curb (like Hobbes, p. 205), but of a necessary instrument for human and individual self-fulfilment.

In Holland, the dominant element in the community was its increasingly wealthy national yet cosmopolitan bourgeoisie. This section of the community, including its regents or town councillors, wanted art, but they wanted it to convey the recognizable experiences of familiar every-day reality: intimate scenes to give pleasure, in contrast with Flemish exuberance and Spanish solemnity – without religious or moral overtones. Never before had there been so many private commissions for intimate easel-paintings of the most varied social nuances, and never before had these been mass-produced for a home market, with painters responding to dealers' requests.

Rembrandt van Ryn (1606-69), after working at his birthplace Leyden, lived from 1631/2 onwards in Amsterdam. His enormous output, comprising three hundred surviving etchings, 1,500-2,000 drawings and 650 paintings, is as universal in scope as its quality is peerless. In male and female portraiture Rembrandt somehow achieves the quintessence of human beings and penetrates deeply into their souls, conveying through his brush an almost more than human knowledge of unsuspected inner feelings and idiosyncrasies. Sixty of his works in this field are the most remarkable series of self-portraits

Opposite: The Opening of the Fifth Seal by El Greco

that have ever been painted; it seemed to him that awareness of others could only be achieved by awareness of himself.

Conveying not only psychology and emotion but the excitement of observed facts – a rare motive for finished paintings before the impressionists – Rembrandt transfigures day-to-day visual experiences by the lofty imaginative perception of his all-powerful eye, and by a startling mastery of light which perhaps owed something, initially, to Caravaggio (p. 188) or his followers. Light washes over forms with a magic, ethereal glow. This endows the prevailing brownness of cloth, flesh, stone or atmosphere with a palpable texture that extracts from the most humble or limited subject a hitherto unimaginable wealth of meaning.

The religious masterpieces painted at several times of his life, such as the *Supper at Emmaus* (1648) which is the most human of all visions of Christ, disclose a personal, scriptural piety that is closer to Comenius' primitivism (p. 209) or Spinoza's natural 'soul that lives in all things' than to the churches of the day. But Rembrandt's whole artistic career was a step-by-step process of liberation through an enormous diversity of experiences, leading towards the last and mightiest and least understood phase in which his imperative quest for inner truth bursts out of the temporal world into sudden dematerialized revelations. He was the first major artist who painted for himself, the first with the independence and urge to pursue his own impulse in subject, treatment and interpretation. The society in which he lived permitted and encouraged this subjectivity, up to a point. But his public was confounded, and unsympathetic, when the *Parade of the Civic Guard* (*Night Watch*) (1642) transformed a typical group scene of Dutch citizenry into a luminous drama weighted with many mysteries.

Rembrandt was not much of a businessman; and his bankruptcy followed (1656). This disaster, occurring at a time when the Thirty Years' War was over and Dutch artistic patronage was actually at its height, proclaimed Rembrandt to be a victim of the modern competitive business of art; although his final manner of broader touch, more solid impasto and deeper knowledge had reached perfection, he had become too far removed from his clients for financial success or retrieval to be possible.

Another such victim was Frans Hals (1580/5-1666), a Fleming who apparently came from Antwerp to the United Provinces, and adapted Utrecht's Italianate school of portraiture to his own more novel ends. His special contribution, achieved by sparkling, impressionist brushwork, was a naturalistic, vivacious gift for catching the fleeting expressions of every human personality, in his or her most transient appearances and moods. Haarlem, where Frans Hals worked, was also the first centre of still life themes (*c.* 1630) and of realist landscape, enriched by Jacob van Ruisdael (*c.* 1629–92) with a gravely luminous, cloud-swept grandeur revealing him as Constable's pre-eminent predecessor in strength of natural vision (p. 250).

Meanwhile at Delft, world centre for blue and white porcelain, Jan Vermeer (1632–75) with his uncannily accurate sense of tone, and mastery of colour values, showed how the illumination of a shuttered, lofty Dutch room could be controlled and studied. There is a curious aloof detachment in the balance and suspense of these hushed, calm, golden scenes, with their occasional distortions perhaps linked with the artist's use of the *camera obscura*. In out-of-doors pictures, such as his unequalled *View of Delft*, Vermeer anticipates nineteenth-century pointillism (p. 245) by his employment of little pearls of paint. His solid precise construction of space arranges its planes to show each foot of depth; and Vermeer places every shape in juxtaposition to its neighbour with an instinctive grasp of interval and proportion that defies all criticism or amendment.

France

As this climactic age of French warfare, power and culture got under way, Sully wrote a Grand Design of European unity implying his country's supremacy over the Hapsburg empire (1638). During the eighteen years in which his diamond-hard, ruthless, subtle mind controlled European history, Richelieu (1585–1642) set out to check that empire; so that the policy of France, in the last long period of the Thirty Years' War (1635–48), was aligned not with its fellow-Catholics but against them.

Despite internal unrest and a sharp decline in real wages, Richelieu laid down the laws of French development for a century and a half to come. Its basis was an exalted royal authority; a churchman, he constructed the system by which the church was to be superseded. Then the Italian Jules Mazarin (1602–61), in addition to drawing the frontier-lines of modern Europe, employed his cynical, courtier elasticity and cunning in order to complete Richelieu's office of midwife to the modern state-system. To the half-Spanish Louis XIV (1643–1715), himself an industrious and farsighted though bellicose administrator, Mazarin handed down the first of Europe's national organizations which was in a position to overshadow the politics of the whole continent. The French government operated arbitrarily and in secret. Princes and other privileged groups, after their abortive 'Fronde' revolts (1648), were tamed, and an experienced royal bureaucracy stood at the helm. It was largely drawn from the upper middle class – a significant creation of the century – which feared the nobles and accordingly supported the Crown. 'You', said Godeau, Bishop of Vence, to the young Louis XIV, 'are the visible and authentic image of God'; and what pleased the sovereign had the force of law. This absolutism incarnate in his person was reflected in solemn ceremonial and etiquette adapted from Spain and Austria to the unprecedented grandeurs of Versailles, where Louis established his court; for, after the Fronde, he distrusted the narrow death-trap streets of his rapidly growing capital, Europe's largest city with its more than half a million inhabitants.

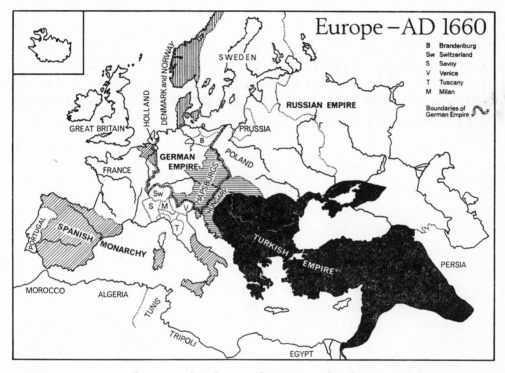

From Dieppe and Rouen for the north, Nantes for the west Indies, Lorient for the Indies, Bordeaux for the Americas and Marseille for the Levant, the French exported linen, cotton, woollen cloth and ever more luxury goods, including especially silk. Louis' indefatigable adviser Jean Baptiste Colbert (1619–83) was the agent of the new protectionist, mercantilist state capitalism, creating hundreds of industries, roads and canals and, despite famines and market shrinkages, controlling all financial life in the interests of the central power.

Funds were provided not only for planned magnificence but for an enormously ambitious foreign policy. France's navy was now the third in Europe; its merchant marine, too, and its colonial empire of Canada and Louisiana, were correspondingly expanded. Louvois transformed a poorly organized army into the best in Europe, numbering nearly half a million troops (1690) equipped from huge armament factories at Nancy. Close-knit and compact, France fought from interior lines, and at its own choice. But its large-scale aggressions caused other European countries to display towards one another an unusual degree of solidarity in self-defence. Before the end of the century, they had united against France in three wars; the last of these (1688–97) was successfully inspired by William III of England (p. 203), owing to renewed Bourbon intolerance towards the Protestants (1685): which cost France 200,000 valuable emigrants and many friends.

The revival of French Catholicism had received humanizing inspiration from St Francis of Sales (1567–1662), who conveys a cultivated, glowing picture of the happy holy life as a means of making the miseries of the world supportable; while St Vincent de Paul (1576–1660) revitalized the priesthood and gave great stimulus to philanthropic activities. Severer, and closer to the Reformation though not within its ranks, was the Abbé de St Cyran (1581–1643), confessor of Port Royal. His stress upon original sin and human degeneracy was derived from Cornelius Jansen (p. 193), who also inspired Blaise Pascal (1623–62). A uniquely comprehensive and penetrating Christian moralist who was also the poetically minded creator of modern French prose, Pascal contested the rising tide of rationalism by his eloquent conviction that truth – which alone may rescue mankind from its miseries – can primarily be known by the heart; so that the only guarantee of human progress is faith.

'I cannot pardon Descartes', said Pascal. For it was René Descartes (1596–1650) who, leaving France for Holland, organized the method of free enquiry that placed man and human reason at the centre of a controlled universe in which all natural phenomena could be reduced to orderly, intelligible, mechanical laws. Descartes invented co-ordinate and analytical geometry as part of his attempt to geometrize all nature. Omnipotent God is demonstrable from our own existence; yet doubt, the appeal of autonomy against authority, seemed to him a legitimate attitude of the human mind. The *Discours de la Méthode* (1637) is written, as no such work had been for over a millennium, for amateur, average readers; and it was in the French language. Thus communicating and diffusing the new intellectual climate which was to become an essential element in the European mind, Descartes reveals a new concern for man himself and his interests, and a unique lucidity and breadth of mental horizon prophetic of modern experimental physics and metaphysics alike.

The supreme dramatists of France, like its architects, rejected baroque for a flexible precision and clarity which, none the less, display a full (though always disciplined) awareness of what can be achieved by the magical baroque interplay of reality and illusion. The bitter violent grandiose men, whose revengeful ambition and ancestral pride are depicted by Pierre Corneille (1606–84), stem from his own age of strife and turbulent excess, and from his personal commitment to a stance that is heroic and sublime. The tragicomedy *Le Cid* (1637), and his tragedies of the following years, caused a sensation with their clanging, sonorous intellectual splendour and their moral clashes between terrible alternatives. The victory goes to *la gloire*; and to human endurance.

Jean Racine (1639–99), in his *Andromaque* (1667) and *Phèdre* (1677), exhibits a new, Elysian faultlessness of polished diction and imagery. His close-knit plots, for all their immediacy, belong to a world out of this world, a timeless classicism whose Greek and Roman robes facilitate the intensest concentration, rejecting every inessential, upon the passionate inner life and white-hot emotional crisis. A Jansenist who quarrelled with Port Royal (p. 198), Racine's exquisite tenderness and subtlety transfigure Corneille's couplets into the introspectively conscience-laden language of the confessional. But above all his concern is with hitherto unexplored psychological depths – particularly the depths of women's sexuality, immersed in the madness of love.

The Parisian Molière (1622–73) wrote comedies of character, of which *Le Misanthrope* (1666) is among the best and *Le Bourgeois Gentilhomme* (1670) the most famous; the Italian-born J.-B. Lully (1632–87), founder of French opera and master of dramatic recitatives, composed music for its accompaniment. Prompted less by ethics than by rational commonsense, the easy topical dialogue of Molière is brought alive by a wonderful creative impulse which utilizes social deformation and excess as a framework for huge ranges of human absurdity – which he views with a moderate, stoical optimism.

Another who commented on men's weaknesses and foibles was Jean de la Fontaine (1621–95). His poetic *Fables* (1668–94) are disillusioned; but amusedly or sadly, with sophisticated charity and tolerance that make the best of things. La Fontaine combines classically familiar themes, ideally adapted to their purpose, with an insight into human nature that is as subtly penetrating as his blend of lyricism and prudence. Human nature, again, was the subject of La Rochefoucauld (1613–80), whose fastidious *Maximes* (1665) interpreted selfishness as the mainspring of human activities. His work is the product of literary *salons*, and so, in their different way, are the spontaneous, vivacious yet reflective letters of his friend Madame Marie de Sévigné (1626–96). Meanwhile Nicolas Boileau (1636–74), in the forcible smoothly elegant prose of his *Art Poétique* (1674), summed up French literary classicism as a code. But its supremacy was challenged, for in the next decade began the 'Quarrel of Ancients and Moderns' (1687).

Widespread diffusion of information, foreshadowed by Descartes, was carried further by the *Pluralité des Mondes* (1686) of Fontenelle (1657–1757), the first important popularizer of scientific knowledge. Then Pierre Bayle (1647–1706), a Calvinist's son, set the tone for the free-thinking century to come with his *Dictionnaire Histoire et Critique* (1697), a vast survey imbued with a moderate scientific scepticism which favoured 'natural equity' and the attitude that governments depend on circumstances. Next François Fénélon (1651–1715) wrote for his pupil the duke of Burgundy a best-selling mythological and political novel *Télémaque* (1699), ostensibly an account of the adventures of Ulysses' son, but in reality a criticism of selfish monarchy. Accepting paternalist government, yet anticipating Rousseau in his fervent advocacy of international peace and natural Utopia, Fénélon marks the transition between old ideas and new.

Yet most of the important literary output of the century had belonged to the earlier times and patronage of Richelieu and Mazarin; and it was in their epoch too, and with the patronage of their civil servants, merchants and financiers, that Nicolas Poussin (1593/4–1665) painted his principal works. Born at Les Andelys in Normandy, he spent most of his life in Rome, where he depicted, initially, religious themes that develop from cooler versions of baroque into superb combinations of classical form and Venetian colour. Then come dramatic groupings, owing more to Raphael and antiquity; and finally, heroic scenes of moral and psychological drama, reflecting, amid the still and spacious nostalgic evening light of those bygone times, the long and passionate meditations concerning nature and destiny that occupied his advancing years.

These groups of figures, as well as the landscapes that form their background, are often composed on a strictly geometrical basis. But this framework of vertical, horizontal and diagonal balances is subordinated to the intensest imaginative power: mathematical order is suffused by an undercurrent of extreme, expectant intensity. Subduing nature to his single-minded, intuitive truthfulness of purpose, Poussin has been variously interpreted as a stern traditionalist and the most fervent of revolutionaries. But above all he is a poetic composer, analogous in his measured rhythms and moral potencies to his country's tragic dramatists whose logical terse economy of expression he shares.

Claude Lorrain (1600–82), born near Nancy, likewise worked at Rome and in the Campagna. His idealized, unlocalized mythical scenes are bathed in the tranquil, mysterious, all-transforming silvery illumination of rising or setting sun. Seeing nature as a series of atmospheric gradations of tone, which he depicted in colours drawn from no formula but from his own lyrical observation, Claude opened the eyes of the world to landscape. There had been important landscapists before him, but for at least a century after his death many Europeans, and particularly English lovers of the picturesque, continued to judge scenery through his eyes.

In these paintings the human form is small and far away. Very different is the sinister intimacy established by the three brothers Le Nain from Laon, whose chilly, naturalistic human dramas contrast sharply with Claude's magical antique world, or with the moral elevation of Poussin, or with the magnificence of the court from which the Le Nains' upper middle class clients were alien and excluded.

This same class, critically intellectual and capable of abstract reasoning, was not without influence upon the development of French architecture. The baroque style, with its assertion of freedom, was too anarchic for the secular designers of seventeenth-century France and the patrons, bourgeois and kings alike, for whom they worked. Increasingly concerned, as time went on, to impress and uplift by absolute, ordered values rather than to amuse or attract, French architects were inclined to take the view that curves were not good taste.

Accordingly, the spirit of the age was expressed by the precise reticent feeling for clarity, space and form of François Mansart (1598–1666), whose colonnaded Chateau de Maisons (Maisons Lafitte) (1642–50) reflected a cool monumental classicism analogous to Descartes and to Nicolas Poussin. Such works prefigure the richer and grander effects of Louis XIV's second period. Vaux le Vicomte (1657–61) near Melun, by Louis Le Vau (1612–70), is conceived as a unity of building and scenery. Its grandiose orders and halls harmonize with the unlimited vistas and water-mirrors of the landscape designs by which Le Notre (1613–1700) conquered a new dimension. Le Vau also finished, after 1661, the three remaining sides of the Louvre (p. 181) – a decisive building at several stages of European art – and he, or one of his fellow-architects Lebrun (p. 202) and Claude Perrault (1613–88), added its east front's twenty-eight slim and coupled podium-based columns, whose magnitude contrasts piquantly with the almost domestic-looking segment-headed windows.

But work on the Louvre was suspended because the monarch lost interest in everything but Versailles. In a new architectural epoch of gigantic disciplined unities, extraordinary lavishness was devoted to the conversion of this palace into a permanent residence for the entire court and government.

Earlier cores (1623, 1661–5) had already been equipped by Le Notre with unsurpassed geometric gardens, conveying the suggestion that the king's rule over men is paralleled by a like domination of nature. But then the palace was reconstructed by François Mansart's quick-minded, versatile nephew Jules Hardouin-Mansart (1646–1708) into an overwhelming composition of masses grouped into distinct wings, baroque in their immensity rather than their decoration. Now, too, was built the Hall of Mirrors (1678–84), with its white marble panels, green marble Corinthian pilasters, gilt-bronze capitals and painted barrel-vault.

The decoration of this Hall was guided by Charles Lebrun (1619–90). Securing advancement through Colbert, of whose Royal Academy of Painting and Sculpture he assumed the directorship, Lebrun virtually became dictator of the arts (1662) and remained in this unparalleled control of artistic taste for two decades or more, until his linear classicism was eclipsed by more sensual styles. Even the stage management of *divertissements*, ballets, triumphs and funerals did not escape the attention of Lebrun, who did much to give French art its characteristic homogeneity; his principal convictions were that nobility and dignity must be primary aims, and that the different arts are inseparable components of a single social unity. Himself a student of Poussin and Cortona (p. 190) and a draughtsman of easy flaring line, he employed at the Gobelins factory fifty painters and an army of artists who spread far abroad their designs for sculpture, fittings and upholstery. From 1697, the factory particularly concentrated on its resplendent royal tapestries, which rapidly superseded Flemish products. Another significant institution of the age was the workshop in which André Charles Boulle (1642–1732), appointed *ébéniste du roi* in 1672, produced for the monarchs his sombre, splendid, inlaid and veneered furniture.

Britain

Under James I, who moved from Scotland to succeed Elizabeth I and founded England's Stuart dynasty (1603–25), there began the journeys of Puritan and other disaffected or discontented emigrants to America. From the voyage of the *Mayflower* (1620) onwards, these migrations became a world-movement exceeding the Spanish and Portuguese exploits of the previous centuries, or even Scandinavian movements of the previous millennium.

Early in the reign of his son Charles I (1625–49), the total tonnage of English merchant ships, which had already increased nearly fivefold in the previous sixty years, was expanding at a still faster rate. But the constitutional

The vast rectangular 'Blue Mosque', built at
Istanbul for Ahmet I by Mehmet Ağa (1609–16),
is supported by four enormous fluted piers and
decorated by blue and green Iznik (Nicaea) tiles
of a calm and restful beauty

ABOVE: The Church of the Intercession of the Virgin at Fili (1693). One of the first Russian centralized churches, this quadrilobe structure surmounted by octagonal pavilions and an onion dome achieves a supremely stimulating blend of Russian and Western traditions, symptomatic of the reign of Peter the Great

LEFT: Peter Rares by shifting alliances maintained Moldavian independence against Germans, Poles and Turks. The admirable, painted exteriors of his distinctively domed churches such as Moldovița (1532) suggest affinities with Novgorodian and Italian, but especially Serb and Bulgar, styles

ABOVE: The cupola of the Cappella della Santa Sindone at the Cathedral of Turin (*c.* 1668–94), capital of rising Piedmont: product of Guarini's esoteric mathematical genius, this receding tunnel of stepped arches creates an illusion of luminous unattainable remoteness

LEFT: Vilnius (Vilna), once capital of a mighty Lithuania and still a rich city in a vast but unsound Poland where Latin and Orthodox traditions met, shows the influence of Borromini or Guarini in these lofty, rippling curves of St John's facade

ABOVE: Bernini's bronze canopy of St Peter's (1633), its four gigantic twisted columns recalling venerated fourth-century pillars, breaks out from Mannerist frustrations into a rush of unrestrained energy and curve

RIGHT: After Inigo Jones had introduced England to Renaissance designs, the steeples of Christopher Wren (1632–1723), variously transfiguring the Gothic spire with classical arcades, gave London as remarkable a silhouette as Cairo or Istanbul
FAR RIGHT: The five-storeyed steeple of the Citadel Church at Riga reflects in its composite styles the political changes of the city, in turn Hanseatic, Polish, Swedish and Russian. More recently it has been the capital of independent Latvia (1919–40)

LEFT: The elegant, rhythmic, graceful magnificence of St Nicholas of Malá Strana, Prague, designed for the Jesuits by the Tyrolean Kilian-Ignaz Dientzenhofer, perhaps from his father's plans (1704-50)

ABOVE: On the Charles Bridge at Prague (1710) the terrible excitement, passionate pathos and desperate suffering of Christ's descent towards St Luitgarde explored the final limits of Bernini's dynamism – and caused the same shock

Baroque artists of the later seventeenth century
working in Portugal have encrusted the Gothic
framework of São Francisco, Oporto, with a
characteristic Iberian wealth of writhing, flounced
surface ornamentation

and financial absolutism which Charles pressed to extremes led to the dis-affection of Parliament's squires and merchants in the Civil War. The self-governing, enthusiastic army of the rebels was victorious, and their success led to a short-lived Republic – which shocked world opinion by executing the king. The Republic's 'Protector' Oliver Cromwell (1649–58) added two hundred warships to the fleet, launched Britain on a career of mari-time imperialism, and greatly strengthened the merchant service also. With cloth to sell in exchange for goods, and no land-front to man, Britain replaced the Netherlands (in spite of a series of evenly contested naval wars) as chief centre of the new transatlantic trade and of the industries; and London, its population approaching half a million – ten times the 1550 total – competed with Amsterdam as the centre of financial operations. Having benefited by its abstention from the Thirty Years' War, England did not participate in the general European economic retrogression. During the century and a half before 1700, although wool remained far the most important source of wealth, there was a spectacular fourteenfold increase in British coal-mining, which was now probably five times as extensive as all other countries' production together, and stimulated a level of iron production with which no country but Sweden could compete.

Cromwell's régime, cementing the United Kingdom (despite atrocities) by his legislative and economic union with Scotland and Ireland, has been described as the crucial break-through of modern capitalism. It also repre-sented the triumph of the middle class administrator whose common law helped to eliminate caste privileges of person and property. Even after the restoration of the exiled Charles II (1660–85) – and consequent reprisals – this basic situation remained intact, and the transfer of power from Crown to House of Commons continued.

During his reign and that of his brother James II (1685–9) the navy raised its total number of warships of over one thousand tons from five to fifty-nine. But Charles' personal policy of friendship with France (1670) resulted in the creation of an anti-Crown party, the Whigs; and then James' reversion to Catholicism compelled his withdrawal in favour of the Stadholder of the United Provinces, William III of Orange (1689–1702), who ruled Britain jointly with his wife Mary II (1689–94), sister to his forerunner. This 'Glorious Revolution' confirmed the supremacy of law over the king – who needed parliament's continued support for his wars – and provided a new pattern of limited monarchy in which an unusual, if still imperfect, degree of judicial impartiality and individual security prevailed. Released from internal politics, English energies could now be concentrated upon the containment and large-scale encirclement of France. This ambitious policy, fought out upon the oceans which were its prize, was organized by a new sort of well-informed English statesman of continental outlook, and paid for by a novel alliance of city financiers with the king, who borrowed their money on long-term loans arranged through the new Bank of England.

At the beginning of the century William Shakespeare (d. 1616) had moved on from his triumphs of the 1590's (p. 175) to a more critical awareness of the disharmonies inherent in contemporary civilization; and to an ever increasing insight into its Machiavellian power-figures, who are flawed and mangled by conflicts of conscience forced upon them, perhaps inevitably and insolubly, by appalling circumstances and the unforeseeable eccentricities of the human soul.

Hamlet (1602), a tragedy of revenge but also of grief and of how men accept it, attains new heights and depths of urgency in its exploration of personality – strained to breaking-point in a Renaissance world where humanism has become melancholic and corroded. Another Renaissance doctrine is the mainspring of *Othello* (1604); for the theme of its compact balanced unity of tight-knit construction is the accumulation of love, hatred, grief and fear to form uncontrollable jealousy. *King Lear* (1606) is written in anger, and about anger. The horrifying, swaying paroxysms of the play's development unfold the grotesque uncharted meaninglessness of human values in a cosmic scheme that has lost its order. These monstrous tumults and excesses are born of some dark fate that speaks of the bleakest pessimism in literature; the corrupt horror, upon which Lear looks, can know neither mitigation nor relief.

The magnificent verse of *Macbeth* (c. 1606) tells of the destructive energies of power-lust, and the judgment that comes upon them; *Antony and Cleopatra* (?c. 1607) is filled with the intensity of passion, and its self-consuming frustration. But *The Winter's Tale* (c. 1610–11) speaks of life which, although shattered, is then renewed in all-understanding forgiveness. Reconciliation, again, and rebirth into new moulds are Shakespeare's testament in the symbolical, idyllic *Tempest* (c. 1611); by the help of destiny, evil is at last over-powered.

With his unending munificence of humanity, self-knowledge and theatrical invention Shakespeare combines an all-embracing genius for applying poetic language and lyricism to dramatic ends. His ear for tone and rhythm – at a time when English music excelled (p. 206) – is only equalled by his eye for character and colour; and this exceptional capacity for sense experience is transmuted, by every resource of intuition and concentration, into imagery that proliferates with unbounded vigour. While soaring far above the common experience, his ever more poignant and penetrative vision nevertheless both mirrored the impulses of mankind and fascinated mankind with the reflection. For Shakespeare, timeless and universal though he is, was inevitably and indissolubly bound up with his times. At a moment when court and middle class were just beginning to move apart, he wrote at many simultaneous levels for a mixed public which comprised every group: the first or only dramatist to transcend all barriers of social division.

John Donne (1572–1631), father of the 'metaphysical school', pondered upon death and the relation between soul and body in urgent nervous lyrics which restlessly fuse intense feeling with the thoughtfulness that these emotions have inspired in him: he covers the whole range of erotic life from sexual celebration to stark disillusion, and broodingly preaches on the journey towards the grave. This period of transition to a more mature and complex linguistic and literary achievement, symbolized by the profoundly influential Authorized Version of the Bible (1611), was also guided by another man of wit and satire, Ben Jonson (c. 1573–1637) – whose urbane, powerful and observant tragedies and comedies, including the vividly realistic *Alchemist* (1610), are each based on one predominant psychological feature.

Psychology of another kind was the theme of Thomas Hobbes (1588–1679). He is the philosopher of power, whose *Leviathan* (1651) sees international relations as a jungle warfare of all against all, in which, for self-defence – anticipating ideas of social contract – power had better be entrusted to the king; though the exiled Charles II did not like Hobbes' additional suggestion that allegiance to rulers bereft of their power to protect their subjects could be abandoned.

Yet Hobbes was tolerated under the Restoration, as John Milton (1608–74) for a time seemed unlikely to be. For to him, defender of the regicides, the monarch's return seemed a Philistine triumph likely to endanger the free speech which his tract the *Areopagitica* (1644) had so eloquently defended. The majestic many-storeyed monument of dynamic, incantatory grandeur that is *Paradise Lost* gave unequalled expression to the Protestant spirit. Blind since 1652, with music his lifelong solace, Milton discovered cosmic evocative powers of language, subtle as well as sublime, in order to create another world that is more durable than ours: a world fit for the magnificence of Satan's heroically evil struggle, the symbol of his diabolical strife with God for man's soul. The battle for souls is again the theme of John Bunyan (1628–88), a tinker and itinerant preacher (imprisoned under Charles II) whose *Pilgrim's Progress* (1678–84) is the first masterpiece of English fiction, a piece of proletarian writing that blends a realistically observant appetite for anecdotic adventure-writing with a Puritan and mystic sense of guilt. More positive and practical was the mysticism of George Fox (1624–91) whose peripatetic, egalitarian missionary activity (1647–) founded the Society of Friends, or Quakers.

In this Dissenting age, a Puritan Republican family produced John Dryden (1631–1700); yet he became a dependent of the Restoration court. Father of English criticism, translator, dramatist – associated on the stage with the no less dramatic, gracefully poignant composer Henry Purcell (1659–95) – Dryden was a new sort of poet in society, exploiting political life with mannerly restraint and with a craftsmanship that achieved the appearance of relaxed good talk. His contemporary Samuel Pepys (1633–1703), one of the founders of the Royal Navy, has exercised a liberating influence on many a human heart by the informal diary in which, within the framework of each day's events, he freely reveals his own faults.

The prevailing fashion for reasonableness was exactly suited by the sensible realism of John Locke (1632–1704), whose *Essay Concerning Human Understanding* (1690) concludes that man has inalienable rights to liberty. Unlike Hobbes, Locke assumes that this is a natural situation; he goes on to emphasize the need for an agreed convention of government, not as a coercive instrument but as an impartial judge based on trust and on consent – which, he added, may if need arise be withdrawn, and transformed into resistance. His analysis continually assumes a separation of political and religious questions that would have been unimaginable even a few decades before. Locke also bases his interpretation of society upon the conviction that understanding must come from experience; this attitude, sweeping away assumptions that there are concepts whose validity requires no proof, reflected the revolutionary scientific progress of previous decades.

For as the century progressed it had witnessed an increasing readiness to challenge established doctrines. These challenges, major landmarks in the history of human thought, had come from a simultaneous combination of speculative thinking, deductive reasoning, blind intuition, and empirical experiment applied to every aspect of nature. Francis Bacon (1561–1626), philosopher, Lord Chancellor and epitome of the English Renaissance, had pronounced through his *Essays* (1597–1615) that science should harness nature for the benefit of mankind; and William Harvey (1578–1657), in his discovery of the circulation of the blood (1623), displayed how to record and implement accurate observations. In mid-century the movement gathered impetus at Oxford, London and Paris, where economically advanced societies encouraged science because of their technological needs. Another spur was Protestant pressure in favour of 'good works', facilitated by scientific improvements. Yet the result was that science gradually replaced religion as western society's dominant theme. The material world was dissociated from the spiritual, and called rational and measurable; and so the crisis of Europe's conscience began. The climactic period was in the 1680's when Isaac Newton (1642–1727) published his *Principia Mathematica* (1687), converting the world into physical and mathematical formulas of measurement based on experiment rather than deduction.

Newton thought highly of the astronomical knowledge of Christopher Wren (1632–1723). But above all Wren was an architect, with a unique capacity for welding diverse elements together. Following upon the departure from medieval styles by Inigo Jones (1573–1652), Wren's varied and graceful London steeples superimposed columnar groupings upon a native tradition of Gothic spires. And above all a novel, English synthesis of classicism and baroque appeared in his reconstruction of St Paul's, with its inventive campaniles and the mathematical wonder of its effortlessly floating dome.

Germany and Scandinavia

The first general European conflagration, known as the Thirty Years' War (1618–48), was fought first between Catholics and Protestants, and subsequently between Catholic Hapsburgs and Catholic France. Its principal phases were German (1618–29), Swedish (1630–5) and French (1635–48). In central Europe, already racked by pre-war as well as wartime economic crises, one third of the whole population was wiped out by fighting, famines and massacres. The most atrocious of these followed the imperial general Tilly's siege of Magdeburg (1631).

During the war Germany's inhabitants, ravaged by droughts as well as devastations, may well have diminished in number from twenty-one to thirteen millions. Furthermore, the Peace of Westphalia (1648), although the stagnation which followed it has been over-stressed, confirmed the emperor's failure to control or unify the German states; which may now have numbered as many as 1,800. Saxony was being outstripped as the strongest of them by Brandenburg-Prussia, under its Protestant Great Elector Frederick William (1640–88), architect of the Prussian military machine and mediator between Calvinists and Lutherans.

The emperors themselves had become little more than adjuncts of Hapsburg Austria, on whose family lands and dynastic connections they depended. After the conclusion of the war, however, their declining power within the empire was offset by Danubian victories outside its borders, won by Prince

Eugene of Savoy the brilliant general of Leopold I (1658–1705). These campaigns, including a second repulse of the Turks outside Vienna (1683),[1] led to the Treaty of Carlowitz (1699), by which the Ottoman empire ceded almost the whole of Hungary to the Hapsburgs. The basic features of the Austro-Hungarian state were now assembled; and Vienna became a capital of exotic grandeur, with Spanish ceremonial and its own courtly form of baroque (p. 222).

More drastic and abstruse than Galileo, Johann Kepler (1571–1630) from Weil in Württemberg, in his *Astronomia Nova* (1609), became one of the inaugurators of the quest for a mechanistic universe.

Later in the century Hans von Grimmelhausen (*c.* 1625–76), adapting the picaresque romances of Spain (p. 169), wrote a great novel, *Simplicissimus*, about a peasant plunged into the Thirty Years' War. At the Saxon court of Dresden, Schutz (1585–1672) fused the musical ideas of his master Gabrieli (p. 167) with German spiritual traditions and a grandiose creativeness of his own. Another Saxon, Samuel Pufendorf from Chemnitz, was the continent's most influential political theorist, optimistically arguing against Hobbes (p. 205) that peace, though precarious, is a more natural state than war (1672).

It was primarily due to King Gustavus II Adolphus of Sweden (1611–32) – now an imperial power – that the armies of the Thirty Years' War, tripled in size since 1500, fought with unprecedentedly efficient powers of movement, devastation, financial and scientific mobilization, and psychological warfare unhampered by ethical qualms.

Sweden's political and military expansion, carried out with the help of many German, English and Dutch mercenaries, was paid for by the production and export of iron on a scale comparable only to England. Extensive gains in the Peace of Westphalia (1648) were again followed by repeated wars, including both ominous clashes with Russia and continual strife with Denmark, which was obliged to cede to Sweden the southern portion of the Scandinavian peninsula (1660).

The century had witnessed the emergence both of a truly representative four-estate Swedish parliament (Riksdag) and of local government; but Charles XI (1660–97) favoured absolutist methods as a means of enabling the country to recuperate from financial and military exhaustion. His Danish contemporary Frederick III (1648–70) likewise brought about an internal reorganization, including the development of a middle class bureaucracy.

[1] For the first, see above, p. 176.

Central and Eastern Europe

It was in Bohemia, with its sharp religious differences, that the Thirty Years' War had begun. Ferdinand II destroyed Bohemian Protestantism (1620), and eliminated Czech culture for two hundred years; the last bishop of the primitivist Moravian 'Unity', J. A. Komensky (Comenius) (1593–1670), spent most of his life in exile, exercising wide influence in England and other countries through his educational ideas.

However, the mercenary general and tycoon Wallenstein (Valdstejn) (1583–1634) from Hermanice made a great profit out of the holocaust. Yet he was also a model Duke of Friedland, a detached political visionary, and the stimulator of Prague's baroque visual arts, initially under Italian and Spanish influences. While the paintings of Michael Willmann (1630–76), a Silesian immigrant, owed more to Rubens, the Catholic convert Karel Skréta of Prague (1610–74) displayed at Zderaz, in the deeply modelled, warm chiaroscuro of his pictures from St Wenceslaus' life, how a new synthesis could be made from the blending of Roman and Bolognese naturalism with the profound emotional expression inherited from the medieval art of Czech lands.

As the serf-owning magnates of Bohemia, as well as of Poland and Hungary, increased their power, the lesser nobility and gentry correspondingly deteriorated; and the position of the serfs, too, became more miserable. In Poland, another result was the decline of central authority, as nobles clung to anarchic feudal decentralization. It was a 'period of deluge' in which Poland lost huge territories to the Muscovites (p. 210); although they then scored a prestige triumph in John III Sobieski's chivalrous relief of Vienna from the Turks (1683), and a more concrete benefit in Augustus II's occupation of a wide strip of Turkish border territory (1699). But these successes were only the prelude to more serious collapse (p. 221).

Like Czechs and Russians, the Poles found their Slav taste responsive to baroque bravura, displayed in the fantastically exuberant uniforms of their Winged Hussars. After imitations of Roman architecture, John III Sobieski (1674–96) decorated his palace and Holy Cross church at Warsaw, which was now the more important city, in the fashions of Dresden and Austria. A third baroque phase developed at Wilno (Vilnius), where no less than twelve churches built by Pac reflected the power and confidence of the aristocracy; while Polish or Lithuanian ecclesiastical art simultaneously produced a more original native style as well.

An independent Transylvania, under the tolerant Calvinist Gabriel Bethlen (1613–29) and George Rakoczy I (1630–48), was for a time the eastern outpost of Protestantism. In Wallachia the warrior ruler Matthias Basarab (1632–54) – warding off continual attacks from Basil the Wolf, Albanian ruler of Moldavia – and the half-Greek art patron Constantine Brancoveanu (1688–1714) promoted new styles of church architecture which specialize in gracefully colonnaded outer porches, blind interlaced arcades, and geometric and floral decoration. A masterpiece of Constantine's reign, and his principal foundation, is the convent church of Hurezi in Oltenia, rich in blue, red and green pictorial decorations which make this a second great age of Wallachian painting.

Russia began this century with a disruptive 'Time of Troubles', including the brief reign of the able but pathologically suspicious Boris Godunov (1598–1605). Michael Romanov (1613–45), under whom the Pacific was reached at Okhotsk, put an end to a brief phase of rudimentary representative government, and acknowledged serf law; while his son Alexius (1645–76) made the landowner unconditional master of the peasants and collector of their taxes. As prosperity increased, Alexius caused the Ukrainian Cossacks under Chmielnicki to transfer their allegiance from Poland (1654), which was also, in the unprecedentedly bloodthirsty Thirteen Years' War (1654–67), compelled to hand over Smolensk and Little Russia. And now the Muscovites were also established, though not yet definitively, upon the disputed shores of the Baltic Sea.

At a time when Moscow's claim to be the 'Third and final Rome' (p. 184) were being stressed, attempts by the authoritarian Nikon (1605–81) to assert the supremacy of the spiritual power cost him his patriarchate (1666); though as a reformer of liturgy and ritual, despite conservative dissent from the Old Believers under Avvakum (1621–81), he was successful. The secular authority finally gained the upper hand under Peter the Great (1685–1725), savage freakish and go-ahead, who inflicted upon his aristocracy, disregarding all their prejudices, a forcible piecemeal programme of westernization based on his military and naval requirements. Although Peter did not try to sweep away the essentials of the old Muscovy or build upon entirely new bases, his intention was to transform his despotism (without intermediate stages or social foundations) into an absolute monarchy of the fashionable European type, which could trade and negotiate on equal terms with the west. By severe exactions, from which the peasantry suffered worst, he founded two hundred factories; and Russia began to constitute a major integral part of the international system.

Moscow's Terem palace (1635–6), though indicative of new luxury, is still medieval in conception. But dynamic developments parallel to western baroque (and, as time went on, adapting its manifestations) were displayed in a variety of original and decorative Russian ecclesiastical architecture: tent-shaped churches with broad-based pyramidal steeples such as St Nicholas at Panilovo (1600), acute-angled gables in Suzdal, elaborate brickwork and coloured tiles at Yaroslavl where the Moscow road crosses the Volga.

Nikon, who deplored the tent-church as a departure from Byzantine precedent, returned from steeples to five sober domes at Moscow and Istra. The Trinity church (1668) at Ostankino near Moscow, like buildings in that city itself, shows intricate, multiple, irregularly massed forms, exploiting the picturesqueness of coloured brick to distract congregations from their miseries. In the Church of the Intercession of the Virgin at Fili (1693), Peter the Great's relatives the Naryshkins achieved a fabulous unification of baroque or Byzantine centralized ground-plan (a quadrilobe placed round a square) with carvings, windows and lacy balustrades of Italian elegance and Russian details – and a dazzling silhouette of Russian miniature onion domes, of which the topmost surmounts one octagonal brick-and-stone pavilion placed upon another.

Russia's development early in the century had been assisted by Turkey's weakness during a series of brief and mainly disastrous Sultanates. But then the Albanian Köprülü family provided a dynasty of five successive Grand Viziers whose direction of the country, to begin with at least, did much to stabilize Ottoman power. Ahmet Köprülü (1635–1676) was the last to extend the Turkish frontiers, by annexing most of Crete; but Kara Mustafa's (1637–91) excessive military ambitions, combined with increasing turbulence among the Janissaries (p. 136), led to failure against the Russians (1681). Repulse followed before Vienna (1683); Hungary and Montenegro were lost; and the frontier with Poland was amended, very much to Turkey's disadvantage (p. 209). These were the first serious rebuffs to Ottoman rule on the European continent. Meanwhile the internal situation, too, had been deteriorating; antagonisms were not racial but social, though they assumed a religious character because of the tendency among the ruling class, whatever their race, to become Moslems.

An earlier Sultan, Ahmet I (1603–17), a religious man who kept his brothers in confinement instead of executing them – so that the succession went to men without experience – gave his name to the 'Blue Mosque' at Istanbul, furnished by his architect Daoud with the grandest of centralized interiors, the stateliest of courtyards and twenty thousand tiles incorporating seventy compositions. Murat IV (1623–40), in one of the bloodiest reigns in history, celebrated victorious wars over the Persians by building in his

Seraglio the rose, blue, white and gold Baghdad Kiosk, a superbly conceived octagon superimposed upon a cross, with a graceful arcaded cloister in a quiet garden.

Murat IV favoured Evliya Çelebi (1611–83), who mingles fact and fantasy in travel-books of tireless curiosity. This was also a classic age of Turkish poetry, including the fierce satires and imaginative Odes of Nef'i (d. 1635), who came from Erzurum to Istanbul; the cheerful sophisticated lyrics of Yahya, leader of the faith (Sheikh-ul-Islam); the fresh yet nostalgic imagery of Naili (d. 1668); and the flowing polished verses of Nabi (d. 1712), whose cerebral adaptations of eastern wisdom to the Asio-European society of Istanbul gained him contemporary popularity. Karib Çelebi (1608–57) of Istanbul, in addition to composing an important bibliography of Arabic, Persian and Turkish works, was the forerunner of westernization in his employment of European geographical sources and defence of scientific research.

8

THE EIGHTEENTH CENTURY

France

Out of approximately one hundred and eighteen million people in Europe in 1700, some nineteen million were French. By 1800, the European figure had risen to about one hundred and eighty seven million, whereas France possessed twenty-seven million inhabitants, including only about two million who lived in towns.

The War of the Spanish Succession was fought not only in Spain, of which the kingship was at stake, but also in Italy, Germany and the Netherlands (1701–14). The menacing French power was confronted by an extraordinary coalition in which Austria was allied with German states, Britain, Holland, Denmark and Portugal. Although France had under arms the unprecedented total of 400,000 men, and terminated the complicated military operations by Villars' important victory over Prince Eugene (p. 208) at Denain (1712), the country emerged from the war weakened, and entangled in financial problems beyond any royal government's power to solve. The long French confrontation with maritime England, in addition to continental Germany, had begun. Louis XIV's policy of European domination had failed to achieve results from his vast output of human and financial resources; and at his funeral there were rejoicings.

During the Duke of Orléans' regency (1715–23) for Louis XV (d. 1774), the cautious Fleury inaugurated a diplomatic recovery. Although government by royal mistresses began, and the War of the Austrian Succession (1743–8) produced no gains, fifty years of merchant capitalism more than trebled the value of French trade. Bordeaux in particular was transformed, and Nantes, St Malo and Marseille likewise made fortunes. Réaumur studied processes for making cast iron and steel (1722); the Ecole des Ponts et Chaussées trained men to make the country's magnificent roads; and Lavoisier (1743–94) discovered oxygen's role in combustion (1772–7).

In the Seven Years' War (1756–63) France reversed the policy of two

centuries by allying itself with Austria, in order to fight England and England's
new associate Prussia. The result, however, for the French was the loss of
Canada and India, and of 200,000 men on the battlefields of Germany.
Meanwhile, at home, all reforms planned by the Crown's advisers such as
Turgot (dismissed in 1776) were opposed by the reactionary, oligarchic
Parlements, notably the Parlement of Paris which had jurisdiction over
one-third of France. Further causes of instability within the towns included
laws made by the oppressive government trade-guilds; and in the country
there were arbitrary state taxes, feudal dues and harvest failures, especially
in 1788.

No important element in the whole land wanted revolution. But it came
because France, while undergoing a social transformation commensurate
with its position as leader of western Europe, adopted for many years a very
aggressive foreign policy which the unreasonable nature of its government,
and the prolonged exclusion of its middle class from privileged positions,
made it impossible to support without the gravest strains. The summoning
by King Louis XVI (1774–93) of the Estates General (three Estates), which
had not met since 1614, brought together – in a power vacuum created by the
king's incapacity – a varied collection of people all eager to overhaul parts of
the system. But their demands could not be met without eliminating
privilege; and so the Third Estate, joined by peasants and craftsmen, asserted
its long-forgotten identity against the nobility and clergy who formed the
other two.

The countryside ensured the revolution success; but the cities, producing
a literature of radicalism and emancipation (p. 217), supplied its ideology,
rhetoric and striking force. As power shifted from government to Assembly
in 1789, modern nationalism emerged. Its hall-marks were dynamic levelling,
and the ruthlessly co-ordinated canalization of mass movements. These
operations were based on the concept that the nation's will is the supreme
law. Following upon the American revolution (p. 228), a novel concept of
human dignity was evident in the Declaration of the Rights of Man (1789),
proclaiming not only national sovereignty but equality, freedom of thought
religion and press, and the limitation of state powers.

The rigorous régime directed by Robespierre (1792) had to combat the
menacing encirclement of France by the English, Austrians and Prussians,
whose troops were only 140 miles from Paris. By national mobilization of a
novel, ominous character, and with the support of the best artillery and gun-
powder in Europe, France hurled them back (1792–3), stopping Prussian
invaders at Valmy, advancing to the Rhine and establishing there a frontier
proclaimed by Danton to be both national and natural. The Parisian mob

lost its temporary pre-eminence to the trained revolutionary army which, nearly a million strong, was led by the rising young Corsican Napoleon to sensational victories against the Hapsburgs in north Italy and Austria itself (1796–7), and then to excursions in Egypt and Syria (1798–9) which were intended to cut Britain's Indian life-line but roused both Russian and Turkish hostility.

Under the Directory (1795–9), property was transferred to the rural bourgeoisie; and the middle class emerged as victors of the revolution. But meanwhile France had provided models of politics, ideology and organization for the rest of the world.

Before the death of Louis XIV, the majestic solemnities of mouldings and furniture had begun to be modified by a lighter and more playful note. Under his successor the town houses now being constructed for the noblemen, with their smaller apartments, rejected the personality cult by introducing themes, colours and fabrics of a more intimate gaiety. The grandeurs of baroque gave place to the sparkling slender curves, delicate foaming waves and asymmetrical twisting sprays of rococo. Men such as Hardouin-Mansart's pupil the Dutch architect G. M. Oppenord (1672–1742), an ornamental designer J. A. Meissonier (1695–1750) from Turin, and the furniture-maker C. Cressent, perfected this art of interior decoration, exploiting porcelain, stucco, lacquers, varnishes and marquetry, and borrowing from Italian grottos and fashionable Chinoiserie in order to achieve a unique, irrational and infinitely varied balance between nobility and graciousness, exuberance and restraint.

This was a Paris of 1,702 couturiers and 1,884 tailors; and of an excellence of cuisine accompanied, now, by the major wines. The musicians who composed for this civilization were François Couperin (1668–1733), an outstanding instrumentalist – at his best on the harpsichord – and Jean Philippe Rameau (1683–1764), a symphonic dramatist of opera who even outdoes his successor Gluck (p. 226) in the richness and variety of his musical language.

A painter whose delicate dreams did much to form the rococo ideal was Antoine Watteau (1684–1721), from the formerly Flemish town of Valenciennes. Amid the shimmering shadowy lights of the *fêtes champetres* which became fashionable partly through his influence, Watteau subtly distilled from Rubens and Veronese a languid, nostalgic, heart-breaking awareness that such beauties will pass; as his life too, amid illness, was rapidly passing. Then François Boucher (1703–70), admirer of Tiepolo's elegance (p. 218), created desirable, impudent girls for a rococo civilization in which women

215

fulfilled a prominent role. The taste of Boucher, and of his patroness Madame Pompadour, pervaded the *rose Pompadour*, *jaune jonquille*, *bleu celeste* and finally *bleu de roi* of the French national porcelain which, under Hellot, took the world by storm from its factories first at Vincennes and then at Sèvres (1756). J. B. S. Chardin (1699–1779), on the other hand, with his still-life and *genre* scenes which appeal to the intellect as much as to the senses, belongs to a different tradition and a more concrete reality, which would emerge again in Courbet and Cézanne (p. 246).

From the late 1750's onwards, rococo gave place to a neo-classicism in which artists and craftsmen, while partially returning to the clarity and realism of the seventeenth century, consciously sought too for purer forms of antique art. Stimulated by remains of Pompeii (p. 33) which came to light in 1748, they were also inspired by Winckelmann's revival of Greek art (1755–6) to discern in classicism (sometimes laced with Egyptian and far eastern motifs) a grandeur and simplicity which seemed the quintessence of tradition and a worthy mirror for the cultural enlightenment of the day (p. 217). The principal Parisian furniture-makers in this style (1770–85), by no means all Frenchmen, included L.-J. Le Lorrain (d. 1759), J.-F. Oeben and J. H. Riesener (1734–1806); while P. Gouthière was famous as a *fondeur-doreur*. Under Louis XVI the style developed more markedly rectangular forms; the antiquarian emphasis was retained, and became even stronger during the subsequent Directoire.

One of the first sculptors to live independently of noble patrons was J. A. Houdon (1741–1828), who combined his devotion to ancient Rome with a vivid observation of nature. From the 1770's onwards he achieved fame by his modish ability to depict the great not as the great, but as ordinary, critically observed specimens of humanity. The leading painter of these years, soon to become the revolution's artistic dictator and founder of a dominant school, was J. L. David (1748–1825), whose monumental, patriotic classicism reflecting heroic Republican ideals of citizenly liberation was already apparent in his Oath of the Horatii (1785). Meanwhile J.-G. Soufflot (1713–80) translated neo-classicism into architectural terms with his Panthéon (Ste. Geneviève, 1755–) – in which he deliberately echoed Gothicism, and so anticipated the Gothic revival that was imminent (p. 233). C.-N. Ledoux (1736–1806) built houses and other buildings to a wide variety of designs; remarkable also are the unexecuted cylindrical and pyramidal plans for the houses of his poetical Ideal City, envisaging a revolutionary social role for architecture, and a concern for the workers whom it served.

In western, central and eastern Europe alike, the language of the French prevailed as the medium of scholarship, diplomacy and polite society. The Abbé de Saint Pierre (1658–1743) made philanthropic *bienfaisance* smart, and spread ideas of progress and European union. Montesquieu (1689–1755) saw Europe as progress and liberty, Asia as stagnation. His *Esprit des Lois* (1748) displays a reason-governed, empirical realism in its interpretation of human life's complex role in society; here is an unfamiliar relativistic understanding of how ideas and institutions are related to their places and their times.

Empiricism, hitherto the prerogative of the English (p. 206), is again the keynote of the *philosophes*, whose writings between 1748 and 1762 signalized the victory of a largely anti-religious ideology of utilitarian ethics based on the conviction that man is the measure of a rational universe. Implicit in their works were warnings against the flaws of French society. For instance the 'physiocrats', guided by Louis XV's doctor François Quesnoy, believed that the best way to increase the community's wealth and welfare was to encourage a natural state of affairs in which no check was placed upon individual economic liberty (1758). Such ideas, and indeed the whole Enlightenment which they represented, were summed up in the *Encyclopédie* (1751–72) of Denis Diderot (1713–84), the 'spokesman of the century' who found social institutions futile, and d'Alembert (1717–83), a tempestuous but doctrinaire mathematician and pioneer physicist.

The programme for the early stages of the revolution was provided by the Encyclopaedists along with Voltaire (1694–1778): though neither they nor he were political revolutionaries. Historian of civilization, the man whose *Essay on Manners* (1756) brought social thinking into fashion, Voltaire personified all the principal ideas and prejudices of this age of reason. Insatiably curious, he was the peerless journalist; in his own day he gained most fame as poet and playwright; the vehicles for many of his principal ideas are his novels, such as *Candide* (1759), with its impatience of Europe's planless confusion. Voltaire's dry, malicious prose breaks down complacency about abuses and, on behalf of the needy and oppressed, goes into battle against religion, intolerance and the old régime.

But the revolution caught its fire from the more emotional J.-J. Rousseau (1712–78) from Geneva, whose study of unnatural human inequality (1755), followed by the *Contrat Social* (1762), heralded the age to come by its ambitious reconciliations between the rights of society and of the individual. The answer seemed to be popular sovereignty, which recalled ancient Rome and Sparta – and could be invoked again by future totalitarian régimes. The noble savage is preferred to conventional society; for feeling, instinct and sensibility are better than thought. Feeling again, a Nordic rather than French preoccupation with the emotions rather than the mind, is the principal theme and component of his romantic *Nouvelle Héloise* (1761), and of his *Confessions* (1764-70) replete with modern self-enquiry and self-pity.

Literature was anticipating politics in its movement towards democracy. *The Marriage of Figaro* (1784) by the watchmaker's son Beaumarchais (1732–99) – following upon his *Barber of Seville* (1775) – has a hero who is more than the successor of Molière's comic servants (p. 199). Figaro has no revolutionary desire to destroy privilege; but he wants a share in it. The moral was pointed by Condorcet (1743–94), to whom not only nations are equal, but classes are also; and there need be no hesitations in achieving whatever changes are desired, for the human soul and body alike are perfectible (1793).

Italy

For the greater part of the century Southern Italy and Sicily remained in Spanish hands. For although by the treaty of Utrecht (1713) Spain lost its Italian dominions to Austria, and lost Sicily to Piedmont and then Austria, Charles of Bourbon, son of the Spanish king Philip V, reconquered both territories (1738) and, like his son Ferdinand IV of Naples and III of Sicily (1759–1805), ruled them as a country independent of Madrid though subject to many of its ideas (later he became Charless III of Spain, p. 219).

Certain Neapolitan thinkers, however, were in sympathy with the Enlightenment: Giambattista Vico (1668–74) founded a new science of humanity blending history and social studies. The Sicilian Alessandro Scarlatti (1659/60–1725) made Naples the centre of a new kind of Italian opera, with its melody directed to emotional purposes; and Giovanni Battista Pergolesi (1710–36) from Iesi (Ancona) added the light freshness of the *opera buffa*. Arcangelo Corelli (1653–1713) was an outstanding early exponent of the violin. He developed the sonorous *concerto grosso*; and Antonio Vivaldi (*c.* 1655–1741), a Venetian who employed the same medium for solo developments, infused his adventurous dramatic contrasts with a lyrical tenderness.

Exempt from foreign occupation for nearly a thousand years, Venice lost its independence forever when Napoleon handed it over to Austria (1797). But before that, despite a seamier side to its life, the city enjoyed a final artistic Renaissance with its comedies of manners by Carlo Goldoni (1707–93), the intoxicating poetical luminosities of G. B. Tiepolo's rococo canvases (1697–1770), and the visions of Venetian buildings and canals by the meti-

ABOVE: Though Caravaggio's religious feeling was intense, one of his revolutionary innovations was to represent Biblical figures, such as Jesus and his companions at the Supper of Emmaus, as ordinary contemporary poor people
RIGHT: Rubens' marvellously constructed *Feast of Herod* (c. 1633–8). His luxuriant fleshy women add glittering lustre to these exuberant, spirally undulating scenes, alive with the movement which he had the supreme power to seize upon the wing

ABOVE: Velasquez, born at Seville of Portuguese origin, sees his models, such as Pope Innocent X (1650), with an abnormally minute and imperturbable scrutiny, and paints them with an intense, imaginative mastery of light and the visible world

RIGHT: Rembrandt's conception of a *Polish Nobleman*. Displaying an indescribable mastery of light and texture, and radiating an unfamiliar excitement of observed and exotic facts, he applies to men's souls an almost more than human knowledge of their inmost idiosyncrasies

NON MARTE   SED ARTE

Unerring in his control of space and interval,
Vermeer 'has retained this early morning innocence
of vision and united it with a most delicate
perception of tone' (Kenneth Clark)

ABOVE: The roof of the Château de Chambord, a royal hunting lodge on the river Cosson freely adapted from the plans of Domenico da Cortona (1519), is a forest of dormers, chimney stacks and stone cupolas, rivalling the most extravagant fantasies of flamboyant Gothic

LEFT: The gardens of Italy, France, England and Portugal are among the major joys of Europe. The Garzoni family bought Collodi Castle, east of Lucca, and started to lay out its spectacular garden in about 1652

ABOVE: Canaletto (d. 1768) conjures up with an increasingly linear treatment (in contrast to the illusionistic bravura of Guardi) the incomparably dramatic central area of Venice, round its fourteenth-century Doge's Palace. These scenic paintings catered for the travellers who now flocked to Italy

RIGHT: The seventeenth-century Vienna theatre: prologue to Lodovico Burnacini's *Monarchina Latina Trionfante* (1678)

culous Antonio Canaletto (1697–1768) and the more impressionistic Francesco Guardi (1712–93), Tiepolo's brother-in-law – a master of transient, luminous atmospheric effects.

Under Victor Amadeus II (1675–1730) and Charles Emmanuel III (1730–73), Savoy or Piedmont (p. 190), the buffer state which controlled the Alps and (since 1720) owned Sardinia, went ahead in road-construction and peasant reforms; it was now the leading Italian power, approaching equality with the major countries of Europe.

It was round Turin, too, that the Sicilian architect Filippo Juvara (1678–1736) built for his royal employers the Superga convent church and Stupinigi Palace (1729–31) which, with their staggering vistas and prolific ingenuities, blend many styles in a final scenographic outburst of Italian baroque.

But enlightened despotism held no attractions for the Piedmontese dramatist Vittorio Alfieri (1749–1803), who spent most of his life travelling abroad. During this time, he produced plays that embody the Italian tragic spirit, incorporating ideas of political liberation which revived the hope that Italy had a national destiny. The scientific revolution, too, was not without its Italian contributors, notably Aloisio Galvani (1737–98) and Alessandro Volta (1745–1827) who pioneered the discovery of electric current.

Spain and Portugal

By the Treaty of Utrecht (1713), King Philip V of Anjou (1700–46) – France's candidate in the War of the Spanish Succession (p. 213) – retained the throne of Spain, but was excluded from Italy and Sicily (p. 218) and lost Belgium to Austria, and Gibraltar and Minorca to the English. Its population three million less than a century before, Spain was driven back upon itself; but any beneficent results inherent in this situation were ruined by the almost unceasing warfare of the reign, in which first French and then Italian interests dominated the ineffective court. Accordingly, Spain continued to remain apart from the progress which other countries were experiencing. Charles III (1759–88), though an honest methodical businessman and one of the ablest European monarchs of the day, was unable to evoke sufficient national response. His incompetent, obscurantist son Charles IV (1788–1808) became subordinated to the French Republican government; the royal adviser Manuel de Godoy owes his title 'prince of the peace' to the treaty which bound Spain to this allegiance (1795).

Yet the artistic field had produced a splendid and widespread efflorescence of Spanish baroque. Highly distinctive in character, this specializes in an abundant all-encompassing decoration which recalls the country's Islamic masterpieces of previous ages. José de Churriguera (1665–1725) filled Salamanca with his masterpieces, not ignoring the basic architectonic values beneath his complex, vibrant surfaces, which seem to echo the local university's involvement in disputations of the most subtle and elaborate kind. The churches designed at Seville by L. Figueroa (d. 1730) are glittering assemblages of sun-dappled reliefs and barley-sugar columns (*salomonicas*). There is less concern for form in the delicate exuberance of F. H. Hurtado (1669–1725) from Cordova, culminating at the Granada's Charterhouse (Cartuja) – deliberately reminiscent of Alhambra traceries (p. 120) – and at a second Carthusian foundation of El Paular, near Segovia. In these chapels, every trace of rectangularity is concealed and eclipsed by dazzling encrustations of ubiquitous ornament; the Sacristy at Granada 'seems to make a perpetual flutter of movement like the foliage of a forest on a breezy day'.[1]

In Toledo cathedral, behind the high altar, Narciso Tomé's *El Trasparente* (1721) violently moulds a vast space into a single explosive, stupefying mass of sculptural ornamentation. At Santiago de Compostela the cathedral façade, known as *El Obradoiro* (1738–49), forms an audacious unity of structural and spiritual contrasts, blending a baroque magnificence with the soaring Gothic verticality of its immense Galician gable. Despite Italian echoes in the Mediterranean churches and palaces of Murcia and Valencia, neither baroque nor rococo could easily retain their Italian, and still less their French, forms in Spain. In painting too, Francisco Goya, at the end of the century, was moving from styles somewhat reminiscent of Tiepolo (with added undertones) to methods that were entirely new (p. 264).

In Portugal, meanwhile, under King John V (1706–50) there was peace, but widespread starvation. The king himself, enriched by Brazilian gold and diamonds and English trade, was not only an active patron of music but inaugurated Portugal's second age of visual splendour. Joaquim Machado de Castro (1731–1822) was a sculptor who handled his surfaces in a rococo style of unusual *panache* and dignity, and Braga is a baroque town where the palaces display a specifically Portuguese (and English), but un-Spanish, love of garden landscapes. Mafra, begun in 1717 by the Swabian J. F. Ludwig (Ludovice), is in size and grandeur a Portuguese counterpart of the Escorial (p. 170), but differs from it by virtue of a greater cheerfulness, expressed for example in an elaborate and original system of inner courtyards. Another, more intimate, manifestation of contemporary architectural talent is the unassuming gracefully tiled Palace of Queluz, begun by Ludwig's pupil Mateus Vicente in 1758.

[1] J. Lees-Milne.

Austria and Germany

The emperor Leopold I declared the Hapsburg domains indivisible (1703), and Charles VI (1711–40) proclaimed his German, Bohemian and Hungarian lands a single state (1713). His annexation of the formerly Spanish Netherlands (Belgium, p. 219) was counterbalanced by failures in a number of subsequent campaigns, and efforts to strengthen his central authority were weakened by the problems of raising war expenses from regional parliaments or Estates.

His daughter Maria Theresa (1740–80) – the first imperial ruler since the Renaissance to be thoroughly German – took steps, with the aid of her adviser Kaunitz, to create a workable, unified Austro-Hungarian state. However, although Maria Theresa's artillery was the most powerful in Europe, the War of the Austrian Succession brought her the loss of wealthy Silesia, with its linen and ores, to Prussia. In an attempt to re-establish her position she switched, in the Seven Years' War, to an unfamiliar French alliance (p. 213) which ended the long Bourbon-Hapsburg rivalry. But Silesia was still not regained.

For a new phenomenon was arising in great-power politics: Prussia, despite its poverty and artificiality, was replacing Austria as the nucleus of German power. Not long after the Prussian rulers had been elevated to the title of king, Frederick William I (1713–40) doubled the size of his standing army from 40,000 to 80,000. Then Frederick the Great (1740–86) more than doubled it again, to a figure of 186,000. He also prompted Maria Theresa and Catherine of Russia to the first of three Partitions of Poland (1772), which shattered world opinion by this unprecedentedly cynical demolition of a historic state. Yet within Prussia, Frederick, the friend of Voltaire, ruled in rapidly expanding Berlin as the model of an intellectually planned and enlightened authoritarianism, aspiring on cold rational grounds towards justice, welfare and universal education.

Maria Theresa's son Joseph II (1780–90) sought to adapt such ideas, in an extreme form, to his own far more heterogeneous imperial territories, by subjecting these to rigorous centralization. But attempts to Germanize the Slavs and Magyars aroused their nationalist feelings; his assertion of the secular authority, combined with a tolerant attitude to Protestantism, antagonized the church; and by abolishing bondage, he incurred the rancour of the still feudal nobility. Before Joseph died, most of his reforms had been withdrawn; but the social system could never be the same again.

His nephew Francis II (1792–1835) began his reign with some inglorious but not altogether unprofitable parts to play. After accepting his share of the major powers' second and third carvings-up of Poland (1793, 1795),[1] Austrian defeats by Napoleon (1797) compelled his acquiescence in a general reshuffle of territories. Austria was to receive Venice (its ancient Republic abolished), Istria and Dalmatia; but it lost Lombardy and Belgium to France.

The early years of the century had witnessed the grave, seemly, imperial architecture of noblemen's palaces and the churches of Vienna and Salzburg. J. B. Fischer von Erlach (1650–1723) of Graz and his son set the artistic seal upon contemporary benevolent absolutism by this tasteful monumental reconciliation of Roman baroque, Venetian sensuousness and French classicism. A livelier magnificence was achieved by Guarini's pupil von Hildebrandt (1688–1745) in the ingenious pavilions and loggias of his patron Prince Eugene's Belvedere (1720–). At Melk, in Lower Austria, the Benedictine monastery-church (1702–14) was redesigned by the Tyrolean Jakob Prandtauer (1660–1726) as a dramatic, twin-towered composition organically growing upon its lofty rock beside the Danube. This majestic exterior has mannerist and medieval reminiscences; but inside are the powerful undulating movements and festive, delicate colours of a new age.

Other German lands produced an even more boisterous, radical baroque, curving three-dimensionally in unrestrained exultation. Such was the Zwinger (1709–19) at Dresden, an orangery and grandstand created with joyful fantasy by M. D. Poppelmann (1662–1736) for Augustus II the Strong (d. 1733), an Elector of Saxony whose prolific building programme sought to efface the ravages of the Thirty Years' War (p. 207). It was, however, the Schönborn family, controllers of the prince-bishoprics of Würzburg, Bamberg and Mainz, who employed the most intellectual of these architects, J. B. Neumann (1687–1753). Beneath its surface ornament's passionate swell and splashing froth, his Vierzehnheiligen church is composed of subtly animated ovals interlocking and responding with the spatial counterpoint of a resplendent fugue. Deeply satisfying, again, are the multiple interplays of rhythmical contrasted lines in churches designed by the Dientzenhofer family, such as St Nicolas de Malá Strana at Prague (1704–50). Prague is also the workshop, not only of an outstanding portrait-painter in Jan Kupecký (1667–1740), but of a sculptural style adapting Bernini with passionate pathos, to provide consolations for a demoralized society. Such is Matthias Braun's crucifixion group of St Luitgarde on the Charles bridge (1710); while the altar-pieces of Peter Brandl (1668–1735), likewise adapting Roman traditions, dedicate their rich flamboyant hues to scenes at the same high pitch of intensity.

[1] Poland's pre-eminent poet Ignacy Krasicki (1735–1801) lived through these events.

But the society which provided the most lavish abundance of this 'radical baroque' was Bavaria, where the tenor of life, although punctuated by occasional great wars, was generally more placid. The patrons were its Wittelsbach kings Maximilian II Emmanuel (1679–1726), Charles Albert (1726–45) and the enlightened Maximilian III Joseph (1745–77). Bavaria was compact and in close touch with the Italians, and its people were peculiarly susceptible to visual effects. At a time when western Europe was turning to the more severe purities of neo-classicism (p. 216), churches in Bavaria were dream-like edifices flooded with unsurpassable colourful gaiety. And yet these feathery illusions of downward streaming light and curving perspective, these 'lacquered arenas and opera-box balconies, coral-reef altars and air-borne seraphs', reflect a conception of divine order which, with the aid of the Virgin Mary, unites earth with heaven. It is the particular contribution of German and especially Bavarian baroque that, even more than the styles of Bernini and Borromini (p. 189), it utilizes all possible artistic devices as contributions to its pictorial worship of the spiritual mysteries. The exciting theatrical display with which this was accomplished took the peasantry out of their dull lives and wedded them to the church.

Court appointments at Munich went to the brothers Asam, who rose at Rohr (1718–25) and Weltenburg (1717–21) far above the village craftsmanship of their origins to extremities of optical illusion and emotional surprise. Coming from Wessobrunn, where there was a leading school for stucco workers, D. Zimmermann (1685–1766) achieved in the oval edifice of Die Wies (1745–54), and particularly in its daringly dramatic pulpit, a forcible impact of unearthly, visionary rapture. Such a fusion of the various arts had not been seen since ancient times. Meanwhile at Ottobeuren (1748), J. M. Fischer (1692–1766) was giving exhilarating expression to his virtuosity in manipulating spatial relations.

It was Saxony and Bavaria again which led the world in the production, not only of painted woodwork, but of small rococo porcelain vessels and figures and groups of supremely *chic* and rhythmical design. At Meissen (Dresden), Augustus II the Strong's jeweller J. F. Böttger invented hardpaste porcelain (1709–19), J. G. Herold produced graceful Chinoiseries for a vast market, and the miniature sculptures of J. J. Kändler (1731–75) exploited the medium's total potentialities of glaze and colour. But after the town of Meissen had been damaged in the Seven Years' War (p. 221), the lead in porcelain design passed to other centres including Nymphenburg in Bavaria, where F. A. Bustelli (1723–63), although an Italian Swiss from Locarno, displayed the most typical and national of all the German styles, reminiscent of Bavarian wood-sculpture. With an inimitably amusing rhetorical sense he catches momentary movement on the wing, and crystallizes it in the crisp fresh brilliance of his plasticity.

However, Germany, in common with other countries, did not altogether resist the change from rococo to neo-classicism (p. 216), of which it produced an unequalled, if frustrated, architectural exponent in Friedrich Gilly (1772–1800). Neither of his two masterpieces of design, the National Monument to Frederick the Great (1797) and the National Theatre of Berlin (1798), were ever built; but their cubic and cylindrical forms, un-pedimented Doric porticoes and semi-circular windows reveal an originality which would not recur for nearly a century to come.

The leading intellectual of early eighteenth-century Germany was Gottfried Leibnitz (1646–1716), whose Slavonic ancestors had settled at Leipzig. His encyclopaedic range has never again been rivalled. Politician, historian, theologian, scientist, inventor of the differential and integral calculus, anticipator of developments in logic, Leibnitz agreed with the baroque church architects in detecting an authoritarian harmony throughout the universe, even if, as Voltaire pointed out, he omitted to determine how evil and free will are reconcilable with this supreme authority. Although the major works of Leibnitz were not published until after his death, his philosophy was popularized and modified by Christian Wolff of Breslau (1679–1754). Wolff's stress on mathematical certitude attracted Frederick the Great. But it offended pietists, and it incurred criticism – from quite a different viewpoint – by Wolff's fellow-Prussian Immanuel Kant (1724–1804). In his *Critique of Pure Reason* (1781), Kant, distinguishing science from philosophy and theology, preferred the former with its empirically verifiable human-founded facts to the latter which speculates upon a God who is unknowable.

As Friedrich Klopstock (1724–1803) revived German poetry with his tender and spiritual love lyrics, his fellow-Saxon Gottfried Lessing created the modern drama of Germany; his *Minna von Barnhelm* (1763–7) is the first significant comedy in the language. At the same time, the East Prussian Johann von Herder (1744–1803) helped to initiate the Storm and Stress movement which, emanating from the middle class, represents the first powerful revolutionary drive in Germany. The Enlightenment, shallow-rooted in that country, was superseded by a romantic, Rousseau-esque insistence upon the dominant role of the elemental subconscious instincts. This movement, linked by Herder with an admiration for what was Gothic and medieval, was more violently irrational than romanticism elsewhere in Europe (p. 232), and impatient of almost all traditional authority.

Two authorities only were revered. One was the still scarcely existent nation, for it seemed to Herder and others, in their admiration for past

German greatness, that the nation is history's guiding force. The other respected authority was Shakespeare, whose dramatic form was established in *Götz von Berlichingen* (1773), spearhead of Storm and Stress and the work which won fame for its young author Johann Wolfgang von Goethe (1749–1832) from Frankfurt-am-Main. While Götz represents the more manly side of the movement, his next hero, in *Die Leiden des jungen Werthers* (1774), stands for its more sentimental, introspective side: Werther with his *Weltschmerz* is one of the earliest psychological studies of a weak character, composed (as it happens) while Kant was preparing his work which gave the individual sovereignty over the universe (p. 224).

At Weimar, the German Athens at which Goethe had been given a post by the liberal Duke Charles Augustus (1775), the study of geology, anatomy and botany awakened in him a fertile new impulse to master and express nature as a whole. But the most influential event in his life was his Italian journey (1786), reflected by the *Roman Elegies* (1790–5) in which Storm and Stress are superseded by neo-classical lucidity. *Wilhelm Meisters Lehrjahre* (1795–6) returns to the theme of a vacillating hero, offering varied and detailed analyses of his moods and motives.

The publication of the first part of *Faust* still lay in the future (p. 260), but meanwhile Wilhelm Meister became the model of every young romantic, introspective novelist. Yet, for the thoroughgoing exponents of romanticism, it still seemed too classical and redolent of the eighteenth century. The leaders of this movement, anticipating modern trends by their realistic psychology, were the brothers Schlegel (1798–1800), who yearned with a frustrated, mock-medieval malaise for the wholly subjective, escapist 'unending process of aesthetic and ethical self-perfection'. The closest approach to their visionary ideal was the poet Friedrich Novalis (1772–1801), an unconscious pagan – with Christian mystical affinities – who derived nihilistic delight from being detached from life. 'Man is a god when he dreams, a beggar when he thinks', said Johann Hölderlin (1770–1843) who, before his reason failed, found the inspiration for his prophetic, pantheistic vision in an ardent love of ancient Greece; romance went back to the classics, though their interpretation had indeed changed since rococo days.

Hölderlin had been influenced by Friedrich Schiller (1759–1805), who came, like him, from the Neckar valley. Moving into the front rank of European dramatists, Schiller created a new genre of historical theatre by his plays *Die Räuber* (1781) and *Wallenstein* (1798–9) – the latter written shortly before he took up permanent residence near Goethe in Weimar. His historical and philosophical contributions and his lyric poetry likewise exercised a wide appeal by their optimism, the clarity of their moral purpose and artistic design, and his enthusiastic contrast of northern gloom with the joyful beauty which he, like Hölderlin, saw in Hellenic antiquity.

Schiller's *Die Räuber* incurred the displeasure of Duke Charles Eugene of Württemberg. Yet this ruler of a not very considerably duchy boasted the best Comédie after Paris, a superior ballet, and the foremost orchestra and opera in Germany.

Music had become the major art of the age, capable of interpreting every human movement and feeling. Georg Friedrich Händel from Halle (1685–1759), an international eclectic who after a period in Scarlatti's Naples (p. 218) settled in England, represents the spirit of the times with the absolutist pomp and grandiose natural conceptions of his colourful, monumental, imaginative oratorios. Far more remote from the cultural *Zeitgeist* is the dense, geometrically piled-up fugal counterpoint in which Johann Sebastian Bach (1685–1750), from Eisenach in Thuringia, clothed his passionate, transcendental fears and hopes. His *St Matthew Passion* (1729) is the climax alike of all Biblical settings, indeed of all vocal melody, and of the German Reformation itself. Christopher Willibald Gluck (1714–87), born in the Upper Palatinate but probably originating from Bohemia (where he studied before settling in Vienna), established modern opera by his *Orfeo ed Euridice* (1762). With fewer characters, larger orchestra and meaningful chorus, Gluck has returned to the grand simple treatment of the ancient Greek dramatists. It was through music, rather than words, that the lyricism and tragedy of his themes was chiefly expressed; yet this music was subordinate to dramatic needs, with useless ornaments and 'dry recitative' abolished.

Josef Haydn (1732–1809), from a Croat peasant family at Rohrau in Austria, clothes his profound imagination and love of life in a highly personal idiom which achieves an unprecedented balance of classical form against romantic feeling. Composed 'to give a few moments of solace and refreshment' – but with little regard for courtly frivolity and etiquette – his prolific output, first for the Esterhazy family (1760–90) and then at Vienna, established the concept and structure of string quartets, sonatas and symphonies alike.

Wolfgang Amadeus Mozart (1756–91) of Salzburg, in his brief frustrated life spent mostly in Vienna, established the concerto form, with its solo instrument mainly the piano which since the '60's was replacing the harpsichord. His last symphonies and string quartets, too, combined pure melody, classical proportion and underlying nostalgia in a heart-breaking amalgam which Goethe viewed as the incarnation of a divine creative force. But even instrumentation seemed to Mozart only another vehicle for song; and his

Opposite: Detail of interior of the pilgrimage church of Die Wies (1745–54)

preferred medium came to be opera, in which he could compass the whole range of human feeling. The *Magic Flute* (1791), foundation of all subsequent German operatic composition, unites every symbol of human desires and dreams in a musical morality-play as sublime as *Faust* or the *Tempest*.

Beethoven (1770–1827) went from Bonn to Vienna (1787, 1792); and already his early works, despite superficial resemblances to the music of the day, disclose a daringly adventurous breadth and epigrammatic grandeur that were beyond the comprehension even of Haydn. But Beethoven's principal life-work, like Goethe's, belonged to a later and different epoch (p. 258). His contemporary Karl Friedrich Gauss (1777–1855), from Bruns-wick, achieved mathematical advances comparable to those of Archimedes and Newton, before passing, at the turn of the century, to astronomy, and later to electromagnetism.

Britain

To fight the War of the Spanish Succession (p. 213) Britain, for the first time since the fifteenth century, mobilized a sizable army; at the battle of Blenheim in Bavaria (1704), Marlborough saved Austria and drove the French armies out of Germany. The Treaty of Utrecht (1713) gave the British a virtual monopoly of the slave market, recognized their entry into the Spanish New World, and heralded their command of the Mediterranean and of Canada. Arranged in London, which was now the world's financial centre (p. 247), England's investments in other countries were without parallel; and so, conversely, were its outgoing loans across the Channel, supplemented and facilitated before long by large-scale developments in private banking and marine insurance.

But the secret weapon of British domination was a successful, complicated relationship between Cabinet policy, Treasury experience and Parliamentary control. The first Hanoverian king, George I (1714–27), contributed to the (slow) growth of government by cabinet through his ignorance of the English language, which kept him away from its meetings. Cabinets were accord-ingly chaired by the Whig Robert Walpole (1766–1745), a master of manipulation who operated a highly profitable policy of peace well into the reign of George II (1727–60). Walpole's retirement (1742), after his defeat in the House of Commons by one single vote, showed that the rudiments of ministerial responsibility were already in existence; and indeed this was a time when the rule of law penetrated to many areas of English life.

The elder Pitt (Lord Chatham), a Tory who believed that his country's destiny was the will of God, saw in the Seven Years' War (with its novel Prussian alliance, p. 214) a chance to further that destiny by the use of sea-power; and the result was England's supersession of France as the principal colonial country, ruling Canada and India alike.

But under the inert Lord North, for all the labours of King George III (1760–1820), these gains were offset by the breakaway of the United States of America (1775–83), whose people could not accept governance from a parliament elected by others. Though many British welcomed this loss – since they realized that the retention of these territories would have meant investing their own government with increasingly autocratic powers – there was strong feeling against the government of Louis XVI which (like the Spanish) had helped the Americans. When the French revolution came, however, hostilities against the new French government, too, became probable when it threatened Britain's Dutch ally; and in the month after the execution of its king, France declared war upon both Britain and Holland (1793). The first phase of the struggle, although Britain won naval victories, brought defeats on land which drove the Dutch out of the war (1795). The second phase eliminated further enemies of France (Naples and Austria), and caused mutinies in the British fleet. But then Nelson's ejection of the French from Egypt (p. 215) by the battle of the Nile (1798), and the British capture of Minorca and Malta, kept the eastern routes open and ensured eventual victory (p. 247).

George III, being now insane, played no part in the conduct of the war, which was directed by the younger Pitt (1783–1801). Long dominant over his Tory colleagues and followers, he effectively asserted cabinet authority. Whatever reverses might occur on the continent could, in the end, be rectified at sea, for the British fleet, with 174 ships of the line and 294 smaller vessels, was now an irresistible force; even sixty years earlier, with 124 and 105 respectively, it had already become the greatest naval power. The carrying capacity of the merchant fleet, too, had multiplied sixfold during the century; and so had exports, from the rapidly expanding harbours of London, Glasgow and Liverpool. Throughout the century the largest English overseas trade was with Ireland, whose elegant capital, Dublin, became the third city in Europe.

John Wilkes (1727–97), demonstrating the inadequacies of Parliament, took significant steps, through the organization of public meetings, to mobilize popular opinion as a political factor. Yet England was still a country controlled by a relatively small landed oligarchy. Nearly half its cultivated soil was occupied by five thousand families; one-fifth of the country belonged to four hundred landlords. None the less, there was a certain fluidity in the class-structure which kept society resilient; this was not a caste-system, for borders were blurred and crossable to an extent that surprised Voltaire.

Until about 1740 population was declining, partly because of high gin consumption. At this period only one London child in four survived – probably fewer in the north, and certainly fewer in Ireland. Yet later in the century, in both countries, improvements in health and food conditions raised the birth-rate to levels higher than ever before. Between 1700 and 1800 the population of England and Wales increased from five to nine million, and the inhabitants of Ireland doubled in number to a total of nearly five million. This Irish population, however, with a standard of living still among the lowest in Europe, depended precariously upon a potato-crop whose failure was to cause catastrophe (p. 248).

For England, too, Thomas Malthus (1766–1834) prophesied famine, owing to over-population (1798); but he underestimated the country's productive power. Distress there was to be, but it came for different reasons (p. 248), and it was accompanied by immense increases in wealth derived from revolutions both in agriculture and in industry. In agriculture grave hardship was caused by landlords' 'enclosure', in mid-century, of no less than three million acres. Nevertheless, English farms were the model of Europe in agrarian organization and research, and by 1800 they produced fifty per cent more per acre than their counterparts in France.

These were also crucial times in chemical research, as Cavendish (1730–1800) explained gases and electricity, Joseph Black (1726–99) measured heat and Joseph Priestley (1733–1804) discovered oxygen. As a prelude to the movement of factories from the south to northern England and the Clyde, Thomas Newcomen's steam-pump (perfected 1711–12) drained the water from coalmines, and Abraham Darby (d. 1717) and his son produced coke for smelting iron at Coalbrookdale. In the last two decades of the century, with the help of Boulton and Watt's steam-engines, output of iron actually quadrupled.

Wool had long been far the most important source of British wealth; but it began to be superseded by a mechanized cotton-industry which, while ruining home industries, so greatly revolutionized production that during the '50's and '60's alone there was a tenfold increase in the export of British cotton, much of the proceeds going to the purchase and transportation of African slaves.

In the 1780's, as inexpensive Irish labour covered Britain with a 5,000-mile network of canals, this industrial revolution gained its full momentum.

With merchants and bankers (including N. M. Rothschild, *c.* 1798) contributing raw materials and capital respectively to large-scale factories, the brake was removed, for the first time, from the productive power of a human society; though, with political revolution across the channel in France, these explosive developments were accompanied by a stringent tightening of laws against sedition and treason.

The national hero on his island, building civilization by his own energy and ingenuity, had been given popular expression in *Robinson Crusoe* (1719), written by Daniel Defoe (1660–1731), a journalist and government spy. Jonathan Swift (1667–1745), in *Gulliver's Travels* (1716), devoted his powerful brain, obsessed with life's squalors, to denouncing the world for its refusal of a rationalist Utopia.

But rationalism was rejected by John Wesley (1703–91). Transmitting to tens of thousands his revelation of faith as a direct supernatural illumination, Wesley made his missionary Methodism, which became a separate body after his death, the best co-ordinated and most dynamic body of religious opinion in the country. The Anglo-Irishman George Berkeley (1685–1753) likewise challenged Enlightenment by denying certainty to the material world and mathematical knowledge.

The high priest, on the other hand, of a rationalistic society and age was Alexander Pope (1688–1744), whose smooth, compact, felicitous poetry (*The Rape of the Lock*, 1711–14) and prose (*Essay on Man*, 1723–4) observed foibles keenly but with a generous social vision. Pope influenced Voltaire and many others by his diffusion of a broadly tolerant, 'natural' religious viewpoint.

The British were now the leaders of Europe in their powerful questionings of human experience; and their pre-eminent philosopher was the Scot David Hume (1711–76), whose *Essays Concerning Human Understanding* (1748) subjected metaphysics and theism to a penetrating yet constructive opposition. Hume's conclusion is that the human mind is inadequate as an instrument for coming to the truth; and his criticism of inductive methods of attempting this task prepared the way for the enquiries into scientific method that lay ahead.

The first important flowering of the English novel began with Samuel Richardson (1689–1761), whose *Pamela* (1740) and *Clarissa* (1748), despite a self-satisfied, almost sadistically calculating ethic, are significant for their detailed examination of the shifts, cross-purposes and changes in human character and feeling. But Richardson's basic situation, according to which female virtue is dramatically pitted against authority, was ridiculed and reversed by Henry Fielding (1707–54) in his *Joseph Andrews* (1742). The first

English theorist of the novel, Fielding, presenting his up-to-date unheroic hero *Tom Jones* (1749), portrays wide regions of contemporary life with an acceptance tempered by social conscience and irony.

Laurence Sterne (1713–68), in *Tristram Shandy* (1759–67) and the *Sentimental Journey* (1761), is a connoisseur of sentimentality and humorous oddity who believed, like Locke, that human ideas follow irrational associations. The Scotsman Tobias Smollett (1721–71), obsessed with dirt like Swift (p. 230), was the last exponent of the picaresque tradition; but his *Travels* (1766) are the first of many modern, bad-tempered travellers' tales, and his tough disillusioned comedy carries unflinching conviction.

Horace Walpole (1717–94) on the other hand, in his *Castle of Otranto* (1764), crystallized, intensified and brought into social fashion the current revival of picturesque, romantic, macabre Gothic, to be cultivated with sensibility. Another criticism of the century's progressiveness, from a very different standpoint, emerges from the neo-classicism of Edward Gibbon (1737–94), whose monumentally elegant and balanced prose, in his *Decline and Fall of the Roman Empire* (1776–88), rejects beliefs in progress and human nature, seeing an approach to perfection not in medievalism or indeed in Christianity but only in the ancient principate of Rome. Though writing as an English Whig, Gibbon participated fully in the cosmopolitanism of the age. So did his Scottish friend Adam Smith (1723–90), typical product of the age of reason and prophet of the middle class. Proclaiming that a government's only duty is to secure justice and defence, and not to adopt mercantilist restrictions or controls of trade (p. 197), his *Inquiry into the Nature and Causes of the Wealth of Nations* (1776) established political economy as a social science. Another of the principal influences on future reforming thought was Jeremy Bentham (1748–1832), whose *Introduction to the Principles of Morals and Legislation* (1789) proclaimed that the test of any institution is its utility in producing happiness – 'the greatest happiness of the greatest number'. For Bentham, inspired by the analogy of Newtonian mechanics, believed that man's pleasures and pains are capable of quantitative measurement.

Utterly opposed, on the other hand, to abstract theory was Edmund Burke (1729–97), a consummate orator whose empirical, conservative reliance on experience led him to defend the American colonists – because his own government's claims regarding them were too high-flown (1774–5) – and yet, by what seemed but was not a paradox, to attack the French revolutionaries, because they were ideological experimenters.

Robert Burns (1759–96) endowed his poems of country life and satire, written in English or in cleverly manipulated Scottish variants of that tongue, with a combination of qualities which raise his traditional themes to a higher power. Conspicuous among these gifts are a distaste for narrow hypocrisy, a spirited, democratic, independent *joie de vivre*, and a general overflow of humanity arising from direct contact with the illiterate poor.

Another who was filled with compassion for the oppressed, but on a totally different and mystical level, was William Blake (1757–1827). Like his pictures (p. 234), the wildly inventive hallucinations of the *Songs of Innocence* (1789) are disconcertingly based not on observation but upon the promptings of an inner eye; and what that inner eye prescribes is uncompromising insistence upon the testing of every standard, and the utter rejection of all ready-made conventions. Spiritually isolated, reacting sharply against the age of reason, Blake is baffled and anguished by the contrast between his own urgent visionary universe and the world.

Blake initiated, and not long afterwards Wordsworth and Coleridge developed, the English equivalent of Herder's romantic movement (p. 224), rating spontaneity, instinct and above all imagination beyond conscious intellect and technical perfection. Valuing nature as the spiritual counterweight to industrialism and artificiality, trusting personal experience against tradition, the romantics rejected rococo frivolity and reason alike in favour of the sensations which they believed would confer insight into a world more complete and satisfying than our own.

William Wordsworth's first volume of *Lyrical Ballads* (1798) was one of the most important events in the history of poetry. Wordsworth (1770–1850) attained ecstatic communion with the sights and sounds of Nature, in which he discerned a fervent inner spirituality that gave his poems their theme and function. Rationalism faded before nostalgia for a lost childhood; and common life must be described in common words, discarding eighteenth-century diction in favour of native wood-notes wild that stood for Rousseau's 'Noble Savage' (p. 217), for hatred of oppression, and for a new sort of plain man's nationalism as well.

While Wordsworth's *Lyrical Ballads* derived moral value from his sensations, the *Ancient Mariner* contributed by Samuel Taylor Coleridge (1772–1834) to the same volume, and his *Kubla Khan* which followed, unveil a life of the senses leading to unearthly and magical regions: regions of subconscious memories and dreams, mirroring guilt and redemption and the loneliness of haunted souls. These were the uncharted territories of human nature and poetry which Coleridge set out to explore. Before embarking upon other careers – as philosopher, journalist, lecturer, preacher and playwright – he, more than anyone else, brought about that literary revolution which caused imagination to be regarded as the all-important creative force at the core of individual personality.

Among architects, the practice of interweaving different threads from the European tradition had been taken up by Nicholas Hawksmoor (1661–1736), whose painstaking yet sometimes poetical virtuosity enabled him to form dramatic blends in which baroque and Gothic themes were intermingled. Sir John Vanbrugh (1664–1726), a fashionable playwright of Flemish origin converted to architecture, displayed at Blenheim (1705) and Castle Howard his mastery of colossal, ostentatious epic-heroic effects. James Gibbs from Aberdeen (1682–1754), whose London masterpiece was St Martin-in-the-Fields with its graceful steeple, had worked abroad in Rome and formed contacts not only with Italian tradition (which earned such architects the name 'Palladian', p. 166) but with the contemporary movement. But it was a speciality of British architects, as of Andrea Palladio and the Portuguese, to treat landscape as an inseparable component of their buildings. Studying Claude and Poussin, William Kent (1684–1748) abandoned their rational order for audacious artificial irregularities. Then Lancelot (Capability) Brown (1715–83) and Humphrey Repton, stimulator of the picturesque as a movement (*c.* 1790), created the sentimentally sweeping lawns and cunningly scattered clumps of trees which made 'informal' English gardens the models of Europe. Squares and Circuses at Bath, designed with Palladian uniformity by John Wood the elder (1704–54), were rows of ordinary town houses conceived as monumental units, but integrated (by his son) with surrounding greenery; and while Ireland received from native and Italian decorators an exuberant rococo and graceful classicism, Horace Walpole's 'Gothic' Strawberry Hill (1750–76) – the first asymmetrical mansion since Tudor times – and William Chambers' Chinese pagoda at Kew indicate a new self-consciousness about styles. There was no longer any single basis or norm of taste to which architects or artists wished to conform.

Robert Adam (1728–92) of Edinburgh developed current tendencies into a novel, exquisite version of classicism in which Roman and especially Pompeian motifs are moulded with quick rhythms and fresh colours into stucco intricacies 'as complex and fine drawn as a spider's web upon a frosty morning'.[1] Interpreting as a single indivisible unity the various arts associated with a house, Robert Adam guided Chippendale, author of an influential work (1754), to produce his best furniture in the '70's. Then G. Hepplewhite's posthumous *Guide* (1788) translated Adam into popular terms and stronger shapes, while T. Sheraton's fluent chair-backs (*Drawing Book*, (1791–4) displayed a somewhat more feminine version of the refinements that

[1] Sacheverell Sitwell.

had become fashionable in France before its revolutionary deluge (p. 216). Meanwhile the raised-anchor and red-anchor Chelsea porcelain, which played a leading part in mid-century, had been eclipsed by the cream-coloured earthenware and 'Greek' black basaltes and 'jasper ware' with which Josiah Wedgwood (1730–95), a large-scale business organizer of labour and industrial research in the Staffordshire potteries, won himself a world-wide market.

William Hogarth (1697–1764), the first British artist to reach a large international audience and to appeal consciously to a public below the highest reaches of society, rescued English painting, engraving and drawing from sterility by his successful satirical prints of moral subjects, *The Rake's Progress* (1735) and *Marriage à la Mode* (1743), animated compositions which convey their sharp message by an accumulation of telling details.

Richard Wilson (1713/14–82), son of a Welsh clergyman, achieved in his views of the Roman Campagna an original form of lush classicism, modifying the traditions of Dutch landscapists and Claude by his own tranquil vision of nuanced, verdant vistas. The portraitist Joshua Reynolds (1723–92), student of Rubens' Anglicized pupil van Dyck and of the antique and the Italians, was the most intellectual painter of the century. Thomas Gainsborough (1727–88), from Sudbury in Suffolk, lived by his fashionably elegant portraits, but did not enjoy this aspect of his work. It was as a magical landscapist that he reigned supreme. What he looked for in a picture, he said, was music; and his instinctive, expressionistic technique – inspired by Poussin's brother-in-law, Gaspard (Dughet), rather than by the Dutch who had taught earlier British landscape painters – conveyed with supreme spontaneity the essence of the English scene. The products of William Blake's brush, on the other hand, like his poems, are outside both place and time – alarmingly idiosyncratic visions of Biblical truth as none but he could see it (p. 232).

Scandinavia

Sweden had her last fling as an imperial power under Charles XII (1697–1718), his country's militaristic, magnetic glory and doom, who beat the Russians at Narva (1700) but was defeated at Poltava (1709), and thereby lost his country its international initiative for ever. His adviser Von Götz attempted novel experiments in state control for which, after Charles' death, he paid with his life.

More fruitful for the future were the factories of Christopher Polhem at

The enchantingly delicate, inexhaustibly imaginative, fantasy of the Amalienburg (1734–9), a hunting lodge beside the palace at Bavarian Nymphenburg, is the masterpiece of the German-ized Frenchman Francois Cuvilliès; the interior decoration was carried out to his design by J. B. Zimmermann (brother of the architect) and J. Dietrich

ABOVE: The ante-chamber to the chapel of
Catherine the Great's palace at Tsarskoe Selo.
The exuberant and exquisite interior decoration
of Rastrelli and Cameron equalled the
graceful productions of the latter's fellow-
Scot Robert Adam

LEFT: The library of Coimbra University was
designed by the Frenchman Claude de la Prade for
King John (João) V, wealthy from Brazilian
mines. Its three rooms are gilded with Chinese
lacquer motifs on light-green, dark-red and olive
backgrounds (1717–28)

RIGHT: Louis Seize furniture. A drop front secretaire
by Martin Carlin, c. 1776, gilded and inset with
plaques of green Sèvres porcelain

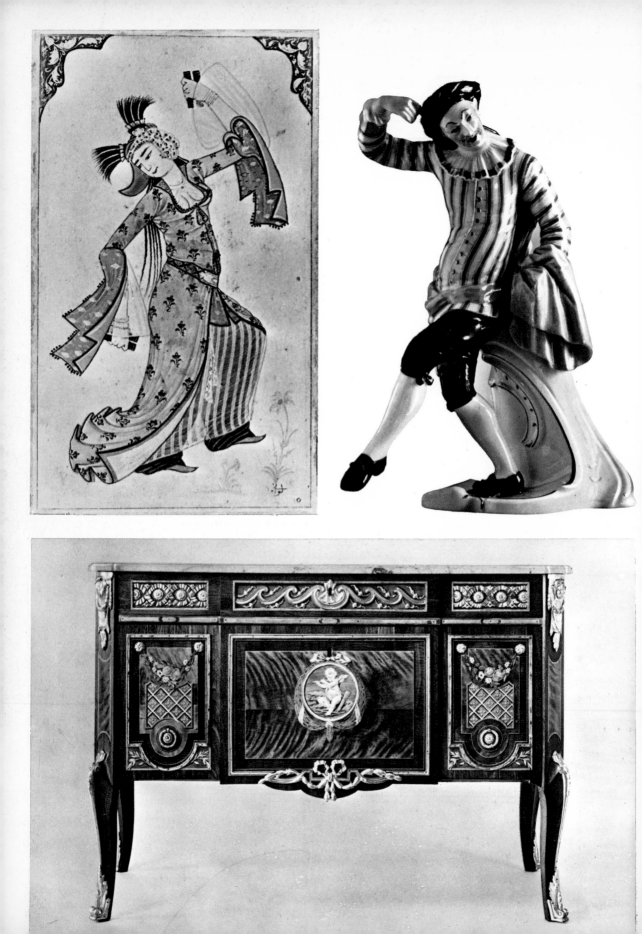

ABOVE LEFT: Under the enlightened patronage of Ahmet III, the most brilliant figure among a galaxy of talent was Levnî (Abdül Celil Çelebi) whose appealing, westernizing miniatures reflect many aspects of Ottoman life and costume

ABOVE CENTRE: Scaramouche, from a set of figures illustrating the popular Commedia dell'Arte by F. A. Bustelli (1723–63), an Italian Swiss whose crisp, fresh, plastic brilliance helped Nymphenburg porcelain to overtake Meissen

ABOVE: Dutch formalism gave way to William Kent's naturalistic interpretations of Poussin and Claude landscapes, 'Capability' Brown's planting schemes, and Repton's masterly designs. Stourhead (1741) was laid out by Henry Hoare junior

LEFT: 'Gustaviansk' commode by Georg Haupt (1780). Gustav III of Sweden was one of Europe's most successful despotic reformers and created a tasteful and distinctive version of Louis Seize furniture

ABOVE: This wing of the Louvre Palace with its rhythmic repetition of columns and pediments, displays the use which architects of the late eighteenth century made of classical features

LEFT: Warsaw's Lazienki Palace (1784) was designed by an Italian, Domenico Merlini, who brought reminiscences of Palladio to collapsing, partitioned Poland

RIGHT ABOVE: Tiepolo's *Finding of Moses* (late 1750's) is a scintillating feat of elegant decoration evoking Venice's golden age. The Princess of Egypt stands with her duenna, page and court dwarf

RIGHT BELOW: *Solitude* by Richard Wilson (1768). He knew his Campagna and Dutch landscapists; his sensuous textures 'fill with an unctuous, tactile pleasure every corner of his fantasies, giving moisture to his verdures, weight to his masonry and body to his vaporous clouds' (M. H. Grant). Constable studied his work

SEI
QUARTETTI
PER DUE VIOLINI, VIOLA, E VIOLONCELLO

Composti e Dedicati
al Signor

GIUSEPPE HAYDN
Maestro di Cappella di S.A.
il Principe d'Esterhazy &c. &c.
Dal Suo Amico

W.A. MOZART
Opera X.

In Vienna presso Artaria Comp.
Mercante d'Editori di Stampe Musica
e Carte Geografiche.

ABOVE: A Concert by Giovanni Paolo Pannini (d. 1765/8). He and Piranesi also created a fashion for picturesque imaginative views of ruins; and Pannini's popular views of modern Rome influenced Canaletto's Venetian scenes
RIGHT: Title page with Mozart's dedication of six quartets to Haydn

Stjärnsund (*c.* 1700) where he pioneered the production of standardized parts, the utilization of specialized machinery, and the systematic distribution of tasks among available labour. Remarkable also, in this century of continental absolutisms, was the constitutional progress of the four Swedish Estates. The only survivors of this ancient system to turn into a modern Parliament on a national scale, these Estates combined English and French techniques in order to maintain a parliamentary party government which was balanced by ministerial responsibility and cabinet solidarity. All this was temporarily swept away by Gustav III (1771–92), whose *coup d'état* established a dictatorial régime. The Act of Union and Security (1789), which confirmed his autocracy, was supported by the unprivileged Estates; but he was murdered three years later.

Not only one of the most successful of Europe's reforming benevolent despots, Gustav III was also the art-loving 'enchanter on the throne' who has given his name to a variant of contemporary French furniture which a white colouring often makes particularly effective. The arbiter of the court's literary taste was the academic poet Johan Kellgren (1751–95), while Karl Mikael Bellman (1740–95) blended humour and pathos in the lyrics he declaimed to the accompaniment of his zither. This, too, was the time of Karl von Linné (Linnaeus, 1707–78), the Swedish botanist whose system of classification the world has followed.

At times during this period Denmark, with which Norway was still united, had the second largest fleet in Europe; in 1759 four hundred of its ships were in the Mediterranean. The country went through a period of headlong reforms attempted by the King's authoritarian German adviser Johan Struensee, who was however executed in 1772.

More typical of a long tradition of moderate scepticism and moderate practical conservatism was the Norwegian writer Ludvig Holberg (d. 1754), a dramatic and satirical genius second only to Voltaire in his generation, who translated the most important European writings into Danish, thus raising it to the status of a cultural language. Later in the century the Danish painter J. A. Carstens (1754–98) achieved a passionate, almost three-dimensional synthesis of classicism and romanticism which produced extensive repercussions upon the artistic life of Germany.

Russia

Peter the Great's reversal of the Narva defeat by his victory over the Swedes at Poltava (p. 234) was followed by the Peace of Nystad (1721), which put an end to the Swedish idea of a Ukraine independent from Moscow. Russia's emergence as a major nation, accelerated by Peter's break-neck methods (p. 210), produced spectacular changes in the balance of European power. Within thirty years (1695–1725) fifty-two new ironworks were opened, one-quarter of them in the Urals; and during the eighteenth century the population of Russia's rapidly extended territories seems to have multiplied threefold, from twelve million to approximately thirty-six.

The period following Peter's death (1725) witnessed cultural evolution on western lines under the foreign influences which inspired Elizabeth (1741–62) to develop new national schools of drama, poetry and architecture, and a university (1755). Russian power did not, at this stage, increase; although the seeds of future pan-Slavism were sown when Russo-Turkish hostilities (1736–9) and other developments caused the Serbs to turn increasingly towards Russia.

Catherine the Great (1762–96) was a farsighted and ruthless autocrat of westernized culture and taste. She was also a massive successful imperialist; Russian southward expansion could no longer be checked by the Turks, whose Christian subjects Catherine ominously claimed to protect (1774). She took her share in the break-up of Poland (p. 221), and incorporated White Russia as part of the motherland (1795). As her forces swept over the Black Sea steppes from Danube and Dniester to the Kuban, their approach to Austria-Hungarian territory posed a new threat to the Hapsburgs. There were hints, also, of Anglo-Russian world rivalry; and the Russians, in their turn, were disquieted when Napoleon invaded Egypt and Syria (p. 215).

The imperial Russian army first appeared in western regions in the 1730's. It then numbered 132,000; by 1796 it had risen to 458,000 and was one of the most powerful in Europe. But the Cossack E. I. Pugachev's dangerous revolt (1773) set back development projects, and Catherine confirmed the domination of Russia's hereditary serf-owners by organizing them into an Estate (1785) of nobility and gentry associated with the Crown. Some ninety-two per cent of the population were serfs: more than four-fifths of these were in private ownership, and the remainder belonged to the state.

Peter the Great's confrontation of the west was symbolized by his foundation of St Petersburg (now Leningrad), on territory conquered from Sweden. Two-thirds of Russia's trade, and most of its Europeanizing influences, passed through this new Baltic capital. In its buildings, native traditions were at first supplemented by Dutch styles or by baroque themes from other lands, which the Ukrainian I. P. Zarudnyi – designer of Moscow's Menshikov tower (1705–7) – blended with motifs inherited from wooden constructions.

Subsequently, Peter tended towards a more French magnificence. But St

Petersburg owed its majesty to the palaces made for Elizabeth by the Italian architect Carlo Bartolommeo Rastrelli the Younger (1700–71). While churches elsewhere, for example at Kizhi (1714) and Podporozhie (1741), play fantastic rhythmical variations on Russian themes, Rastrelli's frontages and columnar groupings at St Petersburg and Peterhof mingle Italian and French traditions and 'Peter's baroque' with his own individual brand of youthfully exuberant contrapuntal rococo, brightly coloured and plastically three-dimensional, displayed upon an immense, imperial scale.

As Catherine the Great interpreted her régime in terms of contemporary neo-classicism, she found in the Rome-inspired Scotsman Charles Cameron an architect and decorator whose elegant, lavish stucco-work at Tsarskoe Selo and Pavlovsk is equal to the choicest performances of his compatriot Robert Adam (p. 233) in imaginative sensitiveness to environment. A leading Moscow classicist, much imitated by subsequent architects, was M. F. Kazakov, whose masterpiece was the Pashkov palace. More eccentric is the Russian version of neo-Gothic which (among work of many other kinds) V. I. Bazhenov (1737–99), an architect often hampered by Catherine's changes of plan, produced for his bridge at the palace of Tsaritsyno.

Sculpture and painting were less prominent than architecture among the arts of eighteenth-century Russia, but they too produced some noteworthy achievements. Carlo Bartolommeo Rastrelli the Elder (1675–1744), father of the architect, gave impetus to Russian sculpture by the dynamic individuality of his baroque bust of Peter the Great (1724). Portrait busts by F. Shubin (1740–1805) too – the son of a White Sea fisherman – show striking psychological truthfulness; and D. Levitsky (1735–1822) was a profoundly observant and influential portrait painter.

Turkey

The reign of Ahmed III (1703–30), recorded by Westerners as a period of sumptuous prosperity, witnessed successes in war and diplomacy under Damad Ibrahim Pasha; and Mahmud I (1730–54), though wars continued, was a lenient administrator, as well as the founder of four libraries. This 'tulip period' of Istanbul – so-called from the fashion for the cultivation of these flowers – was the age of Turkey's pre-eminent lyricist Ahmet Nedim (1681–1760), who employed archaically euphonious language to express his gay, vivacious, colourful personality. The last of the classic poets was the monastery sheikh Galip Dede (Mehmet Esat) (c. 1758–98) who, under imperial patronage, composed an original mystic romance replete with vivid description and elaborate imagery.

Architectural masterpieces of the period, blending native traditions with baroque and rococo ideas, included the pretty pink, green, blue and golden Kiosk of Mustafa Pasha at the Seraglio (restored in 1704), and the huge many-windowed Nuruosmaniye Mosque, 'the light of Osman' (1748–55). A famous miniature painter, who worked for Ahmet III, was Levni (Abdülcelil Çelebi) from Adrianople (Edirne). His highly decorative studies of girls dancing and playing musical instruments have an individual supple grace in which western influences are apparent.

When Russia invaded the Crimea, and Austria invaded Bosnia, Serbia and Wallachia (1736–9), the Turks fought back successfully on both fronts. But as further repeated wars with Russia followed, Turkey proved unable to stand up to the vastly increased resources of Catherine the Great. The Treaty of Küçük Kaynarci (1774) represented a new and serious stage in the diminution of Ottoman power. For this agreement, as well as conceding to Russia the 'protection' of Turkey's Christian subjects, gave the empress a say in the appointment of Wallachian and Moldavian hospodars. These rulers had been Greeks since the beginning of the century; so were the Dragomans of the Porte and Fleet, and many other leading officials.

Under the weak-minded Abdül Hamit I (1774–89) the central Turkish authority began visibly to dissolve. However, the dissolution was to be a prolonged phenomenon, in which every European power had a say and took a hand, hoping either to accelerate or to retard the process. This general, if morbid, interest was reflected by the establishment of Turkish diplomatic missions at Paris, Vienna, London and Berlin. The longstanding alliance with France, however (p. 180), came to an end when Napoleon, in order to sever Britain's communications with its Indian empire, temporarily occupied Ottoman territory in Egypt and Syria.

9

THE NINETEENTH CENTURY

France and the Low Countries

In 1802 Napoleon (p. 215) simultaneously celebrated the pacification of Europe, agreement with the papacy, and the extension of his three-year-old First Consulate into a lifelong office; which was then exchanged for the title of hereditary emperor of the French, combined with the kingship of Italy (1804). For another nine years a continental European empire, culminating in the Peace of Tilsit (1807), was held down by his army, drawn from many nations, sustained on foreign soil, and manipulated by Napoleon's superlative talent for military mobility. But a novel type of commercial warfare, designed to blockade Britain, was frustrated by Nelson's victory off Cape Trafalgar (1805); for French land communications could not eventually prevail against British command of the sea, which required much smaller expenditure.

After failing against British and native resistance in Spain and Portugal (p. 264) and losing half a million men in six months during his disastrous invasion of Russia (1812), Napoleon fell at Leipzig (1813) to a European coalition sponsored by a German liberation movement. Exile at Elba was followed by the 'Hundred Days' of attempted *revanche* which ended with his defeat by Wellington and Blücher at Waterloo (1815), succeeded by internment at St Helena (d. 1821).

As First Consul, Napoleon had seemed to conservatives everywhere a guarantor that revolution was ended; while liberals looked to him for the consolidation of their gains. Carrying out ideas sponsored by the revolution and Directory (p. 215) and transferring them into more authoritative and less adventurous channels, Napoleon displayed his ruthless energetic directness by establishing a utilitarian, efficient, hard-headed police state on unprecedentedly rationalist lines. His lucid legal Codes (1804) were a major bastion of modern society, their recognition of civic equality combined with the maintenance of property rights. His novel administrative institutions and hierarchies, his educational systems, were admired and imitated by the world.

The inherent contradiction between family dynasticism and modern nationalism, which Napoleon never overcame, was intensified under the increasingly ultra-royalist governments of Louis XVI's brothers Louis XVIII (1815–24) and Charles X (1824–30). After economic crises in the '20's, accompanied by the new socialism of Saint-Simon (1760–1825), the excluded and estranged middle class asserted themselves in the revolution of 1830, which was accompanied by similar protests against reactionary rigidity in most of the European states. One result of these events was the break up of the Low Countries (united under Dutch rule after Napoleon), when Belgium asserted its independence under Leopold I of Saxe Coburg (1831–65).

Leopold had appealed successfully to the new French king, Louis Philippe, Duke of Orléans (1830–48), an ex-fighter in the revolutionary army whose citizen kingship tacitly admitted the principle of popular sovereignty. But accelerated French industrialization was accompanied by continued economic slumps and price-rises, together with a fermentation of ideas which made the government react towards greater conservatism. In 1848 the century's most serious wave of European revolutions (p. 257) drove Louis Philippe from his throne. For the first time, in Paris, the working class fought to establish its own régime; but it succumbed to the army, which henceforward supported traditionalism. Napoleon's nephew Napoleon III (1852–70), first established a strong presidential system and then created the Second Empire, which made him the earliest European ruler to owe his power to direct, universal suffrage. He indicated his recognition of this fact, in an age of militant nationalism, by the expert propaganda with which he exploited his economic activity and the glamorous façade of imperial grandeur. Yet although in two decades France had absorbed forty-four per cent of all the gold coined in the world, a quarrelsome foreign policy undermined credit, and war against the new great power of Prussia (p. 258) ended in total French defeat (1870). A revolutionary interlude, under the Paris Commune, was followed by the establishment of the Third Republic, which lasted until 1940. This régime succeeded in launching rapid economic recovery, colonial expansion, and a novel agreement with Russia (1892–3) against Germany. But the end of the century was marked by far-reaching internal splits (1894–1906) between the liberals who supported the Jewish officer Dreyfus and the conservative and military elements who favoured his victimization.

J. B. P. Lamarck's theory of evolution (1815–22) heralded Darwin (p. 252); and a Chair was created (1887) for Émile Durkheim, the pioneer sociologist who devoted fundamental studies to social disorganization. By the end of the century L. Pasteur (1822–95) had identified microbes as the cause of disease. Henri Becquerel (1852–1908) found out the radioactive properties of uranium (1896), and the Curies discovered radium (1898). While Belgium, before and after its independence, already led the way in continental railway construction and energetic industrial and social experiments, French engineers developed the structural uses of steel, building the Eiffel Tower and contributing a masterly Gallery of Machines to the Paris exhibition (1889). Frenchmen made asphalt roads, pioneered reinforced concrete and contributed to the internal-combustion engine (1896–7). Meanwhile J.-N. Niepce (1765–1833) and J.-L.-M. Daguerre evolved photography, and the brothers Louis and Auguste Lumière, adapting the experiments of Thomas A. Edison in America, produced the cinematograph (1895).

The writers of Napoleon's First Empire had mostly been foreigners or émigrés. One of the former was Benjamin Constant (1767–1830) from Lausanne, whose semi-autobiographical novel *Adolphe* (1807) devotes classically lucid analytical powers to the morbid theme of a disunited personality. Among the emigrants was F. R. de Chateaubriand (1768–1848), the magician who preached a return to medieval Christianity and yet introduced an age of anguished sensibility and feeling for exotic nature. Madame de Staël (1766–1817) developed the conception of literary works as products of their environment; leading the international resistance to Napoleon, she introduced the French – and particularly the Swiss, from her Geneva home – to English and Weimar romanticism (pp. 232, 224). Another who gathered up these northern threads to romantic ends, uniting them with Italian and Spanish motifs, was A. de Lamartine (1790–1869), whose evocative, harmonious, spontaneous *Méditations Poétiques* (1820) create a new close bond between author and reader.

Liberalism was gaining ground in public opinion, and by the late '20's Victor Hugo (1802–85) had proclaimed its literary manifestation to be the romantic movement. His outstanding theatrical interpretation of this approach was *Hernani* (1830), which reveals Hugo's supreme, prodigal mastery of stage-craft; though his widest fame was to come many years later from his epic, optimistic, visionary *Légende des Siècles* (1859–83). But as a youth in the '30's this expounder of the eternal properties of human nature, with his unrivalled armoury of words, was already proclaiming the vogue for a superman – ideal of artists and the rebellious young, challenger of a rising bourgeois capitalist society.

A synthesis of this romanticism with native French traditions was attempted by Stendhal (H. Beyle) (1783–1842). His novels *Le Rouge et Le Noir* (1831), linking several explosive themes in an orderly system, and the dazzlingly intricate, surprise-laden *Chartreuse de Parme* (1839), have their roots in the Italian Renaissance and in Voltaire, but display a bitter, brilliant, outsider's understanding of the human heart, combined with an admiration for ruthless, rootless men. In these same crucial '30's, significant portions of *La Comédie Humaine*, a vast series of novels by Honoré de Balzac (1799–1850), constitute outstanding social documents of this age in which literature and art were haunted by the rise of industrialization. His sober erection of facts into living portraits, although these pictures are disconcertingly crossed by fantastic distortions, made him an authoritative figure in the rising history of realism, the most vital artistic force of the century. Moreover, although Balzac was a conservative who believed in authority and the social function of religion, the bitterness with which he unmasked middle-class money-dominated depravities made him the involuntary founder of modern socialistic trends.

Prosper Mérimée (1803–70), in the 1840's, helped to create the pointed, concentrated, rather grim short story. *Les Fleurs du Mal* (1857) by Charles Baudelaire (1821–67) added a novel dimension to literature by the whole-heartedness and fluid imagery with which his astonishing talents bridge the gulf between spiritual and physical worlds. Beneath a surface of morbid obsession and ironical despair, this uniquely lucid and observant intellect identified itself with the world, yet rejected its shallowness with a fierce insistence.

In the French novel at this period, the ascendant realistic movement's unchallenged leader was Gustave Flaubert (1821–80). His *Madame Bovary* (1857) is exhaustive, precise, relentlessly natural, almost sadistic in the professed impersonality of its anti-Rousseau, anti-romantic, anti-melodramatic reaction. Flaubert's three phases of human history are paganism, Christianity and swinishness; and *L'Éducation Sentimentale* (1869) shows how hopes end in the unheroic dignity of gradual collapse. Auguste Comte (1798–1857) saw truth in a new 'positivist', secular religion of science, sociology, human reason and morality, dismissing all *a priori* principle and recognizing only factual observation. The main spokesman of this somewhat chilly post-romantic stress on scientific method was Henri Taine (1828–93), whose search, however, for accurate knowledge of mankind was tempered by a hopeless, resigned horror of the *bête humaine*. Émile Zola (1840–1902) introduced a pseudo-scientific sociological approach into his grandiose, luxuriantly imaginative novels *L'Assommoir* (1877) and *Germinal* (1885), in which the individual is 'stretched out on an accurate historical framework as on an operating table'. While Anatole France (1844–1924) devoted his clever subtle style to sardonic characterizations, Guy de Maupassant (1850–93), Norman master of the realistic short story, subjects his morally deficient, banal characters to merciless intellectual analysis.

Meanwhile Stéphane Mallarmé (1842–98) took refuge in the shimmering, voluptuous fancies of a poetry of negation, conveyed symbolically through new word-meanings and rhythms. The *Romances sans Paroles* written in prison (1874) by Paul Verlaine (1844–96) from Metz wove unheard-of harmonies

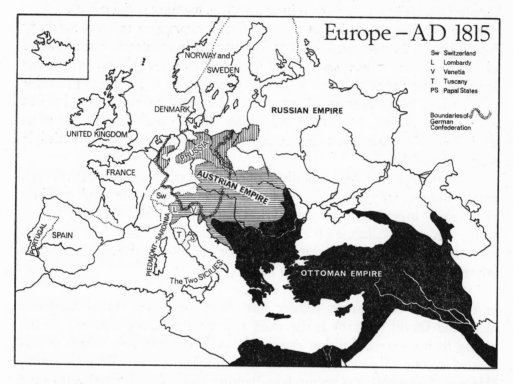

Europe – AD 1815

Sw Switzerland
L   Lombardy
V   Venetia
T   Tuscany
PS Papal States

Boundaries of German Confederation

of sound and mood, conveying a suggestive, symbolic sensibility comparable to contemporary impressionist painting (p. 245); though Verlaine himself preferred the analogy of music as more descriptive of his vague elusive aura of pregnant implications and associations between sound and sense. His friend Rimbaud (1854–91), from the Ardennes, was an arch-rebel and mystic who furiously endeavoured to make literature the direct expression of the heart; his *Saison en Enfer* (1873) views poetry as a 'long, immense and planned disordering of the senses'.

In Belgium Maurice Maeterlinck (1862–1949), of Flemish extraction but writing in French, began his symbolist poems, plays and philosophical works designed to indicate the mysterious, shadowy movements which lie just out of sight, beneath life's outward surface. Meanwhile Émile Verhaeren (1855–1916) wrote colourful and robust French poetry about his native Flanders. Flemish literature, too, gained European stature during the '90's from the contributors to *Van Nu en Straks* (*Today and Tomorrow*, 1893–1901), among whom Karel van de Woestijne incarnated the sophisticated end-of-century spirit in his tortured confessions. Meanwhile in Holland, where Willem Bilderdijk (1756–1831) had achieved an imposing reputation as prophet and lyric poet, a literary revival, sponsored by the review *De Nieuwe Gids* (1885), passed from individualistic to more social trends.

Many of these successive tendencies found expression in contemporary French music. Hector Berlioz (1803–69) was an innovator in orchestration whose *Symphonie Fantastique* (1830) shared Victor Hugo's preference for demonic, enormous themes, lavishing upon them a bizarre, untamable imagination. Meyerbeer and Scribe created French romantic grand opera at the same period, but under Napoleon III's Second Empire the most original artistic product was operetta, spiced by Offenbach with a permissible degree of social satire.

The first steps towards naturalistic opera were taken by Bizet (1838–75), whose *Carmen* (1875) is a forceful and poignant folk-tale rendered into picturesque, ingenious tunes and lyrical harmonies. Then Debussy (1862–1918), who was Mallarmé's friend and set Verlaine and Baudelaire to music, left romanticism and classicism behind for the novel, dreamy, iridescent impressionism of *L'Après Midi d'un Faune* (1894).

In the 1820's the Gascon painter Jean Auguste Ingres (1780–1867) had succeeded David (p. 216) as the chief exponent of neo-classicism, contributing to it a piercing vision conveyed by draughtmanship which subordinated colour to powerful sinuous lines reminiscent of fifteenth-century Florence. Meanwhile the young Jean Baptiste Corot (1796–1875) was fusing an ideal poetical classicism with the misty limpidity of intensely felt romantic moods: the sort of momentary, snapshot moods that were caught by the current invention of photography (p. 241). Théophile Gautier, with his slogan 'Art for Art's Sake' (1832), proclaimed the artist's freedom to choose his own themes and methods, without regard for any sort of purposefulness – or for external influences, since the artist stood on his own: lacking patronage or any other form of security, misunderstood by the bourgeoisie whom he spurned.

Théodore Géricault (1791–1824) both embodied neo-classicism and moved beyond it to scenes of livelier animation, basing his violent Raft of the Medusa (1819) upon observation in hospitals and asylums. Eugène Delacroix

(1799–1863) likewise painted Byronic, Hugoesque themes, poetic but bloody, replete with vivacious and colourfully grandiose excitement. 'The enemy is greyness' – 'the free manifestation of one's personal impressions' is what is wanted; but romantic fervour (with its love-hate relationship towards classicism), and supreme talent as a colourist, were tempered in Delacroix by a brain of exceptional force.

Meanwhile the satirical genius of Honoré Daumier (1808–79) from Marseille, utilizing German lithographic inventions, pointed the way to modern expressionists; and Belgium produced a fantasist of insane power in Antoine Wiertz (1806–65). 'Realism', on the other hand, was a word first used by Courbet in 1850. Bridge between the worlds of Balzac and Flaubert, forerunner of proletarian art in his boast that he alone could relate painting to society, Gustave Courbet (1819–77) in his one-man show of 1855 communicated his robust peasant 'impulse to grasp, thump, squeeze or eat', and an influential urge to employ imagery which would convey the completest possible expression of everyday life. But the nearest of all to total, more than photographic objectivity was Édouard Manet (1832–83): a middle-class Parisian painter of luminous colours and unshadowed modelling who, at the end of the '60's, rallied the younger painters to his conviction, strengthened by studying Goya and Velazquez, that we should trust our eyes, and not our ideas of what things ought to be like. During the next decade, painters – from whom Manet remained aloof although he came to show affinities with their work – echoed contemporary discoveries in mathematics by moving towards the scientific theories of *plein air*, professed by a group of painters first described as Impressionists in 1874. Their aim, long and violently opposed by orthodox opinion, was to achieve even greater naturalism by an exact analysis of tone and colour which rendered the fleeting, instantaneous play of light dancing upon the surface of objects.

Claude Monet (1840–1926) was the most persistent (and paid least attention to the European tradition) in his pursuit of this absolute fidelity to visual sensation, painting directly from the object, often out of doors. 'He is only an eye', said Cézanne, 'but what an eye!' – an individual vision spontaneously recording transient refractions and reflections of light and shade, sub-divided prismatically, during the later '70's, into tiny colour-patches. These led, a few years later, to the 'pointillism' of Georges Seurat (1859–91), who came to abandon the flickerings of *plein air* for a more static, formal type of composition based on mathematical proportions.

Joining Monet in his affirmation of freedom and in his desire to catch the moment on the wing, Edgar Degas (1834–1917) was closer to the sculptor Rodin (1890–1917), or to Japanese colour-print engravers, in his uncannily perceptive, basically realistic observation of the natural, unpremeditated gestures of human beings, foreshortened and in action: a talent which, as Degas painted with acute exactness the society of his day, drew him away from the impressionists to a greater intellectual rigour. Pierre Renoir (1841–1919) on the other hand, though he too started in close association with Monet, was less concerned with purely transitory visual stimuli than with impressionism's other heritage of an enriched colour range. Beginning as a porcelain painter, he adapted his instinctive, sensitive appreciation of surfaces to canvas-painting, and particularly to depicting the solid pink flesh of innocent, massive girls, classic in their sculptural unity yet warmly and pleasurably real.

For it was an urgent task for artists to look behind the manifold appearances of impressionism in search of durable permanent forms. This was the supreme achievement of Paul Cézanne (1839–1906), from Aix-en-Provence. In the late '70's and '80's Cézanne discarded all emotional or intellectual encumbrances in order to achieve a new vision of nature as the mask for an underlying framework of organically solid forms. Cylindrical shapes, in particular, emerged from his desire to achieve recession and the effect of light by the use of primary colours, laboriously analysed and richly uniting pattern and depth. Combining arrogance and humility, frankness and repression, he was at one with his contemporaries Flaubert and Baudelaire in searching for a new way to truth by transforming the unstable romantic equilibrium into a close-knit, durably organized reality – in which man, the subject of Degas' humanism, is now relegated to the level of other things.

Paul Gauguin's (1848–1903) abandonment of western humanism was on different grounds. His greed for rich luxuriant colours led to a 'synthetism' (1889) inspired by Japanese, Romanesque and 'primitive' African models, and welded into an individual flavour by his journey to Martinique (1887) and eventual residence in Tahiti (1891, 1895).

Cézanne and Gauguin were desperately lonely men. So, above all, was Vincent Van Gogh (1853–90) from Groot Zundert in Holland (Brabant). After travelling in the Low Countries, Van Gogh settled in Paris (1886–8) and then at Arles (in which he spent two months with Gauguin) before moving to Auvers where, insane, he shot himself. Yet, amid this tragic record, a frenzied spiritual struggle towards the ultimate purposes of life emerges from his excitedly curling Germanic lines, screaming subjective colours, and restless muscular rhythms – all of which (far removed from a flourishing Dutch school of romantic painting) assault the viewer's emotions with a direct relentless ferocity complicated by the lavish employment of symbolism. When Van Gogh was painting corn, he said simply, 'we are corn' – so passionately does he associate himself with the significance of all he paints, divorcing art from society yet longing to console all humanity by his unsophisticated, self-revealing art intended to 'comfort like music, with something eternal'.

After the Belgian James Ensor (1860–1949) had likewise surprised the late '80's with his exuberantly colourful anticipations of expressionists and surrealists, his compatriot Victor Horta (1861–1947) acclimatized the British-inspired *art nouveau* movement (p. 251) to Belgium, from which it spread to Paris and Dresden (for both of which cities Henri van de Velde (1863–1957) made designs in 1896–7), as well as to Vienna, Barcelona (p. 290), Chicago and many other centres.

Britain

Britain's major share in defeating Napoleon (p. 239) was possible because Nelson perfectly exploited the combination of large guns and sailing ships at Trafalgar (1805); because Wellington's armies in Spain and at Waterloo (1815) were the products of prolonged military reforms (1795–1809); and because the younger Pitt (p. 228), though no strategist, was a persevering and astute administrator and an effective public speaker. Final victory, followed by the Treaty of Vienna (p. 257) to which Wellington and Castlereagh (both Anglo-Irish) made valuable contributions, seemed to justify conservatism; yet social and industrial changes made it impossible to resist the Reform Bill of 1832. This accelerated the transfer of power to the commercial and industrial classes – though forty years later only seven thousand people still owned four-fifths of cultivable England.

Meanwhile, evangelical revival caused Britain to abolish the international slave trade (1807, 1833–4), of which it had been the principal champion and beneficiary. David Ricardo (1772–1823) systematized the rising science of economics; and Robert Owen (1771–1858) stressed the role of labour as the source of all wealth. London, with over a million inhabitants (four million by 1880), was the greatest port in the world, and supplanted Amsterdam as the centre for international financiers, such as the Barings and Rothschilds. With a unique population increase of fourteen per cent in a single wartime decade (1800–10) Britain was forging ahead at an explosive rate of industrialization, half a century in advance of the continent and still well ahead of the Americans, although these were likewise now displaying variety and ingenuity in their industrial inventions.

At the beginning of the century Britain produced ninety per cent of the world output of coal; and between 1830 and 1850 its production rose from fifteen million to forty-nine million tons. Northern coal mines produced the railways which, after a series of experiments (1813–29), led the continent by their fivefold expansion during the '40's. Steam engines could only develop where sheet iron (as well as capital) was made available, and Britain's iron production multiplied sixfold between 1805 and 1840; by the latter date it was three times as great as the output of France. During the next fifty years the British figure again multiplied twentyfold, stimulated by revolutionary aids towards the cheaper mass production of steel, such as Sir H. Bessemer's converter (1855). Other important scientific developments included John Dalton's (1766–1844) pioneer theoretical atomism, Sir Humphry Davy's (1778–1829) electrolytic method for isolating potassium and sodium, J. L. Macadam's (1756–1836) new road surfaces, Michael Faraday's (1791–1867) generator or dynamo, J. Lister's foundation of aseptic surgery (1865–7) and J. J. Thomson's (1856–1940) announcement, deep with future significance, that he had discovered a body smaller than the hydrogen atom, namely the electron (1897).

A merchant navy that doubled in size between 1790 and 1820, and then converted itself rapidly to steam, enabled the cotton worked in Lancashire – the most thickly populated area in the world – to replace wool as the dominant, conquering factor in the British economy (p. 203). Cotton manu-factures rose from £4 million in 1784 to £300 million in 1833; cotton exports, worth £19 million in 1833, had increased by 1870 to £56 million, representing forty-fifty per cent of the total British export trade.

Yet this unparalleled expansion of wealth exacted a terrible price in sweated labour, near-starvation, epidemics of typhus cholera and 'relapsing fever', alcoholism, insanitary residential squalor, sordid urbanization and civil disturbances dating from the Luddite riots of 1811–12 and Peterloo (Man-chester) massacre of 1819. The term 'working class' came into use (c. 1815), and was common parlance by 1832 when the material conditions of the workers were on the downgrade. Early forms of practical socialism date from the same period (p. 240). But as, with the aid of an efficient police force (1829), the new proletarians were broken into their industrial rhythm, social bitterness reached its height in the 'Hungry '40's' and the '50's, when an unstable though dynamic economy produced recurrent depressions and mass unemployment. 1847–8 were bad years, and the first world-wide recession of 1857–8 again had disastrous results. But the worst horror of western Europe was the famine in Ireland where, among an impoverished rural population (p. 229) that had nearly doubled in half a century to a figure of eight million, potato epidemics caused the deaths of one million from starvation and disease, and the emigration of a million more (1846–51).

Yet in England, especially under Sir Robert Peel's premiership (1841–7), this was an age of dramatic reforms – free imports, Factory Acts (1833–) and mine laws, cheap food and Public Health Acts, grants of self-government to Canada and Australia. Moreover, from the fifties onwards a satisfactory balance, bringing gains in wealth to all classes, seemed to have been struck between old and new, agriculture and industry, *laissez faire* and regulation. Queen Victoria (1837–1901) showed a talent for finding the right states-man to orientate her governments as each new current became evident. The dominant politician of the mid-Victorian age was Lord Palmerston (1784–1865). Aggressive abroad with the support of the incomparably powerful Royal Navy, opposed to dramatic change at home, Palmerston effectively manoeuvred a system of administration that was still oligarchic but sensitive nowadays to public opinion. After two breaks in the long-standing peace – the Crimean War (p. 253) with its novel alliance between England and France, and the Indian Mutiny (1857–8) – the '60's witnessed a demand for new and active liberalism; and English cabinet government, regarded as a model of constitutional development, adapted itself to the facts of the industrial revolution. Gladstone – who helped to keep Britain out of the American Civil War (1861–5) – favoured political reforms, while his conservative rival Disraeli preferred improvements in the social sphere. The struggle about Home Rule for the Irish remained inconclusive. But in England the '80's saw the rise of the Labour movement, and the fight for the vote was replaced by conscious questionings and battles about how to use it.

As the European balance of power ceased to be an influence for peace, within two decades (between 1870 and 1890) the great powers multiplied their military expenditure several times over. At the same time, politicians intent upon industrial progress believed that expansion was only possible with new countries as consumers. European capitalism, which largely owed its existence to the exploitation of India and other Asian countries, now carved out spheres of influence in Africa as well. There the British lead, although shortened by rapid continental developments, was reasserted by the unpopular but finally victorious Boer War against Afrikaans-speaking settlers of Dutch origin in South Africa (1899–1902). By this time the population of England numbered thirty-six million, as against nine million in 1800; and the British Empire comprised 390 million people, one quarter of the world's inhabitants.

This was an epoch when the artistic values of the ruling class were only associational and archaistic. Accordingly, the most notable architect of George IV's regency (1810–20) and reign (1820–30) was an eclectic – the clever town-planner John Nash, who could build in the classical, 'Gothic' and Indian styles according to taste. Meanwhile Sir John Soane (1753–1837), under many influences, approached a remarkable new unhampered self-expression (1811–14). However, neo-Gothicism prevailed, and A. W. Pugin (1812–52) made the Gothic revival no longer a style but a religion, enshrined in Sir Charles Barry's Houses of Parliament (1836) and in the second edition (1855) of John Ruskin's *Seven Lamps* (1848). England and Wales continued to develop magnificent gardens (p. 233), but architects ignored the opportunities of the industrial revolution; as they catered for increasingly sterile prevailing taste, innumerable slavishly uninspired neo-Gothic churches, and streets of wholly degraded and uncomfortable small houses, rose throughout the country that so many of them still disfigure.

Yet English painting, which had attained international stature in the previous century, now for the first time produced two outstanding artists in Constable and Turner. The finished, exhibited paintings of John Constable (1776–1837) are master-works deriving inspiration from Dutch seventeenth-century models. But his more lyrical preparatory oil sketches reveal him as a stubborn individualist faithful to his own vision, who wanted, not Gainsborough's traditionally picturesque set-pieces (p. 234), but the 'wet, earthy, romantic and resolute' English truth about the countryside: into which, like Wordsworth, he entered with an unequalled rapturous intensity that transformed the face and future of painting. Describing his landscapes as experiments in natural philosophy, Constable opened up new horizons of realism, impressionism and pointillism by breaking up his colour into fragmentary patches placed densely side by side so that the whole visual world seems to dazzle and vibrate. J. M. W. Turner (1775–1851), unequalled as a natural colourist, was inspired by his Italian travels to develop the landscape and water-colour traditions he had inherited into an atmospheric whirlwind rush of coloured shimmering light and iridescent mist. Within their depths, form is swallowed and dissolved in an evocation of nature which has become a revolutionary vision, defying rational analysis.

The contemporary artistic movement of the Pre-Raphaelites (1848/49–) likewise made use of bright colours, but these, in extreme contrast to Turner, are employed to depict detail, with literary overtones, as in the meticulous Biblical scenes of Leigh Hunt (1827–1910). Feeling that Raphael was over-praised and that seventeenth-century Italians were insincere, the exponents of this style took their title from a theoretical devotion to early Italian painting which was, however, still very imperfectly understood. William Morris (1834–96) believed in regeneration by handicraft, and his Arts and Crafts movement – now mostly noted for its patterned wallpapers – was one

A sketch by Goethe (1749–1832) showing the appearance of the Spirit of Earth in *Faust*. His universal talent encompassed the roles of dramatist, poet, philosopher and scientist

ABOVE: The impact of the industrial revolution, in which England was far ahead of the world, upon the greatest of its painters of light: *Rain Steam and Speed* by Turner (1844), who after visiting Italy expressed his revolutionary visions in form-dissolving, shimmering, iridescent mist

BELOW: John Constable was the last great painter to work in the tradition of the Dutch landscape artists of the seventeenth century. His careful sky studies made under the influence of Luke Howard's *The Climate of London* were put to impressive use in this view of *Weymouth Bay*

TOP: Goya (d. 1828), his visual powers sharpened by deafness, produced exceptional though remorseless portraits, and painted, drew and engraved horrifying studies of the Napoleonic wars – grim reflections on power – before turning, in his later years, to pure nightmare in his 'black pictures'

BOTTOM: 'The enemy is greyness', said Delacroix, who transfigured neo-classicism, combining romanticism with exceptional cerebral force in his grandiose Byronic scenes such as *Ovid among the Scythians*

ABOVE: Edouard Manet, student of Goya and
Velasquez, persuaded young painters to trust
their eyes. This portrait of Zola (1868) was given to
its subject in gratitude. 'We laugh at M. Manet,'
remarked Zola, 'but our children will go into
raptures before his pictures'

RIGHT: Pierre Renoir combined his own unique,
instinctive style of tenderness with a robust feeling
for the warmth of the female form, exemplified
in this pastel of a young girl with black hair (1883)

LEFT: Self-portrait by Paul Cézanne (1880–1), traditional yet revolutionary – at one with his contemporaries Flaubert and Baudelaire in his search for a new way to truth, by transforming the unstable romantic equilibrium into a close-knit durably organised reality

ABOVE: Balzac's prolific novels reflected with realism and fantasy the haunting of art by industrialisation. His portrait was the work of Auguste Rodin

RIGHT TOP: Ledoux's spherical plan for a cemetery at Chaux. He thought out neo-classicism – and every job he undertook – afresh; and used traditional forms with a revolutionary freedom which, if followed up, could have spared the nineteenth century many dull horrors. His *L'Architecture* (1804) presented plans for an ideal city

RIGHT BOTTOM: The new possibilities of iron and steel; vaulting achieved the span of 385 feet in the 150-foot-high Halle des Machines at the Paris international exhibition of 1889, by the engineer Contamin and the architect C.-L.-F. Dutert

Coupe

TOP: The Dresden Opera House (1869–78),
designed by Gottfried Semper

BOTTOM: Photograph of a scene from
Stanislavsky's production of *Uncle Vanya* (1899).
Chekhov's plays and short stories, with their
precise and clinical yet humane analyses of man
and society – including the rising middle classes –
enlarged still further the immense new ranges of
Russian literature

of the progenitors of the *Art Nouveau* style of design: of which the principal novelty resided in a new undulating, writhing and asymmetrically inter-playing ornamentation, naturalistically based on 'the lily's stem, an insect's feeler, the filament of a blossom, or occasionally a slender flame'.[1] Arthur H. Macmurdo (1851–1942), founder of a guild of Morris' followers, pioneered the style in his book on Wren's city churches (1883). While it spread to Belgium (p. 247), Catalonia (p. 290) and elsewhere, Charles R. Mackintosh (1868–1928) gave it effectively original architectural shape in the Glasgow Art School (1893), and it found expression also in the elaborately wrought, stylised, *fin de siècle* black-and-white drawings of Aubrey Beardsley (1872–98).

William Wordsworth, whose gigantic poetical changes had belonged to the last years of the preceding century (p. 232), regarded his *Ode on Intimations of Immortality* (published in 1807) as the crown of his work. Coleridge (p. 232) turned from poetry to many sorts of didactic prose-writing, including the *Biographia Literaria* (1817) and posthumous *Literary Remains* which make him as supreme a critic of English poetry as Lessing and Goethe are of German. Percy Bysshe Shelley (1792–1822), prophet of idealistic romance, believed that poets are above convention. The intoxicating lyrical onrush in his *Prometheus Unbound* (1818–19) – rebel hero of the generation which witnessed the Peterloo massacre (p. 248) – seeks to cure the tyranny and cruelty of humdrum daily life by enormous Platonic schemes of regeneration. John Keats (1795–1821), last-born of the romantics and first to die, innovates in both the form and the spirit of his 1819 Odes: *On Melancholy*, *On a Nightingale*, *On a Grecian Urn*, *To Autumn*. Abnormally receptive to the identity of other beings and things, Keats brought a dis-ciplined sensibility, and richly dense and sensuous imagery, to serve his imagination. This inventive, ecstatic faculty created a radically original response to experience, purely poetical and with none of Shelley's 'palpable design on us'. Byron (1788–1824), hostile to Keats and Wordsworth, was conventional aristocrat as well as rebel and outcast; his masterpiece *Don Juan* (1819–24) is both a realistic satire upon English society and an epic, in which irony tempers his romantic desire that freedom should be bestowed upon himself and others, including the Greeks for whose independence he fought (p. 254). His proud and lonely, destiny-marked heroes formulated the spirit of the age; and the admiration of Goethe and Mazzini testified to the European status and role which English poetry had gained from his pen.

With no such denunciatory intentions, Walter Scott (1771–1832) gave

[1] N. Pevsner.

the British novel also, and his native Scotland, a European reputation and influence. Written shortly after Jane Austen's *Pride and Prejudice* (1813) had shown how the modern personality and its moral dilemmas could be subjected to subtle analysis, Scott's more extrovert *Waverley Novels* (1814–19) inaugurated social fiction with their humorous, worldly wise, convincing presentations of a colourful world rooted in material reality and organically linking man with his community, and past with present. The heyday of the social novel came during the tensions of the late '30's and '40's (p. 248); and its supreme exponent was Charles Dickens (1811–70). Most engrossing of entertainers, writer of the outstanding English comic novel *Pickwick Papers* (1836–7), he not only enjoyed life (his long concealed liaison with an actress gave his later books an improved insight into women) but loathed the English social system – which had inflicted traumatic experiences upon him as a boy. In *Oliver Twist* (1838) and subsequent books he expressed this loathing with phantastic, hallucinatory intensity, spurred by a generous, vague hankering after individual kindliness which reflected the rising conscience of his age. The trenchant prosewriter Thomas Carlyle (1795–1882) took refuge from utilitarian practicality in the dangerous mysticism of *On Heroes and Hero-Worship* (1841). Alfred Lord Tennyson (1809–92), with his exceptional poetic sensibility of eye and ear, was willing to accept his role as the famed prophet of contemporary life, yet sometimes escaped to a beautiful antique world, and only attained conviction of immortality through moods of terror and despair (*In Memoriam*, 1833–50). The single year 1847 witnessed the startlingly powerful novels of the Brontë sisters in Yorkshire – *Jane Eyre* by Charlotte (1816–55), full of terrors and sexual promptings, and the stark mysterious world of Emily's *Wuthering Heights* (1818–48); and contemporary with these were the beginnings of *Vanity Fair*, in which William Thackeray (1811–63) unfolds with unheroic modernity his conviction that men's motives are snobbery and self-esteem. The female novelist George Eliot (1819–80), on the other hand, was a radical Tory whose novels such as *Adam Bede* (1859) subject her characters, within the ordered world she marks out for them, to a relentless intellectual analysis.

John Stuart Mill (1806–73) was a utilitarian but also a romantic, who breathed a new spirit into English radicalism by his works on logic and political economy, suggesting that the good community is one where the human personality is given the freest interplay. But this personality was shown in a new light by Charles Darwin (1809–82), whose *Origin of Species* (1859) – supreme achievement of contemporary urges towards synthesis and progress – demonstrated that all forms of animal life (even those previously regarded as fixed creations) were products of evolution, operating through natural selection as its chief agent. The religion-based position of man was shaken; and Herbert Spencer (1820–93), borrowing sociology from Comte (p. 242), elaborated a system stressing the pre-eminence not only of science over religion, but of the individual over society.

Writing like him in the '60's, the poet Algernon Swinburne (1837–1909) devoted his exciting, melodiously swaying rhythms to another sort of attack upon organized religion, in the interests of liberty and emancipation. On the other hand his contemporary Gerard Manley Hopkins (1844–89), whose sprung rhythm, sensitive language and convictions became very influential after the delayed publication of his collected poems (1918), expressed religious experience more profoundly than any poet since the seventeenth century. Such was the fantastic variety of the Victorian age.

Russia and the Balkans

The officers of Alexander I (1801–25), returning from the Napoleonic Wars to a much enlarged Russia, brought back new attitudes – symbolized by the daring, lyrical, eclectic architecture of A. Zakharov's Moscow Admiralty (1806–15), the European federation schemes of Alexander's chief minister Prince Adam Czartoryski (1770–1861), and the bold ideas of Moscow University's young graduates.

Nicholas I (1825–55) made it his business to freeze these ideas. Seven hundred and twelve peasant rebellions are reported from his reign; after the depressions and famines of 1841–2 and 1846–8 the workers were demanding a change in the social order. An unhappy dependency of Russia was Poland, whose greatest composer F. F. Chopin (1810–49) – arch-romantic, outstandingly original creator of sparkling, lyrical *études* and *nocturnes* for piano – went to live abroad just before a military insurrection of 1830; and the leading Polish poet Adam Mickiewicz (1798–1855), prophet of Utopian socialism, emigrated shortly after its unsuccessful conclusion. Nationalism also grew in White Russia (Byelorussia), where a million and a half Catholics of the Uniate rite were compelled to join the Orthodox church (1839); and in the Ukraine where a secret Brotherhood was forcibly dissolved (1847).

As the Crimean War (1854–6) brought England and France (allies for the first time for centuries) to Turkey's aid against Russia, breaking up the concert of European great powers (p. 257) and bringing defeat to the Russians and discredit to their régime, Alexander II (1855–81), reigning in times of intellectual ferment (p. 255), modified the social pattern, waveringly yet with decisive eventual results. Autocracy remained, yet the emancipation of serfs was proclaimed (1861); though this measure, which raised excessive hopes, was followed within four months by 647 riots.

However, in less than two decades thereafter (1863–79), factory production was nearly trebled, and although the Crimean setback almost excluded the Russians from Europe, their annexation of Vladivostok (1858–60) and Central Asia (1868–85) caused millions, accompanied by missionaries, to migrate south and east. By 1871, the population of the Russian empire had risen since the beginning of the century by 142 per cent, more than twice the rate of any other state, to a figure of eighty-seven millions – and then by 1914 it had doubled again.

A war against the new Turkish sultan Abdül Hamit II (1876–1909) ended in Russian victories both in Europe and Anatolia, and completed the long progression towards independence of Rumania, Serbia, Montenegro and Bulgaria, although the last of these could not sustain its full territorial claims. Greece had been independent since the war of 1821–9. Such countries gradually developed their own native cultural movements, mainly of a patriotic nature;[1] as also did Turkey itself – where Namik Kemal (1840–88) wrote his *Ode to Freedom* – and Finland, annexed by Russia from Sweden (1809) but permitted to retain autonomy until 1899.

In Russia, terrorist and anarchist groups proliferated; pogroms followed the assassination of Alexander II, and Alexander III (1881–94), with the assistance of his clever, bigoted minister Pobedonostsev, concentrated upon repression. Nevertheless the '90's, despite several famine years, witnessed an industrial upsurge, in which capital flowed in from Russia's new ally France (p. 240). Production of iron, coal, oil and cotton increased with exceptional rapidity, and although wheat exports from Odessa reached extensive proportions, the rapidly multiplying urban working class became as significant an element in the state as the peasant. A. S. Popov developed ship-to-shore radio communication; and on land, Asiatic colonization attained major dimensions.

This successive opening up of vast tracts of unexplored territory was paralleled among Russian novelists, whose sweeping range and audacious enquiry formed the main vehicle of criticism expressing the national spirit in these epochs of momentous change. A. S. Pushkin (1799–1837) had witnessed Napoleon's invasion, and during the ensuing disillusionments was exiled. The central national poetic writer of Russia, he is also, with his harmonious sense of measure, the most universal and European – though

---

[1] Mihail Eminescu (1850–84), influenced by Hindu thought, by Schopenhauer and by native traditions, created a new Rumanian poetry.

torn into two by the conflict between his Voltairian aristocratic tastes and a tincture of African blood. *Eugene Onegin* (1823–33) is a 'novel in verse', realistic, sad and witty, emancipated from high-flown diction; while Pushkin's dramatic chronicle *Boris Godunov* (1831) has suggestive breadth and lofty imaginative truth.

Mikhail Y. Lermontov (1814–41), a wild warm-hearted reader of Byron and Shelley yet steadied by a strong infusion of realism, displays as *A Hero of Our Time* (1840) Petchorin, a man of vigour gone to seed in a frustrating society, of which the portrayal helped to establish the Russian psychological novel. Early in the '40's the question how this society should be rescued was violently disputed between Slavophils and westerners, whose leaders, fighting it out in the periodicals, were Belinsky (1811–47), founder of Russian criticism, and A. I. Herzen (1812–70) whose disillusionment after 1848 transforms the rebellious movement, guided by his work *From Another Shore* (1850), out of the romantic and into the revolutionary sphere.

In an epoch when Balzac, Stendhal and Dickens were popular in Russia, the chief founder of Russian realistic fiction was N. V. Gogol (1809–52), arch-romantic as well as disgusted realist, whose exuberantly grotesque, discordant novel *Dead Souls* (1842–) reveals, through the figure of Chichikov, the author's peculiar vision of a spiritually empty community. *Oblomov* (1858), the skilfully and sympathetically depicted anti-hero of I. A. Goncharov (1812–91), is the super-sluggard who 'in a world of planners plans himself asleep'. As industrialism and a new middle-class intelligentsia rose together, I. S. Turgenev (1818–83) mirrored contemporary discontents with a pessimistic yet humane detachment, aware of the role of blind chance; his swift impressionist observation is conveyed by means of strange powers of literary artistry and construction. Bazarov in *Fathers and Sons* (1862) was a tragic Lucifer, a self-styled nihilist (a new word), who died of typhus caught from the peasants. Conservatives said the book glorified nihilism; but revolutionaries felt it libelled their cause.

F. M. Dostoevsky (1821–81) enriched the novel by adding immeasurable new vistas of the human soul's subconscious secrets. *Crime and Punishment* (1866) and *The Brothers Karamazov* (1879–80) are new syntheses of mind and heart which display intimate insight into abnormal pathology, and mark the climax of European naturalism. The brothers, like *The Idiot* (1868–9), reflect with acutely sensitive ambivalence the dilemma between a powerless yet rational rebel and a divine fool merging himself with values beyond human personality and moral barriers. Dostoevsky's merciless, intuitive scrutiny was prompted by an absorption with good and evil and with human misery. Master of depths and heights alike, himself inhabiting an inferno, he blessed life and brought a message of hope and of regeneration through divine love. Passionately devoted to Christ, he saw god-fearing Slavonic Orthodoxy as the salvation from nihilism – and from the liberal western universality for which, though broadminded and cosmopolitan, he felt no affection.

Standing with him at the summit of the psychological novel was Leo Tolstoy (1828–1910), unsurpassed painter and analyst in Russian prose. Exhibiting a realism equal to Stendhal's and a manipulation of masses which Zola could not have exceeded, *War and Peace* (1862–9) is a Russian historical epic into which Tolstoy at two simultaneous levels, personal and national, distils the whole of his experience, in characters drawn from life but evolving according to their own internal laws. *Anna Karenina* (1875–7) is all passion and jealousy; she is punished, for Tolstoy became increasingly moralistic. Yet there is bleak corroding doubt and nihilism in Levin, whose salvation comes through the uncorrupted, Rousseau-esque, anti-cultural wisdom of a peasant. Tolstoy came to see energy, authority and property as the destroyers; the saviours were anarchy, non-violent submission to existence and the unconscious sageness of the race. But the dying *Ivan Ilyitch* (1884) knows that he has nothing to carry with him beyond the annihilating instant of death. And so this most conspicuous literary figure in Europe, with his eagle eye upon all the variety of life, and his devastating power to pierce conventional masks, moved beyond novel-writing to philosophical religion.

The highest literary expression of the intelligentsia, now in the ascendant, was A. P. Chekhov (1860–1904). His short stories and plays of the '90's enlarge the range of Russian literature by depicting this middle class; and humour comes back with these exact, humane but surgically detached analyses of the minutely fragmented stream of life. Though his kind heart hated oppressors, Chekhov had no taste for revolution or economics, seeing men as separated from one another and from society in an unapproachable isolation which only their common humanity can partially bridge. Yet the '90's in Russia were a new era of conscious class-movement, and the largest book-sales (1898) were those of Maxim Gorky (1869–1936), not only a bracing writer about the lawless nomadic freedom of romantic tramps but the precursor of social realism in his restless, intellectual creative urge to overcome social inferiority and the drabness of life (p. 274).

This latter half of the century also witnessed the climax of Russian music. M. P. Mussorgsky (1839–81), attracted like Gogol and Dostoevsky to the national soul's deep forces and passions, based his opera *Boris Godunov* (1874) on Pushkin's dramatic tale (p. 255) in order to compose a powerfully individual musical blend of Russian folk-lore and liturgical echoes. This version of *Boris Godunov*, a model for realists, was revised by N. A. Rimsky Korsakov (1844–1908) whose Symphonic Suite (1888) reflects his membership of a consciously nationalist school. From this movement P. I. Tchaikovsky (1804–93), as western and cosmopolitan as he was Russian, stood apart. His last (Pathétique) Symphony (1893) conveys his melancholic temperament in broad, rich and melodious, vividly scored orchestration ranging from the lightest caressing delicacies to grandiose mass effects.

Germany and Austria-Hungary

The Napoleonic wars broke down the old political structure of Germany, abolishing feudalism, many little states (1803), and the Holy Roman Empire (1806) – whose emperor Francis II became Francis I of Austria combined with Hungary. At the Congress of Vienna (1815) the big four powers, Britain, Austria-Hungary, Prussia and Russia (later raised to five by adding France), imposed 'legitimacy' for half a century and ignored the rising demands of nationality and liberty. Nevertheless, the arrangements enforced by the Congress represented the most thorough attempt that had ever been made to construct new means for keeping the peace.

While Napoleon was still in power, Prussia, guided by H. vom Stein (1757–1831), had already abolished serfdom and class distinctions (1807), established a model university at Berlin (1806–10) and demonstrated unprecedented powers of conscription (1814). After the Congress of Vienna the Prussians continued to forge ahead, ousting Spain as Europe's chief producers of wool and taking the initiative in a Customs Union (1834) which came to include most German lands other than Austria.

The highly conservative Austrian statesman Metternich, who sponsored the Holy Alliance of Austria-Hungary, Russia and Prussia, succumbed in 1848 to a confused three-cornered struggle between liberalism, authoritarianism and newly vocal nationalisms, which convulsed both Germany and his own country. In the latter, starting with the populace of Vienna and Prague, the disturbances spread both to the Hungarian middle classes (under Kossuth) and to the anti-Hungarian Croats. The prophet of nationalist Magyar democracy, following upon a Hungarian literary revival sponsored by Ferenc Kazinczy (1759–1831), was the lyric poet Alexander Petőfi (1823–49). He was killed in the rising; and the musical innovator Franz Liszt (1811–86) left for Weimar to write his Hungarian rhapsodies. Czech culture, too, had been resurgent, since the Byronic lyrical epic *Maj* by Karel Macha (1810–36), and Joseph Dobrovsky's establishment of Slavonic studies (d. 1829). Slovak literature, too, was established by the national epic of Andrej Sládkovic (1820–72), and the revolutionary romantic ballads of Janko Kral (1822–76); while the Croats produced their romantic poet Ivan Mazuranic, and an outstanding symbolist in Silvije Krunjievic.

In 1849, authoritarianism prevailed again in Austria and Hungary. Yet Metternich was now out of the way, and the Act of Emancipation abolished the hereditary rights of landlords. Austria's renewed attempts – which now followed – to create a firmer union with the Hungarian and Slavonic parts of its empire meant that it could no longer claim to possess sufficient Teutonic homogeneity to dominate a Greater Germany. Prussia, instead, went ahead with this task, while its king Frederick William IV, professing the acceptance of liberalism, interpreted this as meaning and requiring national German unity. By 1862, when Bismarck became its Minister President, Prussia possessed the greater part of Germany's developing heavy industries and investor-banks, and was already producing more coal than France and Belgium combined. Denmark succumbed to a Prusso-Austrian alliance (1864); Austria was overwhelmed at Sadowa (Königgrätz, 1866) by Prussian breech-loading rifles and revolutionary methods of mobilization based upon the rapidly expanding railways. Then France's Second Empire of Napoleon III suffered crushing defeat at Sedan (1870), and King Wilhelm I (1861–88) was declared emperor of Germany at Versailles (1871).

Despite serious depressions (especially in 1873), a remarkable period of German industrial growth followed: coal and iron production increased sixfold between 1870 and 1910, and Berlin's population rose sevenfold during the century. Bismarck at last turned to peaceful activities. But he was dismissed by the young emperor Wilhelm II (1888–1918), and the Triple Alliance between Germany, Austria-Hungary and Italy (1882) crystallized a military, and therefore industrial, confrontation of two main European *blocs*, superseding the balance of power concept. Within two decades German army expenditure increased by one thousand per cent.

'All art', stated Walter Pater, 'aspires constantly to the condition of music'; symphonies were now what cathedrals had been to the Middle Ages. At the beginning of the century Ludwig von Beethoven (1770–1827) (p. 227) passed to a novel conception of music as personal revelation and confession, clothing in the closest texture and design not only thought of untranslatable complexity but unequalled emotional power. Terms such as classic and romantic seem irrelevant, since Beethoven was uniquely both, his emotions based on fully conscious intentions and ideas which no art other than music could have expressed with equal range, profundity and dramatic strength.

Opposite: Rouen Cathedral: the porch in morning sunlight, harmony in blue by Claude Monet (1894)

His Third (Eroica) Symphony (1803–4), composed after he had already become partially deaf, represents in its bold, intense conception and construction the most revolutionary step ever taken by a composer. The Fifth is glorious symphonic logic incarnate, and the Seventh a work of gigantic grandeur. The Ninth (Choral) Symphony (1824) broke through the symphonic, instrumental frame with its last movement in which a massed choir sang Schiller's words reflecting the composer's own progressive deism. The densely fugal last quartets, 'dark with excessive bright', reached unimaginable heights of mysterious, poignantly introspective resonance.

Meanwhile Karl von Weber (1786–1826), in his *Invitation to the Dance* (1819), had inaugurated a new era of music linked with dancing; and the magic and horror of Weber's *Der Freischütz* (1821) began German romantic opera. But the principal herald of romantic music was Franz Schubert (1797–1828) of Vienna. His six hundred *Lieder* were the perfect accompaniment for lyric verse – an independent musical form of wide and subtle range which made each song into a miniature drama of successive movements, with changing moods and melodies. As he threw off the influences of his forerunners, the later masses and his Eighth (Unfinished) (1822) and Ninth (C Major) Symphonies, magnificent in their lyrical and elegiac passages, confirm Liszt's description of Schubert as the most poetical of composers. While F. Mendelssohn (1809–47), a Hamburg Jew brought up as Lutheran, tempered his romantic fervour with classical proportions, Robert Schumann (1810–56) was the first composer of piano music to exploit fully its technical possibilities, employing complicated rhythms to express his nervous, sensuous imagination, with its taste for dusk and phantoms and for Byron. Before long the Viennese Johann Strauss (1825–99) was giving his name to the era of the waltz; but Johannes Brahms (1833–97) continued to develop Beethoven's forms with a rhythmical originality revealing, beneath surface calm, a romantic and tragic pessimism.

Yet meanwhile great changes were under way, as Richard Wagner (1813–83) of Leipzig embodied the destiny of man in a new romantic-realist synthesis, a 'seamless tapestry' of music freely interacting with poetry, drama and décor. Unique in its influence upon operatic structure, harmony and orchestration, Wagnerian opera made the Festival Theatre at Bayreuth (1876) the Jerusalem of a new art and religion. In *Tristan und Isolde*, finished in 1859 and performed in 1865, the boiling, shifting, rich violence and subtlety of the music infuses Gottfried von Strassburg's version of the French and Arthurian myth (p. 128) with Nietzsche's melodramatic erotic fervour and the melancholy of Schopenhauer (p. 261). Wagner's most important group of works, however, was *Der Ring der Nibelungen* (1853–76).

This consisted of four operas, including *Götterdämmerung* in which the composer, now at the height of his exceptional constructive powers, created around the vigorous Teutonic heroism of his mythological theme a world of explosive will and passion.

As Beethoven attained his maturity, Schiller (p. 225) also, in his *William Tell* (1804), sought to win for German drama a fertile new field, comprising the national struggle which was to be one of the century's main themes. Meanwhile, Goethe (p. 225) was engaged in that mighty echoing duel of aspirations and despairs, the First Part of *Faust*, which he finished in 1801 and published seven years later. At a time when revivals of folk-lore were in the air, this subject of the sixteenth-century necromancer Faust remained in Goethe's thoughts for more than fifty years; he incorporated within it the intensely tragic Gretchen story which he had composed three decades earlier. Goethe's potent exploring mind extracted from these themes profoundly imaginative speculations concerning man's function and relationship to God; and his unique command of German lyrical expression shaped these thoughts, in immortal universal characters who defied traditional ideas and gave a new structure to romantic Europe. In the Second Part of *Faust* (1825–32), designed more discursively so as to spare no philosophical 'effort to find the supreme manner of life', the most ambitious of many symbols is the union of Faust with Helen, representing the regenerative unification of medieval northern romanticism with the ideals, so beloved by German poets, of classical beauty from the south.

F. Grillparzer (1791–1872), too, fused classic simplicity with romantic melancholy in his fine plays which raised Austrian drama to universal stature. The Jewish intellectual H. Heine (1797–1856) was a lyricist second only to Goethe, and a graceful prose-writer whose mocking, flamboyant, sophisticated wit passed from the Byronic gestures of *Junge Leiden* (1817–21) to the ironic fantasies of exile from a stagnant, despotic fatherland (1831). Later, Stefan George (1868–1933) was Germany's poetic apostle of 'art for art's sake', writing in the nineties as esoteric high priest, prophet and mythmaker of hostility against modern naturalism.

While sensitive early nineteenth-century German architects, C. F. Schinkel (1781–1841) and Leo von Klenze, displayed virtuosity in their variations upon neo-classical and neo-Renaissance themes, romantic painters emerged in the German Swiss Heinrich Füssli (Fuseli) (1741–1825), a visionary poet-painter of macabre horrors who migrated to England; and in Caspar David Friedrich (1774–1840) of Greifswald, who expressed an intensely felt and richly visionary pantheism in his metaphysical, symbolical landscapes contrasting open sea and sky with the deep German forest, of which he is the most exciting interpreter after Altdorfer (p. 177).

G. W. F. Hegel (1770–1831) was another who tackled the habitual German problem of reconciling opposites. His *Phenomenology of Mind* (1806–7) was the most ambitious philosophy of history since Augustine. Yet it shows a conservative regard for tradition, in its endeavours – by means of thesis, antithesis and synthesis – to unify spirit and nature, romance and enlightenment, universal and particular, real and ideal. Hegel optimistically saw these reconciliations achieved by the nation-state, and particularly the Prussian monarchy which thus seemed to him society's final expression of Rousseau's General Will (p. 217).

Arthur Schopenhauer (1788–1860) was the first leading thinker, in his *World as Will and Idea* (1819) (written under the influence of Indian philosophies), to undermine European belief in personal destiny. This subordination of the individual was worked out in terms of the community by the Communist Manifesto in which Karl Marx (1818–83) and Friedrich Engels (1820–95), embittered by the horrors of industrialization, delineated a complete doctrine and strategy of class struggle and social revolution, emphasizing the new self-conscious cleavage between owners and workers (1847). Building upon foundations partially borrowed from Hegel and the classical economists, the first volume of *Das Kapital* (1867) elaborated the basis of modern dialectical materialist communism, with the relationship between classes determined by productive forces. This was during the First International (1864–73), when Marx and Engels made the German Socialist party the strongest in Europe; though it was eventually in Russia instead that these principles, adapted to a new situation, were put into practice (p. 268).

Friedrich Nietzsche (1844–90) likewise rejected Christianity and the western view of history, but did so by reliance upon intuition rather than the intellect. Echoing Plato as well as the ancient east, *Thus Spake Zarathustra* (1873) sought to rise above current complacency, due to recent Prussian victories (p. 258), by demanding the emergence of a new race of supermen created from the ablest. The followers of such ideas, modifying them to suit authoritarian politics, made him appear an advocate of violence; but Nietzchse's main ideas were rather, first, a radical scepticism in the face of all traditional moral concepts, and, secondly, a stress on the moral will.

In these same decades Germany gained steadily on Britain and France not only in industrialization but in scientific discovery. As biological sciences such as physiology and genetics entered a new era from the 1860's onwards, most of their leading exponents were Germans. R. Koch (1843–1910) transformed the immunization of human beings against infection. After H. R. Hertz (1857–94) had demonstrated the existence of electro-magnetic waves and Werner von Siemens introduced the dynamo principle (1866), W. Roentgen (1845–1923) discovered X-rays (1895). Three others whose discoveries were to exercise influence far beyond the realms of theory were Clausius, whose contributions to the First and Second Laws of Thermo-dynamics (1850) and to the discovery of entropy presented new ways of measuring changes in the observable world, Ludwig Boltzmann (1844–1906) who calculated the probable patterns of atom distribution, and G. Daimler (1834–1900) who mounted one of the first successful high-speed, internal-combustion engines upon a motor car (1882–6).

Scandinavia

After the adoption of a new constitution – the oldest written European constitution still to be in force today – Sweden chose one of Napoleon's marshals, Jean Bernadotte, as heir to its throne (1810), which he occupied as Charles XIV (1818–44). Although social progress was beginning and peasants benefited from constitutional reforms (1865), the countryside was insufficiently fertile to prevent overcrowding; and the following twenty years witnessed not only an enormous influx into the Swedish towns – which increased tenfold in size during the latter half of the century – but the emigration of nearly 450,000 Swedes, most of whom went to the United States. Meanwhile, however, Swedish scientific advances, promising well for the future, included the electrochemical theory and chemical formulation system of Jakob Berzelius (1779–1848), as well as J. E. Lund-ström's discovery of safety matches, which developed into a world-industry. After 1870, and particularly after 1890, the opening of new Swedish lands and mines brought about the country's most fundamental economic revolu-tion since the stone age; and it brought in its train religious revivals, develop-ments in social democracy, and temperance and co-operative movements.

The Father (1887) and *Miss Julie* (1889) by Johan August Strindberg (1849–1912) represent landmarks in European dramatic realism; they were ac-companied by important novels and followed by historical dramas and harrowing plays reflecting his own marital, financial and mental tragedy. But an even more significant dramatist had appeared in Norway – restive after its transference from Danish to Swedish rule in 1814 – where Henrik Ibsen (1828–1906) devoted the most gigantic theatrical talent of the century to his interpretation of contemporary moral and communal problems. *A*

Doll's House (1879) and *Hedda Gabler* (1890), dealing with woman's place in society, formidably display his main ideas: the duty of the individual to himself, the supreme importance of self-realization, and the disaster of denying love. In *Pillars of Society* (1877), and again in *When We Dead Awaken* (1899), he attacked bourgeois hypocrisy and cramping convention, both as social evils and as psychological problems affecting human relations. His richest and most fantastic play, *Peer Gynt* (1867), was set to lyrical music by Edvard Grieg (1843–1907), a picturesquely romantic composer of national colouring. Among Norwegian writers the outstanding nationalist was the prolific, volcanic, fighter Bjørnstjerne Bjørnson, 'the sap of Norway's tree'.

Very different was the later Norwegian painter Edvard Munch (1863–1944), who agitatedly clothed the psychological and symbolic aspects of life and love in richly coloured forms, taut and nervous to the point of hysteria. From the time of his Berlin exhibition (1892) onwards, these horror-struck, hallucinatory visions exercised great influence upon central and north European expressionism (p. 287).

Denmark's alliance with Napoleon ended in defeat and the loss of Norway; and then Prussia, supported by Austria (1864), detached Schleswig Holstein too.

Nevertheless the intervening years had witnessed advances by Frederick VII (1848–63) towards constitutional government (1849). The Folk High School was another significant feature of the times (1864). This experiment in popular higher education was the achievement of N. F. S. Grundtvig, who aimed at a reawakening based on the idea that future greatness lay in the individual qualities of men, however humble. Another important national development was the co-operative movement in Danish farming, which underwent radical reorganizations in production methods (*c.* 1880).

While H. C. Oersted (1777–1851) proved the relation of electricity and magnetism, human profundities were explored by Sören Kierkegaard (1813–55). Deploring metaphysical speculation, he concluded with agonized faith that 'truth is subjectivity' – whereas 'objectivity', science, mistakenly shirks the necessity of choosing for oneself. Kierkegaard became the teacher of Heidegger (p. 280) and one of the founders of present-day existentialist method. A powerful modern response has been evoked by his iconoclastic diagnosis of contemporary spiritual sickness; this penetrating analysis of the deficiencies of contemporary faith, in works such as *Training in Christianity* (1850), exerted a revolutionary influence on Protestants such as Karl Barth.

In Iceland, which after political convulsions received limited self-government from Denmark in 1874, the most important poet in a new lyrical movement of the '80's was Hannes Hafstein (1861–1922).

Spain and Portugal

When Napoleon's armies invaded Spain and Portugal (1808), he was faced in Madrid by the first national resistance movement, resulting eventually in his ejection from the peninsula by Wellington and the Spaniards and Portuguese. Meanwhile, however, the Spanish colonies on the American mainland set up royalist and then national *juntas* which secured independence one after another in the 1820's; while Portugal recognized Brazilian independence in 1825.

Spain sank into extreme reaction under Ferdinand VII (1814–33). His marriage in 1829 provoked attempts upon the throne; these caused a series of dynastic (Carlist) disturbances under Isabella II (1833–68), whose abdication was followed by a short-lived Republic (1873–5). Before Alfonso XIII (1885–1931) came of age, Spain was defeated by the United States and lost Cuba, Puerto Rico and the Philippine Islands (1898). Portugal, on the other hand, had secured international acceptance for its claims to the enormous African territories of Angola and Mozambique (1886–91).

Francisco Goya (1746–1828) was uniquely pitiless as painter to the depressing court of Ferdinand VII, exploring as it would seem to us (though apparently not to their dissatisfaction) the weakest points of his sitters' personalities. His visual powers sharpened by total deafness, he had painted and drawn terrifying, spontaneous, horrors of war – reflections upon the nature of power suggested by the Napoleonic occupation; and in his later years, although he continued to paint official portraits, the nightmare element reached a crescendo in the 'black' paintings now in the Prado. Goya had killed the tradition that painting was *intended to please*; he also created another precedent by depicting female nudes, but viewing them as a stranger – that is to say, he differentiated sex from intimacy. 'Last of old masters and first of moderns', student of Velazquez and eighteenth-century Italians and the link between these and Picasso, he introduced a new age by his assertion that the painter was free to depict private visions as only poets had depicted them before. The naturalistic immediacy, mastery of form and colour, and psychological insight with which Goya perpetuated his intense revelations transformed artistic outlooks for a century.

The Byronic poet José de Espronceda (1808–42) stood at the Paris barricades in 1830 (p. 240), but Spanish romanticism was to be seen less in literature than in the excitable court life of Isabella II. Prose writers included the venomous satirist Mariano de Larra (1809–37) and Benito Perez Galdos (1843–1920) whose diffuse exuberant talent, and interest in abnormal psychology, were lavished upon many novels dealing with historical, social and religious themes. Meanwhile Portuguese poetry and drama had been revived by the romantic exiled liberal J. B. de Almeida Garrett (1799–1854); and Antero de Quental (1842–91) wrote the best sonnets since Camoes, intimate and exact. C. Castelo Branco (1825–90), a novelist of extremes, described the regional scene with prolific impressionism, while J. M. de Eça de Queiros (1843–1900) was a realist of sensitive and imaginative spontaneity and technical finish.

Italy

Not only Germany, but Italy found national unity during the nineteenth century – for the first time for fourteen hundred years. Napoleon, bringing a breath of fresh air, had simplified the country's political structure, improved its communications and introduced commercial banking and codes of law. Although, after 1815, the Austro-Hungarian empire regained Venetia together with Lombardy, a revived Piedmont gained Liguria; the Papal States remained weak, and revolutionary plots fanned outwards from Naples into the Sicilian and mainland revolutions of 1848.

'The sole idea now fruitful and powerful in Europe is the idea of national liberty . . . of citizens speaking the same tongue'. These were the words of Giuseppe Mazzini (1832), who set up a short-lived Republic at Rome (1849). Later, the Piedmontese minister Camillo Cavour invited the intervention of Napoleon III to weaken the Austrian hold on north Italy (1859), so that Lombardy was ceded to Piedmont. Then Giuseppe Garibaldi ended Bourbon rule in Sicily and Naples (1860) and in the following year invaded the Papal States. Victor Emmanuel II of Piedmont was declared King of Italy. Defeated by Austria at Custozza (1866), the Italians nevertheless profited by the Austro-Prussian war (p. 258), and Napoleon III's encouragement, to annex Venice; and in 1870, despite the opposition of Pope Pius IX, they occupied Rome, which replaced Florence as capital of the country.

In 1882 the Triple Alliance (p. 258) was signed between Italy, Germany and Austria; and in the same year Assab (Eritrea) was declared a crown colony. But Italian claims upon Tunisia and the Trentino remained unsatisfied, and the attempt to conquer Abyssinia was defeated (1896). In the same year, however, Italy won laurels in the scientific field, when Guglielmo Marconi (1874–1937) established a radio wave-link spanning the Thames – and five years later it was the Atlantic that was spanned.

Italian literature assumed both personal and patriotic forms. In the finest Italian lyrics written for half a millennium the despairing, mocking individualist Giacomo Leopardi (1798–1837) devoted an unrhetorical, economic solemnity to his traumatic depiction of loneliness, misery and disillusionment with nationalistic impulses. The counter-note of patriotism was struck by the poets Ugo Foscolo (1778–1827), Alessandro Manzoni (1785–1873) and Giosuè Carducci (1835–1907), all manifesting a romantic spirit in forms dependent upon the classical tradition. Foscolo, like many of his contemporaries, passed from admiration of Napoleon to ardent nationalism, which he preached with exhortations of hope and endurance. Optimistic, also, is Manzoni's single masterly novel *I Promessi Sposi* (1827), a serious and reflective adaptation of Scott's historical romances (p. 252) which displays belief in the success of a good cause and the comforts of religion. Carducci's powerful political odes made him the quasi-official poet of the modern Italy. Meanwhile, however, the Sicilian Giovanni Verga (1840–1922) was showing another side of the picture by devoting his talents as a novelist to the private lusts and vendettas of peasants, amid economic conditions against which they were not strong enough to prevail.

But the characteristic expression of nineteenth-century Italy was the flourishing art of opera, for which Gioacchino Rossini (1792–1868) gained an unprecedented public, particularly with *William Tell*, performed with a French libretto in 1829. *Don Pasquale* (1843), by Gaetano Donizetti (1797–1848), was the best of all *opera buffas* (p. 218); and Giuseppe Verdi (1813–1901) explored new ranges of pathos, lyrical passion and virile inventive vitality in *Rigoletto* (1851). Another of his operas, *La Traviata* (1853), was the first successful operatic attempt at domestic tragedy, reflecting the composer's desire to bring the singers closer to their audience. These two works were adapted from Victor Hugo (p. 241) and Alexandre Dumas respectively; but then, in his old age, Verdi collaborated with the librettist Boito to compose two works on Shakespearean themes which are the finest of all operatic realizations of great plays – *Otello* (1887), which raised the form to hitherto unexplored heights, and the masterly imaginative comic tableau of *Falstaff* (1893) with its swirling gaiety that contrasts with Verdi's own dark pessimism. Meanwhile a new movement of *verismo*, displayed through violent plots in sordid surroundings, was launched by Mascagni's *Cavalleria Rusticana* (1890), Leoncavallo's *Pagliacci* (1892), and the powerful dramatic sparkle of Puccini's *La Bohème* (1896).

10

THE TWENTIETH CENTURY

Twentieth-century Europe

The years that preceded the First World War were a period of abundant economic prosperity for the richer sections of Europe. Through free trade and middle-class efficiency, exports rose by fifty per cent in a single decade. Britain was still the most powerful industrial country, with one third of its commerce going to its own possessions; by 1910 this British overseas traffic had doubled and not far from tripled within fifty years. Thirty per cent of the world's power and forty per cent of its spindles were in Britain, and from Britain came most of its loans. London was still unrivalled as financial centre and commercial harbour (p. 247), and more outward trade passed through Liverpool than through any other port in the world.

However, the collapse of European supremacy was foreshadowed by Japan's successful war against Russia (1905), indicating that Europe's weapons could be used against itself; this demonstration was a stimulus to nationalism in British India, French Indo-China and the overseas possessions of other powers. Within the European continent, despite moves towards international institutions such as the Permanent Hague Court of Arbitration (1907), the traditional balance of power gradually polarized into two armed camps. William II speeded up Germany's industrialization, so that its iron and coal production and export trade trebled in twenty-five years (1888–1913). The British, their misgivings about continental entanglement overcome by these German threats, confirmed their alliance with France and Russia (1904, 1907; p. 240).

In the First World War (1914–18) Germany fought alongside Austria-Hungary and Turkey (the Central Powers) against France, Britain and Russia, joined by Japan, Italy (1915) – which had abandoned its Triple Alliance with the other side (p. 258) – and the United States (1917). The war was caused by hysterical nationalisms, unworthy politicians and diplomats, and the inadequate control of armed forces by civilian authority. This was the first general conflict among states possessing all the panoply of modern organization, and controlling, from their mainly European centres, the greater part of the world, so that the scale of operations was vast enough to shatter the old international pattern of economy. Moreover, since whole peoples were involved, industry and morale became important factors in the conduct of hostilities. With the aid of new weapons such as the aeroplane, submarine, tank and poison gas, of which the lethal effects were supplemented by unimaginative incompetence in the high commands, destruction was without precedent since the days of Genghiz Khan or Timur. Out of sixty-five million men mobilized, perhaps ten million were killed or died, twenty-one million suffered from wounds, and nearly eight million were captured or missing, making a total, in the armed services of the various nations, of about thirty-nine million casualties. Perhaps eight or ten million civilians also died from causes resulting from the war. A very large proportion of all these casualties was European. Moreover, the deaths of twenty million people were caused by the 1918 influenza epidemic, the worst of all time; twelve and a half million of these died in India, but the scourge also caused enormous casualties in Europe.

The worst hardships took place in Russia, which lost nearly four million soldiers within ten months. Oppressive and inefficient government had already, before the war, led to the birth of Bolshevism (1903), which broke away from the less thoroughgoing Menshevist opposition to the government; Bloody Sunday (1905) was followed by strikes rising in number from 222 in 1910 to 4,098 in January-July 1914. During the war, capable Bolshevik propaganda helped to create the Russian revolution (1917), which brought about the abdication of Nicholas II, followed, a few months later, by the installation of a Communist Soviet régime, its withdrawal from the war, and the tsar's assassination. Other causes of the revolution included successive military disasters, a catastrophic war-time economy, agricultural failures, and the concentration of impoverished and exploited workmen in the factories of Petrograd, the former St Petersburg – soon to be Leningrad.

V. I. Lenin (1870–1924) alone knew what to do; and he set about adapting to contemporary Russian conditions (by the regulation of all human activities) the Utopian ideals of equality and social justice put forward by Karl Marx (p. 261). One of Lenin's own contributions to this doctrine was his theory of revolutionary strategy and tactics, applicable not only to Russia but to infiltration throughout the capitalist world, which he believed to be on its last legs. Lenin's version of the dictatorship of the proletariat was also original. Master of every technique for maintaining as well as seizing power, he disbelieved Marx's view that the coercive power of the state would be able to wither away, instead interpreting the Communist Party as a 'van-guard' which must forcibly manipulate the masses in the direction of socialism. Such views, contrary to those of his colleague Trotsky, were stimulated by the desperate total dislocation which Lenin inherited, including three years of internal 'White' resistance – sponsored by the western allies and overcome by Trotsky's Red Army – and a drought on the Lower Volga (1920–1) which caused five million deaths and brought the total population deficit of the country, after seven years of war and devastation, to twenty-eight million.

Because of such conditions, Marxism had to be adapted so that the proletarian revolution should come first and the broad industrial base for socialism later; and the New Economic Policy (1921–4) was obliged to compromise temporarily with capitalism by allowing a limited amount of private enterprise and profit. Under Stalin (d. 1953) a series of Five Year Plans achieved, from 1929 onwards, vast new exploitations of natural resources, brought about by the expansion of heavy industry with machine-building as its backbone. Improvement in living conditions came more slowly, while individualism in agriculture, industry, trade and opinion was crushed in the interests of centralized control, and the Party turned into an all-powerful, hierarchical bureaucracy.

While Russia was still out of action, the victorious allied powers, meeting to dictate the Treaty of Versailles and divide Germany's colonial spoils, set up the League of Nations (1919), designed to prevent aggressive war. Its Council of nine was to include representatives of France, Great Britain, Italy and Japan. The United States, also, were intended to be among its members, but they repudiated Woodrow Wilson's policy of European co-operation and intervention, and never joined.

Germany recovered sufficiently to join the Locarno Pact (1925) and the League (1926). From the liquidated Turkish empire emerged Kemal Ata-türk's compact national, authoritarian republic of Anatolia and eastern Thrace, the first Islamic country to commit itself to secular, occidental industrialization, and yet at the same time the barrier which kept Europe from expanding eastwards. But what changed the face of the continent most was the collapse of Austria-Hungary. This disintegrated into the states of Austria (Germans), Hungary (Magyars) and Czechoslovakia (Bohemians, Moravians, Slovaks and Ruthenians); while Croatia and Slovenia joined the Serbs to form a new south Slav kingdom of Yugoslavia, and Galicia (like part of east Germany) went to a revived Poland which was detached from Russia; as also were Finland, three Baltic countries (Estonia, Latvia and Lithuania), and other more ephemeral states including, momentarily, the

Ukraine. Twenty-six of the thirty-two counties of Ireland also became independent of Britain. This multiplication of new units, many of them very weak, made the traditional European balance of power almost impracticable. Moreover, the novel effort to redraw frontiers in accordance with self-ruling nationalities could never satisfy all minority groups. Nevertheless, more Europeans now lived under the rule of their own compatriots than ever before.

But the exigencies of the First World War had placed new possibilities of mass-control in the hands of governments, and nationalism was parting company with the liberal ideas to which, in the previous century, it had been linked. In Italy, disappointed by its limited gains from the Treaty of Versailles and explosive with overpopulation and industrial unrest, Benito Mussolini (1883–1945) established under a monarchic façade his Fascist régime, with the trappings of ancient Rome and imprecise echoes of various ideologies. In the years that followed, dictatorial governments of similar pattern displaced parliamentary systems in a number of European countries. This tendency gained force from the widespread instability produced by alternate booms and slumps, culminating in a violent economic crisis which shattered western and central Europe as well as the United States (1929–32), inflicting thirty million unemployed upon the world and leading to the conclusion that states must intervene to prevent its repetition. Soon afterwards Germany, indignant about its losses and full of an embittered, impoverished middle class, came under the control of a far more thorough-going totalitarian régime than Italy's, the Nazi government of Adolf Hitler (from Austria) which lasted from 1933 until 1945. With a wide measure of popular support, reinforced by relentless mastery of communications and police media, Hitler imposed an unprecedentedly brutal regimentation appealing to fanatical nationalist, militarist and anti-Semitic prejudices and instincts. Without any intervention from other countries, he broke the Treaty of Versailles in order to reoccupy the Rhineland (1936), seized Austria (1938), and – undeterred by his four-power Munich agreement with France, Britain and Italy in the same year – used the German (Sudeten) minority in Czechoslovakia as a pretext for the dismemberment of the country (1939).

His subsequent attack on the Poles precipitated the Second World War (1939–45), which Britain and France entered in their support. However, Poland was at once partitioned between Germany and its new ally Russia, which also defeated Finland in the Winter War (1939–40) and annexed the three other Baltic states (p. 269). Aiming to make huge areas of Europe a single political and economic unit, the Germans next occupied Denmark, Norway, Belgium and Holland, and eliminated France (1940). Large British and French forces, however, were able to escape from Dunkirk to Britain: which, bombarded from the air, now stood alone. The Spaniards, though their dictator Franco had been helped by the Germans and Italians to win his recent civil war (1936–9) against the Russian-supported Republican government, remained neutral. But Italy, shortly before the French armistice, joined Germany, and attacked Greece. Although this attack was successfully resisted, Greece and Yugoslavia were overrun by the Germans (1941), who had also drawn into their alliance Rumania (with its oil wealth), Bulgaria

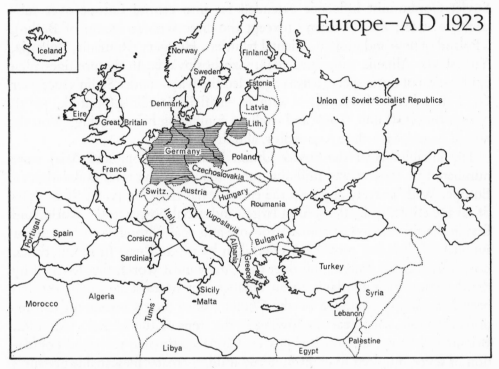

Europe–AD 1923

and Finland. The war was enormously extended in this year by the German invasion of the Soviet Union and the attack by Japan (at war with China since 1937) upon the United States fleet at Pearl Harbour. The turning of the tide came with the surrender of the Germans' Sixth Army at Stalingrad (Volgograd, 1943), followed by their ejection from North Africa, the U.S.-British landings in France (1944) and invasion of Germany, the Russian capture of Berlin (1945), and Japan's surrender following the use of American atomic bombs at Hiroshima and Nagasaki: the product of researches going back to the revolutionary physics of Max Planck, Rutherford and Einstein. The Second World War caused at least twenty-two million deaths, a quarter of them non-combatants – excluding the six million Jews, out of a total of 8,300,000 in Europe, who were killed by Hitler's government.

Such was the last, so far, of the conflicts between mass-mobilized European nations which had been inaugurated by the French revolution. On this occasion, only one country in Europe emerged as a first-class power, and that was the most seriously damaged of all, the Soviet Union. Despite losses estimated at seven and a half million people (and creating, all told, a population deficit of some forty-two million), and despite the destruction of one-quarter of all Soviet property, the end of the war saw eleven million Russians still under arms, immense potential resources still untouched, and Soviet Communist influence extended far into central Europe over subordinate states: East Germany (except the three western sectors of Berlin), a Poland of new and more occidental frontiers, Hungary, Rumania, Bulgaria, Yugoslavia, Albania and, since 1948, Czechoslovakia. In the prestige-laden exploration of outer space, Russia again led the way – under Stalin's successor N. S. Krushchev (1953–64) – with its artificial satellites (Sputnik, 1957), cosmic rockets (Lunik, 1959) and satellites containing human beings (Vostok, 1961); America is a close competitor, and the only one.

The inhabitants of the Soviet Union itself (in Europe and Asia) were numbered in 1963 at 225 millions, more than half the total population of Europe. With scarcely any help the country has risen, by twenty-five years of savage effort, to be the second largest industrial power in the world, and first in the production of cotton, iron-ore and coal; although coal, as major supplier of fuel, has now been overtaken by oil and gas. In recent times, however, Russian domination over the Communist world, first lessened by the defection of Yugoslavia to an independent Marxist stance (1948), has been increasingly contested by the Chinese, since their Communist revolution in the following year. Following in the steps of the U.S.A., U.S.S.R., Britain and France as a nuclear power, China's estimated mainland population of seven hundred to eight hundred million creates inescapable pressures along the frontiers both of India and of underpopulated Asiatic Russia.

Although a European conflict, the Second World War, with its fifty-seven belligerents, was more truly a World War than its predecessor; and one of its results was that after four hundred years the centre of gravity, now split into two, had shifted away from the historic western European powers, not only to Russia but to another continent: from which the United States both politically and economically dominates western Europe. The United Nations (1945) sought to bring all countries, large and small, together, and many steps have been taken in the direction of an international and sometimes federal outlook. But owing to rapid post-war deterioration in the allied relations precariously maintained by Stalin, Roosevelt (d. 1945) and Britain's saviour Churchill (d. 1965), most of the resultant organizations, civilian as well as military, have been restricted either to U.S.-influenced western Europe or to Russian-controlled eastern Europe. A few countries are neutral, and there is at present on both sides a 'polycentric' loosening of ties within the formerly monolithic blocs – thus returning to the millennial, anarchical, European pattern; in the west, the protagonist of this national view is De Gaulle, the French war-time resistance leader, recalled to a new strong presidency in 1958.

A decisive change has been the loss by the colonial powers Italy, Britain, France, the Netherlands, Belgium and Spain of their possessions in Asia and Africa. This process, sometimes peaceable and sometimes forcible, has enormously swelled the number of independent nations. Yet, with a revived west Germany taking the commercial and industrial initiative, European trade has in general kept a strong lead over the former dependent territories, most of which, politically independent though they are, are within a few years doomed by their explosive increases in population (unless aid-programmes on a quite revolutionary scale are introduced) to catastrophic outbreaks of famine which will have direct repercussions upon Europe itself, as well as America.

In this, as in other forms of international co-operation, Europe's traditional dilemma is about to enter into its acutest phase. Still the most important single strategic area in the world, it cannot without greater unification exert an influence proportionate to its resources and experience; and yet the civilizations of Europe have always been nourished by diversity, and would not flourish without it. However, the alternative has not yet been put to the test, since the various unifying institutions within the continent have so far been of limited scope and effectiveness – though the European Common Market is believed to convey a potential message of greater universality.

In spite of continued national fragmentation, the changes of the present century, during the intervals between cataclysms of war, have already included hitherto unimaginable benefits. For a variety of reasons, including vast and sensational scientific developments and more enlightened social thinking, material standards have risen, often spectacularly, in almost every part of Europe; though the peaceful use of nuclear energy is still in its infancy. An unusually advanced régime is the humane, egalitarian 'industrial democracy' of neutral Sweden, which, with its employers, trade unions and government working as a triumvirate, has achieved the highest living standards and productivity in Europe, based on a combination between socialism and private enterprise producing a relatively equitable distribution of the country's resources. Eleven per cent of the Swedish national income is spent on social welfare; and Denmark too is advanced in social security legislation, backed by a uniquely developed agricultural export industry, largely dependent upon small-holdings. Norway has the largest annual output of electrical energy per head in Europe; the most extensive forest growth per head is found in Finland which, recovering rapidly from two disastrous wars with Russia (p. 270), has tripled its industrial workers in half a century.

In many other non-communist countries the trade unions have now become a match for industrialists in bargaining power. But meanwhile, in these as in communist areas, the increased interdependence which scientific techniques have forced upon society's various parts has speedily caused all organizations and pressure groups – unions, co-operatives and political parties alike – to throw up new specialized, indispensable *élites* replacing by a novel oligarchy, and fresh rifts, the old social gaps between leaders and led. In this as in other respects Europe has continued, as always, not to 'preserve' its heritages, but to reshape their components into a partially unfamiliar and living pattern, adapted to constantly changing conditions.

Writing

In Russia Maxim Gorky (1868–1936), who had already gained fame as a short story writer (p. 256), became the first consciously proletarian novelist and playwright, breaking new ground by introducing the humblest, most suffering and most degraded human beings. Abroad from 1922 onwards, Gorky wrote penetrating, ruthlessly realistic biographical and autobiographical essays and novels on the problems of society, and then received a warm welcome on his return to the Soviet Union (1928). Writer and man of action, a link (like the historical novelist Alexei Tolstoy) between old and new, he helped intellectuals of the bygone order and yet formulated the social realism which proclaimed it the writer's task to portray Soviet man and his moral qualities, 'promoting socialism through the depiction . . . of facts, people, and relations between people, engaged in labour processes'. This doctrine was enforced with particular vigour in 1928–32, and again in 1946–8.

The supreme Russian poet of the century has so far been Alexander Blok (1880–1921), who personified the whole symbolist movement and illuminated revolutionary themes with his exquisite mysticism, rhythmical talent and brilliant exploitation of catchwords, slang, street-talk and songs. Deeply opposed to symbolism, on the other hand, was another master of proletarian poetic language more violent in his imagery, the Georgian Vladimir

Mayakovsky (1894–1930), a sledge-hammer innovator of genius whose desire to inflict *A Slap in the Face of Public Taste* (1912) was subsequently superseded by revolutionary exposition. 'It's my revolution!', he proclaimed.

I. G. Ehrenburg (b. 1891), now the doyen of Soviet letters, showed his lethal talent for sardonic, paradoxical exposés in *The Extraordinary Adventures of Julio Jurenito* (1919). The revolution was popularized, in what seemed too wayward and bizarre a fashion, by the experimental, ingenious young individualists who called themselves the Serapion Brethren (1921). One of their founders was the Ukrainian Mikhail Zoschchenko (1895–1958), whose melancholy, uncompassionate humour was deployed to depict the eternal Russian Philistine, with the old bourgeois Adam still inside his heart. Anna Akhmatova (b. 1888) wrote poignant, intimate poems which have now been reinstated in official favour. Boris Pasternak (1890–1960) has become internationally famous for his novel *Dr Zhivago*, with its strangled cry transcending mechanistic materialism; but he was more noteworthy for the fresh and original poetry of his youth, which belonged to the main European stream of the time. Konstantin Paustovsky has written an illuminating *Story of a Life*.

Yevtushenko, interesting for his not uncharacteristic blend of rebellion and conformity, represents the emergence of a fresh outlook on the world, and a new creative wave among the younger generation. A. I. Solzhenitsyn (b. 1918), in *One Day in the Life of Ivan Denisovitch* (1962), displays in his sparing but adroit characterization a marked sense of actuality combined with an unusually strong conviction of the goodwill and generosity of ordinary people, whose intentions he conveys with a sure ear. While Nagibin is a vivid narrator of sympathetically imperfect characters, Yuri Kazakov (b. 1928) explicitly stresses his concern with honesty towards himself and his readers, and yet argues against the idea that literature directly affects men's lives and ethics. The restless stylist Vassili Aksyonov (b. 1933) is likewise opposed to moralizing and didacticism, though interested in the technological intelligentsia as a theme; they are envisaged as potential readers by Pasternak's poetic pupil Andrei Voznesensky, born in the same year, who claims that a poet can communicate with them most directly since the immediacy of his form meets the urgency of their need. Meanwhile, new literary movements are arising among many of the fifty peoples of the Soviet Union who now have written languages when they had none, or only primitive ones, before.

While the Belgian Maurice Maeterlinck reacted from his earlier mystic and fatalistic tendencies (p. 243), in France Henri Bergson (1859–1941), half Pole

half Irishman, stressed the importance of intuition against scientific deter-
minism, bequeathing to literature the *roman fleuve* with its 'stream of
consciousness' and *élan vital* which can guide either an individual or society.
Paul Claudel (1868–1955), reinstating classical religious tragedy, sought to
recreate Catholicism along patriotic lines. More complex was André Gide
(1869–1951), famous from the '30's, within whose supple, experimental heart
and writings warred Protestant Puritanism and homosexual amorality.
Another homosexual was Marcel Proust (1871–1922) whose quasi-autobio-
graphic work *A la Recherche du Temps Perdu* (written from 1909 onwards)
submerges us in his almost total recall of a vast cycle of remembered time,
a departed, decaying aristocratic society patiently and protractedly re-
gathered into perspective and rethreaded into simultaneity with the subjective
present. Novelist turned dramatist, François Mauriac (b. 1885), studying sin
and guilt in south-western France, is classical in his rejection of wide romantic
themes; classic, too, is the synthesis of intellect and sensuousness achieved by
Paul Valéry (1871–1945) in his lucid, narcissistic poetry and prose. Jean
Giraudoux (1882–1944) was foremost among a number of thought-provok-
ing dramatists who utilized mythological and biblical themes to set within
a timeless framework the dilemmas of contemporary destiny. Another playwright of similar themes, as well as a powerful novelist of violence, is Jean
Paul Sartre (b. 1905). Socially committed and preoccupied with the problem
of sincerity, Sartre, in his adaptation of the existentialism derived from
Kierkegaard by Heidegger (p. 280), emphasizes our immersion in a hostile,
alienating world, where we must fend for ourselves – for there is always
stress on man's freedom of choice: 'I am what I choose to be' is the keyword
of this new, chilly humanism. Eugène Ionesco, a Rumanian whose sinister
farces are in French, is the humanist of absurdity – displaying the futility of
conversation, the cross-purposes of dogmatists and the lamentable contrasts
between man's deliberate irrationalism and his fatal passion for logic.

In the '50's has come the French *nouveau roman*, abandoning all conventional landmarks of character and plot. Alain Robbe-Grillet's elaborate,
quasi-scientific, painter-like, visionary descriptions are purged of recognizable psychological content, obsessively deploying long series of nouns with
repetitive, hallucinatory shifts of focus which seek to avoid the pitfalls of
introspection by showing that the world 'quite simply *is*', independently of
human emotions. The grotesque images and hyperbolic moods of Nathalie
Sarraute are indicative of a nightmarish, derisive vision of existence, mocking
our conscious values by absorption in the 'infra-psychological' reality lurking
beneath our smallest gestures and responses. These anti-novels hope by such
harsh means to rescue fiction from its mirror of external illusion and to set

free human possibilities that have not hitherto been permitted to see the light. Meanwhile in Africa and the West Indies French language and idiom, like English, are being employed and extended to express profoundly un-European ranges of experience.

Ireland, reappearing on the world scene (p. 270), contributed a number of specific notes to English literature. G. B. Shaw (1856–1950) came to England where he reflected his broad social enthusiasms – detecting the world's evils with unusual clarity – in the comedy and verbal wit of his argumentative plays. W. B. Yeats (1865–1939), hating destruction yet admiring barbaric energy, distilled from the mythology of Ireland, with increasing strength in his later years, an austere and beautiful poetry that is Irish in utterance yet based on Anglo-Irish culture and upon an unbroken English literary tradition. J. M. Synge's dramatic dialogues (1871–1909) clothe in richly flavoured poetic prose a sense of reality and of the common human lot, which enables him to penetrate deeply into the Irish peasant soul. His compatriot James Joyce (1882–1941) was an unequalled interweaver of comedy and epic whose *Ulysses* (1922) employs linguistic and incantatory rhythms to communicate layer upon layer of stream-of-consciousness associations and cross-references. Through these he conveys, in contemporary Dublin, his sadly realistic, dispassionate estimate of human life and drift. Joyce's friend Samuel Beckett, writing in English as well as French, created one of the most influential plays of the '50's, his desolate, nihilistic *Waiting for Godot* (1955).

In England Henry James (1843–1916), an American of northern Irish extraction, enlarged the modern novel by his subtle nuances of sentiment and human relations within an idealized and invented European aristocratic world, consistently built up in elaborately insinuating language. The Pole Joseph Conrad (1857–1925), among whose novels *Nostromo* (1904) is outstanding, clothes extreme exotic situations, moral dilemmas and intensities, heroisms and disgraces, in an articulate rhetoric tempered at times by irony. H. G. Wells (1866–1946) wrote his novels such as *Kipps* (1906) and *The History of Mr Polly* (1910) with the intention, like Shaw, of emancipating society by the popularization of his ideas; prominent among these were hostility to convention and class, and belief in science. D. H. Lawrence (1885–1930), too, was a powerful transmitter of his own unresting energy. In *Sons and Lovers* (1913) and his other novels he sought to liberate from sexual repression and cramping industrialism the submerged seven-eighths of man's personality and the 'primitive' wisdom and passion allegedly latent within the blood. E. M. Forster (b. 1879) adopted more subtle and humorous means to show the interactions of the two types of mankind who live by their emotions and their intellects respectively.

Popular novelists of the 1920's, such as Aldous Huxley and Evelyn Waugh, employed the satire of comic anarchy to purge the contemporary English *malaise*. This disquiet, due to a sense of hopeless drift without a positive faith, is incarnated in the novel poetic suppleness, disturbingly close to speech rhythms, of the expatriate American T. S. Eliot's *Waste Land* (1922). His meditative poems *Four Quartets* (1943) are bafflingly rich in depth and complex meaning. Eliot's revivals of verse drama (since 1935), in plays revealing an inner and edifying message beneath the surface theme, have reverted towards the Christian humanism traditional in western Europe, though without making direct use of its symbols. The writers of the '20's had turned away from the problems of the time in disgust or mockery, asserting instead the sensibility of the individual; but poets of the 'serious' '30's such as W. H. Auden, with his piquant blend of extreme technical virtuosity and northern commonsense, forced their readers' attention back to the public world and to more or less leftist, didactic images of danger and courage fashioned to combat its flabbiness and psychological and social sterility. George Orwell (1903–50) manifested a bitterly human nihilistic viewpoint, Grahame Greene a tormentedly analytical Catholicism. Meanwhile philosophers such as G. E. Moore (1904), the former Austrian Wittgenstein (1921), and A. J. Ayer (1936), attacked the flaccid attitudes of the age in their own way. Seeing the problem of language as central and using philosophy to explain what language is unable to state, such scholars urged the abandonment of metaphysical jargon and pseudo-entities. The speeches of politicians and other public figures, particularly inept at that time, consequently incurred a colder and harder look.

The novel of the war-time '40's shrank back from *engagement* to the warmth of personal relationships; and the years since then have been conspicuous for cunning or razor-sharp practitioners – including C. P. Snow, Iris Murdoch, Ivy Compton-Burnett, Muriel Spark, Angus Wilson – who in their ruthless, economical portrayals of a limited sector of society identify themselves, critically yet sympathetically, with the sensitive and more or less bewildered characters they portray. In poetry, the fiery, passionate images of the Welshman Dylan Thomas (d. 1953) display an almost mystical concern with the central themes of birth, love and death. The poetical movements that followed have been conspicuous for a class-conscious, almost surgical distrust of any group fantasy or private heroism.

Since 1955 there has been a vigorous revival of prose drama; its themes, calculated to disturb social or personal complacency, represent a break-through into the new age produced by half a century of rapid social evolution. John Osborne's method has been described as the anti-stock-response – the popular women's magazines in reverse; Jimmy Porter in *Look Back in Anger* (1956) is the spokesman of his generation, blowing off his top about everything. Arnold Wesker, preoccupied with themes of integration and with the working class ethos, urges that brotherly, socialist concern for other men should be extended into the whole of life; Harold Pinter's plays are about people frighteningly incapable of reasonable discussion about purposes and ideas, or about society.

In Vienna, the operations of the human mind were illuminated by the psychoanalytical studies inaugurated by Sigmund Freud (1856–1939), a Jew from Moravia who lived in the Austrian capital from the age of four. During the first decade of the century, he explored and underlined the dynamic influence of the unconscious, opening it up to rational enquiry and destroying, first, the illusion that people's actions are explained by the motives that they believe or allege to inspire them, and secondly, the no less illusory assumption that they possess co-ordinated characters responding intelligently and predictably to the happenings of life. These conclusions have had far-reaching and permanent results upon twentieth-century literature, thought and artistic development. Among the internal conflicts to which the mind is subject, Freud invested infantile sexuality with a prominence regarded as excessive by his pupil C. G. Jung, who transferred his attention from the personal to the collective unconscious. Nevertheless, despite these and other reservations, including those of the social anthropologists who found his approach too biological, it was Freud, employing new techniques such as free association in order to overcome psychological resistance, who invented the first instrument designed for the scientific examination of the human mind. Only Einstein could compare with him in influence, by his creation of the theories of relativity.

Of Vienna, too, was Hugo von Hofmannsthal (1874–1929), whose accomplished, conservative lyrics, lyrical plays and librettos exemplified the supreme place occupied by poetry in German literature. R. M. Rilke (1875–1926), born at Prague, blended symbolism of authentic grandeur with a unique delicacy in his myth-creating *Duino Elegies* and more exuberant *Sonnets to Orpheus* (1922), one of the most notable sequences in modern poetry. Rilke possesses a mastery of the external world, yet he is also mystically indifferent to social reality.

Thomas Mann (1875–1955), almost the first German novelist to make a European impact, revealed a preoccupation with the fevers of decadence;

and his repeated contrasts between spirit and flesh, the normal man and the artist, discipline and the outsider, reflect his heirship to the pessimism of Schopenhauer (p. 261). Franz Kafka (1883–1924), on the other hand, was the supreme expressionist among novel-writers. 'Sometimes', he said, 'I feel I understand the Fall of Man better than anyone'; and his world full of bad dreams, horrible unanswered questions and grotesque realistic details, balefully conveys the generalized anxiety which weighed upon his generation. Kierkegaard (p. 263) had expressed this disquiet philosophically, and under his influence Martin Heidegger (b. 1889) describes the same feeling of *Angst* as our sole guarantee that we exist – having been unaccountably placed in this unwelcoming world to fend for ourselves; a theme worked out in various literary media by Sartre (p. 276).

The German theatre's outstanding figure Bertolt Brecht (1898–1956) sought to destroy the stage-illusion in order to make his audiences think. Despite self-contradictions, the thought that this universal experimentalist and adapter hammered into their minds, in the *Dreigroschenoper* (1928) and *Mutter Courage* (1941), was that people have material motives based on selfishness or social class: but that our rational communication with one another, though hazardous and precarious, can on occasion with difficulty be achieved. Günter Grass (b. 1927) and Uwe Johnson (b. 1934) have resuscitated the German novel with their abundant ingenuity and linguistic fertility. Johnson sensitively studies east and west; Grass is a versatile prodigy who directs his militant surrealist humour against bourgeois weaknesses. So do two vigorous German-Swiss playwrights – Max Frisch (b. 1911), also architect and novelist, and Friedrich Dürrenmatt (b. 1921), once a Protestant theologian. Since their launching at Zürich, both these dramatists have unmasked the pious commonplaces of comfortable people with an aggressive, inflammatory, and mercilessly mordant wit. But Frisch is an elegant, gentlemanly satirist with a concern for the human soul; whereas Dürrenmatt is 'the gloomy penitential preacher of modern drama', with a frightening destructive taste for monstrosities.

In Italy, hampered for decades by unfavourable Fascist influences upon the arts, the principal literary figures were the voluminous philosopher Benedetto Croce (1866–1952), conscious of an instantaneous present ceaselessly engulfed by the past and melting away before our eyes, and Gabriele d'Annunzio (1863–1938), sultry luxuriant poet, playwright of sensation and protagonist of nationalism in action as in words. The plays, novels and short stories of Luigi Pirandello (1867–1936) adapted current metaphysical discussions in order to emphasize the inconsistency of the world, a labyrinth in which his characters cannot track their path. The novels of Cesare Pavese

(1908–50) were brief, bitter and poetical; those of Alberto Moravia are based on a situation of *La Noia* – boredom, the title of a book (1962) – signifying indifference to everything real, and the denial, despite erotic preoccupations, of any definable state of mind.

The leading Portuguese poet of his generation was Fernando Pessoa (1888–1935), a complex personality sensitive to many current influences. The work of his successors ranges from the extroversion of Miguel Torga, poet and short-story writer, to the introspective religious perplexities of José Régio's poems, novels and plays. Spain's theatrical authors have included Jacinto Benavente (1866–1954), a prolific and lightly satirical playwright who brought the national theatre back to reality, and Federigo Garcia Lorca (1899–1936), a tragic dramatist who has however won greater fame, especially since his death, from his traditionally stark, compressed poetry inspired by Andalusian noble savagery and preoccupied with death. Andalusian, too, was J. R. Jimenez (1881–1958), whose subtle cadences fuse the landscapes of his native land with French symbolist and other influences which had been earlier, though less organically, incorporated into Spanish poetry by the Nicaraguan Rubén Dario (1867–1916). Poetry in Spanish America has been very active; in Spain, an early pupil of Dario was the subtle and contemplative Antonio Machado (1875–1939), who adapts the new movements to the traditional rhythms and spare images of his native Castilian.[1] In a later generation, including poets of heartfelt simplicity and feeling, Camilo José Cela (b. 1916) has drawn a grim and disgusted picture of squalor in country and city, enhanced by sordid dialogue.

In Catalan poetry, a new level of achievement was apparent in the profound, distinctive spirituality of Joan Maragall (1860–1911). But the problem of assessing the relative significance, within the general European framework, of literary works in non-international languages is an almost insoluble one, particularly in this increasingly literate century when writers from all the numerous European nations and cultures have, with varying degrees of selfconsciousness, sought their own specific articulacy and self-expression. The existence or absence of foreign translations, or even the extent to which works are translatable at all, are equally inadequate as criteria of quality; and the barriers erected by international politics are almost as impenetrable as those of language. Yet these national literatures, however parochial their tongues, cannot be neglected, since, in an increasingly uniform age, their local undertones provide channels by which a writer can still have authentic private communication with his readers.

[1] Jorge Guillen, author of *Cántico* (1919–50) with its drive towards unified perception, lives in America.

In Greece, before and after the First World War, the spoken language fought a keenly contested but more or less successful battle with the scholarly, classical tongue. Kostis Palamas (1859–1943) played a prominent part in this movement; yet there is classical restraint in his patriotic poetry. He also recreates the atmosphere of Byzantium: and so does Constantine Kavafy (1863–1933), poet par excellence of the Greeks in Egypt, ironically realistic, homosexual and compassionate. The Cretan Nikos Kazantzakis (1885–1957), although a novelist, chose to reinterpret the *Odyssey* not in the prose-fictional form of James Joyce but in a thirty-thousand word epic, with a hero who, shouldering the burden of contemporary perplexities and aspirations, is intensely aware of living in an age between two cultures. George Seferis (b. 1900), too, sees Odysseus as one whose wanderings never end, his past and present coexistent in our minds and hearts.

Elsewhere in eastern Europe much literary talent, though not all, has been devoted to patriotic and ideological problems. In Turkey Ziya Gökalp (1875–1924), combining nationalism with pan-Turanian ideas, gave spoken Turkish dignity as a literary language, while Ahmed Haşim (1883–1933) westernized the languors of his native Damascus by adding the *malaises* of Franco-Belgian symbolism. Yahya Kemal Beyatli (b. 1886), with his dual allegiance to classical and modern Turkish, embodied the nationalist literary spirit, exercising a dominant influence upon the poets of Atatürk's régime. Fazil Hüsnü Daglarca (b. 1912) is a versatile, restless Turkish lyric and epic poet who confronts the linguistic reforms and controversies of his country with a freshly original style; and the free verse of Nazim Hikmet (d. 1963), who spent much of his life in prison and exile, is a forceful blend of dialectic and lyricism which at times achieve a poignant humanity.

In Bulgaria the versatile Ivan Vazov (1850–1921), active in many branches of literature, had summed up the events before and after national independence. Pencho Slaveykov (1866–1912) added a universal note to Bulgarian poetry, and P. K. Yavorov (1877–1914) incorporated the methods of symbolism. The modern Croat lyric is represented by a group of poets including the constructive, energetic Vladimir Nazor (1876–1949), guerrilla warrior and lover of Dalmatia and its islands; while Ivo Andric contributes a restrained psychological realism, and beauty of expression, to his evocations of his native Bosnia. Miroslav Krleža (b. 1893), ideological dramatist, essayist and novelist, made dark tempestuous farces of rebellion, humorous yet tragically pessimistic. The most influential Slovene poet of the early years of the century is Oton Županic, a master of form; his realist and symbolist contemporary Ivan Cankar (1876–1918) wrote lyrical prose searching for the manifold intricate relations that ought to bind one person

Detail from the unfinished church of the
Sagrada Familia at Barcelona by Antonio Gaudí
(d. 1926), whose soaring vitality transfigured into
fantasy an explosive blend of *art nouveau* and Gothic
and oriental traditions

ABOVE: 'What gives our dreams their daring is that they can be realised', said Le Corbusier whose Unité d'Habitation on the outskirts of Marseille, with its sculptural eye for spatial relations and for the new engineering aesthetic, was a step towards his concept of a 'Ville Radieuse' for three million people

RIGHT: The Phoenix Rheinrohr building in Düsseldorf (1960). Pioneered in America by a series of architects who successively advanced their mastery of technical means, skyscrapers have persuaded all but the most closed of minds that towering verticality can achieve great beauty

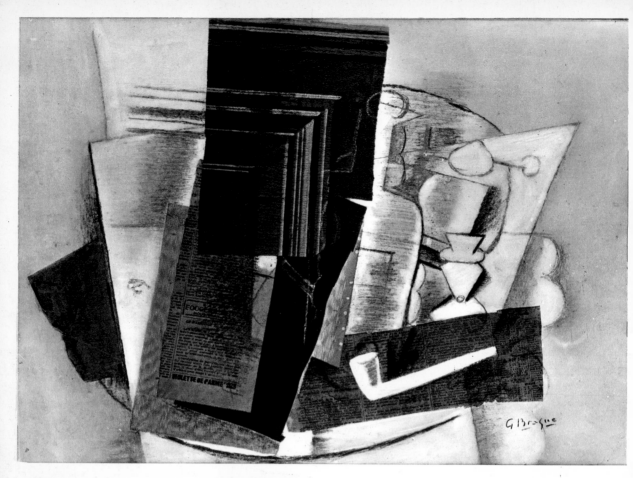

ABOVE: Under the influence of Cézanne's structuralism and of Negro, Sumerian, Mexican and Peruvian motifs – now more familiar through photography – Braque (with Picasso) disintegrated his figures – eliminating perspective – and then moved from analytical Cubism to a synthetic, two-dimensional stage represented by this *Bottle, Glass and Pipe* (papier collé, 1913)

LEFT: Piet Mondrian carried the process of abstraction to the limits in his return to cool, classical simplicity and flat surfaces of pure colour, arranged in a perfect geometrical balance

RIGHT TOP: The alabaster Reclining Female Figure (1929) of Henry Moore, who once expressed the view that modelling sapped the manhood out of western sculpture. His first concern is with his material – to find out what the stone wants

RIGHT BOTTOM: The inexhaustible force and variety of the Catalan Pablo Picasso has granted civilization one of its epoch-making revolutions – or a series of them. This lino cut based on Manet's *Déjeuner sur l'herbe* is one of many variations which Picasso has made on earlier works of art – imbuing them with his own vitality, yet retaining the spirit of the original

ABOVE: The programme heading for the Russian Ballet's performance of *The Firebird* (1909). The ballet, with music by Stravinsky, was choreographed by Fokine, with Tamara Karsavina dancing the title role

BELOW: Scene from the German film *The Cabinet of Dr Caligari* (1919): a masterpiece of expressionist line. The director was Robert Wiene

RIGHT: Scandinavia is far ahead of the modern world in domestic design, which contributes to happiness. Swedish Orrefors glass combines sparkling purity with elegant functionalism, traditional form and concern for its materials

FAR RIGHT: *Penguin:* a black-and-white 'ryijy' rug by Lea Eskola (1962). Since 1910 the Finns have superbly applied subjective free-colour artistic themes to the old handicraft skills of their textile and ceramic industries

BOTTOM RIGHT: Part of an electronic 'score' (or rather diagram) by Karlheinz Stockhausen (b. 1928), pointillist exploiter of the twelve-note idiom of Schönberg and Webern

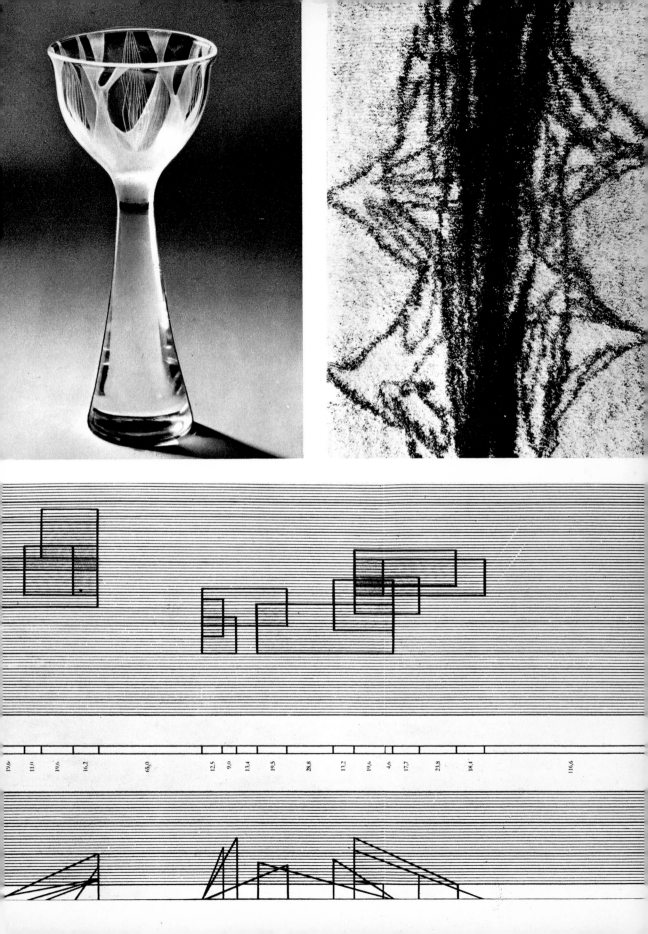

Bicycle Wheel by Marcel Duchamp (1913). Duchamp was one of the founders of the Dadaist school, which shocked the art world in the early part of the century. What seemed to be a dead-end in twentieth-century art has recently been taken up and adapted by a new generation, and the 'ready made' has an established part in the contemporary scene to another, and hesitating between helplessness and a protest rooted in bitter misery. Subsequently, the lyric tradition of Slovenia has been maintained by Alojzij Gradnik and Anton Podbevsek. The Serbian novelist Borislav Stankovic (1876–1927) contributed a starkly realistic note in his erotic psychological novel *Tainted Blood*.

In Poland Stanislaw Wyspianski (1864–1907) turned from painting to the theatre, for which he wrote powerful and prophetic historical and patriotic tragedies. Jaroslaw Iwaskiewicz (b. 1883) ranges from poetry of the human body, obsessed with decay and death, to his massive three-volume novel *The Fame and the Glory* (1955–8). Maria Dabrowska (1892–1965), epic novelist and social publicist, is one of several distinguished Polish woman writers who have illuminated the inter-war period (when Cracow became *avant-garde*) and then the new order since 1945. Another unusual writer of fiction is Jerzy Andrzejewski, who has evolved a complex literary originality from apprenticeship to many national traditions in addition to his own. A number of poets inspired by the Second World War, notably Tadeusz Rózewicz, have treated the themes of battle and occupation with ironical, doom-struck fantasy verging upon surrealism.

The Czech Karel Capek (1890–1938) gained an international reputation from his novels and particularly from the plays which devoted a warm and whimsical fantasy to attacking the mechanization of the age. Yet the leading feature of Czech literature remained, as it has always been, lyric poetry. The hermit Ottakar Brezina (Václav Jebavý) (1868–1929) wrote hymn-like, philosophical compositions of scintillatingly inventive imagery. Vitezslav Nezval (1900–58) achieved a highly personal, surrealist (p. 000) exuberance in the 1930's; while Josef Hora (1891–1945), inspired by the working-class struggle, produced his most powerful lyrics under the tragic stimulus of the war years. The Slovak lyric had a prolific exponent, during the earlier part of the century, in Hviezdoslav (Pavol Orszagh) (1849–1921). As the literature of his country expanded prodigiously after the liberation of 1918, the two volumes of poetry of Ivan Krasko (Ján Botto, 1876–1958) attracted attention, and the next generation produced further lyricists in E. B. Lukác (b. 1900) editor of the literary magazine *Elan*, J. Smrek (b. 1898) who wrote of the sensuous and sensual pleasures of life, Frantisek Halas (1901–49) and Jaroslav Seifert (b. 1901).

The poet who, after Eminescu (p. 254), has evolved a new Rumanian lyric poetry is Tudor Arghezi (b. 1881); and the national Transylvanian bard Octavian Goga (1879–1938) became another spokesman for the same generation. Mihail Sadoveanu (1880–1961), faithful to his country's Communism, was outstanding among the prose-writers of the same period for his prolific and vivid delineation of Moldavian peasant life; and in the younger generation there has been a plentiful supply of novelists.

In Hungary Endre Ady (1877–1919) initiated a new era by the passionate and original lyrical poetry and prose in which he gave weight to topical revolutionary thinking. Zsigmond Móricz (1879–1942) was an author of realistic novels about the conflicts that divide one man from another, and Deszö Szabö (1879–1945) wrote novels and short-stories of rebellious, vituperative vividness. Another writer of fiction, as well as essays and plays, Laszlo Nemeth, concludes his study of the transmutation of Communist life into human life (a theme garishly illuminated by the rising of 1956) by urging Hungarian youth to 'use what you have'. György Lukács (b. 1902) is a major literary critic who has moved from admiration for Nietzsche to various interpretations of Marxism. Among poets, Gyula Illyés (b. 1902) devotes his talent to themes of nature complicated by undercurrents of withdrawal from clear-cut social solutions; and Attila József (b. 1905), before committing suicide in 1937, displayed rare imaginative grasp and originality in his representation of working men's life upon the outskirts of a big city. The national genius for lyricism has reappeared in Ferenc Juhász (b. 1928), whose poem *The Boy Changed into a Stag cries out at the Gate of Secrets* is described by W. H. Auden as one of the most remarkable poems of the age.

In the north, there are the same problems of assessing literatures in a non-international language, though here they are not so often accompanied by the further complexities of mutual politico-social incomprehension. In Norway Knut Hamsun (1859–1952), an outstanding novelist in the traditions of Nietzsche and Strindberg, ignored the problems of society in favour of individual human beings exerting themselves against physical hardship. Social injustices, on the other hand, concerned the Dane H. Pontoppidan (1857–1943); and his compatriot J. V. Jensen (1873–1950) likewise dwelt on the poor, reinforcing his biologically-based humanism by an extraordinary ability to recollect sensory perceptions. In a Danish literary Renaissance which began to develop towards the end of the Second World War, pride of place went to Martin A. Hansen (1909–55), whose novels and essays nostalgically set the divisions of modern civilization against the imagined integration of medieval culture.

The Swede Sigrid Undset (1882–1949) likewise looked back to the past in her historical novels, as well as courageously handling an erotic subject (1912). Hjalmar Bergman (1883–1931) lavished upon his stories a fertile and vigorous imagination; Pär Lagerqvist's (b. 1891) novels *The Dwarf* (1944) and *Barabbas* (1950) are moving studies of evil and violence. The poetry and even more striking prose of Harry Martinson (b. 1904), a self-educated proletarian, occupy a unique place in Swedish literature.

In Finland Juhani Aho (1861–1921) moved from a realist technique towards romanticism, and Yrjö Hirn (1870–1952) belonged to the central humanist tradition. The country's nationalist poet was Eino Leino (1878–1926), whose best-known works were his historical ballads written early in the century; while F. E. Sillanpää (b. 1888), following a persistent Scandinavian tradition, has derived poetic insight and inspiration from the Finnish countryside and its inhabitants. Yrjö Jylhä wrote a remarkable poem *The Purgatory* about the traumatic Winter War against the Russians (p. 270); and Paavo Haavikko is both a novelist and one of the leaders in a strong lyric movement dating from the 1950's.

An important Dutch poetic revival, inaugurated before the turn of the century (p. 244), continued with the mystical symbolism of P. C. Boutens (1870–1943). Both wars, in addition to the inter-war period, produced further activity in this field; notably from the subtle and versatile poet and essayist Simon Vestdijk (b. 1898). In Belgium, from early in the century, Stijn Streuvels saw the countryside of west Flanders through visionary eyes, and between the wars several writers contributed to an original *avant-garde* Flemish theatre.

The Arts

The most important cultural developments in modern Europe belong to the various branches of science, which have witnessed by far their greatest changes of all time. Scientific knowledge, despite uncertainty whether it will lead us to utopia or an holocaust, is the dominant philosophy of European civilizations, and they are committed to its advancement and application. For better or worse, these revolutionary developments have absorbed talent which, in other centuries, would have been devoted to the arts or to literature; and that is partly why those traditional humanities have failed to shape the basis of a new society. Yet, even if they have fallen short of this, the advances that they have registered are in some respects as significant as those of any previous century.

This does not, however, perhaps quite apply to music, though here too there have been extensive changes. In France Claude-Achille Debussy (1862–1918) composed a revolutionary opera *Pelléas et Melisande*, of which Maeterlinck wrote the libretto (1902). Debussy evolved a new approach no longer based upon narrative or dramatic romanticism, but recording instantaneous impressions, on the analogy of the impressionist painters (p. 245). This method was worked out in more clear-cut fashion by Maurice Ravel (1875–1937), whose *Spanish Rhapsody* (1907) and ballet *Bolero* (1928) display his orchestral virtuosity.

Ballet had come to be regarded as a major European art largely as a result of Russian successes, stimulated at first by the Frenchman Jean Petipa (d. 1910). At a time of creative activity both in Stanislavsky's theatre at Moscow and in Meyerhold's at St Petersburg, Diaghilev's team of dancers, including Nijinsky whose stylized, angular movements were far ahead of his time, conducted their first Paris season in 1909. Their scintillating choreographer was Fokine, whose *Prince Igor* illustrates his theory that ballet should flow uninterrupted, with its whole theme or story expressed through the dance. Diaghilev enlisted Benois and Bakst among his artists, and commissioned Igor Stravinsky (b. 1882) to compose *The Firebird*. Stravinsky's *Petrouchka* (1911) followed, and then (for an enormous orchestra) the savagely orgiastic incantatory *Sacre du Printemps* (1913), of which the rhythms, overpowering melody, and harmony echo folk-themes and Jung's collective unconscious. Dmitri Shostakovich (b. 1906) made his name by his First Symphony (1926) but is best known for his wartime, programmatic Seventh (Leningrad) (1941). Soviet music is officially set the task of optimism, 'rallying the people, singing free labour, calling for heroic effort'.

Johan Sibelius (1865–1957), a Finn who studied in Berlin and Vienna, celebrated his native country in *Finlandia* (1900) and *Tapiola* (1926), works which reveal his imaginative powers of expression and individual close-knit technique. In Germany, Richard Strauss (1864–1949) followed up experiments in musical realism by operas that seemed to contemporaries violent and sensational. *Rosenkavalier* (1911) is the best known, but the more intimate *Ariadne auf Naxos* followed (1913), and then, most profound and thoughtful of all, *Die Frau ohne Schatten* (1919). Classical yet colourful, hard-hitting, and continually developing his gifts, Strauss achieved towards the end of his life a balanced synthesis between the contrasting elements in his temperament.

Meanwhile, however, Arnold Schoenberg (1874–1951) had reflected the unrest and suffering of the expressionist movement (p. 287) by attempting something new. This was his atonality or keylessness (1908), seen in *Pierrot Lunaire* (1912) and later developed further towards complete abstraction in a twelve-note technique (*c.* 1923) which killed classical music by its acceptance that each of the twelve chromatic semi-tones is of equal significance. The Hungarian Béla Bartók (1881–1945) likewise cultivated atonality and dissonance, though combining these tendencies with lyrical tastes which draw upon the unclassical, flexible melodies of Magyar folksong; his collaborator Zoltan Kodaly (b. 1882) blends this traditional material with rich harmonics that achieve emotional strength by less harsh and explosive means. The Greek composer Nikos Skalkottas (1904–49), manifesting a multi-dimensional, concentrated power to fuse folklore traditions with his own forward-looking clarity, moved from lyric settings of medieval love poems to the ironic twists that marked his collaboration with Bertolt Brecht (p. 280), and to atonalities derived from studying with Schoenberg.

But European music since the Second World War has been preoccupied with opera; in England, for example, Benjamin Britten gained fame from his tragic *Peter Grimes* (1945). Influenced by Purcell as well as Stravinsky, Britten prefers 'clean slender sounds', and chooses themes of compassion and the destruction of innocence, such as the American Herman Melville's *Billy Budd*. Meanwhile the more ambitious symphonic and chamber compositions of the '50's have tended to be introspective and eerie works displaying an international style of strong chromatic and rhythmical complexity, with a minimum of historical or stylistic reference.

Russia's first individualistic painter M. Vrubel (1856–1910), a tragically intense genius closer to the visionary Blake (p. 234) than to impressionism, brought Russia to Gautier's doctrine of art for the sake of art (p. 244), which was also the slogan of Diaghilev and his friends (p. 286). The years between 1905 and 1911 were a period of significant artistic fermentation. Painters in Central Europe and elsewhere, cognisant of Freudian psychoanalysis (p. 279) and influenced by the art of *naifs*, of children and of the non-European traditions which photography had made more familiar (p. 241), were exploiting the use of exaggeration and distortion – liberating objects from their accidental aspects – in order to convey emotional impact. This expressionist movement is the opposite to impressionism, since it does not try to shape impressions on our senses from without, but (leaving it to the photographers to represent nature and fulfil the social duty of recording objects and events) prefers to distort, as our feelings and memories distort, in order to give an outer shape to our inner and often unconscious experiences. G. Rouault (1871–1958), the most significant religious painter of the century, employs these forceful means to set Christ against the vices and lies of society.

This desire to intensify emotional communication by the unrestrained interplay of lines and colours led towards abstraction. Paris was interested and shocked by the 1905 exhibition of various painters (Les Fauves) who displayed various different aspects of these revolutionary tendencies – including the vividly rhythmical colourist Matisse (1869–1954), whose later and more abstract paintings were to prove an important source of inspiration to artists after the First World War.

But it is the Catalan Pablo Picasso (b. 1880) whose versatility, curiosity and inexhaustibly inventive powers of transformation and animation have subjected the vocabulary of art to a revolutionary enlargement. The fractured postures of his *Demoiselles d'Avignon* (1907), stimulating the superb harmonizer of colour and design Georges Braque (1882–1963) who not long after collaborated with Picasso, proclaimed the arrival of a new era – under the influence of negro and other non-European artistic traditions (Sumerian, Mexican, Peruvian, etc.), as well as of the structural theorizings inherited from Cézanne. The same figure is shown from two or more simultaneous viewpoints, emancipated from the conventional fixities of perspective; and soon, as this analytical cubism gave way to a synthetic stage (1910–12), such three-dimensional elements as remained in the design were replaced by two-dimensional colour patterns or series of planes, compressing time and space (as Einstein also did) into a single formula in which the physical object is increasingly disintegrated and reconstructed in freely associated, decorative, geometrically intricate mutations, sometimes variegated by the adhesion of paper, cloth or metal *collages*. 'When a form is realised', said Picasso, 'it is there to live its own life . . . you paint not what you see, but what you know is there.' At long last, perceptual art in Europe had been superseded by a conceptual approach which compels the observer to share, no longer in fine sentiments nor in the chance naturalistic realities of being, but in the intellectual, transcendental truth which underlies all such feelings and objects.

While the poet F. T. Martinetti (1876–1944) published his dynamic manifesto (1909) erecting this cubist fragmentation into the philosophy of Futurism – translated by Umberto Boccioni (1882–1916) into painting and sculpture – Vassili Kandinsky (1866–1944), moving from Moscow to Munich, broke away altogether from the representation of familiar things in order to paint combinations of shapes and colours bearing no intentional resemblance to any natural object (1910). These abstractions, restoring a tradition which had vanished from Europe for many centuries (p. 72), are composed of rhythmically balanced, lyrical and almost musical designs, dependent upon the assumption that specifically artistic values belong to forms and colours in their own right. Kandinsky's Swiss associate Paul Klee (1879–1940) described his own style of emancipated fantasy as 'taking a line for a walk'; the Dutchman Piet Mondrian (1872–1944), whose influence helped to make America a leading centre of post-first-war painting, favoured a peculiarly rigorous geometrical abstraction. This novel search for the spiritual values behind the world of appearances makes a direct appeal to the viewer's sensibility without any conventional intermediary.

While O. Kokoschka (b. 1886) ranged over a wide expanse, identifying man's relations with the elements by means of landscapes based not on classical perspective but on elliptical patterns, the nihilistic Dada school founded at Zürich during the First World War (1915–22) sought to shock and scandalize by opposing all the dictates of artistic custom and of commonsense. Dada and Cubism, together with earlier European painters of the macabre and grotesque such as Brueghel and Bosch, were the forerunners of André Breton's Surrealist group (1922) including Max Ernst (b. 1891), who had introduced Dadaism to Cologne, and the Spaniards Salvador Dali (b. 1905) and Joan Miró (b. 1893). Surrealism, in its perversion or transmutation of models, has been described as a logical attempt to push the illogical to its extreme limits. Following upon Breton's study of psychoanalysis, these painters and their Belgian successors the fantasist René Magritte, the more explicitly Freudian artist Paul Delvaux, and Octave Landuyt who is grotesque in a more indigenous Flemish tradition, clinically exploit the unconscious in all its disregard for beauty, morals and logic. This they have done with a chilly exactitude of finish that paints familiar things in acutely recognizable detail yet combines them in irrational relationships; employing photographic meticulousness in pursuit of an aim beyond the reach of any camera, and making use of a private language which symbolizes the total incomprehension of current artistic change by public taste. Yet the permanent value of the initial movement lay in its renewal of the function and significance of imagery: Dali's bent and flopping clock, like the earlier designs of the synthetic Cubists (p. 288), reflects Einstein's curved time-space.

In the world after Hitler and the atom-bomb, attempts at traditional harmonies have been explicitly rejected as a 'dishonest extenuation'. In the Netherlands Karel Appel (b. 1921), following the American Pollock (1912–56), dismisses such romantic illusions by 'action-painting' (or *tachisme*, from *tache*, a blot or stain), namely the unpremeditated splashing and dribbling of paint upon canvas at the dictates of the unconscious: a technique owing debts to Kandinsky (p. 288) and culminating in the German Fred Thieler's measured solemnities and large luminous *collages* of glass-like brittleness.

The sculptors of the present century have been less prominent than the painters, whose tendencies they have in some degree followed. Aristide Maillol (1861–1944) reacted from Rodin's dramatic, fluent forms (p. 245) towards the static monumentality of ancient Greece. The Croat Ivan Mestrovic (1883–1962) devotes to his wooden medium an acute and powerful sense of design. Constantin Brancusi (1876–1957) from Rumania transferred abstraction from painting back to sculpture – the African medium from which Picasso, Matisse and others, before their abstract periods, had derived their inspiration. Jacob Epstein (1880–1959), who likewise admired these Africans, displayed a creative versatility and emotional sympathy ranging from colossal stylized figures (which earned him the usual Philistine ridicule) to superb, rough-cast characterizations – closer to the classical European tradition – of calm and sensual women, and of men who, in the opinion of Henry Moore, are even better, because they are more objectively rendered. Moore (b. 1898), whose hieratically posed figure-compositions aim at power rather than beauty, is above all truthful to his material, profoundly concerned with its inner nature as the medium and vehicle for his spatial, three-dimensional creations. Milanese sculptors exploit bronze with great effectiveness; the best work of Marino Marini (b. 1901) is potent and urgent, and Giacomo Manzù (b. 1908) adapts the Italian humanist tradition to his studies of human features.

In the shaping of domestic objects most countries lag far behind Scandinavia. Its designers of furniture, glassware, ceramics, metal-works, floor-coverings and fabrics have since 1930 blown away the cobwebs by their elegant functionalism, combining traditional solidity with daring yet economic form moulded by the need to save material, and admirably suited to the techniques of modern industrial production. Swedish engraved glassware sparkles with breath-taking, ice-sharp purity; designs based on old handicraft skills lend distinction to the textiles and ceramic industries of the Finns; and the Danes have a word 'hygge' for the quality of pleasant, relaxed comfort and well-being with which they brighten the objects of their everyday life.

An outstanding architect of the first years of the century was the Catalan Antonio Gaudí (1852–1926) who, working in and around Barcelona, turned from neo-Gothic to an *art nouveau* (p. 251) infused with orientalism and the soaring exuberance of his own imagination, which exploited curves and diagonals with explosive, sensational vitality.

In an age of major American advances, Frank Lloyd Wright (1869–1959) expounded the doctrine of 'organic architecture' that would harmonize with its users and environment; building was again, at long last, recognized to be a social art related to the life of the people it serves. Walter Gropius (b. 1883), developing the thinking of the de Stijl group (which Mondrian

(p. 288) had helped to found and Wright influenced) in wartime Holland, proclaimed the need for architecture to come to terms with the industrial civilizations of the machine. His own University of Design, the Bauhaus at Weimar (1919) and then at Dessau, was built to prove that the various arts, and particularly architecture and engineering, could benefit one another and need no longer be estranged. After moving to the United States (Harvard, 1937) Gropius contributed largely to the skyscraper's new functionalism, closely related to new building materials (concrete, steel, glass) and environment. Another German emigrant to America (Chicago, 1938) was Mies van der Rohe (b. 1886), who after the First World War had designed tall buildings of radical novelty and clarity, making sensitive and daring use of materials, space and proportion.

Finland was another country where architectural values grew out of products of technology and industrialization. Eliel Saarinen (1873–1950) moved from a national romantic conception – 'a heavy rain-shower that washed away the dust of the previous century and watered the soil' – towards, though not all the way to, functionalism.[1] Alvar Aalto (b. 1898), distinguished for his imaginative use of the national product of wood, has extended these principles to exhilarating town-plans.

Le Corbusier (b. 1887) emphasized the beauty of machines (1922), proclaimed that the house is a machine for living in (1923), and advocated the total elimination of ornament. Yet he himself, however rational in principle, is prevented by his poetic, individualistic imagination from carrying to rigorous extreme the functionalism that he preaches. At first Le Corbusier seemed to seek contrast rather than correspondence with nature; but since about 1930, in sympathy with the ideas of Wright, he has moved towards a greater harmony with the materials he employs. Employing novel geometric designs suggested by Cubism, and subsequently interpreting his architectural forms in sculptural terms, he has described proportion as the 'divine nothing which is everything and gives life to all'; and this emphasis is reflected in the bold verticality of his sensitive spatial relations that prefer unrestricted freedom to rigidly defined interior divisions.

It is as tempting for the *avant-garde* to overestimate modern architects, painters and sculptors because they are new, as it is for the public to mock them for the same reason. It must, however, be recorded that, in spite of the artistic popularization which is characteristic of the age, and although in past epochs inspiration has sometimes benefited from disturbed conditions, the current blend of unprecedentedly destructive mass-warfare with

[1] He went to live in America, where his son Eero also achieved architectural distinction.

mass-communications makes it harder for artistic originality to emerge than in any previous century.

Nevertheless, these same mass-communications, created by the electronic development which is bringing us into the computer age, have provided the twentieth century with its characteristic cultural media of the cinema, broadcasting and television. The cinema is not only an art but an industry, and an entertainment as well. Yet some of its products have also ranked high among the public or private artistic experiments and achievements of the time. A film's limitations are clear. It is not the unaided work of a single person's creativity; it is ephemeral, and once it loses topicality is unlikely to become topical again; it contains a strong mechanical (photographic) element which limits the imaginative factor; and only about sixty per cent of its contents are seen by the observer at the first viewing – this proportion having decreased since silent films gave way to sound. Above all, more than any previous artistic medium, the cinema is vulnerable to cheap commercialism. Nevertheless cogent arguments for its artistic value were put forward by the American pioneer D. W. Griffith (1875–1948), and then in the '20's and '30's by outstanding Soviet directors and aesthetic philosophers of the film: protagonists of the view that it must not merely represent a happening but must shape it, and express an attitude about its nature and significance. Encouraged by Lenin's dictum 'of all the arts, the most important for us is the cinema', Sergei Eisenstein (1898–1948) put these theories into sensational effect in his film *The Battleship Potemkin* (1925), followed by *Alexander Nevsky* (1938). Such films give life and blood to Eisenstein's view that the juxtaposition of two film-shots, artistically designed, is not merely the sum of its parts but an original creation impelled by the director who guides the spectator's associations.

V. I. Pudovkin (1893–1953), although his main early achievement lay in silent films, saw the sound film as the supreme art of the future: a heady, unique and hazardous creative adventure, synthesizing every artistic element, oral, visual and philosophical alike. During the '30's many other countries produced an experimental *avant-garde* cinema, but the home of intellectual film-making was the France of René Clair, Jean Renoir, Marcel Carné and Jean Vigo. At the end of the Second World War, the honours went to Italy, where Rossellini and de Sica introduced the moving neo-realism of films such as *Bicycle Thieves* – voted the best film ever made in 1952, and the sixth best ten years later. By the early 1950's, while Alfred Hitchcock experimented succinctly with incongruities in America, new Italian directors such as Michelangelo Antonioni with his empty streets and long blank passages, and Federico Fellini with his shiftless young men in frustrating provincial towns, reflected the current breakdown of communications between man and man, and man and woman. These films no longer imposed an emotion upon their viewers, but cut out a slice of experience and left us to interpret it.

Latterly a lively school of cinema has been created in Poland, where Andrzej Wajda fertilizes obsessions with the war-theme by his own heady blend of intellectualism and nervous, melancholy romance; Andrzej Munk's film *The Passenger* (started in 1961, and completed by Munk's collaborators in 1963 after his death) is a remarkable study of the precariousness of civilization as laid bare by atrocities. But above all in Sweden Ingmar Bergman (b. 1918), linked to able predecessors by his brilliant company of actors, has combined in the trenchant photography and symbolism of *The Seventh Seal* (1956), *Wild Strawberries* (1957), *The Virgin Spring* (1960) and *Silence* (1963), every traumatic contrast of innocent delight and brutal sadism, pain and unbearable relief, puritan morality and ungovernable sensualism, savage realism and desperate illusion.

Electronics can bring these masterpieces to the millions, just as millions buy the cheap paper-back books which, launched in Britain and expanded in America, have now completed their third decade. Broadcasting, too, has set many aesthetic problems and recorded many achievements, since its creation by American pioneers (1906) and first scheduled programmes at Pittsburgh (1920) and in Britain (1922). Although the radio's need for universal symbols and passively shared experiences are stimuli to infantilism, there are peculiar artistic and dramatic possibilities in this medium's illusion of reality and intimate presence, and in its concentration upon the single sense of hearing which allows audiences to shape from the programmes their own escapist or therapeutic or artistic fantasies: for from the overwhelming suggestiveness of words, as Alberto Moravia remarked, there can be no awakening.

But the widest vistas in the territory of mass communications are those opened by television, developed by the Scot J. L. Baird (1888–1946) and C. F. Jenkins of America and first programmed during the late '30's in the United States and England. The larger audiences reached by television can mean fewer and simpler ideas, conservative form and social content, conformity to the lowest common factor – and a relatively low level of attention. Moreover, although the individual has strong defensive mechanisms, modern means of organizing and controlling mass opinion bring insidious temptations to exploit unreason. In particular – and especially in times of crisis – there is, in many countries, the haunting, unverifiable possibility that viewers may be subjected to subliminal flashes of unrecognized and unwanted persuasion.

Yet this is the channel through which the public wishes to receive its entertainment; because of television, the total number of cinema tickets sold in Britain has gone down by three-quarters during eighteen years. There is also a ready public for cultural TV (in addition to actual instruction, on open or closed circuit, in which the United States are the pioneers). It is, however, a necessary proviso that this should be treated not as an extension of stage, cinema or sound broadcasting, but as a new artistic medium with a specific character shaping both the substance of its message and the form in which it is expressed. This importation of cultural topics and standards into millions of homes, though rarely evocative of durable original creation, may well become revolutionary in its supply of suggestive stimuli and interpretations. For the provision of these, Europe, like all other parts of the world where this medium is to be found, still depends not only upon the elaborate team-work required, but also upon the existence, discovery and encouragement of individuals possessing exceptional talent.

The British Isles

Atlantic Ocean

North Sea

Inverness

Aberdeen

Falkirk
Glasgow
Kirkcaldy
EDINBURGH
R. Clyde

Belfast

Carlisle

Newcastle
Sunderland

Middlesborough
Scarborough

Lancaster
Blackpool
Preston
York
Blackburn
Leeds
Hull
Liverpool
Halifax
Manchester
Grimsby
Stockport
Sheffield
Lincoln
Nottingham
Grantham

Irish Sea

Monasterboice

Dublin

Stafford
Derby
Leicester
Norwich
R. Severn
Birmingham
Great
Yarmouth

Waterford
Lismore
Cork

Gloucester
Cambridge

Swansea
Cardiff
Oxford
Windsor
LONDON
Thames
Bristol
Bath
Greenwich
Canterbury
Dover
Calais
Salisbury
Winchester
Exeter
Southampton
Brighton
Folkestone
Plymouth
Portsmouth
Boulogne

English Channel

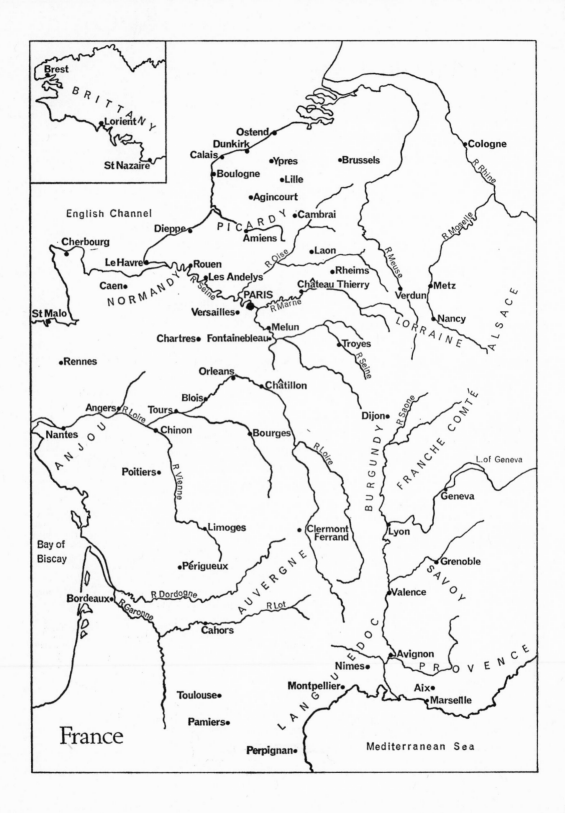

Brest

B R I T T A N Y

Lorient

St Nazaire

Ostend

Dunkirk

Calais

Boulogne

Cologne

Ypres

Brussels

Lille

Agincourt

English Channel

P I C A R D Y

Cambrai

Dieppe

Amiens

Laon

Cherbourg

R Oise

Le Havre

Rouen

Rheims

R Moselle

Metz

Les Andelys

Château Thierry

R Meuse

Caen

R Seine

PARIS

Verdun

Nancy

N O R M A N D Y

R Marne

St Malo

Versailles

Melun

L O R R A I N E

A L S A C E

Chartres

Fontainebleau

Troyes

Rennes

R Seine

Orleans

Châtillon

Blois

Dijon

R Saône

F R A N C H E   C O M T É

Angers

R Loire

Tours

Chinon

Bourges

B U R G U N D Y

L. of Geneva

Nantes

A N J O U

Poitiers

R Loire

Geneva

R Vienne

Bay of
Biscay

Limoges

Clermont
Ferrand

Lyon

Périgueux

A U V E R G N E

Grenoble

S A V O Y

Bordeaux

R Dordogne

Valence

R Garonne

R Lot

Cahors

L A N G U E D O C

Avignon

P R O V E N C E

Nimes

Toulouse

Aix

Montpellier

Marseille

Pamiers

France

Perpignan

Mediterranean Sea

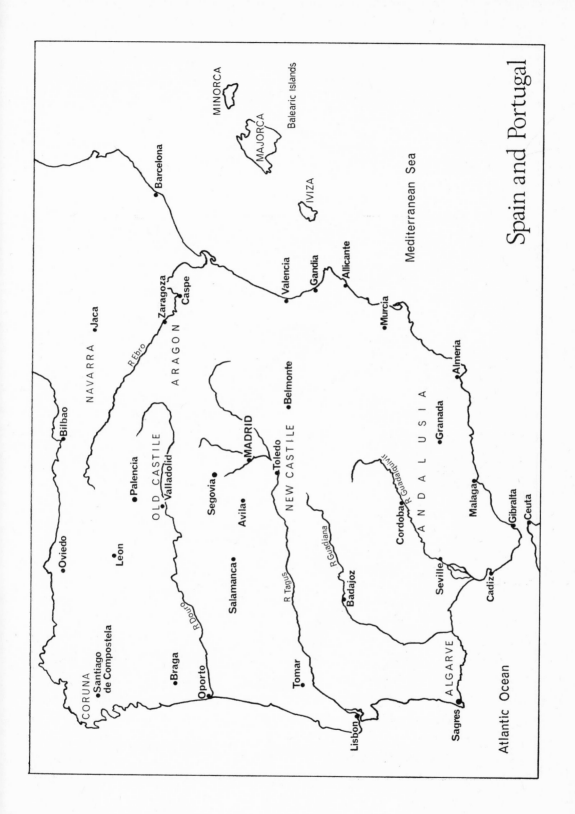

Spain and Portugal

Central Europe

The Low Countries

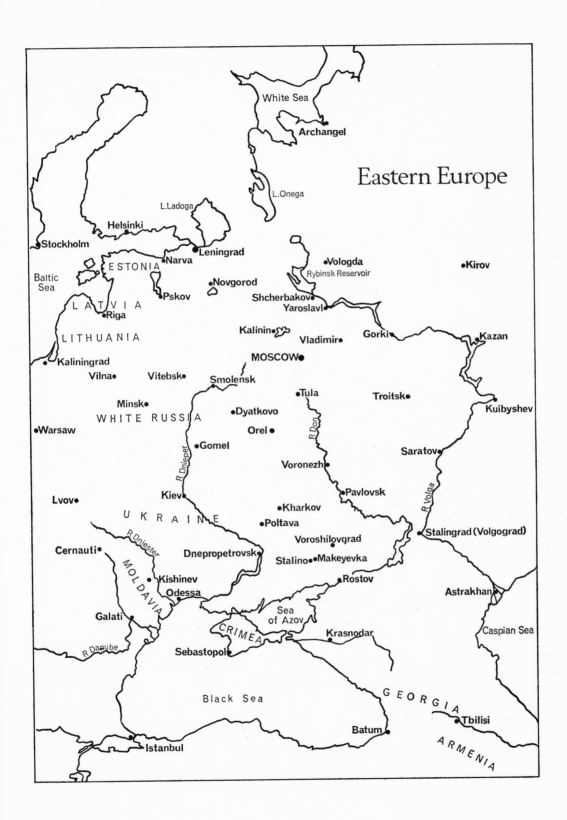

The Balkans

INDEX